States of Emergency

Cultures of Revolt in Italy
from 1968 to 1978

◆

ROBERT LUMLEY

V E R S O

London · New York

First published by Verso 1990
© Robert Lumley 1990
All rights reserved

Verso
UK: 6 Meard Street, London W1V 3HR
USA: 29 West 35th Street, New York, NY 10001-2291

Verso is the imprint of New Left Books

British Library Cataloguing in Publication Data
Lumley, Robert
    States of emergency : cultures of revolt in Italy from
    1968 to 1978.
    1. Italy. Social movements, history
    I. Title
    303.4'84

    ISBN 978-0-86091-969-8

Library of Congress Cataloging-in-Publication Data

Lumley, Robert, 1951–
    States of emergency : cultures of revolt in Italy
    1968–1978 / Robert Lumley.
        p.   cm.
    Includes bibliographical references.

    1. Italy–Politics and government–1945–1976. 2. Italy–Politics
and government–1976– 3. Students–Italy–Political activity–
History–20th century. 4. Working class–Italy–Political
activity–History–20th century. 5. Social movements–Italy–
History–20th century. 6. Italy–Social conditions–1945–1976.
7. Italy–Social conditions–1976– I. Title.
DG577.5.L86   1990
945.092'6–dc20

Typeset in September by Leaper & Gard Ltd, Bristol
Printed in Great Britain by Bookcraft (Bath) Ltd

States of Emergency

V

contents

acknowledgements

The bulk of this book was first written as a Ph.D. thesis (finished in 1983 with the title 'Social Movements in Italy, 1968–78') at the Centre for Contemporary Cultural Studies, at the University of Birmingham. The research work was done in Milan in the late 1970s and early 1980s. Although that work has been revised and updated, my debts go back to my time in Birmingham and Milan. It was the support and good company of Charlotte Brunsdon, Myra Connell and Janice Winship which made it possible to sustain momentum when writing. I want also to thank Paul Ginsborg, who gave me invaluable help and advice when it was most needed, Liliana Grilli for her kind hospitality in Milan, and Antonietta Torchi for continuous encouragement and ideas. Whatever the value of the book for others, for me the experience of writing it has been important in introducing me to Italian people and their culture. For this I am deeply grateful to Italian friends, and to all those who helped me so generously with my research. Finally, I'd like to say how much I owe to Richard Johnson, who was a stimulating and caring supervisor, to members of the Magpie discussion group, especially Martin Chalmers and John Solomos, and to Malcolm Imrie of Verso, without whom this book would probably have remained a thesis. While I am responsible for what has been written (warts and all), I hope that those who have given me a hand will find something in it which will interest them.

The author and publishers would like to thank the following for their kind permission to reproduce illustrations: Alfredo Chiappori ('In the commune . . .', 'Calm down . . .', 'Culture must be defended'); Altan/ Quipos ('The cost of living . . .', 'Hello . . .'); Giorgio Forattini ('I was white . . .', Marx crucified); and Elfo ('Identities, Secrets'). Every effort has been made to trace the copyright holders of illustrations: we must apologize to those we have been unable to contact.

glossary of organizations

Since the reader may not be familiar with the trade unions and political organizations in Italy, which are often referred to in the text using abbreviations (e.g. PCI, instead of Italian Communist Party), this glossary provides a brief guide. It is not comprehensive, but covers those organizations most frequently mentioned.

The Unions

Italian unions are divided into three confederations:

Confederazione Generale Italiana dei Lavoratori (CGIL)
Confederazione Italiana dei Sindacati Liberi (CISL)
Unione Italiana del Lavoro (UIL)

Each of these in turn is divided into 'categories' according to industry (hence FILTEA–CGIL is the textile workers' 'category').

CGIL   is the biggest trade union organization, with 2½ million members in 1968. Communist and Socialist parties (⅔ and ⅓ respectively) are heavily, though not exclusively, represented at all levels.

CISL   is the second union organization with about 1½ million members in 1968. It was formed as a result of a breakaway from the CGIL in 1948 and for many years it was dominated by the Christian Democrats, though its basis is not confessional.

UIL   is the third union, with about half a million members in 1968. It includes Socialists (45%), Social Democrats (30%) and Republicans (25%) in its leadership.

In the engineering sector attempts to overcome this tripartite structure saw the establishment of the *Federazione Lavoratori Metalmeccanici* (FLM) in 1972, but the majority of members belong first to an affiliate 'category' and those who only hold cards of the FLM are a minority. The affiliate categories are:

FIOM (*Federazione Impiegati Operai Metallurgici*) is composed of engineering manual and white-collar workers and is part of the CGIL. In 1968 it had 271,000 members.

FIM (*Federazione Italiana della Metallurgia*) is part of the CISL. In 1968 it had 170,000 members.

UILM (*Unione Italiana dei Lavoratori della Metallurgia*) is part of the UIL. In 1968 it had 103,000 members.

ACLI (*Associazioni Cristiane Lavoratori Italiani*) was founded in 1944 to organize Catholic workers separately from the CGIL. Dominated by Vatican and Christian Democrat Party influences, the ACLI became more independent in the late 1960s.

MO (*Movimento Operaio*) is the generic term meaning the official workers' movement. Its British equivalent would be the 'labour movement'.

Workplace Representation

Internal Commission (*Commissione Interna*) factory-based representative bodies elected by all workers irrespective of union membership. Their bargaining role was heavily circumscribed and by the late 1960s they were often out of touch with shopfloor opinion. Hence their replacement by Factory Councils post 1969.

Delegates (*Delegati*) the nearest British equivalent is the shop steward, but they do not in the Italian case necessarily belong to a union. They are elected representatives who came into being during the Hot Autumn mobilizations, and were later made official.

Factory Council (*Consiglio di Fabbrica*) the successor to the Internal Commission, it is composed of delegates and represents all workers in a workplace. Set up in the wake of the Hot Autumn, it was, however, much more firmly based on the shopfloor.

CUB (*Comitati Unitari di Base*) rank-and-file workers' organizations set up independently of the unions in 1968–9, mainly in large factories in the North. After 1969 they were increasingly dominated by political organizations.

Zone Council (*Consiglio di Zona*) set up in the early seventies as part of the unions' campaign for social reforms. They were composed largely of delegates from Factory Councils in an area. However, the Zone Councils remained on the drawing-boards, and never took root.

Employers' Associations

Confindustria (*Confederazione dell'Industria Italiana*) is the organization of private employers, although up until 1969 it also represented the state sector.

Intersind is the body representing state sector employers.

Political Parties

DC   (*Democrazia Cristiana*) has been the party of government since 1948. Its membership is almost exclusively Catholic and its support comes from different classes, although its policies have favoured free enterprise capitalism. In May 1968 it won 39% of the vote, and 266 seats in the Chamber of Deputies.

PCI   (*Partito Comunista Italiano*) the largest working-class party with a membership of 1½ million in 1968, and 27% of the vote and 177 seats in the May 1968 election. It was in the government from 1945 to 1947, but otherwise represented the main opposition force. The party paper is *L'Unità*.

PSI   (*Partito Socialista Italiano*) the first workers' party in Italy, was greatly weakened by fascism. In 1947 a social democratic grouping broke away, rejoined the party in 1966 and then left again in 1969. In 1968 it got 15% of the vote and 91 seats in combination with the PSDI. The PSI participated in government from 1963 to 1972. The party paper is *L'Avanti*.

MSI   (*Movimento Sociale Italiano*) a fascist party. It got 4% of the vote in 1968, and 24 seats.

PRI   (*Partito Repubblicano Italiano*) a historic lay centre party which took part in the Centre–Left government from 1963. It got 2% of the vote in May 1968, and 9 seats.

PLI   (*Partito Liberale Italiano*) a historic lay right-wing party. It got 6% of the vote in May 1968, and 31 seats.

PSDI   (*Partito Social Democratico Italiano*) a breakaway from the PSI. In the April 1963 election it got 6% of the vote, and 33 seats.

PSIUP   (*Partito Socialista di Unità Proletaria*) was a left-wing split from the PSI following its entry into government in 1963. Its strength was in the CGIL. In May 1968 it got nearly 5% of the vote, and 23 seats.

Il Manifesto was a left-wing split from the PCI of 1969 grouped around a journal of that name. It was important as an intellectual current rather than as an organized political force. It theorized a council communism of Gramscian inspiration.

AO (*Avanguardia Operaia*) was set up in 1968–9. Although it had roots in Trotskyism, it called itself Marxist–Leninist. It was closely associated with the factory rank-and-file committees (CUBs) in Milan. From December 1968 it published a bi-monthly journal called *Avanguardia Operaia*.

LC (*Lotta Continua*) was formally constituted in 1969 as a fusion of elements (ex-members of Potere Operaio, student movement activists), and identified itself with a variety of social movements, of which the Fiat rebellion of 1969 was the most formative. From November 1969 it published the weekly paper *Lotta Continua*.

PO or Pot. Op. (*Potere Operaio*) founded in Tuscany in 1966–7 by activists associated with the reviews *Quaderni Rossi* and *Classe Operaia*. Important for its theroetical positions and for isolated but well-publicized interventions in factory conflicts in 1967–8. From September 1969 published a weekly paper called *Potere Operaio*.

ML (*Marxisti–Leninisti*) there were several groups which claimed to be faithful to the political line of the Communist Party of the People's Republic of China, although only the PC d'I (*Partito Comunista d'Italia* – not to be confused with the PCI) was officially recognized. In October 1968 the Unione (*Unione dei Communisti Italiani Marxisti–Leninisti*) was founded, with the paper *Servire il Popolo*, but fell apart in 1969. In that year *Movimento Studentesco* was set up in Milan. Based in the State University it took its name from the student movement but was a rigid ML sect.

PRI (*Partito Radicale*) first set up in 1955, it was more a current of opinion than a party. Refounded in 1967 it campaigned chiefly on civil rights issues and against the fascist hang-overs in the institutions (laws, Church privileges). Its influence grew in the 1970s when it promoted referendum campaigns on abortion and other issues.

Today the political arena is covering over with a new flora; we should savour while we can the heady scents of these wild flowers and unruly weeds, so invigorating after so much deodorant and disinfectant. The functionaries and doctrinarians of the former social movements rub their eyes in bewilderment: these struggles are not in the place reserved for them; they do not speak the language they learnt in the last century.[1]

If the multiple points of social contact once characterizing the city can be reawakened under terms appropriate to affluence, then some channels for experiencing diversity and disorder will again be open to men. The great promise of city life is a new kind of confusion possible within its boundaries, an anarchy that will not destroy men, but make them richer and more mature.[2]

1. Alain Touraine, Zsuzsa Hegedus, François Dubet and Michel Wieviorka, *Anti-Nuclear Protest: The Opposition to Nuclear Energy in France*, Cambridge 1983, p. 180.
2. Richard Sennett, *The Uses of Disorder*, London 1971, p. 92.

introduction

By this time one thing was clear in those mass meetings. The impression all the workers had was that this was a momentous point in the conflict between the bosses and us, a decisive moment . . . And in fact during the meetings frequent mention was made of the word revolution.

We made holes in all the wire mesh grilles and then we made the torches the torches were made with bits of sheets tied tightly together and then soaked in oil and for this too we agreed a time in the middle of the night we all lit the oil of the torches and we pushed these brands through the holes in the grilles but there was no one there to see this either the torches burned for a long time it must have been a beautiful sight from outside all those torches flickering against the black wall of the prison in the middle of that boundless plain but the only ones who could see the torchlight were those few people driving their cars that sped like tiny darts in the distance on that black ribbon of the motorway several kilometres from the prison or maybe an aeroplane flying above but they fly very high up there in the silent black sky and they see nothing

The above quotations come from two novels by Nanni Balestrini: the first from *Vogliamo tutto*, published in 1971, and the second from *Gli invisibili*, which came out in 1987.[1] They deal respectively with the beginning and the end of the period and the movements that are the subject of this study – a beginning that is bright and vibrant with hope and expectation as protest spreads and individuals find themselves through collective action; an end that is filled with a sense of personal isolation, despair and darkness.

Balestrini's interpretation is, of course, highly individual, and he uses the licence of fiction. Nonetheless (and this is the reason for starting with his words), he reminds us of the point of view, thoughts and feelings of the participants of the movements, those who, in the Italian expression, lived the experience 'on their skins', often paying a heavy price for their illusions and their commitment.

However, it has perhaps become possible in the last few years to gain a more detached and analytic understanding of the post-'68 decade without losing a sense of what it meant at the time. There is now no longer the same obligation either to celebrate and justify in the name of a cause or to condemn '68 and all its works as the postwar equivalent of the Fall. While this divide characterized much of the literature at the time of the tenth anniversary, in 1988 a number of studies appeared which were historical rather than polemical in approach.[2] Indeed, a note of irony and self-consciousness has crept in, sometimes bordering on cynicism, and this marks a change in what Raymond Williams calls a 'structure of feeling'.[3] Until 1980–81 (though it is difficult to pinpoint a date), there was a certain continuity in people's conceptions of themselves with the ideas identified with '68, especially among those who had been participants. Then, from the early 1980s onwards, that past came to resemble a foreign country. It is as if a frontier had been crossed and the language and points of reference had changed.

However, in the Italian case, the significance of the years 1968–9 as a watershed has been hard to forget. The student revolt, followed by the Hot Autumn of industrial disputes in 1969, shook the foundations of the Republic, leading to a decade of intense conflicts. These brought both positive and negative consequences. For a summary of the beneficial effects, it is worth quoting Umberto Eco: 'Even though all visible traces of 1968 are gone, it profoundly changed the way all of us, at least in Europe, behave and relate to one another. Relations between bosses and workers, students and teachers, even children and parents, have opened up. They'll never be the same again.'[4] As for the regressive developments set in motion in the wake of 1968, the most obvious example is the rise of 'black' and 'red' terrorism and the formation of a clandestine Italy bent on the destruction of the country's democratic institutions – what Giorgio Galli has called *L'Italia sotterranea*.[5] And although parliamentary democracy survived these threats, the adoption of draconian legislation and repression produced cruel distortions in the administration of justice, increasing the rights of the state at the expense of the citizen.[6]

The events of 1968–9 can be said to have led to contradictory developments: on the one hand, to modernization, democratization and the growth of civil society; on the other, to endemic social conflict, continued institutional blockage and a polarization of politics into repression and terrorism. However, it is easy and misleading to construct a simple schema of cause and effect. The problem of analysing the continuities and

2

breaks in the forms of oppositional politics, and assessing the extent to which they contributed to a more open or closed society is a key one for this book. Its focus, however, is on social movements.

Social movements, of course, entered centre stage in this period, not only in Italy but in many other countries.[7] The student and worker movements of the late sixties were joined by movements of women, youth, homosexuals, ethnic minorities and others. This phenomenon was important not just for the social groups in question, but for the political, social and cultural life of the societies involved. The meaning of democracy, for instance, was made a matter for debate by the advocates of 'direct democracy' in schools and workplaces,[8] whereas feminists began to redraw the boundaries of the 'public' and the 'private'. Social movements can be seen, therefore, to offer an ideal vantage-point for looking at the changes being brought about in a society, and for understanding the reactions to them. At the same time, the movements are themselves often laboratories of experimentation, incubating future ideas and forms of behaviour.

The Italian case is especially interesting from the point of view of social movements. In the post-'68 period in Italy they were more extensive then in many other countries, spreading into every area of society; they were also often more intensive, including extreme forms of action, and more sustained, lasting for a longer period of time. Whereas, for instance, the May mobilizations in France were short-lived, in Italy the *maggio strisciante* was drawn out until the end of 1969, if not longer.[9] The movements, moreover, took particular forms because of the peculiarities of the national history and development, as witnessed by the role of southern immigrants in the strikes of 1969, or by the role of Catholicism. While the Italian case belongs firmly to the kinds of social movement which arose in Western Europe, it had specific characteristics.

The key importance of social movements in recent Italian history can be appreciated in the rich and intelligent reflections and discussions to which they have given rise. These range from debates in the world of art and design,[10] through to those in works of fiction, political theory, sociology and semiology, a point that is illustrated by the career and writings of Umberto Eco.

Eco in the early 1960s was a member of an avant garde circle that promoted the subversion of literary orthodoxies and aesthetic canons; in 1968 he championed civil rights and was a participant and interlocutor in the struggle to change universities, teaching practices, and how the idea of culture was understood; subsequently, as a columnist, he commented on the methods, objectives and messages of the social movements that traversed Italian society. His *The Name of the Rose*, published in 1980, can be read as a political allegory in which the debates about poverty, authority, inquiry and persecution set in a medieval monastery deal with issues raised by the conflicts of the seventies, especially terrorism.[11]

However, the most developed considerations on social movements have come from Italian sociologists. Their empirical studies and theoretical work are remarkable by any standards, and hopefully, if it does nothing else, this book will show the value of their contribution. The most impressive single research project is the study of industrial conflict carried out under Alessandro Pizzorno at the State University of Milan and published in six volumes called *Lotte operaie e sindacato, 1968–72*.[12] Otherwise, the leading writers in the field include Alberto Melucci, whose work is slowly becoming available in English, and Francesco Alberoni, whose *Movimenti e istituzioni* represents a landmark.[13] Pizzorno, whose approach helped create a school of sociology, developed analyses based on concepts of 'representation' drawn from Gramsci and Durkheim. Melucci, on the other hand, has switched attention away from the relationship of social actors to the political system or market, and towards exploration of the networks of meaning elaborated by and within social movements. In fact, it would be possible to reconstruct the close relationship between the evolution of the movements and the evolution of sociological theory, showing the interaction as a two-way process. Whereas in the early 1970s the sociologists' interests broadly corresponded to the political orientations of the movements (in the sense of their relationship to the political system), by the end of the decade the concern with subjectivity and social and cultural identity expressed within the movements seemed to make the previous model redundant.[14]

Yet while there is now a considerable literature in Italian on social movements, there has not been any attempt to provide a synthesis which looks at their development historically. The movements have also tended to be taken singly rather than as an ensemble. One of the objectives of this book is, therefore, to give an overview and to make some critical assessment of the literature in the light of its reconstruction and interpretation of the movements for the period 1968–78.

States of Emergency is more or less chronological in structure. Part I covers the period prior to the events of 1968 and aims to uncover the latent tensions which later erupted into open conflict. It provides an introduction to the peculiarity of the Italian crisis, relating it to the country's historical development as the 'first of the last, and the last of the first', a country which only became predominantly urban and industrial in the late fifties and early sixties. Parts II and III deal respectively with the student and workers' movements in the years 1968–9. This section forms the core of the book as these two movements, it is argued, established the coordinates for the direction political opposition would take in the following decade. It was not just a matter of what actually happened, but of the mythic status that the late-sixties revolt acquired. Part IV is, in fact, more concerned with the appropriation of that legacy than with measuring the accuracy of reflections on the previous movements. It takes the examples of left-wing terrorism, the youth movement and the women's movement as three case studies. The focus here is on the formative years of terrorism (rather than its point of maximum development), the so-called 'movement of '77', which saw the emergence of a 'youth politics', and the campaigns over abortion, which marked a crucial stage in the development of a feminist politics in Italy. In the final chapter, some concluding observations are made about the relationship of the language of politics in the 1980s to that of the earlier movements.

This study, however, makes no claim to be comprehensive. It is, above all, a study of social movements in the northern Italian city of Milan, although observations are made about the Italian experience more broadly. This requires a word of explanation to help put the Milan movements in a national context.

Taking Milan as the vantage-point from which to survey Italian social movements as a whole inevitably involves difficulties. In fact, the Milanese experience cannot be said to typify or represent national developments. These varied from city to city (not to mention towns and villages). Milan is a city with its own particular social and economic structure, and political and cultural traditions. However, its importance to Italian life, and its role as a centre for a great diversity of activities, meant that Milan was also a centre of social conflict.

Milan has been called the 'real capital' (*il capitale morale*) of Italy because it is a major commercial and industrial centre where many multinational companies have their headquarters, in preference to Rome. Apart from being the home of La Scala, the opera house, and *Il Corriere della Sera* (the Italian equivalent of *The Times*), Milan has a complex cultural infrastructure. This includes publishing houses (these accounted for half the capital and a quarter of the employees in the sector in 1968); three leading universities; and numerous theatres, cinemas, and so on. Historically, Milan had a crucial role in the formation of the nation-state, while its geographical position has helped make it a communications crossroads and the most cosmopolitan of Italian cities.[15] In the early 1960s, Milan was the symbol of the 'economic miracle' and progressive modernism. But at the end of the decade it became a theatre of urban conflict.

Because Milan was a cultural, economic and political centre in the 1960s and 1970s, it was also a site of a wide range of social movements. The universities and engineering factories were in the eye of the storm in 1968–9, and in the following years urban conflicts over housing and other resources were an important feature in the city's life. The various movements, notably the feminist movement, built up networks and counter-cultural activities so that an 'alternative Milan' came into being.[16] Thus, although the Milanese case cannot be taken as representative in a simple sense, the rationale for studying this city lies in the range of the movements which developed there, and the fact that it constituted a point of reference for opposition forces elsewhere in Italy. In 1968–9 only Turin could contest Milan's primacy.

This study is provisional in many respects, and cannot claim to be definitive. While it aims to provide a historical perspective, it is unavoidably conditioned by the contemporary nature of the events and processes being described and analysed. The difficulties have already been alluded to in commenting on pendulum swings in how '68 has been viewed from one anniversary to another. The proximity of the events also means that the sources on which this study is based are restricted. Use has been made mainly of contemporary published material – daily papers, magazines, journals, and emphemera such as leaflets, manifestos, and so on. Nor was it always easy to get access to documentation. Libraries and institutes are only just beginning to collect and organize archives for the period, and no serious attempt has been made to build up oral records.[17] Therefore, private collections were used, along with tape-recorded interviews and fieldnotes, particularly for Parts II and III; Part IV is more dependent on secondary sources. Future historians will have the advantage of archives, but material will not be available for some time to come (thirty years for the state archives; over fifty years for the Vatican archives). They will also have access to more personal documents: letters, diaries, photographs, and so on. Although much can be done in the interim in terms of oral historical work, its validity depends on being able to test it with reference to other sources.[18]

There is growing recognition within Italy of the need to gain a better understanding of this period of turbulent transition running from the late 1960s to the end of the 1970s. A number of conferences organized in 1988 and 1989,[19] and a spate of new publications are signs of this new interest.[20] Moreover, it is a period which is receiving increasing attention from English-speaking scholars.[21] I hope, therefore, that this study will feed into this work. I hope also that it will make a contribution towards current debates about the changing nature of oppositional politics in contemporary Europe,[22] and put the spotlight on the cultural as well as political dimensions of social movements.

Notes

1. Nanni Balestrini, *Vogliamo tutto*, Milan 1974, first edn, 1971, p. 106; *Gli invisibili*, Milan 1987, p. 280; in English translation by Liz Heron, *The Unseen*, London 1989.

2. Perhaps the most interesting book to come out in Italy is Peppino Ortoleva's *Saggio sui movimenti del 1968 in Europa e in America*, Rome 1988.
3. Raymond Williams, *The Long Revolution*, London 1971, first edn. 1961, pp. 64–88.
4. Scott Sullivan, 'Master of the Signs', *Newsweek*, 22 December 1986, p. 49.
5. Giorgio Galli, *Italia sotteranea. Storia, politica e scandali*, Bari 1983.
6. The novelist, Leonardo Sciascia, went as far as writing: 'If in reply to those in Italy (and I include myself) who ask about Sakharov and the plight of Russian dissidents Chernenko was to suggest looking rather at what is happening to our administration of justice, it would be a correct and well-deserved answer'; *Nuovi Argomenti*, October–December 1984.
7. The metaphor of the stage should perhaps be replaced by that of the television screen ‚since this was the first time in history that protest across the world was beamed almost live from continent to continent; see Anthony Smith, *The Shadow in the Cave*, London 1973, pp. 73–111.
8. For the best critical account of the theories of democracy under discussion, see Norberto Bobbio, *The Future of Democracy*, Cambridge 1987.
9. For a comparative study of social conflict in this period, see Colin Crouch and Alessandro Pizzorno, eds, *Resurgence of Class Conflict in Western Europe*, London 1977.
10. For the debate on the politics of design, see Penny Sparke, *Italian Design*, London 1988, pp. 161–97.
11. The relationship between Eco's cultural analyses and the social movements is most evident in the anthologies of his articles: *Il costume di casa*, Milan 1973; *Dalla periferia dell 'impero*, Milan 1977; and *Sette anni di desiderio*, Milan 1983.
12. The findings of the research are contained in the last volume: Alessandro Pizzorno, ed., *Lotte operaie e sindacato: il cicio di lotte 1968–72*, Bologna 1977.
13. For the importance of the concept of 'social movement' to the development of sociology in Italy, see Paolo Ceri, 'I quattro volti dell 'anti-sociologia', *Quaderni di Sociologia*, 4–5, 1985, pp. 53–96; and Carlo Carboni, ed., *Classi sociali e movimenti in Italia. 1970–85*, Bari 1986.
14. See Alberto Melucci, ed., *Altri codici*, Bologna 1984.
15. E. Dalmasso, *Milan: capital economique de l'Italie*, Paris 1971.
16. A new development in the genre of the guidebook in the mid seventies, the 'alternative guide' provided a map of this other city; for Milan, see Giuseppe Ricci, Claudio Marras and Mauro Radice, *Milano alternativa*, Milan 1975.
17. I mainly used the library of the Fondazione Feltrinelli. Hopefully, in the wake of the twentieth anniversary of 1968 more will be done to collect material.
18. For the foremost work in the fields of oral history in Italy, see the studies of Luisa Passerini: *Storia orale*, Turin 1978, and her semi-autobiographical *Autoritratto di gruppo*, Florence 1988.
19. For example, the conference organized by the Department of History of the University of Turin in November 1988; 'Università e società italiana. Le culture e i luoghi' and conference organized by the Istituto Lombardo per la storia del Movimento di Liberazione in Brescia in March 1989.
20. The anniversary year, 1988, was marked by a deluge of anniversary editions in the Italian press, especially the weeklies, *L'Espresso* and *Panorama*, the best of which were found in the special numbers of the daily paper, *Il Manifesto*. Books include celebratory ones, like Mario Capanna's *Formidabili quegli anni*, Milan 1988, and Nanni Balestrini and Primo Moroni's *L'orda d'oro*, Milan 1988, but also Ortoleva's *Saggio sui movimenti del '68*.
21. The most notable recent work on the period is Sidney Tarrow's *Democracy and Disorder: Protest and Politics in Italy 1965–1975*, Oxford 1989, which came out as this book was going to press. The publication in the very near future of Paul Ginsborg's *Italy since 1943*, and Stephen Gundle's study of the Communist Party and cultural change, will represent major contributions to our understanding.
22. A debate promoted by writings such as John Keane's *Democracy and Civil Society*, London 1988, and Boris Frankel's *The Post-Industrial Utopians*, Cambridge 1987.

7

PART I

origins of the crisis of 1968-9

In 1968–9 Italy experienced an 'organic crisis', in which there was a massive withdrawal of support for the structures of representation, and an abrupt increase in political demands. The crisis of 1968–9 arose within specific institutional contexts, especially in the universities and schools, and in the factories, as will be shown in subsequent chapters; but to understand its dimensions it is necessary to look at its historical origins. This is not to say that the crisis was an inevitable outcome of Italian historical development; rather, the aim is to highlight some of the features, especially of the postwar period, which help explain the range of probings and testing of the 'social contract'.

This background to the main study of the social movements will be divided into three chapters. The first will look at the relationship of the subordinate classes of Italian society to the state, taking a cue from some of Gramsci's writings on the question. The second will deal with the organizations of civil society; it will focus in particular on relations between employers and workers, and between the working class and its representative bodies (the unions and left-wing parties). The third chapter will concentrate on the perceptions of injustice and the formulation of 'standards of condemnation' which anticipated and prepared the mass social awakening and mobilization at the end of the 1960s.

This outline of the period before the eruption of the social movements is necessarily selective and partial; it attempts to delineate developments leading up to the crisis, not to provide a historical account of the postwar period.

Themes are introduced in these chapters from a historical perspective which are taken up and developed in parts II and III. The crisis of reformism is discussed in detail in chapter 4, in terms of the educational policies of the Centre–Left government which provoked a storm of protest from students. Distrust of the state is explored in chapter 11 with particular relation to the conflicting conceptions of law and order thrown up by the student and workers' movement. The 'moral outrage' expressed in the slogans of workers' demonstrations is connected up in chapter 16 to historical grievances. The importance of the historical legacy will be seen in how the social actors perceived injustices and how the social movements drew on the past to make sense of and ennoble their struggles.

1

a distrusted state

Recurrent questions in Italian historiography and political discussion have included: Why is the Italian nation-state so lacking in social and political cohesion? And what has led to the incapacity of the ruling bloc to modernize Italy's institutions? Some writers have traced the roots of the problem back to the failure of the attempt to found an absolutist state in Italy in the late Middle Ages, but the usual point of departure for analyses is the *Risorgimento*, the movement of national unification in the mid nineteenth century. The key theses setting the agenda for debate were set out in Gramsci's *Prison Notebooks*.[1] For Gramsci, the model bourgeois revolution – the French Revolution – was the yardstick for assessing the *Risorgimento*, which he called a 'failed revolution' (*rivoluzione mancata*). According to Gramsci, the failure of the Italian bourgeoisie to form a national-popular alliance, involving the subordinate classes in the struggle against the backward landowners, meant that the unification remained formal rather than real. The division between north and south, corresponding to the compromise between northern capital and the southern *latifondisti*, and the exclusion of the great mass of the population from participation in the political life of the new state, meant that a conservative settlement was reached at the expense of economic and social progress. For Gramsci only the Italian proletariat, in alliance with poor peasants, could make a nation out of Italy. Whether Gramsci's analyses withstand criticism by historians today is a matter for debate, but the liveliness of the discussion since the mid sixties suggests that they are useful in giving pointers to understanding the contemporary crisis of the Italian state.

One of Gramsci's concerns, the externality of the popular classes to the formation and subsequent history of the Italian state, is of particular interest. The southern peasantry exemplified this hostility or indifference to nationhood. It was tied by intense local and family loyalties, and shared cultures and dialects having little affinity with a national culture. This peasantry did not identify with Italy as a state, and saw its utopias in the Americas rather than in the peninsula. But the working class of the north, despite its relative privileges, also found itself in conflict with a repressive state.[2] The experience of universal suffrage was an interlude between periods of government exclusively by and for social elites. There were only two free general elections before the Fascists took power in 1922. In other words, the Italian working class before 1945 did not develop a strong sense of citizenship through participation in political parties, elections, voting and celebrations of formal freedoms and equalities.

The other major processes whereby the working class in Western Europe was 'nationalized' – education and war – affected Italian workers less than those of other countries. Education had little impact on the predominant use of dialect, and acted more effectively as a channel for middle-class social mobility than as a means of promoting mass civic consciousness. Wars mobilized sections of the population in a way only paralleled by spurts of industrialization, and aggravated class tensions, creating horizontal solidarities that threatened the unity of the state. The debacle of late-nineteenth-century Italian imperialist expeditions at Adowa, the mutinies and non-collaboration during the 1914–18 war, and the disastrous Fascist military campaigns, all proved counter-productive for the ruling bloc. They also fuelled opposition to nationalism in the form of anti-militarism, anti-statism and internationalism. The persistence of anarcho-syndicalist tendencies within the working class and the widespread identification of the state with all society's evils testify to the traditions of popular anti-statism.

In the post-1945 period the relationship between the working class and the state changed. The establishment of a democratic republic changed the rules of political conflict, and the major parties and unions of the working class made themselves the upholders and interpreters of parliamentary democracy. The principal protagonist of the Resistance, the Communist Party, took a leading part in 're-educating' the working class into this role. Togliatti's reading of Gramsci (whose *Prison Notebooks* were published between 1948 and 1951) centred on the idea that the working class had the task of forging a national solidarity that the weak bourgeoisie was incapable of doing. It had to represent the 'national-popular' and lay the foundations of social and economic reconstruction, as the transitional stage to the construction of a future socialist society. In a speech of June 1945, Togliatti claimed that:

> the democratic revolution in our country has never been completed or seriously

developed .... In demanding the Constituent Assembly, we find ourselves in the company of the best men of our Risorgimento – in the company of Carlo Cattaneo, Giuseppe Mazzini and Giuseppe Garibaldi, and we are proud of it.[3]

But the Communist Party rank-and-file had to be taught that the new parliamentary state was 'theirs' and that they had to act responsibly – a task that was not always easy. A report at the 6th Congress stated:

The persistence of sectarian positions ... is seen in the tendency to disrupt other political meetings ... singing songs with words in bad taste ... leaving work early to attend meetings, the use of banners without the *tricoleur*.[4]

For many, the leadership was only saying these things so that it could fool the other parties, which, it seemed, were happy to work with the Communists for as long as it suited them.

The landslide election victory of 1948 for the Christian Democrat Party finalized the expulsion of the Left parties from government. At this crucial conjuncture democracy as an idea was linked to the Western 'camp' and to the defence of Catholicism. Future governments worked to impose their definitions of what constituted 'democratic' and 'anti-democratic' forces; the Communist Party was treated as alien, while the CGIL was treated as its instrument in the workplace; meanwhile, the 'apolitical' and 'free' trade unions were encouraged. Systematic repression and discrimination and propaganda campaigns were used by governments and by managements in the factories to undermine working-class representative structures.

The close cooperation between the state and the employers' federation (Confindustria), and the exclusion of the working-class parties from government were the two axes on which Italian 'democracy' revolved in the period 1948–60.[5] Although the basic democratic freedoms were observed, there were some continuities with the Fascist state that help explain the ways in which those freedoms were circumscribed and curtailed. In this perspective, it is the period of postwar collaboration and reconstruction which appears as an aberration. The personnel of the state apparatuses had been mostly employed by the previous Fascist regime, and the Republic inherited laws that were the very antithesis of the constitution. The Rocco Penal Code, for example, includes among its list of crimes: the membership of anti-national and subversive associations, the incitement of 'class hatred' and the defamation of state institutions.[6] Although there were few laws controlling labour disputes, industrial conflict was heavily policed through instructions contained in the reports of the procurators-general, and in the circulars, letters and telegrams sent to them and to the prefects by the ministries of justice and of the interior.

During Scelba's period as minister of the interior these were directed almost exclusively against forms of picketing and 'political' strikes.[7] From 1948 to 1954 an estimated 75 were killed and 5,104 were wounded as a result of police action directed against forms of protest.[8]

If the politicized and organized sections of the working class were the targets of repression, governmental policies encouraged private initiatives detrimental to all wage-earners. Laissez-faire economic policy subordinated all state intervention to the immediate needs of private capital. Whilst in other Western European countries reconstruction was carried out with the objective of ensuring full employment and full utilization of capital resources, in Italy a policy of deflation and the containment of demand through a regime of low wages and high unemployment was actively pursued by Einaudi and his successors. State expenditure went towards the construction of motorways that suited the needs of Fiat rather than towards the creation of a welfare state.[9]

The beneficiaries of this economic policy were the big companies and sections of the middle classes. Internal consumer expenditure rose for the small minority of the population that could afford to buy the goods (televisions, cars, fridges, and so on) that symbolized the reign of plenty. In 1960 only 11 per cent of the population owned a fridge. Otherwise production was oriented to the world market. The so-called 'economic miracle' was attained on the basis of increases in productivity much greater than increases in wages. In addition, it entailed the mass migration of labour from the south to the northern cities, and to northern Europe.[10] The 'miracle' aggravated social tensions, making the existing political arrangements untenable.

In 1953 the Christian Democrat government tried to introduce a law (the so-called 'swindle law') that would ensure the permanent majority which it had failed to win in the elections, but the attempt failed in the face of a mass national campaign of opposition. From 1953 to 1963 the Christian Democrats maintained power through coalition governments in which they were always the dominant partner holding the key ministries. In 1960 this politics, based on the exclusion of the Left parties, was put into crisis. The possibility of further alliances with parties to the Right was blocked by mass mobilization against Tambroni's attempt to form a government with the neo-fascist MSI, and a wave of strikes showed the strength of the industrial working class, and the need to win its goodwill.

The nature of these mobilizations gives some indication of the evolution of the working class's relationship to the state. The response to the calls by the parties in 1953 and 1960 shows that there was a strong desire to defend democratic institutions from manipulation and authoritarianism. However, the actions were largely defensive. They were a response to a continuous war of attrition waged against workers' organizations. Their point of reference was the Liberation and Reconstruction period, of which the celebration of 25 April and the battle to apply the spirit of the Constitution were important aspects. By way of contrast, the factory mobilizations of 1960–63 were offensive actions. Their chief objective was wage increases, but the mass street demonstrations signalled a revolt against conditions inside and outside the factory.

The Socialist Party response to the working-class mobilization was to use it as a bargaining counter with the Christian Democrats. It claimed to have a programme of radical reforms and economic planning which would make capitalist development 'rational' and beneficial to the working class as a whole. However, the only reforms which the Socialists succeeded in carrying out as promised were in education and in the nationalization of the electricity industry. The 1969 Forecasting and Planning Report revealed that achievement of objectives for 1966–8 was as low as 11 per cent for urban transport, 16 per cent for hospital building and 22 per cent for school building.[11] This failure was doubly serious because of the inadequacy of state provision of services and their farming out to private agencies. The movement of two million Italians from south to north between 1960 and 1970 created a demand for housing, services, education and basic infrastructures that a laissez-faire government policy had not been able to cope with.

The Centre–Left government created hopes of changes that would bring Italian living standards into line with northern European countries. However, its actions were heavily circumscribed. For the Christian Democrats there was no question of allowing the destruction of the state clientelism that provided one of its power bases (sottogoverno), and for them the inclusion of the Socialists had more to do with isolating the Communists and securing an incomes policy than with a strategy of structural change based on a high wage economy.[12] The imposition of a deflationary policy in 1964 had the political aim of undercutting wage demands by increasing unemployment. This measure effectively asserted the continuity of a low wage regime, and prevented further reforms on the pretext that reform had to wait for more prosperous times.[13]

The Centre–Left experiment contained elements of a longer term strategy for bringing the working class into a collaborative relationship with the state, but there was the minimum of institutionalization. Tripartite talks between unions, private industry and the government were rarely carried out, and then outside the planning framework.[14] Although the Communist Party cooperated with legislation in parliament, it and the CGIL resolutely opposed an official incomes policy. It spoke instead of the need for more structural reforms, but little working-class mobilization took place around the issue of reforms.[15] However, the idea of reform spread, and citizenship came to be considered not just in terms of formal legal and political rights, but in terms of material well-being and rights to housing, education, health facilities and other services. The 1963 general strike over housing represented an important step in this direction.[16] What was in question during the late 1960s was how changes could be brought about; whether a central government dominated by the Christian Democrats, or indeed any government, had the will and capacity to reform. If it did, how could sufficient pressure be brought to bear on it to do so, and, if it did not, what alternative strategies were open to the working class.

The rigidity of the political structures and their acknowledged inability to reform themselves fed popular distrust and suspicion of politicians and the political system. Power remained firmly in the hands of the Christian Democrats, who successfully prevented an alternation of parties in government. The resulting operation of the Italian parliamentary system has been compared to that of Namier's eighteenth-century English parliament in which there were 'ins' and 'outs', and politics consisted of 'place-seeking' and cynical manoeuvring. Percy Allum writes:

> the lack of an electoral alternative has led all parties to viewing their role as the occupation of as many posts as possible in the state institutions not for the purposes of transforming society but of accruing patronage ... this operation has reduced them to being the defenders of sectional interests.[17]

For a short time, it seemed that the Socialists would be different, but the gap between their promises and their achievements widened the longer they stayed in the office. Giuseppe Tamburrano, who was closely involved with the Centre–Left experiment, attributed its demise in the final analysis to the Socialist Party's failure to mobilize support within the country for its reform proposals. Instead of doing this, it lost itself in a maze of bureaucracy. Its experience seemed to prove the old adage that power corrupts, rather than its own thesis that real changes could only be brought about by being the 'control-room' (*stanza dei bottoni*). Moreover, this failure of the Socialist Party's reform programme discredited 'reformism', and it strengthened the hand of those who advocated extra-parliamentary action and revolutionary politics.

Notes

1. For an excellent summary of Gramsci's writings on the subject and assessments of them, see John Davis, ed., *Gramsci and the Passive Revolution*, London, 1979. Diana Pinto has written of the way Italy, which in the 1960s was held up as a model of 'modernization', quickly became a focus of attention because of its crises: 'Seen as the "sick man" of Europe, Italy has been studied recently as a special case among Western

democracies and advanced industrial nations. Indeed its very claim to membership in the 'club' has been at times reconsidered by Italians and non-Italians alike . . . when Italy was doing well she could be pointed out as an example of Western strength and success; when she was doing badly, the specificity of her "case" had to be stressed so as not to bring in question the entire Western frame of reference.' D. Pinto, ed., *Contemporary Italian Sociology*, Cambridge 1981, pp. 1–2.

2. 'Italian workers in general, like the hand-loom weavers of Biella . . . had their political sensibilities sharpened by always seeing beside the factory-owner . . . the police representative, the "carabinieri" . . . and behind them the procurator to the king . . . the prison . . . that is, state violence'; Vittorio Foa, 'Sindacati e lotte sociali', in *Storia d'Italia*, vol. 5, 2, Turin 1976, p. 1788.

3. Paul Ginsborg, 'Gramsci and the Era of Bourgeois Revolution', in *Gramsci and the Passive Revolution*, p. 43. For an outline of the development of Communist Party strategy in this period, see D. Blackmer and S. Tarrow, *Communism in Italy and France*, Princeton 1975.

4. Giorgio Galli, *Storia del PCI*, Milan 1977, p. 298.

5. G. Pasquino, 'Capital and Labour in Italy', *Government and Opposition*, 3, Summer 1976.

6. Percy Allum, *Italy – Republic Without Government*, London 1973, p. 207. See also C. Pavone, 'Sulla continuità dello Stato (1943–45)', *Rivista di Storia Contemporanea*, 1974.

7. Umberto Romagnoli and L. Mariucci, 'Ordinamento sindacale e sistema economico nella Costituzione', in U. Romagnoli and L. Mariucci, *Lo sciopero dalla Costituzione all'autodisciplina*, Bologna 1975.

8. D. Blackmer, 'Postwar Italian Communism', in D. Blackmer and S. Tarrow, *Communism in Italy and France*, p. 47.

9. M. De Cecco, 'Economic Policy, 1945–51', in Stuart Woolf, ed., *The Rebirth of Modern Italy*, London 1971.

10. See A. Graziani, *L'Economia Italiana 1945–70*, Bologna 1972, especially the introduction; also M. D'Antonio, *Sviluppo e crisi del capitalismo italiano, 1951–72*, Bari 1973.

11. Gianfranco Pasquino and Umberto Pecchini, 'Italy', in J. Hayward and M. Watson, eds., *Planning and Public Policy*, Cambridge 1975, p. 138.

12. P. Farneti, 'Partiti e sistema di potere', in V. Castronovo, ed., *Italia Contemporanea*, Turin 1976, pp. 72–3, p. 81.

13. See A. Graziani, 'Aspetti strutturali dell'economia italiana nell'ultimo decennio' in A. Graziani, ed., *Crisi e Ristrutterazione nell'Economia Italiana*, Turin 1975.

14. I.F. Mariani, 'Incomes Policy and Employment Policies in Italian Economic Planning', in *Planning and Public Policy*.

15. Giuseppe Tamburrano, *Storia e cronaca del centro sinistra*, Milan 1971, p. 30; Farneti, 'Partiti e sistema di potere', pp. 82–3.

16. P. Ceri, 'L'autonomia operaia fra organizzazione del lavoro e sistema politico', *Quaderni di Sociologia*, 1, 1977, pp. 28–63.

17. *Republic Without Government*, p. 92.

2

civil society and its discontents

The brevity and fragility of the experience of parliamentary democracy in Italy before 1945 had severe consequences for the nature and development of civil society. The parties, unions and other organizations of the working class had a longer struggle to establish their rights to exist and operate freely than in other capitalist countries. It was not until after the Milan massacre of 1898 that the ruling bloc recognized the need for a strategy designed to limit class conflict through the legitimation of some of its forms. Giolitti had to teach sections of capitalists that it was in their interests that the state did not involve itself in labour disputes. He personally tried to strengthen relations with the reformist wing of the Socialist Party and the trade unions. However, the primary role of the Socialist Party in promoting unionism, the stress given to general class representation in the context of uneven, regionalized industrialization and of a working class in the early stages of its making, and the continued resurgence of insurrectionary syndicalism – all these factors politicized industrial relations in country and town. In these circumstances, the formal distinctions between the political and economic roles of party and union, which characterized a reformist politics found a difficult terrain in which to grow. Revolutionary ideas flourished.[1]

The 'Red Years', 1919–20 were characterized by the confusion of the roles of union and party, and by the rise of the new factory councils that claimed to combine their functions. It was a remarkable experiment in workers' control which remained a much discussed experience, especially in the light of Gramsci's writings.[2] Its defeat, however, opened the way to a wholesale destruction of parties and unions, rather than to a redefinition of their roles within the terms of a parliamentary democracy. The fascist regime replaced them by state-controlled surrogates. The objective of the ruling bloc had become the very abolition of civil society as a sphere of independent activity on the part of the subordinate classes. Even leisure, sporting and extra-work pursuits that had previously been carried on through the political parties were subjected to state organization and supervision. Within the workplace a new ideology of labour was constructed by the employers.[3]

The success of the fascist regime in actually creating its own culture, and in actively intervening in reshaping everyday customs and practices was in many ways limited. However, its destruction not only of organizational structures of opposition, but of a popular memory on the part of the young and of traditions and skills of organization, had lasting effects. Through the anti-fascist struggle and the period of reconstruction, the working class had to recreate its own organizations, and to rebuild the fabric of civil society itself.

The framework for this activity was established by the winning of political freedoms and civil rights, but the power of the working class lay in its extensive network of local organizations. In particular, the political parties played the leading role. The Communist Party in Milan organized in every quarter of the city and extended its control through recreational centres, cooperatives and organizations like Unione delle Donne Italiane (Union of Italian Women, UDI). Certain working-class areas in Milan like Sesto San Giovanni (nicknamed 'Stalingrad') and Rogoredo became Left strongholds. The PCI implanted its cells in the factories; in Milan in 1945 it had 360, and by 1947 these had tripled in number. It has been estimated that by 1948 80 to 90 per cent of Milanese engineering workers were in the CGIL.[4]

As has been noted, working-class organizations developed a defensive rather than offensive strategy in the Reconstruction period. Nevertheless, this imposed limits on managements' 'right to manage' in the factories; workers blocked redundancies, imposed consultation and, in the early stages, purged fascist personnel.[5] The concerted political offensive against the Left, that resulted in the 1948 election landslide, was followed by a longer term and more difficult war against working-class organization in civil society. The political victory had immediate pay-offs for the landlords and property owners, who, with police protection stepped up the rate of evictions, cleared squats and affirmed the rights of property.[6] In the factories the opposition was more tenacious.

The years from 1950 to 1959 were characterized by a long-term decline in working-class organization and resistance in the face of the employers' attacks. In January 1955 Dott. Borletti, vice-president of the Confindustria, the national employers' organization, spoke of their objectives; he said:

We need to bring order back into the factories by re-establishing those forms of discipline without which it is impossible to work; we must eliminate all those deviations and political interferences that the war, the postwar period and revolutionary illusions have introduced into company life.[7]

The first and crucial step was the imposition of mass redundancies. This enabled employers to sack leading militants and to threaten workers as a whole with the prospect of losing their jobs. High unemployment throughout the fifties put pressure on the employed to conform to the orders of management. Those militants who survived found themselves continually under surveillance, moved from one section of the factory to another, and increasingly deprived of rights to represent or be represented in an effective as well as formal sense.[8]

The dismantling of the workers' representative structures allowed management the freer use of labour within the productive process, and employers increased absolute exploitation by introducing longer and more flexible hours. Managements also brought in new machinery and corresponding hierarchical regimes of control to increase the rate of relative exploitation. The weakening of the nucleus of politicized skilled workers meant that resistance to Taylorization had been undermined. In turn, the changes in the productive process lessened the need for those workers through de-skilling, and opened the doors to the unskilled unemployed. Martinoli, a director of Pirelli, put the case for technological change at a conference on workers' conditions in industry held in Milan in 1954:

it provides the optimal conditions for the achievement of higher levels of employment because a number of workers look favourably and almost with a sense of liberation on monotonous work; this work does not require responsibility, a spirit of initiative and the obligation to make decisions.[9]

The system of industrial relations created in the 1950s was paternalistic. It heavily circumscribed workers' freedoms, and punished behaviour which threatened its authority. Independent and active unionism was not recognized. The PCI was excluded from participation in parliamentary government and the CGIL from participation in negotiations within the factory. Union officials did not have permission to enter most Milanese factories between 1948 and 1968. The rights to freedoms of speech and organization sanctioned by the Constitution could not be exercized in the factory. Instead, discrimination and sackings and the careful screening of new employees prevailed.[10]

But paternalism also had its philanthropic aspects. It combined older ideologies of 'family' cultivated by earlier generations of *entrepreneurs* with modern theories of human relations. Companies needed not only to suppress class ideologies but to rearticulate class relations as relations of non-antagonistic reciprocity between employer and employee; the words *operaio* and *classe operaio* had to be substituted by *lavoratore*; a collective identity had to be replaced by individualism. To this purpose companies increased differentials between groups of workers and the variable proportion of the wage linked to piece-rates.[11] The power of foremen to grant personal favours in the shape of job allocation and promotion was increased.[12]

This incentivization of self-interest had a gloss of neo-capitalist consumerism in the bigger, impersonal firms like Pirelli where the management aspired to American Taylorist models in which autonomies and controls in the workplace were exchanged for higher wages.[13] The vogue for human relations spread, but with the emphasis on maximizing productivity through time and motion studies rather than through strategies of job enrichment. Moreover, the tendency was to hold wages down as far as possible, especially among the smaller companies. Older forms of Catholic paternalism held sway especially in the family companies that were still intact in the 1950s. Giovanni Falk, for example, who inherited the Milanese steel dynasty, had a vision of his company as a 'little country with its enlightened governors and faithful subjects, its glorious history and values to be handed down from generation to generation'.[14] Falk, in his eyes, was the symbol of work and harmony, a solid pyramid that threw out a large and protective shadow. Companies provided nursery schools (usually run by a religious order), holiday homes for children, medical services and child allowances. The provision of services was especially designed for women workers, to enable them to work, but also to bind them into the company's family by appealing to them as wives and mothers.[15] The hold of the company ethos, however, was strongest among the white-collar workers, who tended to think of themselves as middle class, and who enjoyed monthly salaries with special secret merit awards for the diligent.[16]

The paternalist strategy aimed to abolish social contradictions. In fact its inflexibility and authoritarianism invested those differences of interest at an economic level with the very questions of power and politics that it aimed to eliminate. Even the big companies did not have the economic resources to act as little states, and gave priority to profit-making. The attempt to cultivate the 'free' trade unions, the predominantly Catholic CISL and the Social Democrat and Republican UIL, had some success,[17] especially among white-collar workers, but managements preferred to establish clientelistic relations with them rather than to encourage collective bargaining. They therefore built up memberships as a result of preferential treatment, bribery and discriminatory recruitment policies. Whilst this divided and weakened workers' overall organization in the short term, it did not help create a viable alternative to the left-wing CGIL. Neither did the backstairs bargaining provide an adequate mechanism for dealing with widespread shopfloor discontent. Thus, when conflict occurred in circumstances more favourable to workers, it involved fundamental issues concerning rights and it was infused with political significance.

Statistics on industrial conflict, membership and elections to the internal commissions indicate the extent to which the employers' offensive did paralyse and dismember the union organization built up before 1948. Strikes caused the loss of 64 million hours a year in 1948–9 and an average 22 million for 1950–58.[18] Industrial conflict in Milanese industry was sustained for a longer period, and the figures for union membership are less disastrous than for some cities. Nonetheless, the percentage of the unionized out of the total employed in the engineering sector fell from 61 per cent in 1951 to 23.7 per cent in 1958.[19] A central factor in eroding unionization was the increase in the number and percentage of unskilled and semi-skilled workers being taken on, especially women and youth.[20] The nucleus of the unionized was based on the skilled section of the workforce who had been the leading protagonists in the antifascist movement. Repression reinforced division between the skilled and unskilled, whilst the growing white-collar section of the workforce remained largely untouched by unionism.

The unions' response to the employers' attacks was heavily conditioned by the unfavourable conditions in which they operated during the 1950s. In the CGIL, memories of that period evoke pictures of steadfast heroism. The union activists paid dearly for their beliefs, and it was the strength of their convictions that drove them on. Not surprisingly, therefore, it was party members who made up the backbone of the union organization.[21] A young woman organizer who worked at the Borletti factory from the end of the decade remembers:

> Almost all the activists were in the Communist Party. Firstly, they trained in Party schools and then they took their battle into the union ... many were regularly sacked ... it was really a way of selecting militants; the more the bosses hit them, the more they became true political militants.[22]

However, the strengths of the inner core of the union did not compensate for its relative isolation from the majority of workers nor for serious inadequacies of analysis and policy.

Some of the deficiencies can be attributed to the very influence of the parties: party political issues such as the Korean War and general programmes for economic renewal did not connect up with bread-and-butter questions: ideological divisions got in the way of organizing around common interests; union activities were constantly liable to outside party pressures. But these have to be related to the fact that most activists were skilled male workers who had participated in the Resistance, whilst the majority of newly recruited workers were younger, unskilled and unpoliticized. These divisions along the lines of age, gender and union experience were aggravated by employer policies of divide-and-rule, and by the introduction of new technologies, which greatly changed labour processes, and therefore relations between sections of workers. The failure by the CGIL to develop analyses and appropriate strategies meant that it was marginalized from the everyday problems and experiences of the workplace.[23] The cultural backwardness (a looking-back to older models of class unionism and Marxist orthodoxies) furnished mobilizing ideals, but weakened the CGIL's capacity to meet the needs of a new generation of workers.

The CISL, by contrast, took the American unions as its model, and tried to break with the Italian tradition of left-wing trade unionism in the name of modernity. It represented its members only, and concentrated on productivity bargaining at local levels. In practice, the CISL was anti-Communist. It was tied to the Christian Democrat Party and under the influence of the Catholic Church. Moreover, its predominantly white-collar membership within industry and the service sector made it even more prone to management pressures. The CISL's negotiation of agreements for its members that excluded the CGIL, its dependence on discriminatory recruitment for its membership and its refusal, as far as possible, to go on strike made it a *de facto* form of company unionism in the 1950s.[24]

Between 1960 and 1963 this system of industrial relations based on paternalism was challenged from below. The defeat of the Tambroni government due to mass mobilizations, gave workers a sense of power. The decline of unemployment and the economic upturn put workers in a position to bargain with employers. The economic transformation of the 'miracle' years increased the numbers of workers and their relative importance as a group in society in the northern triangle. At the same time, huge increases in investment, productivity and profits had been achieved without reform of a low wage regime guaranteed by authoritarianism within the factory. Rebellion in the factories, starting with the militancy of the young workers in the electrical engineering sector in Milan in 1960, expressed a demand for a share in the newly created wealth. They called for wage increases and succeeded in winning considerable concessions. In the struggles the union succeeded in using wage demands as a means of unifying different sections of workers. Differentials were reduced, the principle of wage parity for women over eighteen was established, and a two-hour reduction of the working week was won. On the shopfloor, engineering workers experimented with short, sharp strikes, backed by the

CGIL, in addition to the use of national general strikes and demonstrations, which were the traditional form of mobilization. The latter were on a scale that had not been seen on the streets of the big cities since 1948. Students too marched alongside workers.[25]

The shift in the balance of class forces in Italy was reflected in the increased percentage of the Gross National Income accruing to the working class. However, it was a temporary advance that was reversed from late 1963 to 1967. Deflationary policies increased unemployment and employers clamped down on wage increases. The gains were whittled away through inflation and once more productivity increases exceeded those of wages.[26] The government did not succeed in establishing an incomes policy, and instead provided the conditions for the strengthening of management's hand. The unions were too weak to mobilize effective resistance. Above all, the unions within the factories had failed to build up their organization; membership did not increase proportionally to the increase in the working population, and continued to depend on the male, skilled and older section of the workforce for its leadership. Measures of union recognition and agreement to plant bargaining by the internal commissions were circumscribed by both management and union preference for centralized negotiation at higher levels.[27] The unskilled and semi-skilled, the women, younger workers and immigrants were the most exposed to the pressures of the labour market and to changes in the labour process. These workers' interests were inadequately represented. Union analyses of changes in the labour process led to policies of accepting technical change as good in itself rather than as inherently structured by capitalist relations. Bad working conditions were accepted in exchange for monetary compensation. Wage differentials were accepted as a reflection of objective skills together with the introduction of new grades for the highly skilled.[28] In short, the key mechanisms of division and hierarchical control within the factory were not comprehensively challenged by the unions. The anger and explosive militancy of the most oppressed and exploited sections were treated as an abberration, as evidenced by the celebrated Piazza Statuto incidents in Turin in 1962.[29]

In the mid sixties economic development centred on restructuring and rationalization of plant to maximize the rate of relative exploitation,[30] without increasing capital investment to the level of the 1951–63 period. Speed-ups of the line and increases in workloads reached intolerable levels in some factories. Managements replaced women and older workers by young semi-skilled men because of their physical endurance.[31] The atmosphere in the factories was no longer one of fear and intimidation, but unions had still not been readily accepted as bargainers within the workplaces. Leopoldo Pirelli, vice-president of the Confindustria, publicly espoused enlightened acceptance of trade unionism, whilst within his factories he withheld recognition from the CGIL. The idea that the factory was exclusively under management control and that it was vital to defend the conquests of the 1950s in this sphere was shared by the 'enlightened' vanguard of Italian industry and the small company owner alike. Negotiation was limited to powerless joint consultative bodies. Repression had become more selective, and management was more self-conscious about control techniques, but otherwise the paternalist model remained intact.[32]

The contradictions within the factory were not, however, displaced into the market, nor were workers' struggles for higher wages transformed into a mechanism for expanding the home market. Carli, president of the Bank of Italy, did not pursue a Keynesian economic policy characteristic of other advanced capitalist countries. The brief experience of a higher standard of living was cut short. The language of class consciousness promoted in the propaganda of the CGIL connected up with widespread resentment over social inequalities. The propagation in the newspapers and on television of ideas about Italian prosperity, and invocations to spend produced 'needs' and expectations that were frustrated by the meagreness of the wage packet.[33]

The relationship between the capitalist interest groups and the government was also fraught with differences. The reemergence of industrial conflict and the demise of an earlier industrial and political equilibrium made some leading sections of the capitalist class look to government for solutions. Fiat and Pirelli promoted the idea of a trade-off involving reforms in exchange for lower wage increases. For these big companies, planned wage increases and additional taxation were worth conceding if they sought social peace, because their chief concern was with the costs of running capital-intensive plant. Moreover, their representatives, like Pirelli, prided themselves on being long-term thinkers and modernizers. On the other hand, the smaller companies that dominated the *Confindustria* in the 1960s depended on keeping wages to a minimum, and had a laissez fairist hatred of government interference and taxation. The hostile campaign of the *Confindustria* against the nationalization of the electrical industry, and its attempt to block reforms characterized its unrelenting efforts to sabotage the Centre–Left government.[34] This lobby proved more determined and influential than the reformers.

The big companies did little to support the government reforms, and went along with deflation because the buoyant international market provided an outlet for their goods.[35] The half-hearted attempt to delegate the task of managing consensus to the state was ultimately a failure because the ruling bloc was not prepared to allow it sufficiently autonomy to act against some of its immediate interests. However, there were no comprehensive, alternative approaches to industrial relations within the private companies; no policy of greater flexibility was designed to involve the unions themselves in the disciplining of their membership. The relative ease with which the counter-offensive of the mid sixties was carried out gave management the illusion that their prerogatives were safe from serious threat.

The unions and the nuclei of militants formed in the struggles of 1960–63 were thrown into confusion by the downturn in their fortunes. Rifts reappeared between the confederations; the CISL and UIL supported the Centre–Left government and its proposed incomes policy, whilst the CGIL was split between its PCI component, which opposed wage control without adequate guarantees that there would be far-reaching reforms, and the Socialists who were loyal to their government. In the interests of formal unity the CGIL ended by expressing opposition without mobilizing it.[36] Attention focused on the development of national negotiations, whilst the politicking dissipated the fragile unity among the rank-and-file.

The gap between the representative structures of unions and Left parties and sections of the working class widened. The unions' introduction of new factory-based forms of representation remained on paper,[37] whilst the internal commissions did not revive their plant-bargaining activity because of the limits set by national contracts. Within the factories the PCI cells withered, and many of their papers ceased publication.[38] Outside the factory, neither unions nor parties tried to organize the unemployed. The transformation that had changed the composition of the working class through reorganizations of the labour process had also radically altered its housing and living conditions. Massive urbanization and growth of the northern industrial cities destroyed the roots of older political sub-cultures.

In the 1950s the grassroots structures of the political parties – the parish structure on which the Christian Democrats depended,· and the sections of the Left parties – had adapted to the relatively slow demographic changes. A political geography of 'red' and 'white' zones had been fairly clearly delineated and the associations of civil society were permeated by political affiliations. Especially in the case of the PCI, party life defined social horizons, and an intense and embattled community spirit was formed. Much political mobilization and activity was functional to the preservation of the organization. In the cities there were quarters where the urban space (the courtyards of the tenement houses, the local *osteria*) served to underpin social solidarity. However the rapid urbanization of the 'miracle' years provoked the decomposition of these communities.[39]

The bases of the Left parties were hit in several ways. Thousands of migrants, particularly from the south, went into peripheral areas of the cities where the parties had no preexisting organization, or into inner city areas that became heavily overpopulated.[40] The party sections were used to relating to relatively stable communities of families, and were ill-prepared to cope with the needs of the solitary male immigrant. The Church organizations for immigrant workers and the Christian Democrats had more adequate ways and means for dealing with immediate material wants. The letter of recommendation for the job and the provision of charity fitted with paternalist practices in the factory. Then the immigrants themselves made up for all the shortcomings of the welfare services with the organization of self-help, usually on a family basis. In an atmosphere that was often one of discrimination against the Southerner (*terrone*), solidarity among immigrants led to a certain 'ghettoization'.[41] The incapacity of the Left parties to respond to the needs of these people by fighting for the provision of housing, against high rents and for real equalities of living conditions with the older generation of inhabitants meant that they were not attracted to the existing political structures.

Urban development also involved a progressive undermining of the traditional working-class strongholds. Previously peripheral areas of the cities suddenly became relatively central, and prone to 'gentrification' by the middle classes, whilst the centre was monopolized by the office blocks and big shops.[42] Then more general changes in society overtook the parties. Within the working class a gap grew up between the fathers whose politics were formed in the period of the Resistance and Cold War, and children who were becoming adults within a world of East–West detente and relative international capitalist growth. Both the ideologies of a Stalinist Marxism that forecast imminent economic collapse, and of traditional Catholic morality were losing their relevance.[43] Communist Party membership figures show a steady decline for the period 1954 to 1968. As a percentage of the industrial working class it was falling, but the fall in the membership of the youth federation (FGCI) was even more dramatic.[44]

The inability of the PCI, and of the PSI (which was ceasing to be a mass party), to recruit, represent and mobilize workers, and particularly immigrant workers, youth and women, signalled a failure to deal with the major social transformations of postwar Italy.[45] Taylorization, urbanization, mass schooling and mass migration were important aspects of the remaking of the Italian working class in the postwar decades. Yet, the Communist Party did not know how to organize around the social conflicts they engendered. The parties' and unions' inability to interpret and represent discontent in civil society was accompanied by their tendency to look to parliament and the state to resolve or alleviate the contradictions that had been accumulated in the period of economic boom. Action in civil society was subordinated to parliamentary manoeuvres, electioneering and forms of pressure-group politics. The PSI was immobilized from 1963 because of its involvement in government, and owed its influence in the CGIL to its personnel in the leadership rather than on the shopfloor, whilst in the constituencies it too used the spoils of office to cultivate a clientelist vote. It underwent the classic Italian political process of 'transformism'.[46] The PCI remained in official opposition, but within parliament cooperated in drafting legislation. Whilst the PCI remained a mass party of the working class, and its leaders stressed the importance of membership and implantation in civil society, in the period 1954 to 1968 it was undergoing a process of 'electoralization'. The party's votes marginally increased, but its membership declined.[47] In 1968 the PCI's capacity to mobilize subordinate groups had seldom been weaker. It followed rather than led the mass social movements of 1968–9.

This incapacity of the political parties of the Left and the unions to articulate and represent discontent within civil society meant that when people mobilized, they resorted to disruption rather than to the ballot-box or to petitioning. The claims of the politicians and trade unionists about the importance of organization, discipline and alternative reforms went unheard. Where the official organizations in centres of discontent (like large factories and universities) were weakest, the forms of protest tended to be the most unruly. One of the most dramatic examples which showed this in 1968–9 was social conflict in Turin; the very factors which had weakened the resistance of workers and subordinate groups – immigration, repressive paternalism, scientific management, depoliticization – created the conditions for a highly radicalized revolt. The steady erosion and destruction of the sense of community within the workplace and the city created a need to build that community through collective resistance. However, there was nothing automatic about this process. Resistance grew up because of changes in how individuals and groups perceived their situation.

Notes

1. Giovanna Procacci, 'Caratteri dello sviluppo economico in Italia dalla fine del secolo alla prima guerra mondiale', *Archivio Sardo*, 4–5, 1975, pp. 81–135.
2. See Gwyn Williams, *Proletarian Order*, London 1975.
3. Adrian Lyttleton, *The Seizure of Power*, London 1973; Luisa Passerini, 'Work Ideology and Consensus under Italian Fascism', *History Workshop Journal*, 8, Autumn 1979, pp. 82–109.
4. S. Vento, 'Milano', in R. Rugafiori, F. Levi and S. Vento, *Il Triangolo Industriale*, Milan 1974.
5. One worker from the Sit Siemens in Milan recalled that some managers were not allowed into the factory unless they were carrying a copy of *L'Unità*, the Communist daily; see I. Regalia, 'Sit Siemens', in A. Pizzorno, ed., *Lotte operaie e sindacato in Italia*, vol. 4, Bologna 1975, p. 34.
6. G. Consonni and G. Tonon, 'Aspetti della questione urbana a Milano dal fascismo alla ricostruzione', *Classe*, June 1976, pp. 43–101.

7. *Scintilla*, April 1955, Factory paper at Borletti's in Milan.
8. See E. Pugno and S. Garavini, *Gli anni duri alla Fiat*, Turin 1974; Giuseppe Della Rocca, 'L'offensiva politica degli imprenditori nelle fabbriche', *Annali della Fondazione Feltrinelli*, 1974–5, pp. 609–39.
9. Giuseppe Della Rocca, 'L'offensiva politica degli imprenditori', p. 612.
10. The 1957 Parliamentary Commission on working conditions in factories found many instances of abuse of workers' rights; one testimony went: 'Before being employed information is asked on your opinions about politics, the unions, and family life. On being employed, the worker must present two photographs for the company files. It is as if he is about to enter a prison rather than a factory.' *Libro Bianco della Gioventù delle Officine Borletti a cura della Commissione Giovenile FIOM*
11 A. Illuminati, *Lavoro e rivoluzione*, Milan 1974, p. 129; M. Regini and E. Reyneri, *Lotte operaie e organizzazione del lavoro*, Milan 1974, pp. 17–30.
12. For a fascinating account of relations between male workers and foremen which tells of picnics in the countryside as well as of arbitrary despotism in the factory, see Franco Platania, '23 years at Fiat', in Red Notes, *Working Class Autonomy and the Crisis*, London 1979.
13. P. Bolchini, *La Pirelli: operai e padroni*, Florence 1967, p. 97.
14. G. Manzini, *Una vita operaia*, Turin 1976, p. 110.
15. Scuola Serale CNAS, *Borletti*, Milan 1970.
16. Aldo Marchetti, 'Linea sindacale e reorganizzazione del lavoro negli uffici, 1948–75', *Classe*, 13, February 1977, pp. 172–3.
17. See glossary for brief outline of differences between the union confederations.
18. Bianca Beccalli, 'Scioperi e organizzazione sindacale', *Rassegna Italiana di Sociologia*, XII, 1971, pp. 91–3.
19. Ibid., pp. 101–2.
20. The number of women employed in the province of Milan rose from 1950 to 1960 by 22%. The increase was mostly in factories requiring seasonal labour (for example, ice cream production), the telecommunication sector's assembly lines where women predominated, and in the service sector. Women's patterns of employment typically met the requirements of cheapness, seasonality and flexibility.
21. Alessandro Pizzorno, 'Sull 'azione politica dei sindacati', *Problemi del Socialismo*, 49, November–December 1970, pp. 880–84.
22. Interview with Rina Barbieri, 25 March 1978.
23. For analyses of the traditional Left's failure to grasp the changing nature of postwar capitalism, see the writings of Raniero Panzieri; *La Ripresa del Marxismo–Leninismo in Italia*, Milan 1972, and, *Lotte operaie nello sviluppo capitalistico*, Turin 1972. Also Illuminati, *Lavoro e Rivoluzione*, pp. 78–93.
24. 51% of national membership was white collar; five out of nine members of the secretariat in the early fifties were members of the Christian Democrat Party; see Pizzorno, 'Sull'azione politica dei sindacati', pp. 887–90. For a history of Catholic unionism, see D. Horowitz, *The Italian Labour Movement*, Cambridge, Mass. 1963; and G.P. Cella and B. Manghi, *Un sindacato italiano negli anni sessanta. La FIM–CISL dall 'Associazone alla classe*, Bari 1972.
25. D. Grisoni and H. Portelli, *Le lotte operaie in Italia dal 1960 al 1976*, Milan 1976, pp. 77–9; P. Bolzani, 'Le lotte di fabbrica dal luglio '60 al centro sinistra', *Classe*, 16, December 1978, pp. 51–86.
26. M. Salvati, *Il sistema economico italiano: analisi di una crisi*, Bologna 1975, pp. 41–3.
27. Foa, *Sindacati e lotte operaie: 1943–73*, pp. 120–21.
28. Illuminati, pp. 147–9.
29. Young Fiat workers attacked the headquarters of unions opposed to strike action and brought the wrath of the CGIL as well as the other unions down on their heads. See Dario Lanzardo, *Piazza Statuto*, Milan 1981; Foa, *Sindacati e lotte operaie*, pp. 130–32.
30. Salvati, *Il sistema economico italiano*, pp. 30–31.
31. Massimo Paci, *Mercato di lavoro e classi sociali in Italia*, Bologna 1973, pp. 272–5.
32. A handbook giving advice on how time-and-motion men should behave towards the

workers is instructive about techniques of self-presentation to the point of absurdity. 'Young technicians', it begins, 'cannot have a profound knowledge of Man and therefore can lack tact when dealing with workers; this can result in damaging their morale and professional stature ... 24 points are listed that, whilst appearing puerile, are a fundamental guide to living on the shopfloor: (i) Show yourself full of energy; (ii) Walk quickly; (iii) Don't assume airs; (iv) Don't keep your hands in your pockets; (v) Don't dress too elegantly; ... (viii) Don't use excessive amounts of aftershave; (xi) Don't suck sweets; (x) Show no interest in the opposite sex; (xi) Display interest and not bewilderment in front of productive processes and machines seen for the first time; (xii) Stand in a comfortable position that is not disrespectful towards the worker; (xiii) If smoking offers occasion for reflection, offer a cigarette to those engaged in the job in question; ... (xv) Don't ask the worker what you should already know; ... (xviii) Don't greet superiors in a servile manner and (xix) Speak in Italian.' An extract from 'Comportamento del cronotecnico' by Dott. Luigi Novellis in *Corso di cronotecnica* (1964), quoted, with irony, in *Megafono*, June 1970, the Borletti workers' paper.

33. The Italian working class tended to buy consumer durables by cutting back on expenditure on food and housing, showing how a new idea of 'necessity' was being constructed; A. Graziani, *L'economica italiana*, pp. 46–9.
34. G. Tamburrano, *Storia e cronaca del centro sinistra*, Milan 1971. pp. 241–56.
35. A. Graziani, 'Aspetti strutturali dell'economia italiana nell'ultimo decennio', in A. Graziani, ed., *Crisi e Ristrutturazione nell'Economia Italiana*, Turin 1975, pp. 28–32.
36. Sergio Turone, *Storia del sindacato in Italia, 1943–69*, Bari 1976, pp. 383–418.
37. Tiziano Treu, *Sindacato e rappresentanze aziendali*, Bologna 1971, pp. 49–76.
38. From 1954 to 1967 the number of factory cells nationally fell from 11,495 to 3,013; see M. Barbagli and P. Corbetta, 'Partito e movimento: aspetti e rinnovamento del PCI', *Inchiesta*, 31, January–February 1978.
39. G. Sivini, *Partiti e partecipazione politica in Italia*, Milan 1969.
40. For all the provinces of the industrial triangle 77% of the rise in population (by 1,439,013 between 1951 and 1961) was due to immigration. Half of the immigrants went to Milan. See E. Dalmasso, *Milan: capitale economique de l'Italie*, Paris 1971, pp. 452–80.
41. For a fascinating analysis of the experience of a group of Southern women in Turin, see Gabriella Gribaudi, 'Reticoli sociali e immigrazione: relazioni di scala', in E. Beltrami et al, *Relazioni sociali e strategie individuali in ambiente urbano: Torino nel novecento*, Turin 1981.
42. M. Boffi, S. Cofini, A. Glasanti and E. Mingione, *Città e conflitto sociale*, Milan 1972.
43. E.G. Della Loggia, 'Ideologie, classi e costume', in Castronovo, *Italia Contemporanea*.
44. Working-class membership: 1947 – 958,596; 1950 – 886,000; 1959 – 690,000; mid-60s – 650,000. 'From 1954 to 1962 the PCI is reduced to having not 3 but 1 worker member to every 10 employed workers.' Centro G. Francovich, *I. Communisti in Fabbrica*, Milan 1967, pp. 8–9. From 1954 to 1968 membership of the FOCI fell from 430,000 to 125,000 – a loss of 70.9%; M. Barbagli and P. Corbetta, 'Partito e movimento', p. 8.
45. 'Political participation was higher for the skilled than for the unskilled, and for factory workers than non-factory workers. It was minimal for the "peripheral" groups'. G. Martinotti, "Le Caratteristiche dell 'Apatia Politica", *Quaderni di Sociologia* XV, 1966, pp. 288–309.
46. *Trasformismo* is the term used to describe the process whereby a party's political programme converges with that of its opponents. It was used first to describe how, when the Left came to power under Depretis in 1876, the latter began to recruit his ministers indiscriminately from both sides of parliament.
47. This needs to be put in the context of the PCI's strategy for broadening its support within civil society by winning over other social groups; see S. Hellman, 'the PCI's Alliance Strategy and the Case of the Middle Classes', in D. Blackmer and S. Tarrow, *Communism in Italy and France*, Princeton 1975.

3

the agitators and moral outrage

From the end of the 1950s Italy was a country undergoing simultaneous major upheavals in its social and economic structure, so that it experienced change with a sudden intensity. John Low-Beer writes that the

> innovative militancy of the Italian labour movement since 1968 may be explained partly by the conjunction of a number of changes in the society in the previous years: the rapid growth of manufacturing in the North and the concomitant immigration from rural areas of the South to the industrial cities of the North; and the increase in the student population and in the number of technicians in the advanced sectors of industry. The spread of values particular to postindustrial society thus coincided with the large influx of young immigrants into semi-skilled jobs. In Britain or the United States, these changes were separated by at least a generation. Their overlap proved to be an explosive situation.[1]

As has been seen, the reorganization of the workplace and the city had contradictory effects; thus, the labour militancy can in part be ascribed to the discontent of the immigrant workers, but immigration also had consequences of making organization and resistance more difficult. The changes provoked fractures between the parties of the Left and the unions and their constituencies, and made their analyses of social realities hopelessly inadequate. So there was nothing automatic about the emergence of the spirit of collective protest and opposition. It grew first of all on the margins of the organizations and in the minds of dissident and disaffected individuals. These figures will be the subjects of this section; firstly, in the shape of intellectuals and, secondly, in that of the worker-militant.

A Dissident Intelligentsia

The period of the 1960s was characterized by a ferment among intellectuals on the Left reacting against the Marxism of the Communist and Socialist parties, and searching for a revitalized theory. Groupings which became known as the New Left set themselves a historic task; it was, in Giovanni Bechelloni's words:

> a political culture which aimed to break with the heritage of idealism (a heritage which appeared in the thinking of the Left parties in the shape of historicism, Gramscianism, neo-realism and philosophical Marxism); to do this, it re-read Marx as the sociologist of capitalist society, but the return to Marx was characterized by a tension between theoretical inquiry and political commitment.[2]

This project's outcome can be examined in different ways, but here the primary concern is with the New Left's critique of the organizations claiming to represent the working class, and with its role in promoting social mobilization. The focus will be on its reviews, and on the political initiatives emerging from them.

The importance of the review in the 1960s needs to be related to the particular role of intellectuals in Italian society, especially on the Left, and to the political debate of the period. Firstly, it is worth noting that the idea of the review as a privileged format for theoretical/political intervention sprang up within the milieu of the city intelligentsia. Becchelloni describes it as being composed of groups of people peripheral to the political parties, who teach in universities, often on a temporary basis, or in a *liceo*; they have connections with publishing houses, live in the cities of the Centre and North, and many travel to the United States, Britain, France and Germany.[3] Their marginality is significant in that it is also the result of a choice that involves an alternative intellectual route, which is cosmopolitan. It holds the promise of a future that others might not be able to see. In this spirit Franco Fortini wrote in a letter published in the first edition of *Quaderni Piacentini*:

> The history of contemporary Western societies is the history of individuals and minorities who decide not to bow to the inevitable ... those who in their isolation have decided not to remain alone.[4]

In a similar vein, characteristic of the significance of the visionary in the mythology of the Left, Danilo Montaldi wrote of Lenin as someone who 'did not accept "reality", and by "dreaming" realized what no "realist" succeeded even in imagining'.[5] The roles assigned to the intellectual were as numerous as the different currents within the New Left, but there was a shared belief in the power of ideas and hence, even if implicitly, in that of their authors and disseminators. A high moral tone and deep seriousness emanated from the pages of the reviews, and dominated the oppositional culture.

It is significant, however, that in the 1960s it was largely through reviews rather than through books that cultural exploration was pursued. This particular cultural vehicle was more suitable to the needs and aspirations of a new brand of intelligentsia. It facilitated the expression of a collective as opposed to individualistic ethos such as that celebrated in the dominant culture's conception of the artist and thinker. Goffredo Forfi has remarked on the peculiar value of the review:

> I have always been convinced that reviews, more so than books, 'make culture', if only because very few really important books get published. . . . Working on a review requires practical knowledge and abilities; there is the exchange of opinions between people, the taking up of positions, the making of decisions in relation to what is happening, the capacity to reason and to choose between proposals.[6]

The importance of the reviews and the sense that intellectuals had something important to contribute related to the context of rapid social change, which seemed to call for new maps and compass readings. Bechelloni lists six reviews as being the most influential: *Quaderni Rossi*, *Quaderni Piacentini*, *Classe e Stato*, *Classe Operaia*, *Contropiano* and *Nuovo Impegno*. Of these, attention will be given to *Quaderni Rossi* (*QR*) and *Quaderni Piacentini* (*QP*), which first came out in September 1961 and March 1962 respectively, and to *Classe Operaia*. The first task faced by the reviews was to make a comprehensive critique of the traditional Left, and the second (though it did not necessarily follow) was to elaborate alternatives. Bechelloni has written:

> The history of the reviews and of the relations (or lack of them) with the parties and organizations of the Workers' Movement can also be studied as the history of the incapacity for renewal and openness on the part of the leaderships of the latter.[7]

This blockage became particularly evident in the post-1956 renewal of debate on democracy, though it should be pointed out that this was most lively in the Socialist Party where there was a greater range of opinion from pro-Soviet to social libertarian than in the Communist Party. Leading spirits within *Quaderni Rossi*, like Raniero Panzieri, were former members of the PSI or part of critical minorities within it, like Vittorio Foa. The entry of the party into government in 1963 and the subsequent foundation of the PSIUP further distanced the intellectual dissidents.[8]

There was no equivalent split in the Communist Party until the Manifesto group's formation in 1969, although prestigious individuals like the philosopher Lucio Colletti left in protest against Stalinism.[9] However, it was an obligatory point of reference and target of criticism as the biggest party and the custodian of Marxist orthodoxy.

The critiques made of the parties were predominantly of what was seen as their 'social democratization'. This was most evident in the case of the Socialist Party, but was also thought to apply to a Communist Party that was oriented to parliamentarism and losing touch with the industrial working class. This line of analysis had a long history in the writings of the Bordigist and Trotskyist organizations, which claimed to be the genuine heirs to Marx and Lenin. For them, the key to revolution lay in the role of the party and the adoption of the 'correct political line'. In the 1960s this approach was given a new lease of life with the popularity of the Chinese model following the Cultural Revolution of 1965–6. The Chinese model answered a call for orthodoxy and the wish to believe in a promised land. However, the critiques developed by the *Quaderni Rossi*, and by Raniero Panzieri in particular, departed from this sterile tradition. They questioned elements of the tradition itself as well as what were seen as its deformations at the hands of the Socialist and Communist Parties.

Panzieri's critique was far-reaching and had lasting effects precisely because it did not recapitulate the attacks on the parties for 'betraying' the working class or for deviating from the orthodoxies. He said quite simply that the problems went back to the founding fathers themselves, whose object of analysis had been laissez faire capitalism. A consequence of this was that they gave disproportionate importance to planning and to the common ownership of the means of production as the defining features of socialism. It was, then, these aspects that predominated in the thinking of the modern parties. They espoused the vogue for technological change, planning and modernization, thereby subordinating themselves to the logic of neo-capitalist development.[10] Panzieri did not spell out his own position, but in his writings others found critiques of the vanguardist conception of the party, ideas for council communism, and the brief for Italian appropriations of Chinese experiments in breaking down divisions of mental and manual labour. Panzieri did not live long enough to see this happen, and was not a person lightly to dismiss the parties and unions with which he had worked for so long. However, a younger generation had less caution and greater expectations.[11]

The question of alternative organization and concrete political intervention haunted the intellectuals associated with the reviews. Above all, they accepted the Marxist insistence on the unity of theory and practice. However, they were more in agreement over their differences with the traditional Left than in how to act on their ideas. The problem was less pressing for *Quaderni Piacentini* which assumed the role of a forum and published articles from a range of viewpoints, including the first appearances in Italian of writings by Marcuse, Horkheimer and Habermas. For the *Quaderni Rossi*, on the other hand, disagreement ended in splits and the launching of *Classe Operaia*. The editorial group was divided in its estimation of whether the time was ripe for setting up a revolutionary organization; Panzieri and Vittorio Reiser referred to the engineering contract of 1962 as a defeat for both the unions and the working class, while for the future founders of *Classe Operaia*, Romano Alquati and Mario Tronti, the former had indeed been defeated, but the working class had made a 'qualitative leap'.

The fate of *Quaderni Rossi* and *Classe Operaia*, neither of which survived longer than a couple of years, would be of little interest but for their place in the history of the Italian New Left. Their role has retrospectively acquired mythic qualities. Particularly celebrated were Tronti's articles: 'Lenin in England', 'Factory and Society' and 'The Strategy of Refusal', which proved to be founding documents of Italian *operaismo*.[12] A key formulation was:

> We too have worked with a concept that puts capitalist development first and the workers second, and this is a mistake. Now we have to turn the problem on its head ... and start again from the beginning: and the beginning is the class struggle of the working class. At the level of socially developed capital, capitalist development follows hard behind the struggles....[13]

From this perspective, the history of recent capitalist development was rethought; the major economic transformations, mass production and state initiatives to underwrite wage gains and job security were seen as responses to working-class insurgency in the period following the Russian Revolution. These, in turn, created the conditions for new levels of class struggle. The mass worker of the modern factory, unlike the craft worker of an earlier stage of capitalist development, expressed a radical antagonism to the production process itself. The 'strategy of refusal', to use Tronti's words, entailed the refusal of production obligations (through strikes, sabotage and manning struggles) and the escalation of wage demands. Tronti interpreted these tacit and tactical practices as workers' struggles to make the fulfilment of needs independent of capital's requirements. For him the mass worker short-circuited union representation, and traditional party policies.

The concept of workers' autonomy (*autonomia operaia*) was not invented by Tronti, but he had an important role in defining a term which was to become a touchstone of revolutionary politics over the next ten years. (A mapping of the different uses to which the term has been put would make an interesting study in its own right.[14]) It was important not only for political activists but set the terms of wider cultural debate. In the mid and late sixties workers' autonomy was understood to mean autonomy from capital (the refusal of workers to define their need and demands according to capital's need for labour power subordinate to the rhythms of the production process), and autonomy from external organiz-ations (workers' independence from the parties and unions which were seen to be subservient to capital). As such, it represented the most absolute and essentialist conception of social movement.

However, the problem of assessing the influence of the new ideas about political movements remains. How significant were people like Panzieri and Tronti, who were the outside agitators? Did they undermine the old inevitability, and were they also 'the travelling salesmen of the new inevitability'?[15] Most people, if they had been asked this question in 1967, would undoubtedly have dismissed as irrelevant the reviews and the alternative organizations of the New Left. The circulation of the former were highly restricted; in late 1967 *Quaderni Piacentini* sold 4,000 copies, and *Classe Operaia* sold a maximum of 5,000 before it ceased publication in 1966.[16] The organizations were weak. An inquiry by the review *Nuovo Impegno* in 1967 found that they numbered eighteen, but they had 'virtually no workers inside them, and little effect on struggles or presence in the factories'.[17] Bechelloni writes that

> this political culture was developed in restricted intellectual circles, and, during the 1960s, had only the faintest of echoes in political and cultural debate and in political events.[18]

Moreover, the reviews were taken by surprise by the sudden rise of the student movement. They had paid little attention to the problems inside the educational institutions, or to the protest in the United States. A certain fixation with the factory conflict produced myopia in relation to other social tensions. Moreover, the reformist and modernizing ambitions of the government were taken at face value as the manifestation of neo-capitalist planning, so that their demise was not seriously considered.

However, measurement of influence by circulation and membership figures can be misleading. *Quaderni Rossi* illustrates this. It was a review with a small circulation, but a disproportionately large readership. It played a seminal role in the emergence of a sociology of the workers' movement, but the review was also a point of reference and inspiration for a generation of political and trade union activists. It gave dignity and significance to workers' opinions and experience.

An interview recorded in 1967 with a union activist at the Sit Siemens electrical engineering factory in Milan is interesting on this point. She recalls that when she went to complain to Communist Party officials that they had not understood the problems on the shopfloor (tens of women had been suffering fainting fits and hysteria because of the pressure of work, but the union agreed to compensation rather than a reduction of line-speeds):

> they came back at me with 'that's what the *Quaderni Rossi* people say' and so on. I, poor thing, hadn't a clue who these people were, so I went to find out.

She described how, when she went to speak about working conditions at meetings, 'an official was sent with me so that I bore witness to my experience, and he drew the political conclusions'.[19] The *Quaderni Rossi* experiment, in other words, proposed an alternative method of political work which attempted to overcome this division of labour.

The ideas coming from the New Left need to be put in the broader context of their intellectual significance, and their fashionableness. They presented challenges to the orthodox readings of Marx, Lenin and Gramsci. They were like a breath of fresh air. For example, Asor Rosa's *Scrittori e Popolo*, which attacked neo-Gramscian accounts of the Italian literature, and Tronti's *Operai e Capitale* were intellectual landmarks for the younger generation in the universities.[20] Publishers who sympathized with these views, saw the market possibilities opened up by interest in such radical political texts. They promoted and capitalized on the emergence of a new market, and fed the immense hunger for cultural and political discussion with a flow of new publications. Primo Moroni and Bruna Miorelli have written:

> A great laboratory was formed in which Stalinists, libertarians, council communists, Leninists, *operaisti* and 'spontanists' all took part. Their strictly political themes mixed with Marcuse, Laing, Cooper, the Frankfurt School. Remember the enormous impact of don Milani's *Letter to a School-Teacher* which was printed by a miniscule publisher with organic ties with the community. If it now seems little more than ... populist, at the time it gave vent to an aggressive radical opposition to the system. Books and symbols of the international struggles in China, Vietnam and Cuba were readily consumed. The Feltrinelli bookshops sold literally tons of Che Guevara posters. The old public made up of intellectuals, trade unionists and party officials was joined by a new type of purchaser – the student and young worker ... The old eighteenth century idea of the bookshop as a place of culture was superceded by the modern one of the market opening on to the street.[21]

Of the more established publishers, it was Giangiacomo Feltrinelli who proved most adept at sowing the seeds of new-leftism and reaping the subsequent harvest in the wake of 1968. His story is both intriguing and illuminating.

Feltrinelli, the millionaire owner of one of Milan's largest publishing companies, was fascinated by the Latin American revolutionary movements and dreamt of imitating its methods of guerrilla warfare in Italy. He was, therefore, attracted by elements of the New Left who looked to Cuba and the Third World for inspiration, rather than by the traditional Left. An article in the review *La Sinistra* in July 1967 drew a picture of Feltrinelli:

> His hair, long and disorderly like a beatnik's, his moustache drooping and wearing a very colourful tie . . . he spoke to us of his conversations with Fidel, and of the uplifting experience of a people ... who generously supported the fight against Yankee imperialism.[22]

Although Feltrinelli's relations with the New Left were full of contradictions on account of his wealth (these came into the open when a student meeting greeted him with the slogan: 'Two, three, a thousand million'), nevertheless his readiness to publish its documents and to provide financial support should not be lightly dismissed.

Firstly, Feltrinelli, along with smaller publishers like Samona and Savelli, pioneered the opening up of a new market, and, in the process, gave currency to the new ideas. Thus, the social movements were able to make use of already existing networks linking political initiatives to the publishers.[23] Secondly, Feltrinelli's attraction to the revolutionary cause illustrates the way that romance and adventure were fashionably associated with the Left in this period. His case is exceptional, but the phenomenon of 'defections' by the sons and daughters of the wealthy and influential in Italy was to take on scandalous proportions.[24]

In early 1967 the New Left was marginal to political and intellectual life in Italy, but it was perhaps not as marginal as might at first be imagined. Clearly, the reviews were the preserve of a tiny minority, and the established parties dominated debate. At the same time, as analysis of the student movement will show, the new ideas made considerable inroads into the acceptance of the parties as the inevitable representatives of opposition in the country. More generally, the New Left was a symptom of wider shifts of opinion. Many of the themes developed by the New Left on the nature of modern capitalism and on the reorganization of the factory, touched on problems that were preoccupying people who had to live with worsening working conditions and falling wages. The themes developed by *Quaderni Rossi* and its *operaist* offspring were in many ways prophetic. A marginal grouping of intellectuals managed to put their finger on the pulse of discontent and to identify its causes in the transformations of the labour process in the factories, but in addition they anticipated the radical demands. In the mid sixties few listened, but by the end of the decade the call for the abolition of grades, for lump sum wage increases, for the elimination of piece rates, for direct workers' democracy, were heard in hundreds of workplaces.

However, workers, who had little enough opportunity to come into contact with the new Left ideas before 1968, arrived at radical analyses of society by other routes. For them, the older traditions of resistance – Socialist, Communist and even Catholic – and the 'moral economies' of workplace and community – were more important in shaping their rebellion. These agitators were, moreover, insiders rather than outsiders.

Worker Agitators

The agitators within the factories in the period before 1968 were mainly drawn from, or had been within, the ranks of the Communist Party, and were the backbone of union organization. They were especially well qualified for this role for a number of reasons, which related mostly to their political rather than their trade union identities. Above all, these people resisted the pressures of everyday experience that seemed to say that nothing could really be changed. A woman militant recalls the positive aspects of her experience of the party, which she subsequently left in 1967; to the question: 'Did you always believe in revolution and the overthrow of the state?', she replied:

> Yes, ... it seemed that at a certain moment along the road something could happen that had never happened before ... at one level, ingenuously, I believed that this society is not ours, and we must create a society of our own that is different. This is what the PCI taught and it did it well. It is not by chance that it took the best part of the working class because of its sense of responsibility ... the militant had to be very serious, honest, humble, conscientious, and present himself to the workers by putting himself at their service.[25]

The life of this particular agitator bears witness to her words, in that she was sacked several times for her activism (a penalty she viewed as an ordinary part of her 'training'), but her struggle was also against the 'sense of resignation ... the feeling that as a woman you have to accept what you're given'.

The Communist Party membership and background was, however, no automatic guarantee of a militant's ability to represent and mobilize fellow workers. When ideology was separated out from, and even counterposed to the 'moral economies' of groups of workers, then it could function repressively as seen in the instance of the response of PCI officials to emotional reactions to working conditions, which was regarded as an economic issue to be resolved by monetary agreement. In the mid to late sixties, a number of agitators found themselves in conflict with the party, which seemed incapable of organizing the intense feelings of resentment and outrage on the shopfloor, and which they felt had reneged on its promise to bring about radical change. For them, immersion in the daily realities of the factory was also an act of purification and a return to the roots of the Communist project. The role of these agitators was enhanced by their political connections, which linked them to outside networks, giving them additional resources of information and moral and intellectual support.

The Marxist tradition, in all its many variants, was undoubtedly the most significant ideology in encouraging the idea of social transformation in the 1960s. A whole history, as has been mentioned, lies behind this legacy. Catholicism, by contrast, was predominantly associated with social and political conservatism. However, radical interpretations of Catholic belief, often influenced by Marxist thought, took shape among workers as well as among intellectuals. Interesting light can be thrown on the role of agitator as evangelist by the autobiography of Antonio Antonuzzo, in whom life in the modern factory provoked deep-felt moral outrage.[26]

Antonio Antonuzzo was Sicilian in origin, but his family transferred to Tuscany in search of work, a search that eventually took him to Milan. In 1961 he got a job at Alfa Romeo. For the first three years he was the typical, obedient hardworker. He got the job after receiving help from the Christian Democrats and a charity organization for immigrants, and gained promotion to skilled status because of his good relations with the foreman. At work his main concern was self-advancement through hard work, and, although not a scab, during strikes he went with his friends (mostly *meridionali* like himself) to 'seek out a woman with a good heart who sells the wares of love'. Their idea of collective action did not rise above bargaining the rate with the women concerned.

Antonuzzo does not point to a single incident as precipitating a change from an individualist, deferential consciousness to a belief that 'there was a collective way of struggling to save the working class from its subordination'. He writes of becoming aware of the disproportion between wages and work done, but more significant is a sense of revulsion at the inhumanity perpetrated in the factory: 'When a machine broke down, you became aware of how little you mattered to the management: a series of technicians rushed to get it working, whilst when a worker had an accident or could no longer work they replaced him by a more efficient one.'[27] It shocked him that such things were tolerated by the Catholic Church; 'in the name of Christ they justified the injustices suffered by the exploited.' But it was through the radicalized Catholic FIM–CISL that Antonuzzo became a militant. He applied himself assiduously to unionizing others, using his mobility as a 'jolly' and his speed as a worker to travel around the factory. Often he wrote articles for the factory union paper in the lavatory. In an attempt to buy him off, management offered Antonuzzo a foreman's job, but he had already decided against the individualist option so that the offer could only increase his angry determination to foment revolt. His account of the treatment meted out to scabs during the 1966 industrial dispute celebrates an old ritual of collective theatre in which the 'Judas' is paid off:

> I collected five *lire* from every worker on my team and I said to every one of them that they should shout 'scab' when I threw the money on the bench in front of him.[28]

For Antonuzzo the discovery of the union coincided with the creation for himself of a new identity and sense of belonging. It was deeply personal:

> until I joined the union I saw the family as a personal matter. After joining, I came to think about it as something I shared with other people.[29]

His conception of society and of his place in it had been transformed. The experience was something that he felt the need to communicate to his fellow workers. When in 1967 he became a full-time organizer for the FIM–CISL, he was given the possibility of dedicating himself completely to the cause he had espoused. He experienced the joys of evangelism: 'when I went among the workers ... I had a host of things to say because I felt one of them and I was happy because they listened to me with attention.' Antonuzzo's rebellion against injustice was very particular and his conversion to socialism was minoritarian. It was especially marked by his Catholic faith and his southern origins, and it took place in a period in which the majority of workers appeared to accept their lot. However, his anger and thirst for action were not isolated and hidden obsessions; rather, Antonuzzo could sense himself giving vent to collective feelings. It was a time when the rumble of popular protest could be heard under the surface of the society; it was a time that agitators dream of.

Cracks in the Fabric

In 1968–9 Italy experienced what Gramsci termed an 'organic crisis'. Social movements broke the mould of institutional definitions of politics, and the insurgency in civil society put the authority of the ruling bloc in question. But, as has been shown in this chapter, the mould was already badly cracked before it was put under the intense pressure of new political demands. There was a massive withdrawal of support and delegation with respect to the structures of representation, especially in the light of the failure of the Centre–Left government to live up to its promises. It was a clear case of the 'ruling class failing to achieve a noteworthy political enterprise for which it had demanded their approval'. Disappointment and disillusionment were registered in the general elections of May 1968 when the Socialist Party votes fell dramatically, and the small rival to the left, the PSIUP, won ground. However, the rift between representatives and represented went further. Emilio Colombo's summary of the cause of the crisis in progress, given to the national council of the Christian Democratic Party in January 1969, is instructive:

> Where have we fallen short? It seems to me that reforms have got nowhere, so the structures of civil society have aged and the whole fabric has deteriorated. Social forces have not found suitable channels for the expression of their sense of freedom. That's why the moment of pluralism ... is becoming, in our society, a moment of disorder. The wave of unrest, and even irrationality, is all the more disturbing when sectors which are by nature given to reformist action pursue revolutionary objectives because of their profound disillusionment with the methods and timing whereby reforms have been carried out by the politicians.[30]

The failure of the Centre–Left reforms had particularly serious consequences given the scale and stressfulness of the socio-economic changes following the 'miracle' years. There was the growth of widespread scepticism about the possibility of redressing injustices and reducing inequalities through parliamentary measures. The Communist Party, too, was affected by this mood, which strengthened the hand of its left-wing and dissident members. In this context, the revolutionary option did not seem very much less realistic than the reformist one, particularly when Italian history seemed to suggest that sudden and dramatic popular mobilizations produced more results than gradual parliamentary reforms. The social contract, in other words, could it seemed, only be redrawn through the actions of social movements. This tradition of popular protest was part of a rich historical legacy that still had adherents within a Communist Party that had been systematically excluded from government since 1947. It was, moreover, the moving force behind the agitators who were heretics looking for an authentically revolutionary communism. With the demise of the political parties, the idea of political action that dealt on the spot with problems and injustices acquired its rationale and legitimacy, even though it appeared irrational to government ministers.

The ideologies of resistance and rebellion, and the moral economies of groups of workers were of great importance to the process of social mobilization which began in late 1967. Without them, the crisis of representation would have produced disillusionment without hope in change. As the interpreters and propagandists of discontent, the agitators played a crucial role, especially in the early stages of the movements. Although the surge of collective defiance surprised most militants in the factories in 1968, nevertheless they were ready, in that they looked to their fellow workers rather than to the organizations as the force for change in the world. Similarly, among students it was the exponents of the New Left who were most prepared to initiate disruption and construct alternatives. The role of the agitators was undoubtedly positive in many respects, though with the proviso that they were in many respects the revivers of an older faith rather than apostles of a new one.

Notes

1. John Low-Beer, *Protest and Participation: the New Working Class in Italy*, Cambridge 1978, p. 237.
2. Giovanni Bechelloni, *Cultura e ideologia nella nuova sinistra*, Milan 1973, p. xii.
3. Ibid., p. xii.
4. Ibid., pp. 32–3.
5. D. Montaldi, *Lenin Bisogna sognare*, 1958. Quoted by Stefano Merli, *L'altra storia, Bosio, Montaldi e le origine della nuova sinistra*, Milan 1977, p. 7.
6. Goffredo Fofi, 'Piccola editoria: errori manifesti e virtù latente', in *Quaderni Il Lavoro dell'Informazione*, 1, 1981, pp. 79–80.
7. G. Bechelloni, *Cultura e ideologia*, p. xxxvi.
8. For details on PSIUP see glossary.
9. Lucio Colletti, 'A Political and Philosophical Interview', in *New Left Review* 86, July–August 1974, pp. 3–9.
10 R. Panzieri, 'Surplus Value and Planning', in GSE Pamphlet Number 1, *The Labour Process and Class Structure*, London 1976.
11. See S. Mancini, *Socialismo e democrazia diretta, introduzione a Raniero Panzieri*, Milan 1977.
12. The term *operaismo* can be literally translated as 'workerism'. However, since the English carries certain pejorative connotations which the Italian term does not have, an anglicized version of the original word has been adopted.
13. Mario Tronti, 'Lenin In England', in Red Notes, *Working Class Autonomy*, p. 1. Tronti's articles were collected together and published by Einaudi under the title *Operai e Capitale*, Turin 1966.
14. It would be possible, for instance, to trace developments through the writings of Mario Tronti, which lead to theorizations of the 'autonomy of the political' and positions within the cultural–political arc of the Communist Party; or, to follow the trajectory of Toni Negri's thought, which in the mid 1970s attempts to redefine workers' autonomy in relation to social conflicts outside the factory. However, the term's usage needs also to be explored in less theorized forms (for example, in the 'commonsense' of the social movements). For some further reflections see Toni Negri, *Dall'operaio massa all'operaio sociale*, Milan 1979, and M. Tronti et al., *Operaismo e centralità operaia*, Rome 1978. Also Lumley, 'Working Class Autonomy and the Crisis: Italian Marxist Texts of the Theory and Practice of a Class Movement: 1964–79', in *Capital and Class*, 12, Winter 1980/81, pp. 123–35.

15. 'Since the time of the Apostles no social movement has been without its army of preachers and militants.... It is the activist minority that promotes and promulgates new standards of condemnation ... very frequently they are outsiders. They do the hard-sell of undermining the old sense of inevitability', Barrington Moore, *Injustice*, pp. 472–73.
16. G. Bechelloni, *Cultura e ideologia* p. 31.
17. Ibid., p. 167.
18. Ibid., p. xii.
19. Silvana Barbieri in an interview (May 1967).
20. Although these books were not studied in courses on literature and philosophy, they were often read by alternativist study-groups. Very few books in fact circulate in this way, being continuously lent and re-lent. Take one of them out of a library and you will usually find it bears the marks of heavy use. In Britain in the mid sixties E.P. Thompson's *Making of the English Working Class* was such a book. The significance of the intellectual excitement generated by such moments of discovery has too often been overlooked. Richard Johnson observes rightly: 'The elements of really useful knowledge that do exist in schooling occur in the cracks of the system and in spaces won away from, or in tension with, its main pressures. What happens here is an appropriation and transformation of elements of the approved disciplines and curricula, a hard, bitter and very contradictory struggle to produce critical knowledge'; R. Johnson, 'Educational Politics: Old and New', in James Donald and Ann Marie Volpe, Eds, *Is There Anyone There from Education?*, London 1983.
21 Primo Moroni and Bruna Miorelli, 'Storia e problemi della piccola editoria', *Ombre Rosse*, 30, September 1979, pp. 93–103. For don Milani's *Lettera a una professoressa*, see part II, chapter 6, pp. 82–3.
22. *La Sinistra*, July 1967; see also Silverio Corvisieri, *Il mio viaggio nella sinistra*, Milan 1979, pp. 77–81.
23. For example, Feltrinelli asked Fernanda Pivano to edit a series for him called 'books for peace', though this particular initiative came to nothing; Fernanda Pivano, *c'era una volta un beat*, Milan 1988, pp. 84–5.
24. These deflections are part of the history of the Left which is often overlooked or dealt with simply in terms of rational intellectual choices. Yet they had important effects; for example, Giovanni Pirelli liquidated his share in the company and financed the publication of *Quaderni Rossi*.
25. Rina Barbieri interview.
26. Antonio Antonuzzo, *Boschi, miniera, catena di montaggio – la formazione di un militante della nouva CISL*, Rome 1976.
27. Ibid., p. 175.
28. Ibid., p. 184.
29. Ibid., p. 196.
30. G. Tamburrano, *Storia e cronaca del centro sinistra*, pp. 322–33.

PART II

the student movement

The student movement in Italy, as in other Western European countries, became the archetypal movement of opposition of the late sixties. It came to represent and symbolize new forms of rebellion and discontent as it was not a residue of older historical antagonisms, and arose in a period of relative growth and prosperity. Education was widely heralded by governments and parties, especially of the social democratic Left, as the means of levelling social differences, broadening the basis of citizenship and guaranteeing future prosperity. However, it produced the bitter fruit of conflict. Youth – the generation destined to create the future utopia – turned into a social problem and the angry conscience of a divided society.

The impact of the student movement owed much to the fact that it was an aspect of an organic crisis. Students were the first social group to mobilize *en masse* when conflict in the workplaces and in society as a whole was at its lowest level since the mid fifties. Moreover, it was the first time that students emerged as a social subject in their own right. Previously they had acted in support of other groups in a subordinate capacity. They had taken up general political questions. Now, students were important numerically. They were part of a new social grouping – youth – that came into being with the extension of schooling. But the student movement's novelty and its significance as a model of social action gave it a historical role out of all proportion to the students' relatively marginal position in society.

In this section, the student movement will be analysed in the period starting from its origins in the early 1960s to its eclipse by the workers' movement in 1969. Chapter 4 deals with the educational reforms of the Centre–Left government, which created or aggravated many of the conditions that provoked the student revolt. Subsequent chapters deal with the movement in the universities, and the emergence of a specific 'student politics', with case studies of the movements at the Catholic and State Universities in Milan in 1968–9. In addition there is an examination of the movement in the Milanese schools. Lastly, there are chapters on the student movement's impact on the education system, and on its more diffused effects on political and cultural life in Italy. Although student politics grew up within the institutions, the development of the theme of 'student–worker unity' led logically to more general political orientations. The popularization of ideas about 'cultural revolution' meant that the activities of radical intellectuals working not only within fields like theatre but also in the professions were rethought, with important consequences for the spread of conflicts into every sphere of Italian society.

4

from mass schooling to mass protest: failures of the education system

Defining Education

A logical starting point for an analysis of the student movement is the 1962 education reform that established mass secondary schooling in Italy, and led to an expansion of the intake of the further education sector. However, some introduction of concepts is necessary to put the reform in proper analytic and historical perspective. To begin with, as Richard Johnson insists in his important work on the history of education in Britain, 'education' and 'schooling' need to be distinguished.[1] The two terms tend to be treated as synonymous, thereby assuming that knowledge is primarily acquired within the four walls of an institution. This idea exists not only in the definitions given by teachers and policymakers, but in the commonsense notions of everyday speech. The conflation of education with schooling seems to be a 'natural' fact, whereas it is the result of a historical process with important consequences for how society's conceptions of knowledge are constructed. Richard Johnson writes that it has practical effects:

> it tends to naturalise existing educational arrangements, and to marginalise and devalue less formal means of learning. It constructs a sharp divide between school (where we learn/are educated) and life outside those institutional walls (where we work/play). It tends to enhance the role of the professional teacher and the organised curriculum over other sources of wisdom and more practical knowledges. Above all, it tends to hide from view a whole history of the construction of schooling or encourages the belief in some simple history of progress, a history with no costs, no struggles, no ambiguities.[2]

Richard Johnson goes on to develop two other categories from British historical examples to describe the political strategies involved in the social construction of education and schooling.[3] They are the substitutionalist strategy, which conceives of education in non-institutional terms, and the statist strategy that focuses on schooling.

Historically, the pursuit of substitutionalist ideas and practices of education arose with the popular movements of the first half of the nineteenth century. In them, learning was a group activity related to class and human emancipation. Knowledge was valued for its usefulness in changing the world, and education was thought of in the broadest sense as the acquisition of skills and learning through everyday experience as well as through books.

The statist strategy emerged at a later point when 'capital had secured a tighter control over the conditions of labour', reducing the margins of autonomy and the resources of time and income necessary for the earlier experience of popular self-education. It was directed towards increasing state educational provision and access to it for the working class. By contrast with substitutionalism, the statist approach tended to identify education with schooling, and to delegate power and responsibility to others, namely the public authorities and the teaching profession. Richard Johnson remarks that:

> Most forms of statist strategy ... deepen the separations which constitute the specifically educational forms of oppression. They deepen the divisions between adult and child, between education and the rest of living, and between professional educators and their curricula and the knowledge that is produced outside the academic institutions.[4]

However, he is careful to stress that the strategies should not simply be counterposed or oversimplified; the statist approach has not concentrated exclusively on the question of access, but has involved struggles over the control of institutions and the nature of the curriculum and of teaching. The very creation and extension of state provision makes certain forms of substitutionalism anachronistic, and substitutionalism has tended to become compensatory. However, Johnson insists that it is not therefore defunct as a strategy. Indeed it can be said that the student movements of the sixties put these questions back on the agenda. But before looking at this movement, it is necessary to outline the previous struggles over education in Italy, and at the reforms carried out by the Centre–Left government.

Reforms

In an earlier period when the mass of the population was excluded from the vote on the grounds of illiteracy, and when educational provision was minimal, not the school, but the Socialist Party and other popular organizations in Italy were the people's 'educators'. An account of pre-1914 struggles for knowledge stresses its political dimension:

> Socialism is a school because the leaders of the party are interested in enrolling the greatest number of voters ... then, for the workers better to absorb the principles of socialism, it is necessary they acquire the habit of reading. Already among the working class itself new personalities are arising who live the same lives as the workers and yet because of their greater intellectual achievement, they become the pioneers.[5]

In this practice of education, learning was collective and functional to the needs of the group rather than to individual self-advancement. It also contained an idea of learning through social practice, which was the aspect elaborated by Gramsci in his factory council writings when he counterposed the real knowledge and control of the production process by the workers, to the intellectual bankruptcy of the capitalists.[6]

This substitutionalist strategy, which concentrated on creating alternative educational organs such as newspapers, training militants and fostering a socialist culture, was dominant within the working-class movement when it was excluded from full citizenship. With the establishment of schooling for all and universal suffrage in 1945, substitutionalism became a secondary and to a large extent residual element of the strategy of the Left in the educational field. However, it was not entirely superseded. Christian Democrat control of the educational system, the deficiencies of state schooling and the implantation of the PCI as a mass party excluded from participation in government made it both feasible and desirable to sustain some elements of an alternative educational practice. In the 1960s there was a marked decline in the PCI's activity in this sense, but groups of dissident intellectuals to its Left were active in reviving ideas of autonomous workers' education.

For the parties and trade unions of the Left a statist strategy prevailed over the substitutionalist. The realization of the demand for free, compulsory state education, even if inadequate and deformed, set the terms for an approach to education based on demands for its extension and reform as a public service. In the immediate postwar period, they lost the opportunity provided by extensive working class mobilization and presence in government to push through radical reforms; the primary objective was to make the existing system function. Lucio Lombardo Radice of the PCI wrote:

> It is not a question of whether it is just or not that the best elements of the working classes are excluded de facto from secondary and further education, but of whether the Italian school, as it is organized today, is an efficient instrument for the reconstruction of the country.

This approach meant accepting ruthless selection and the fundamental division between training and education.[7]

This failure to reform the educational system had long-term consequences. The tripartite division inherited from the Gentile reforms remained intact; five years of compulsory schooling for all, in which the post-elementary stage was divided into lower secondary and training. Further education was divided into the *liceo* and technical institutes, and then there was university for a privileged minority. The class character of the system was very marked, although it was entirely state controlled except for a few Church-controlled schools and the nursery sector.[8] In 1959–60, only 20 per cent of thirteen- to fourteen-year-old children got the lower secondary certificate, and at thirteen 49 per cent of children left school. In the fifties an estimated 18 per cent of the population used Italian rather than dialect as their main language; Italian-speakers were largely those who had passed through further education.[9] The Idealist tradition, which drew a sharp distinction between a humanist education and technical training, and gave absolute priority of the mind over the body, had its economic rationale too. Demand was for cheap, unskilled labour, on the one hand, and for an educated minority for the liberal professions.[10] Literary subjects (the classics, history, literature, were taught, though sociology and economics did not appear on the curriculum) were privileged over the sciences. The exercise of the body was not included within school activities; not even prestigious *licei* had sports facilities. There was no form of sex education, while the teaching of moral values owed much to the Church, which had reinforced its position in the postwar period. It exercised its influence through compulsory religious education, strict censorship of textbooks and interventions in policy-making in the Christian Democrat Party. This also contributed to the patriarchal regime in which the teacher stood in for the father (the vast majority of teachers in secondary schools were male), and ruled with iron discipline. The forms of control extended directly to the family, in that from elementary school onwards all marks on tests and on behaviour were taken back to the parents; this practice was inherited from the Fascist period.

The strategy of the Left parties in the early fifties was based on criticizing the ideological content of education, in particular its subjection to Church influence. In 1959 the PCI moved from a defensive position to the formulation of reform proposals for secondary schooling. It advocated a single compulsory school for all, the raising of the leaving age to fourteen, the abolition of compulsory Latin and the extension of science teaching.[11] The idea of comprehensive education contained in the proposal, which was substantially made law in 1962, was advanced in comparison to other European school systems; Giorgio Ruffolo writes that the reform envisaged:

> The introduction of a wide variety of subjects related to the lived culture of our time, the granting of a certain independence to departments, the establishment of extra schooling, and differentiated classes and special classes for pupils in difficulty.[12]

In effect, the reform brought Italy into line with other industrial capitalist states by transforming an elitist into a mass secondary schooling system. The numbers attending secondary school increased from 1,150,000 to 1,982,000 between 1959 and 1969.[13] Between 1966 and 1970 education moved from the fifth to the first most important item of government expenditure – 6 per cent of the Gross National Income, as compared with 5.6 per cent in Britain and 4 per cent in France, was spent on education.[14]

The major shortcoming of the strategies of the PCI and PSI, which were the chief parties promoting educational reform, was their almost exclusive focus on 'access'. For them the problem was to extend the benefits of secondary schooling to children who had previously been excluded from the system or restricted to training for skilled manual work. The quantitative demand for more schooling and more facilities prevailed over qualitative demands. The issue of control remained marginal, and was framed in terms of public versus private provision, which was significant only in relation to the nursery sector. The curriculum was modernized and made more relevant through the inclusion of more science teaching, but forms of pedagogy were not discussed. Under the rhetoric of egalitarianism that proclaimed education as a 'right for all', there was a strong current of meritocratic and technocratic thinking that clouded any perception of the emergence of new forms of discrimination and selection within the reformed secondary school. Moreover, analysis of the relation between the more qualified youth and the availability and types of work in the economy was scanty or utopian. The Project '80 government forecast, for example, projected a single education system up to the age of sixteen for 80 per cent of youth on the assumption that there would be a massive expansion in demand for technically qualified manpower.[15]

The limits of the reform were also manifested in the forms of action that the parties and unions adopted in campaigning for it. Mobilization tended to be external to the educational institutions themselves. The issue was raised at election times. For the unions, education was significant in that educational qualifications provided the basis for enlarging their definition of 'skill' as a bargaining counter with the employers. Otherwise, the unions delegated responsibility for education to the parties, which privileged parliamentary and legislative activity.[16] It was the complex task of winning assent among the parties which shaped legislative decisions, rather than popular mobilization and debate. The strike wave of the 1960–63 period did not impinge directly on the education issue, though it provided the conditions for the formation of the Centre–Left government. The eclipse of substitutionalism as a popular form of educational practice, and hence the decline of a sense that there were alternatives, meant that critiques of the state system lost a popular and radical dimension. Reform was carried out over and above the heads of the mass of the population.[17] Moreover, the lack of a consistent pro-reform current within the secondary schools themselves, and the weakness of unionization by the confederations in the educational institutions, meant that there was no effective alliance between progressive politicians and the profession.[18]

In consequence, the implementation of the 1962 reform largely escaped the control of its political advocates. It was conditioned rather by the traditionalism of the authorities within the schools, by the rightward shift in government policies, and by the changes in the labour market. Contradictions arising from the perpetuation of practices inherited from Liberal and Fascist regimes combined with new ones to produce a long drawn-out crisis in the system.

The majority of teachers resisted the changes in order to defend privileges acquired when they were the prestigious representatives of the state in a largely illiterate rural society. The autonomous professional associations concentrated on representing their corporate interests and did not participate in constructing the reforms. Their relatively light teaching load, averaging fourteen hours a week, was not increased, but the additional work was done through the use of part-time and temporary teachers.[19] The relationship between teachers and pupils in the secondary school kept many of its authoritarian features, which headmasters jealously guarded.

Government policies did little to alleviate or improve the situation. No comprehensive programme of teachers' training was established, and investment in infrastructures to cope with the increased intake was inadequate. There were serious shortages of textbooks, and class-rooms; by the next decade 14 per cent of elementary schools worked a double shift system or rented rooms. The burden fell particularly on the working-class children, especially those of the south; in 1966–7 failures to get the elementary certificate included 15 per cent of children from secondary schooling.[20] In 1971 three-quarters of Italians did not have a qualification higher than an elementary certificate; 14.7 per cent had a secondary school qualification.[21]

The restriction of reform to the secondary school put great pressure on the upper secondary school (*scuola media superiore*) and the university. The upper secondary school had a structure which was a century old. In the upper secondary sector, the main division was between the *liceo* (of which were of two types – the *liceo classico* for the humanities and the *liceo scientifico* for the sciences), and the technical institutes. The former tended to have a predominance of students from middle-class families, with only 10 per cent of working-class background compared with over 30 per cent in the technical institutes. It was these institutions that had to deal with the influx of students from the reformed secondary schools, who were choosing to continue their studies rather than enter the job market. In 1960, 82,000 out of a total of 311,000 left school for work, whilst in 1968 only 91,700 out of 507,000 did so.[22] The numbers going to the upper secondary school had doubled. The structures, however, were ill-adapted for such changes; a high degree of centralization prevented flexibility: teachers had little autonomy, syllabuses were set by the ministry of education, and heads were directly responsible to the ministry. The result was a fall in educational standards measured in terms of attendance and the 'drop-out' rate; a report of 1969 spoke of 10 per cent of *liceo classico* and 24 per cent of the *instituto professionale* students leaving at the end of the first year.[23]

The universities also enormously expanded their intake; the number of students increased from 268,181 in 1960–61 to 404,938 in 1965–6. Legislation opened access to science faculties to students from the institutes in 1961, and in 1965 entrance by examination and the fixed quota (*numero chiuso*) were abolished. The number of students from the working class thereby increased from 14 per cent in 1960–1 to 21 per cent in 1967–8. However, the privileged point of entry into the university was through the *liceo*. The term 'mass university' was misleading when only one in sixteen went to university.[24] The number of women students doubled between 1960 and 1968, but in 1968 accounted for just under one third of the intake.

Although the social base of the university had been broadened, a social and economic selection replaced one imposed by examination structures. The institution functioned as a sort of funnel that was wide at the point of entry and narrow at the exit. The drop-out rate, length of time for course completion and examination results showed up the disadvantages suffered by students of working-class origins. An average 14 per cent of students dropped out, though many fewer did so in the faculties of law and medicine which were predominantly middle class in composition. The problem of course completion was chronic, with two-thirds not finishing in the prescribed time. Examination results and future prospects related to class origin, with a higher success rate in the courses preparing students for the liberal professions.[25] Guido Martinotti compares the Italian and English universities of the late sixties in terms of their social function:

> In 1966 about 81 per cent of those with a secondary school certificate went to university, but only 44 per cent succeeded in getting a degree. A comparison between the two systems shows how the two results are virtually identical; whether the selection happens prevalently before or after university, a large part of the student population does not reach the end of the period of study. In the English system this takes place through an evaluation of merit (since the selection largely precedes the university due to a limitation on student numbers). Meanwhile, in the Italian case, selection is left to the game of chance, or, to put it more exactly, to the social factors that intervene to regulate it.[26]

Since only 5 per cent of students received a grant, which was in itself insufficient to cover the costs of maintenance and study, the poorer students were forced to work in order to study. An inquiry in 1965–6 in five universities found that 14 per cent of students were in this situation, whilst 66 per cent depended entirely on their parents for maintenance.[27] The consequences were lived out in lower educational achievement and the abandonment of further study. Private means grew in importance as the quality of public provision declined. The staff–student ratio worsened to reach 1:60 in the early 1970s, and library facilities and building did not expand to meet the increased demand.

Corrosion and Landslides in the Educational System

The reform and expansion of the education system proved a bitter disappointment to the leading reformers themselves, who had hoped it would lead to the modernization of Italian society. They made up for the shortage of skilled manpower and technicians that had been identified as a bottleneck in the economy in the early 1960s. Yet, in the process, the supply increased well in excess of the demand. Although the reformed secondary school played its part in satisfying demand for young male workers who were better qualified and more versatile, the rise in educational expectations meant that the secondary school acted as a point of departure for further education rather than as a terminal point.[28]

Although economic considerations were important in educational policy-making, these have to be placed in the context of the political calculations and cultural orientations of the politicians themselves. Above all, education as an issue involved the winning of consent and the forging of alliances. When education was made more widely available it created expectations and hopes of betterment that were important elements in legitimating the system. The Christian Democrats were particularly conscious of such considerations.[29] A humanist political culture was combined in the Christian Democratic Party with a sensitivity to the requirements of patronage. Everything was done to avoid damaging vested interests. After the concession of the 1962 reform, which was one of the conditions for Socialist Party's participation in government, further changes were piecemeal compromises designed to keep alliances intact. The expansion of state employment (which absorbed 80 per cent of graduates) and of the tertiary sector have been interpreted as an aspect of a strategy of the ruling bloc to maintain its hegemony over the educationally qualified sectors, who were a potential source of social tension. This particular concern for winning over intellectuals has a long history in Italy. A remark by Gonella, minister of education in 1946, is telling:

> the social order can be destroyed not only through the revolutionary agitation of the masses, but also through the slow corrosion and the consequent landslide that undermine the moral defences represented by the intellectual classes. If those defences fail, a society can tumble into disorder.[30]

This phenomenon of corrosion and landslide took on crisis proportions in the late sixties, and, because of the education reforms, involved a much wider section of society than that represented by the privileged intelligentsia of which Gonella was thinking. The reforms created a whole series of new problems as well as leaving old ones unresolved. Since only the secondary school was changed, leaving the further education system unreformed, imbalance and bottlenecks developed. The universities could not cope efficiently with the massive increase in intake, and then produced graduates in excess of the requirement for qualified employees.

In the 1960s, it was more the problems within education than what happened afterwards that preoccupied students. There was considerable frustration over petty inequalities and officiousness; for example, students going to university from technical institutes could only study science subjects, whilst those from a *liceo* could study whatever they wished. But there was also a feeling that this, like the organization of exams, was symptomatic of the irrationalities of the education system. The aura of the university was tarnished in overcrowded lecture theatres where doubts were spread as to the intellectual merits of the professors. The committed students who read the latest publications (Asor Rosa's *Scrittori e popolo*, for instance) found themselves better informed than some of the lecturers. The crisis in the institutions was also a crisis of cultural legitimacy; that is to say, of their claim to be society's depository of knowledge.

To understand how this crisis came about it would be necessary to chart the changes within intellectual fields; to see how orthodoxies were being challenged from within a discipline, or how new sorts of knowledge were being championed. Some idea of what this involved can be seen in the case of sociology.

The first faculty of sociology was set up in 1962 at the University of Trento on the initiative of progressive elements within the Christian Democratic Party. They wanted to 'help Italy catch up with the other advanced countries, creating a new means of managing a society whose complexity was beyond the comprehension of orthodox economic liberalism'.[31] The model was American. The sociologists at the time looked for a 'prince' in the form of government policy-makers, and they defined themselves as 'experts rather than committed participants of social action'.[32] However, by the mid to late sixties, the founders' project went very wrong. The faculty at Trento became the epicentre of student protest. Moreover, a second generation of sociologists, sharing in the growing disillusionment with the Centre–Left government, began to look for a new role for the discipline, as a force for social change from below rather than from above. There was increasing criticism of the functionalist school of Merton and Parsons, and a re-reading of the classics, Durkheim and Weber, and a new interest in developing a Marxist sociology. The discipline promoted to help understand and solve the problems produced by the economic miracle became a seedbed of dissident opinion.

However, the 1960s was a period when orthodoxies were widely under threat, and developments within the field of sociology are only one extreme example of this process, about which some general observations can be made. Firstly, in the Italian context there was considerable criticism of how appointments were made on the grounds of political affiliation rather than of merit. It seemed that culture was being debased (losing its essential qualities of autonomy and impartiality) in the political market-place. Secondly, the courses were criticised for being out-of-date. The age of academic staff became a metaphor in a conflict in which a younger generation sought to represent modernity and the future society-in-the-making. Thirdly, there was mounting discontent over what was seen as the remoteness of universities and further education from the rest of society. Their outdatedness was related to their self-containment, and their attachment to a mandarin ethos at a time when knowledge and culture were being opened up to previously excluded groups.[33] These conflicts concerned the education process and some of the earliest forms of 'contestation' (for example counter-courses) focused on this. But they also became connected with broader political and social questions; the major mobilizations centred on education as a social and political right.

Student grievances accumulated over a multitude of issues, but it took opposition to the Gui bill to bring them into focus. This bill was designed to restrict entry to the universities by fixing quotas. Students denounced the objective as a betrayal of the ideals promoted by the new government itself. They led the first major opposition to the Centre–Left government. Ironically, it was in the field where it had achieved most that the government was challenged.

Educational reform, not economic policy, provoked a storm of moral outrage from the social group to which the PSI looked for support. To explain this, it is perhaps useful to think of de Tocqueville's observation about how the French king's attempts to alleviate his subjects' sufferings made them more not less aware of the injustices. Educational reforms, by improving the chances of young working-class people going to university, drew attention to the fact that very few did. Students went to university with great expectations and found a tawdry reality. Guido Martinotti summed up the contradictions at the heart of the situation:

> The clash is between the expectations created by social demand for education and by the egalitarian ideology implicit in the educational system, and today's realities of social inequalities that deeply structure the university system. The university has been turned from being the means of substituting economic conflicts, into the site of some of the most violent conflicts in society.[34]

Writing of the French situation in the late 1960s, Pierre Bourdieu gives an analysis of the relationship between the expansion of the student intake and the crisis of the value of educational qualifications which is equally applicable to Italy:

> The increase in pupils and the concomitant devaluation of educational qualifications (or the educational position to which they provide access) have affected the whole of an age group, thus constituted as a relatively unified social generation through this common experience, creating a structural hiatus between the statutory expectations – inherent in the positions and diplomas which in the previous state of the system really did offer corresponding opportunities – and the opportunities actually provided by these diplomas and positions in the moment in question.[35]

The crisis in the educational system was, therefore, part of a wider crisis, indeed it formed a meeting point for a range of social, political and cultural conflicts, which will be examined in the chapters that follow.

Notes

1. Richard Johnson, *The State and the Politics of Education, Units 1–2 of Educational Studies: A Third Level Course: Society, Education and the State*, Milton Keynes 1981, p. 13.
2. Ibid., p. 13.
3. Ibid., pp. 28–9.
4. Ibid., pp. 28–9.
5. Luigi Einaudi speaking of his visit to Biella in 1897, quoted by D. Horowitz, *The Italian Labour Movement*, pp. 46–7.
6. G. Williams, *Proletarian Order*, p. 106.
7. G. Dorigotti, 'Il PCI e la sculoa', in L. Balbo and G. Chiaretti, eds, *La scuola del capitale*, Padua 1973, p. 113. The meritocratic approach of the PCI and PSI had class connotations, however, in that it counterposed the hardworking son of the people to the lazy sons of the middle classes; 'The time has come when the portals of the university will be free of noisy vagabonds and crowds of idlers and when they will hear yet unknown footsteps – those of the worthy sons of working people', a PCI parliamentarian quoted in M. Barbagli. *Disoccupazione intellettuale e sistema scolastica in Italia (1859–1973)*, Bologna 1974, p. 441.
8. L. Balbo and G. Chiaretti, 'Le trasformazioni del sistema scolastico italiano', in *La scuola del capitale*, p. 18. Gentile was minister of education in the Fascist State.
9. Tullio De Mauro, 'La Cultura', in A. Gambino, *Dal '68 a oggi: come siamo e come eravamo*, Bari 1980, p. 191, p. 199.
10. Paci, *Mercato di lavoro*, pp. 255–79.
11. Dorigotti, pp. 113–47.
12. Giorgio Ruffolo, *Riforme e controriforme*, Bari 1975, p. 83.
13. M. Miegge, 'Sviluppo capitalistico e scuola', in *La scuola del capitale*, p. 49.
14. Ruffolo, pp. 89–90.
15. L. Balbo and G. Chiaretti, 'Le trasformazioni del sistema scolastico', in *La scuola del capitale*, p. 19.
16. Vittorio Foa, Introduction in G. Levi Arian, *I lavoratori studenti*, Turin 1968, pp. 34–5.
17. Ibid., p. 37.
18. Contrast with the British case, see Centre for Contemporary Cultural Studies, *Unpopular Education: schooling and social democracy in England since 1945*, London 1981, pp. 89–93.
19. A leaflet written by students at the Catholic University claimed: 'Part-time or temporary teachers are a reserve army of white-collar workers who are easily manoeuvred. They make up about 70% of the teaching staff and yet cost the state less than all the full-time staff.' *Proposta per un collegamento studenti-insegnanti – Commissione 'Collegamenti lotte sociali'*, undated (1968–9?). These teachers tended not to be in the unions at all, whilst full-time staff was organized in autonomous professional associations which were not affiliated to the main confederations.
20. L. Balbo and G. Chiaretti, 'Le trasformazioni del sistema scolastico', pp. 93–4.
21. Ruffolo, p. 191.
22. Paci, *Mercato di lavoro*, p. 277.
23. Ruffolo, p. 86.
24. Guido Martinotti, *Gli studenti universitari*, Milan 1969, p. 5, p. 54, p. 30.
25. Ibid., p. 96, p. 120.
26. Ibid., pp. 92–3.
27. Ibid., pp. 162–69.
28. Paci, *Mercato di lavoro*, pp. 277–78.
29. Ibid., pp. 263–64.
30. Barbagli, *Disoccupazione intellettuale*, pp. 394–5.
31. Alessandro Silj, *Mai più senza fucile alle origini del NAP e delle BR*, Florence 1977, p. 34.

32. Diana Pinto, 'La sociologie dans l'Italie de l'après-guerre, 1950–1980', *Revue Française de Sociologie*, XXI, 1980, pp. 234–41.
33. On the specifity of cultural conflicts, see Pierre Bourdieu, 'The production of belief: contribution to an economy of symbolic goods', *Media, Culture and Society*, 2, 1980, pp. 261–93. An ex-student of the faculty of architecture at Turin University remembers: 'He was really ancient, the head who had been head for thirty years, an ultra-conservative man. There were courses which were clearly absurd, and lecturers who were capable only of teaching those courses'; R. Gobbi, *Il '68 alla rovescia*, Milan 1988, p. 24.
34. Martinotti, *Gli studenti universitari*, p. xxii.
35. P. Bourdieu, *Homo Academicus*, Cambridge 1988, p. 163.

5

the end of respectability: the student movement in the universities

Crisis of the Old Organizations

Both legislation on education and counter-proposals coming from the left failed to take into account the opinions of the students themselves. Students were treated as the objects of pedagogic practices and the passive recipients of knowledge. Students in the late sixties rebelled against this paternalistic approach to their problems and asserted their own needs and identities. This rebellion took the form of a social movement which expressed new demands, but not before the older forms of representation had proved incapable of channelling and interpreting student activism.

The first protests against government educational policies emerged from within the student organizations connected to the main political parties. The most radical organization was the Unione Goliardica Italiana (UGI) which grouped together adherents of the PCI and PSI; the Intesa represented the Catholic students and had links with the Christian Democrats. From 1948 to 1968 these organizations took part in the Unione Nazionale Rappresentativa Italiana (UNURI), which was an officially recognized body within the universities and spoke for student interests. In 1963 it negotiated grants with the government. The ethos of these organizations derived from the world of the political and cultural elite; the preamble of UGI's charter read:

> 'The university spirit is composed of culture and intelligence. It is love of liberty and consciousness of one's responsibilities.... And lastly it is the veneration of the ancient traditions handed down by our free universities.[1]

The politics of the active university students reflected those of the national parliament. UGI and Intesa stood for election to the Organismi Rappresentativi (OORR), which acted as forums of debate. The elections to the OORR in 1964–5 still showed the predominance of conservative opinions among students; UGI received an average 17 per cent of the vote, which was little more than the fascists and just under half that of Intesa. However, there were signs of change in student politics. During the strikes of 1960–63 large contingents of students participated in the mass demonstrations, and in 1963 all the architecture faculties of Italian universities were occupied. Above all, mobilization against the Gui bill had national dimensions and a high level of participation, culminating in a march in April 1965. This bill for university reform proposed to limit student intake to the universities and to establish three types of course from one year diplomas to the full degree course. It was attacked by UNURI as unjust, and a committee for the 'reform and democratization of the university' was set up in cooperation with lecturers to oppose the bill.[2]

The architecture faculties were especially lively centres of student politics in the mid sixties. This seems to have been due to their keen and critical interest in the Centre–Left experiment, for which planning and building programmes were touchstones. At the Polytechnic's faculty in Milan, study groups analysed the political functions of architecture and criticized courses and learning methods. In particular, students demanded the coordination of subjects into coherent programmes of study, the integration of research and teaching, and the introduction of collective study. The emphasis was on education as process rather than product.[3] Radical students connected the role of the institution to national politics. Thus, the Centre–Left was increasingly criticized for its failures to introduce urban planning and to improve working-class housing, and the Gui bill was criticized for the way it threatened to separate research from teaching and 'technicize' the study of architecture. In 1967 opposition to the government turned into a fifty-five day occupation at the Milan faculty. This in many ways anticipated future student actions. An environment was created which was 'functional to collective living, debate and shared work'; all major decisions were taken by the general meetings rather than by UNURI; commissions were set up to examine political and educational issues with the participation of some lecturers. The authorities ended by conceding to demands for seminars and for greater choice of courses.[4]

Events in Milan, however, were eclipsed by student actions in Pisa which brought the crisis of UGI to a head, and radicalized opposition to the government. The Pisan students put themselves on the political map by stepping up the campaign against the government's reform proposals. In February 1967 they disrupted a conference of university heads, who were meeting in Pisa, occupied some buildings and clashed with police.

Throughout the events the official student bodies were bypassed by the activists, and decisions on action were taken at open general meetings. But what made the Pisan students' initiatives especially important for the development of the movement was their theorization of a new approach to student politics. The 'Pisan Theses' became one of its most influential manifestos.

The Theses applied an *operaist* analysis inspired by the *Quaderni Rossi* to the student situation. They maintained that the transformation of a free market into a planned capitalism required more highly qualified labour power to meet the needs of advanced technological production, as outlined in the government's Pieraccini plan. Therefore students, who were now defined as the future qualified workers, were no longer a privileged elite, but were 'objectively' members of the working class. The political problem, according to the Pisan argument, was to create awareness among students of their real class position, and that this could best be achieved by fighting for student wages. The struggle would bring students and workers together against the common enemy – capitalism and the state.

Although the demand for student wages was not widely taken up, the Pisan approach had a strong appeal, especially among dissident Communist and Socialist aligned students. Like the Marxist heresies of the mid sixties from which they originated, the Pisan Theses promised a certain ideological purity in their militant refusal of parliamentarianism and reformism. At the Rimini conference of UGI in May 1967 the Pisan Theses formed the basis of a current of opposition to the leadership coming from the PSIUP and the left wing of the PCI.[5] The narrow victory of the leadership in the voting of the motions turned out to be pyrhhic; the failure to respond positively to the growing radicalization among students sealed the fate of UGI, Intesa and UNURI. Attempts to provide new organizational solutions fell on deaf ears; the idea of a student's union in 1967, of a constituent assembly in early 1968 and finally of an 'organization of Communist university students' in March 1968 all remained a dead letter. By the end of 1968 all the organizations had formally dissolved themselves.

The fate of the para-party student organizations, however, served to conceal the degree to which the new generation of activists was formed within them. Like many of the reviews and political groupings, to which it was closely related, the new wave of student opposition to parliamentary reformism took the form of Communist heresies. This is very evident in the case of the Pisan student movement, which was dominated by the *operaist* theories which emanated from the *Quaderni Rossi* grouping at nearby Massa, and which was among the first to get actively involved in industrial disputes, making links directly with workers rather than through the unions.[6] This early association of student politics with workers' struggles and the popularity of the proletarianization thesis gave the Italian movement its most distinctive character, and had lasting effects on its orientations. However, this approach also tended to obscure the problems faced by students themselves, and it was not until these were addressed that the movement was able to take mass forms.

Student Identity and the Politics of Violence

In the winter of 1967 and the first quarter of 1968, student agitation in the universities grew to national proportions. In November the universities of Trento, Turin and Genoa and the Cattolica of Milan were occupied, and in December the movement spread to the south with the occupation of Naples university. In January 1968 thirty-six universities were occupied. The common denominator of the movement was opposition to the Gui bill under discussion in parliament, but, as Rossana Rossanda writes: 'the students were first of all against the logic that had produced the bill, the political, academic and social mechanisms that generated it'.[7] At a student movement conference in Milan in March 1968, Mauro Rostagno outlined the nature of the conflict in progress:

> The new type of mass social struggle reveals the nature of the new type of social system; it is a social system that tends to destroy independent areas of activity, subjecting them to a centralized, rigid and planned control. Distinctions between the superstructures and structures, between economy and politics, between the public and private no longer make sense.... Study, work, consumption, free time, personal relations ... all of them enter into a scheme of inputs and outputs that allow conflict but will not tolerate antagonism.[8]

The new conflict involved all spheres of life and helped forge a student identity and politics. This process will be examined in this chapter in relation to the themes of political violence, and fashion, which provide important insights into the movement's image of itself in its formative period. (Analyses of the movement at the Catholic and State universities of Milan in the following sections will give a more concrete and detailed picture of its development.)

The student movement's antagonism to the state had been a major source of its unity ever since the Centre–Left government had tried to reform the universities. Anti-reformism was almost an article of faith. However, it became more vivid, immediate and impelling when students and police joined battle in Rome on 20 March, 1968. Student defiance of a ban on demonstrations was met with tear-gas and truncheon charges.

That was no novelty; the difference on this occasion was that the students fought back and drove the police off the streets. *La Sinistra* wrote:

> The fight against 'academic' and 'societal' authoritarianism is now visibly unified; the whole state apparatus is behind the academic structures not only culturally but physically. The truncheon reinforces professorial concepts, the water-cannon speaks for parliamentary majorities, and the old-style exam stands behind the blanket of tear-gas.[9]

The battle of Valle Giulia was a turning point for the student movement. Guido Viale writes:

> The government and the movement, from this moment, found themselves face to face as protagonists of a conflict with national dimensions.... The government did not miss another opportunity to force showdowns with students and workers. And the students responded by forming 'defence organizations' (*servizi d'ordine*) to keep control of the streets. At Pisa, a few weeks later, a student demonstration, which ended by occupying the railway station, was organized and well-equipped; everyone wore the same crash-helmets as the Japanese and German students.[10]

On 25 March 1968 Milan had its 'Valle Giulia'. Students at the Catholic University, who had been locked out by the authorities following their eviction from the premises, decided to reoccupy the buildings near Sant' Ambrogio. Previously conflict had always been non-violent; on the one hand, the police treated students with the respect they traditionally paid to the middle classes and the commissar of police maintained an understanding with student leaders. On the other hand, the students themselves used passive resistance and tried to win public sympathy for their cause. However, on this occasion, these rules of the game were broken as both sides resorted to violent means. Although the majority of the six thousand student demonstrators came to protest peacefully, the politicized activists were determined to reoccupy even if this meant a battle. Mario Capanna, one of the leaders, delivered a dramatic speech and ultimatum to serried ranks of police guarding the university gates, saying: 'We are giving you ten minutes to leave the premises that you are illegally occupying, or we will have to evict you' (*'Vi diamo dieci minuti per sgomberare'*). The students, in other words, were assuming the role of the police and claiming the right to restore order. The police replied to the provocation with violent charges. The kid gloves were taken off, and the peaceful demonstrators, along with the more militant ones, were severely beaten and terrorized. Sixty students were imprisoned, and forty-eight were charged with serious offences. So, in the wake of Valle Giulia, the terms of student–police conflict changed dramatically. For students, the police became a hated enemy, against whom it was legitimate to use force; whilst the police lost all respect for people they regarded as *figli di papa* (the spoilt children of the privileged), and willingly taught them a lesson.[11]

Guido Viale's analysis, according to which the government went out of its way to provoke confrontations, needs, however, to be given more precision. Distinctions have to be made between and within the different state apparatuses which were neither uniformly conservative nor completely controlled from above by the executive. It seems that the Centre–Left government had little to gain from violent showdowns with the student movement, and preferred compromises; following the Valle Giulia events it ordered the release of all those arrested and encouraged the university rector to negotiate with the movement. However, within the state's repressive apparatuses, conservative and right-wing opinion favoured the use of force to put down disorders. In the heat of events, the latter were able *de facto* to impose their policies of strong policing, and then to oblige the minister of the interior to defend their actions. The toll of deaths and injuries due to police charges, tear-gas canisters and use of firearms escalated as a consequence, especially from the beginning of 1969.[12] At the same time, it should be noted that the student movement as a whole did not make distinctions between the good intentions of ministers and the actions of the police in Italy. Rather, the bloodshed appeared to confirm analyses of the state, according to which it was an instrument of class rule which was fundamentally repressive. The words of one of the movement's most popular slogans, 'Smash the state, don't change it' (*'Lo Stato si abbatte non si cambia'*), reflected this view.

The logical consequence of such thinking about the state was the evolution of theories and strategies within the student movement which made political violence a central problem. Pacifism was pronounced dead by common consent; as graffiti put it 'A revolutionary pacificist is like a vegetarian lion.'[13] Student activists learnt how to make Molotov cocktails as part of their trade, and readers of *La Sinistra* could find diagrams and instructions to help them.[14] The idea of violent and armed struggle appeared in the movement's songs and slogans. A list of the most popular slogans in the movement, compiled by the magazine *L'Espresso*, shows how dominant the theme of violence had become by the end of 1968

Revolution, yes – revisionism, no (*Rivoluzione si – revisionismo no*)

Workers' power – arms to the workers (*Potere operaio – armi agli operai*)

Power comes out of the barrel of the gun (*Il potere sta sulla canna del fucile*)

The Vietcong win because they shoot (*Vietcong vince perché spara*)

Violence in return for violence (*Violenza alla violenza*)

Two, three, lots of Vietnams – two, three, lots of Valle Giulias (*Due, tre, molti Vietnam – due, tre, molte Valle Giulia*)

War, no – guerrilla action, yes (*Guerra no – guerriglia si*)[15]

Furthermore, the most popular song of the student movement was *La Violenza*. A verse celebrates clashes with the police: 'Today I have seen a demonstration – smiling faces, fifteen-year-old girls and workers along-side the students,' then 'I saw armoured cars overturned and burning, and many, many, policemen with broken heads' (*tanti e tanti baschi neri con le teste fracassate*). The chorus-line makes clear that 'whoever wasn't there this time, won't be with us tomorrow' *La violenza, la violenza, la violenza e la rivolta; chi non c'era questa volta non sarà con noi domani*).[16]

The violence practised by the student movement in its formative stages can be referred to as 'expressive behaviour' as defined by Pizzorno, in that the conflicts with the authorities tended to be ends in themselves and often did not rely on processes of negotiation because their true objective was the constitution of a new identity.[17] But violence was exalted within the political culture of the student movement for several reasons. Firstly, violence, real and symbolic, made it easy to distinguish friends and foes. It drew lines of battle, and enforced alignments. It was a litmus test showing the difference between revolutionaries and reformists. Violence, it was thought, showed the state's apparatus in its true colours (in *La Sinistra*'s words, it exposed the 'truncheon behind the professorial concept').[18] Secondly, violence had a shock effect that was conceived by the movement to be therapeutic. It not only distanced the students from the bourgeois values of their families, but served to root them out from the inside. Notions of legality, it was thought, had to be overcome, otherwise nothing would change. Thirdly, violence created solidarity: 'Whoever wasn't there this time, won't be with us tomorrow.' It was a test that required people to prove themselves. Che Guevara's 'new man' had to be created in the heat of battle, and to be like Guevara meant following him down the violent road for, in the words of a '68 slogan: '*Guevara non parla, spara*', (Guevara doesn't talk, he shoots). Violence meant 'putting yourself on the line', and so 'being taken at your word'. It was a test of trustworthiness 'now', in a moment of crisis, and the anticipation of 'tomorrow's' society of fraternity. Moreover, the act of collective violence was an intense physical and emotional experience that summoned up total commitment to the group on the part of the individual. Lastly, violence was group power in action, and the means of its extension. The broken heads of the police showed what could be done if only the oppressed fought back. It was only the beginning, but it was also the prefiguration of future revolt and insurrection. Violence was conceived of as a detonator that multiplied itself and generalized struggles, starting with 'two or three' and growing into 'many' revolts.

The theme of political violence was crucial to the student movement's development, but it would be misleading to take it literally by removing it from its proper context. It was by no means the only or predominant political focus, and was more verbal and symbolic than physical and organized.[19] It was, above all, a means of self-differentiation in its extremest form. In this respect it can be compared to the use made of fashion by the student movement, which served to *épater le bourgeois*, and to assert a common identity.

The Politics of Student Dress

The first shock waves to pass through *il Milano perbene* (well-heeled Milan) were generated by Italian 'beatniks'. Their tent-village *New Barbonia* (New Bumsville) on via Ripamonte provoked hysteria at the *Corriere della Sera*, whose headlines on the Milan pages played on the fears of the readers for the safety of their children: 'The Longhairs of New Barbonia Even Celebrate Sacrilegious Weddings'; 'Provos and Longhairs Threaten A "March on Milan" Tomorrow'. A description of their eviction stresses the danger they represent to public health: 'Police, waste-disposal services and health officers finally managed to clean up, spraying some 500 litres of disinfectant over the area'.[20] The beatniks' long hair, in particular, was used to conjure up images of dirt, primitivism, and sexual depravity.

The beatniks were part of a bohemian world which, in Milan, found its centre of gravity in the Brera district and its headquarters in the Bar Giamaica. For them, lifestyle and appearance were at one with their anti-bourgeois, anti-institutional ideas. However, their brand of shock tactics was an extreme form of a more generalized use of clothing and appearance for expressive purposes. There was an extraordinary coincidence between the rise of the movement and the mass purchase of new items of clothing. The rapidity of the changes in appearance can be seen by looking at photographs taken in 1967 and in 1968. Photographs of the Architecture Faculty occupation in Milan in early 1967 show clean-shaven male students dressed in jackets and ties. Their dress is of sombre hue – browns and dark greens – and little that is sartorial distinguishes them from the rest of the city's middle class. Pictures taken a year later show a very different image of the student. This time the Cuban-style beard is in fashion, many men and women students are wearing *blu-jeans* (as they are known in Italian), men are not wearing jackets, unless they have a military look with cap to match. Some have red handkerchiefs tied around their neck, but the tie has been dispensed with. The colours are brighter.[21] A similar comparison of 'before' and 'after' can be made with the class photographs of a city *liceo*; that of 1967 is formal and everyone has a neat appearance, whilst in the 1968 picture the young students look scruffy and wave their clenched fists at the camera.[22]

For demonstrations the movement developed its own sort of uniform. In winter, everyone wore khaki *Eskimo* jackets, trousers and long scarves. The common rationale given for wearing this clothing was that it was practical; the *Eskimo* had lots of pockets and was tough, warm and water-proof, and the scarves were useful for masking the face and for protecting the eyes against teargas. However, this does not explain how a certain wardrobe and repertoire of hairstyles and gestures developed within the movement. To do so, it is necessary to look at the emergence of its image of itself, and its attempt to define itself in the eyes of the world. The dress of the Italian student movement was marked by the desire to project a political self-image. Style took on political connotations, in that the activists often wore their clothes as if they were carrying a banner. Commitment was worn on the sleeve for all to see. Politics was no longer invisible to the eye, a private matter of conscience to be guessed at by the curious stranger; it was made public for all to see. Whilst in previous political movements people had worn emblems, carnations for instance, usually the class connotations of appearance were already sufficiently identifiable; workers, for example, frequently attended demonstrations in their overalls. For students, however, it was vital to dress differently in order to distinguish themselves from the middle classes from which most of them came. In fact, it was almost obligatory not to dress in a traditional manner in the student ambience to avoid being taken for a Fascist.

The new appearance cultivated by the student movement was experienced as an immense release from the constraints of dull respectability. Young men experimented by wearing bright colours, which had long been denied them. For women, the new fashion of the natural appearance released them from the pressures to use make-up and wear high heels (many wore trousers and did not wear a dress again for several years). For the men it led to the cultivation of the wild and unkempt look, especially on the more libertarian fringes. The movement, in addition, encouraged a certain theatrical imagination, which perhaps explains the temporary vogue for Carbonaro-style mantles that evoked romantic images of revolt.[23] However, the movement also created models of what a comrade should look like, and implicitly invested them with moral values. In fact, this will to set up new standards, as well as the willingness to criticize the dominant codes, differentiates the relation of fashion to a social movement from other forms of fashion. Thus, it was not like those fashions described by Alberoni in which: 'every individual, although behaving in the same way as the others, is, in reality, concerned only about himself', because the style for the student movement was a means of 'participating in a wider solidarity'.[24] Then, unlike deviancy, there was not only a conscious breaking of the hidden rules governing appearance, but an alternative set of norms. Interestingly, in Milan a strange man known as Sacha took particular pleasure in attending student demonstrations and occupations dressed in the height of elegance in a blue suit with shirt and cravat, or wearing a smoking jacket.[25] His deviant imagination could be satisfied only against the backdrop of a student generation that had turned its back on middle-class fashions. Although there were some who delighted in cutting a fine figure, the moment for doing so had largely passed (such a moment was Feltrinelli's return to Italy from Bolivia at the beginning of the previous year dressed with Cuban flourishes); now it was more important to share a common identity.[26]

The student movement dealt with the question of fashion in largely negative terms. Appearance and clothes became issues in as far as they represented the consumerism, wealth and ostentation that the movement opposed. Thus, before the Christmas of 1968, students picketed the department store Rinascente, not only in support of the striking shop-workers, but to oppose Christmas consumerism. Earlier in the month they attacked the opening night of La Scala in protest at the luxury and finery exhibited by the Milanese bourgeoisie. A strong streak of puritanism ran through the movement, which also reflected a masculine ethos according to which expenditure on clothes and appearance was fundamentally wasteful. It was basically thought that clothes should be practical and economical, and that appearance should be natural. The utopian idea informing the new fashion was that in an ideal society there would be a rough-and-ready equality; dress would really be of little importance in judging and distinguishing people. It was an artifice that had to be minimized in order to achieve a collective identity. The movement's idea of clothing and appearance, in other words, was an aspect of a naturalistic aesthetic which aspired to make the relationships between people transparent.[27] Ultimately, the movement condemned the very idea of fashion, and would have liked to have abolished it as seemed to have been done in China.

A Moral Panic

By the first months of 1968 the student movement in Italy had radically transformed the student image and identity. Students looked and behaved differently from the sons and daughters of the middle class who had gone to the *liceo* and the university before them. Over the period 1968–9 students became both hate-figures and fashion-setters in the eyes of the media-consuming public. Liberal progressive opinion, represented by the weeklies *L'Espresso* and *Panorama*, was given pictures of an exotic and exciting world and of struggles against the conservative establishment. *L'Espresso* specialized in guides and maps designed to help the reader decode the movement's signs (the insignia of different political organizations, their origins, and so on).[28] By contrast, *Il Corriere della Sera*, the Milan-based daily, thrilled and shocked its readers in turn with stories about student outrages. Whilst *L'Espresso* tried to make the phenomenon comprehensible, the *Corriere* dwelt on its incomprehensible features.

The campaign of the *Corriere della Sera* had all the characteristics of what Stan Cohen has called the 'moral panic':

Societies appear to be subject, every now and then, to periods of moral panic. A condition, episode, person or group of persons emerges to become defined as a threat to societal values and interests; its nature is presented in a stylized and stereo-typical fashion by the mass media; the moral barricades are manned by editors, bishops, politicians and other right-thinking people; socially accredited experts pronounce diagnoses and solutions; ways of coping are evolved or (more often) resorted to; the condition then disappears, submerges or deteriorates and becomes more visible. Sometimes the object of panic is quite novel and at other times it is something which has been in existence long enough, but suddenly appears in the limelight. Sometimes the panic is passed over and is forgotten, except in folklore and collective memory; at other times it has more serious and long-lasting repercussions and might produce such changes as those in legal and social policy or even in a way society conceives itself.[29]

In England the 'folk devils' studied by Cohen in the late sixties were mods and rockers; in Italy, the reds were traditionally the devils, but in 1968 students assumed the role, provoked a panic about the infiltration of Communism and permissiveness into Italian institutions. The *Corriere della Sera* usually referred to movement activists as 'the Chinese' (*i cinesi*) – a term which conjured up the red menace and the yellow peril in one. Its coverage of student politics gained a certain notoriety for its sheer vituperation. However, it was not only the right which condemned the movement.

The moral panic was mainly felt by the political and religious establishment and traditionalist middle class, but it also cut across political

cultures. One of the most notable statements directed against the movement came from Pier Paolo Pasolini, who was a Communist Party
sympathizer. In June 1968 he wrote a poem expressing his loathing for the
figli di papa:

> Now all the journalists in the world are licking your arses ... but not me, my
> dears. You have the faces of spoilt brats, and I hate you, like I hate your
> fathers.... When yesterday at Valle Giulia you beat up the police, I
> sympathized with the police because they are the sons of the poor.[30]

In the same month Giorgio Amendola, a leading member of the PCI,
described the student movement as a re-edited version of irrationalism and
infantilist, anarchist extremism. He called for a fight on 'two fronts',
which meant counterposing the patrimony 'accumulated by us over tens
of years of hard struggles' to dangerous student extremism.[31]

In 1968 it is possible to speak of a moral panic of which the students
were the principal protagonists. They aimed to shock and disgust sections
of public opinion and they succeeded. But unlike the folk devils studied by
Cohen who delighted in infamy without pretending to destroy society, the
student movement was a movement and not a set of deviant activities. It
aimed to subvert the existing institutions, and, if possible, to bring about
revolutionary changes. By themselves students were powerless, and their
actions provoked a moral panic of limited proportions. But when they
joined forces with the workers' movement that panic became more
general; it became a 'crisis of hegemony'.

Notes

1. Franco Catalano, *Il movimento studentesco e la scuola in Italia*, Milan 1969.
2. Ibid.
3. *Libro bianco sulla Facultà di Architettura di Milano*, Milan 1967.
4. Ibid., pp. 1–2.
5. Marco Boato, *Il '68 è morto: Viva il '68*, Verona 1979, pp. 100–28, p. 141.
6. See Massimo Bertozzi, 'Teoria e politica alla prova dei fatti. Il "Potere Operaio" pisano (1966–1969)', *Classe*, 17, June 1980, pp. 298–307.
7. Rossana Rossanda, *L'anno degli studenti*, Bari 1968, p. 38.
8. Boato, p. 209.
9. *La Sinistra*, 9 May 1968.
10. Guido Viale, *Il sessantotto*, Milan 1978, p. 43.
11. Reconstruction from interviews especially with Antonia Torchi, 1982; also *Corriere della Sera*, 26, 27 March 1968.
12. A publication of 1970 listed the death toll from April 1968 to mid July 1970: (Paolo Rossi, university student (aged 20) killed during a student demonstration on 26 April 1968; Angelo Sigona and Giuseppe Scibilia (aged 27 and 48 respectively), farm-workers killed during clashes at Avola on 2 December 1968; at Battipaglia the apprentice typographer Carmine Citro (aged only 13) and the teacher Teresa Ricciordini

were killed; at Rome on 1 March 1969 during clashes at the university occupation Domenico Congedo (aged 20) died; on 28 October 1969 Cesare Pardini (aged 22), a student was killed by a tear-gas canister in Pisa university. . . .' In all, there were twenty-eight deaths and hundreds of wounded. 'Corrente' Proletaria dei Lavoratori Studenti', *Le lotte dei lavoratori studenti*, Milan 1970, pp. 9–10.

13. Emilio Tiberi, *La contestazione murale*, Bologna 1972, p. 120.
14. *La Sinistra*, 16 March 1968.
15. *L'Espresso*, 15 December 1968.
16. Guido Viale, *Il sessantotto*, p. 49.
17. 'When a mass of individuals, who belong to an occupational group, or class fraction, or who have common objective interests, are excluded from the system of representation but find themselves in favourable circumstances for mobilization . . . the conflict which ensues in their struggle for recognition tends to be more intense than over normal demands. . . . For example, conflicts are often ends in themselves (and sometimes no specific demands are made) . . . because the real objective is the constitution of a new identity'; Alessandro Pizzorno, 'Le due logiche dell'azione di classe', *Lotte operaie e sindacato*, vol. 6, p. 13.
18. *La Sinistra*, 9 March 1968.
19. For an interesting discussion of the slogan as a cultural vehicle, see Aldo Marchetti, 'Un teatro troppo serio', *Classe*, XIII, June 1982.
20. Fernanda Pivano, *C'era una volta un beat*, Milan 1988, p. 107.
21. Interview with Stefano Levi, student leader at the faculty of architecture of Milan Polytechnic.
22. A study has yet to be made of the photographic representations of the social movements in Italy using private snapshots, news photographs, etc. The main collections of photographs are those of professional photographers, for example, Uliano Lucas, *Cinque anni a Milano*, Turin 1973.
23. The Catholic University leader, Mario Capanna, is said to have had a penchant for this look.
24. Francesco Alberoni, 'Movimenti e istituzioni nell'Italia tra il 1960 e il 1970', in L. Graziano, ed., *La crisi italiana*, Turin 1979, pp. 223–34.
25. He had become such a well-known figure that an obituary was published on his premature death; *Corriere della Sera*, 13 May 1978.
26. The importance of context for the meaning of dress is wittily illustrated by Umberto Eco: 'She is wearing a mini-dress: she's a girl of easy virtue. In Catania. She's wearing a mini-dress: she's a modern girl, Milan. She's wearing a mini-dress, in Paris: she's a girl. She's wearing a mini-dress, in Hamburg, at the Eros: maybe it's a man': Umberto Eco, 'L'abito non fa il monaco', in Francesco Alberoni et al, *Psicologia del vestire*, Milan 1971, p. 9.
27. 'In revolution, therefore, the questions of how one will make sense of momentary encounters, how one will know whom to believe, become all-important. Codes for making sense of appearances by strangers acquire an inflated importance as history is speeded up and time suspended'; Richard Sennett, *The Fall of Public Man*, New York 1977, p. 226.
28. In March 1968 *L'Espresso* presented a map entitled 'Their Prophets': 'What we give you here is a sort of ideological atlas, a genealogical tree of the principal positions of the student movement. It would be excessive to attribute to it absolute scientific rigour'; quoted in *I dieci anni che sconvolsero il mondo*, Florence 1978, pp. 11–13.
29. Stanley Cohen, *Folk Devils and Moral Panics: the Creation of the Mods and Rockers*, London 1972, p. 28.
30. Pasolini's poem/pamphlet was first published in *L'Espresso*, 16 June 1968, with the title: 'Il PCI ai giovani!!' It was followed by articles by Vittorio Foa and others criticizing it in the editions of 23 and 30 June; Enzo Siciliano, *Vita di Pasolini*, Milan 1978, pp. 322–3.
31. Giorgio Amendola, 'Necessità della lotta su due fronti', in *Rinascita*, 23, 7 June 1968; quoted in Boato, p. 234. The official position of the PCI, however, was to give full support to the student movement; Luigi Longo, who was on the left of the party, spoke

of this movement as 'posing a series of problems of tactics and strategy. We have to recognize that it has shaken up the political situation and has been largely positive ... in undermining the Italian social system'; Ibid., p. 235. His arguments prevailed over those of Giorgio Amendola. *L'Unità* in 1968–9 carried out a struggle on one front only, and hardly a critical remark was made about student politics; see Grant Amyot, *The Italian Communist Party*, London 1982, p. 175.

6

religion and student politics: the catholic university

Conflicts within the Catholic World

The occupation of the Catholic University (the 'Cattolica') on 18 November 1967 sent shock waves through Italian Catholic society. Until then the university had not been touched by the political ferment of the state-controlled institutions. It was set up by the Church in 1921, as a crucial part of its strategy to create a nucleus of Catholic intellectuals to intervene in lay culture and politics. Secondary education was largely in the hands of the state, so the Church attached particular importance to control over its own university. It had always remained under the close supervision of the bishop, and many of the leading members of the Christian Democrat party were its former students.[1] The authorities reacted to the prospect of 'subversion' and the infiltration of Marxist ideas into the cloisters of Sant' Ambrogio by calling in the police.[2] The 'ringleaders' were expelled. However, what was seen by the authorities as an alien intrusion was the product of conflicts within the Catholic world in the 1960s. The student movement at the Cattolica is of particular interest for understanding the change of conscience into political consciousness, and tracing the development of Catholic radicalism.

In the immediate postwar period the Catholic Church in Italy had to defend itself from three chief threats – Marxism, demands for the ending of the Concordat, and the secularisation of society (what Pius XII referred to as *lo spirito del secolo*).[3] This it did with remarkable success through a full-scale mobilization of the faithful in the parishes – a success which was crowned by the Christian Democrat electoral victory of 1948. The PCI was isolated (Communist voters were threatened with excommunication), the Concordat renewed, and sections of the middle classes previously aligned with the secular Liberal and Republican parties shifted their allegiances, and educated their children according to Catholic principles. It was not until the thaw in the Cold War and the more liberal policies of Pope John XXIII, who lifted the veto on the Communist vote, that Catholics were able to speak more freely about their tasks in society.

Within the Church the most important developments occurred in Latin America, where some priests were active among peasant movements and theorized convergences between the teachings of the Gospel and of Marxism.[4] Given the especially strong links with Italian missionaries, and the sympathy aroused for Latin American struggles against imperialism they became a point of reference. Exhibitions mounted at the Cattolica in 1967 publicized the suffering and oppression of the Third World, and appealed strongly to themes of social commitment.[5] Dissent within the Church in Italy, however, was marginal and heavily dealt with by the hierarchy. It was only able to come into the open when the 'ice' of conformity had already been broken by the social movements. One of the most celebrated cases of dissent was the rebellion of don Mazzi, a young priest at Isolotto, a working-class parish in Florence. When the bishop sent him a letter warning him against the use of the Church for political purposes, radical Catholics occupied Parma Cathedral in protest.

However, the major source of dissent was not within the Church, but among lay Catholics. On the one hand, there were shifts in middle-class opinion away from subordination to clerical influence expressed by the spread of ideas of 'modernism' (especially those of the 'permissive society'); on the other hand, the very success of the Church intervention in politics had had a secularizing effect on its own conduct and image because of its involvement with the Christian Democrat party and big business. The 'revolt' among sections of the laity can be seen as part of an older cycle of disenchantment based on the discrepancy between the morality of the Gospels and the activities of the Church. What gave it political significance in the late sixties was the tendency towards independent action by lay bodies with close affiliations with the Church, and towards the setting up of new lay groupings. An inquiry of 1968 into the formation of groups and associations spontaneously set up on direct democratic lines and with left-wing political projects showed that 36 per cent were of Catholic origin.[6]

The CISL, which did not recruit on the basis of religious beliefs, but which had the mass of its support among Catholic workers, had already committed itself to joint action with the Communist-dominated CGIL in response to pressures from its membership.[7] What was more serious for the Church was the radicalization of the Associazione Cristiana Lavoratori Italiani (ACLI) which was the Catholic pressure group within the world of organized labour. In 1968 it broke its links with the Christian

Democrat Party.[8] The emergence of 'class' and 'exploitation' as terms within Catholic denunciations of capitalist society, showed how Marxist ideas were being taken up, sometimes with even greater enthusiasm than within the historic organizations of the Left.

Within the Catholic student organization, Intesa, there had been a tradition of cooperation with the Left, which became closer with the increasing disappointment in the government. The Gioventù Studentesca (GS), a Catholic association of students which had no official political orientation, became a cauldron of open debate and discussion at the Cattolica. The return of sponsored missionaries from Brazil, the summer work camps in the poverty-stricken areas of Calabria and the initiation of play projects among the children of the Milanese hinterland – all these experiences, which had been promoted out of a spirit of *caritas*, excited 'Communist sympathies' among students in the context of the growing dissent among Catholic intellectuals and organizations. Humanist and populist ideas linked up with Marxist theories, and evangelism took on the form of overtly political activism.[9]

Mobilizing Moral Outrage

The flashpoint at the Cattolica was the issue of a 50 per cent increase in student fees. The university already had higher fees than the average, and the cost seemed greater because an unusual number of the 20,000 students were from outside the province, and there were 8,500 'worker-students'. However, it was not so much the sum of money involved by the autumn rise in fees as the principle at stake which concerned most students. There was widespread anger at what was seen as hypocritical behaviour by authorities who prided themselves on providing an educational ladder down to the poorest parishioners. It was described as an attack on the right to education (*diritto allo studio*). The student representative body organized an extraordinary general meeting of all student organizations, the publication of a report (*libro bianco*), a public debate and a demonstration of protest. It won the backing of the youth federation of the Christian Democratic Party as well as that of the PSIUP.[10]

The first protests, in the shape of strikes during lectures and examinations, were not popular because they were identified as 'left-wing', and education was not yet seen as political. But when the rector refused to enter into dialogue with the students, a call for an occupation won the support of two-thirds of the students. When police arrived on the scene, there was outrage at the authorities' readiness to use force, break the rights of sanctuary, and to involve the state despite the university's continuous reiteration of its free and independent status. The use of passive resistance, following the example of the US movement, under-scored the legalism and the peaceful intentions of the Cattolica students, and highlighted the hypocrisy of the rectorate. A motion approved by the general meeting of the students in occupation expressed: 'indignation, suffering and deeply troubled human, civil and Christian feelings in response to the authorities' behaviour towards the occupation.' It went on to say that police intervention 'is particularly offensive to our university, which likes to regard itself as free and Catholic'.[11] The degree of support for the action, which split the teaching staff, reflected the injured sensi-bilities of middle-class adults, who resented being treated like children. Had the police not been called, it seems likely that the mobilization would have fizzled out, especially in the absence in mid November of a wider national movement.

The occupation was the form of action that served most to group together the dissident students. The first occupation in November 1967 involved from 100 to 200 activists, who were prepared to defy not only the authorities, but their own families by staying overnight in the univer-sity. With the closure of the Cattolica for a week after the eviction of the occupiers, they carried out an information picket (*picchettaggio di informazione*), and distributed a daily bulletin. The main decisions were taken at the general assemblies of all the students, whilst a committee of agitation ran the everyday activity. 'Commissions' were formed to hold seminars and organize specific activities. The movement began a protest guided by the belief that the authorities would see reason, and act accord-ing to their educational and moral ideals. However, through the occu-pation it developed its own structures and independence based on direct democracy and self-managed learning.

A motion put to the general meeting of the Cattolica by students repre-senting the student movement (*movimento studentesco*) slate in the university elections shows a particular concern for the issues of selection and authoritarianism. It was passed. It lists the demands of the movement as follows:

On Autonomy

1. The recognition of the autonomy and self-government of the student movement.
2. The withdrawal of disciplinary proceedings against activists.
3. Freedom of speech.
4. Provision of facilities and timetabling for student movement activities.

Teaching

1. The recognition of experimental courses promoted by the student movement.

2. The generalized use of seminars.
3. Free debate within courses.
4. The establishment of inter-disciplinary and experimental courses open to all.
5. The democratization of all controls (over attendance and examinations).

Political Relations

1. The recognition of the power of the student general meeting over all important decisions concerning administration, teaching, etc.
2. The publication of all official documents.

The Right to Study

1. The progressive reduction of all fees.[12]

The ideas of anti-authoritarianism and democratic self-management were particularly central to the student movement at the Catholic University. The whole political style was very different to that of the movement at the other institutions. There was no left-wing tradition; no Marxist intellectuals like Stefano Levi, a leader in the architecture faculty of the Polytechnic who was called in to advise during the first occupation; no experience in political organizing. But these deficiencies were made up for in other ways; the politics were less orthodox and more experimental. This can be seen in the charismatic leadership of Mario Capanna.[13] He spoke in a way that everyone could understand and yet his speech was full of irony and vivid imagery. He made people laugh, and made them feel they had something to say. His flair for invention contrasted with the monotonous rhetoric of a Left which aped a humanist model *da foro* (based on the forum ideal). Capanna succeeded in interpreting an untutored enthusiasm for politics, which expressed itself in a movement and not in a party political form.

Anti-authoritarian politics was especially important at the Cattolica because it related directly to the students' resistance to surveillance and control by the authorities, who were concerned about the souls of their pupils as well as about their education in a narrower sense. Much of the student movement's stress on free speech and debate within courses was informed by a struggle against religious dogma. This concern with the religious question was peculiar to the movement at the Cattolica. It is worth considering not only as a special issue, but in relation to how politics itself was invested with 'religious' meanings.

The challenge to Catholicism by the students was aimed against the Church as an institution rather than against religion. Students occupied churches and interrupted masses with iconoclastic enthusiasm.[14] Censorship and the sterility of cultural conformity were attacked in *Dialoghi*, a student paper; one issue protested against interference by consisting entirely of blank copy. Demands were made for the end of Church juridical control over the university, and for the abolition of the requirement that entrants should be Catholics. A student leaflet pointed out that, in the Gospels, it was the poor and oppressed who were the chosen ones.[15] Students demanded the right to control Gioventù Studentesca, the student organization, without interference from the bishop. Proposals were also put for seminars on the Faith to replace the theology lectures. Demands focused on the accountability of the hierarchy, and on the need for the Church to fight oppression in the world. However, it is notable that the movement made no mention of the Church's crucial role in the regulation of sexuality in the university and in society generally. Rigorous moral codes were applied within the institution; lecturers and students found to be 'living in sin' were expelled, and women students living away from home were placed with families to prevent them falling into sin. Although women participated in the movement (a fact which shocked the authorities), there is little sign that feminism played any part in the demands or actions of the movement.

The simplest course open to dissident Catholic students was to resolve or relegate the religious question as a priority by ceasing to attend Mass. Thereby, belief was either made personal and withdrawn from the Church's tutelage, or it was discarded. This step was one taken by many young Italians in the 1960s, and was one aspect of the secularization of the society.[16] However, in the late sixties, energies and enthusiasms that had previously been channelled through the Church's organizations took political forms. This development has already been mentioned in relation to the radicalization of the Catholic-based lay bodies such as ACLI, the CISL and various community ventures, but it was also a more general phenomenon that affected secular politics. This can be shown by looking at *Letter to a School-teacher*, which was possibly the single most influential text in the student movement, and by showing how radical Catholic and Marxist ideas converged in this period.

Letter to a School-teacher denounced the selective and discriminatory nature of education, using the experiences of the small Tuscan village school at Barbiana. The themes being dealt with had a direct relevance to a movement which was fighting for everyone's right to education, and which had made teaching into a political issue. Indeed the book anticipated the movement. It was easily translateable into Marxist terminology, and was adapted and selectively used by its extensive readership. However, much of its appeal derived from its difference from standard Marxist accounts, which spoke of the objective mechanisms whereby capitalism reproduced its labour power (for example, the Pisan Theses). The Barbiana letters focused on the individual experience of education and spoke through the voices of children excluded not only by economic but by cultural processes. Tullio de Mauro has suggested that don Milani's discovery of the politics of grammar, and of the knowledge and use of words resulted from his critical appropriation of his priestly functions.[17] Firstly, the Church taught don Milani 'intimately to adhere to linguistic obedience'; the Church's language, which served to bring individual consciences into conformity with etiquette and principles of belief and to free its own functionaries from the ties of social and geographical origin, taught don Milani about the power of words. He rebelled against that use of language, but with the power of having mastered it. Secondly, don Milani, according to De Mauro, was above all a preacher who wanted to change things. In this respect too, the 'linguistic school of the Evangelists' prepared him in that it insisted on the power of 'the word', and on the need to emancipate the oppressed from the burdens of cultural deprivation. For don Milani it was vital that the poor should rely on their own powers to speak and write, and should free themselves from the oppressive notion of 'correct Italian';

> We need anyway to understand what is correct language. The poor create languages and then continue to renew them. The rich crystallize them so that they can take advantage of whoever doesn't talk like they do. Or they fail them in exams.[18]

In his work at Barbiana, he attempted to overcome these inequalities by encouraging collective authorship and linking learning to a participatory notion of democracy.

Although not exclusive to a Catholic culture, don Milani's sensitivity to certain forms of oppression was perhaps best represented by radical Catholic currents. It was characterized by attention to culture as a political problem which required specific forms of action and analysis and by its focus on experience and the personal dimensions of oppression. Moreover, don Milani's example stood out for its moral commitment and appealed to feelings among students that the culturally privileged should 'go to the people'. Rossanda wrote that the letters from Barbiana were perceived as evidence of the need for an Italian version of the Chinese Cultural Revolution. Yet, by contrast with appropriations of Chinese slogans and sloganizing style, don Milani offered a vivid insight into the lived experience of injustice. The book touched a generation's sense of moral outrage and had echoes far beyond the world of the university activists. It showed the power of a religious culture to generate and activate moral standards of condemnation.

There were specific reasons for the popularity of the *Letter to a School-teacher*, but these need to be placed in the broader context of the convergence of radical Catholicism and Marxism in the late sixties. This relationship has not received much critical attention; Catholic intellectuals have perhaps shown more interest in the interaction of religion and politics (or in the similarities of political and religious militancy) than Marxists, who have been anxious to defend 'science' from 'contamination'.[19] Whilst it is true that many of the overtly religious elements that appeared in the movements of opposition were of tangential significance, the 'religious structure of feeling' was of considerable importance in the making of 1968. This structure of feeling had been a part of Marxist and Socialist movements from early in their history, but it had been contained and marginalized by parliamentary parties that feared uncontrolled enthusiasms.[20] In 1968 it was recreated and reactivated in the student movement.

In this light it is possible to understand how the radicalization in the Catholic world could lead to a *rapprochement* with Marxism, without requiring the total abandonment of a structure of feeling based on faith and commitment to an ideal. Indeed, it could be argued that politics offered even greater possibilities for self-sacrifice, the service of others and for apostolic militancy and, therefore, for being a more genuine Christian. However, the majority of new adherents to revolutionary politics experienced their conversion as a break with Catholicism and with their own pasts. They turned religion on its head, and dismissed it with Marx's peremptoriness as an opiate. This had serious consequences for the student movement, and generally for the relations between Catholic and Marxist cultures in the subsequent period. The moment of *rapprochement* was succeeded by one of division and mutual animosity.

The crisis and decline of the student movement at the Cattolica was bound up with this breakdown in dialogue between Marxists and practising Catholics among the students. In the early stages of mobilization in 1967–8 the militant and politicized minority had been sensitive to religious feelings and beliefs. Thus, after the clashes with the police in March 1968, meetings were held of the Assemblea Ecclesiastica, and care was taken to elaborate biblical justifications for rebellion and for the use of violence. However, splits developed among activists on whether to continue to organize around religious issues, and between the politicized minority and the mass of students at the university. By the end of 1969 religion was no longer a terrain of struggle between dissident students and the authorities, largely because radicals directed their attention to other problems without linking them up to Catholicism. Above all, they abandoned the university and student struggles in favour of political agitation around the factories, which became the centres of social conflict from the autumn of 1968. Thus, the movement evacuated its own stronghold and left a free hand to the authorities to restore the status quo.

The rector at the Cattolica had consistently opposed the student movement, and had frequently resorted to repression in attempts to root out dissent. Over two years tens of students were expelled from the university. The police barracks, which conveniently faced the main entrance to the university, acted as a constant pillar of strength to the authorities. There was no question of giving way to the student movement and allowing the university to be subverted from within. There was too much at stake. The importance of the university to the Catholic Church was evidenced by the national annual *Giornata della Cattolica*, a day given over to collecting funds from the faithful to support their institution, and by its function in educating its lay political elite. The weakening of the students' movement was therefore seized on by the authorities to drive it from Sant' Ambrogio as Christ had driven the money-lenders from the temple. Over a two year period it disappeared from the Cattolica and Catholic dissent irremediably lost a crucial stronghold. Instead the university became a springboard for the launching of Comunione e Liberazione. This was the Catholic Church's successful youth organization, which showed a skilful adoption of themes and structures developed by the student movement for the purposes of re-establishing the role of religion in daily activities. Although Catholic dissent continued to grow in the wake of the social movements, and gave rise to organizations such as Christians for Socialism, the cruel irony of the dramatic echoes of the student rebellion at the Cattolica was that the Church learnt more from it than did its opponents.[21]

Notes

1. F. Schianchi, *La Università Cattolica*, Milan 1974, pp. 149–59.
2. Guido Viale, *Il sessantotto*, pp. 22–3; Schianchi, pp. 176–7.
3. G. Poggi, 'The Church in Italian Politics, 1945–50', in S. Woolf, ed., *The Rebirth of Italy*, London 1971. The Concordat was drawn up between the Fascist state and the Church, making Catholicism the state religion.
4. Francesco Alberoni, 'Movimenti e istituzioni nell'Italia tra il 1960 e il 1970', in L. Graziano, ed., *La crisi italiana*, Bologna 1979, pp. 253–5.
5. Interviews with ex-Catholic University students show that there were considerable differences in how the Third World issue was interpreted. Ida Regalia, a member of the Intesa group, stresses the importance of the missionaries, and makes links between the politics of radical priests in Latin America and work with the urban and Southern poor in Italy. Ex-students who identified more immediately with the Left (Antonia Torchi, for example) made Vietnam and Che Guevara their examples of Third World struggles, and counterposed the politics of guerrilla warfare to Catholic pacifism. Even so, Leftists were careful to exploit Catholic 'consciences' to the full, rather than to alienate support, at least in the earlier stages of mobilization; Interview with Ida Regalia, April 1978; interview with Antonia Torchi, August 1982.
6. Franco Rositi et al, *La politica dei gruppi*, Milan 1970, pp. 140–41. See also L. Tomasi, *La contestazione religiosa giovanile in Italia (1968–78)*, Milan 1982, pp. 42–62; F. Garelli, 'Gruppi giovanili ecclesiali, *Quaderni di Sociologia*, 3–4, 1977,

pp. 277–81; Percy Allum, 'Uniformity Undone: Aspects of Catholic Culture in Postwar Italy', in Z. Baranski and R. Lumley, *Culture and Conflict in Postwar Italy*, London 1990.

7. See part III, chapter 11, p. 170.
8. S. Turone, *Storia del sindacato*, pp. 404–5, pp. 414–16.
9. Ida Regalia interview.
10. 'Perchè si è giunti all'aumento delle tasse' in *Dialoghi*, undated.
11. Mozione approvata dall'assemblea generale degli studenti occupanti, 19 November 1967.
12. Proposta di mozione presentata dal MS all'Assemblea Generale, 2 April 1968.
13. Mario Capanna was a Catholic University student who became the best known student leader in Milan. (These observations on his role come from a taped interview with ex-students, Aldo Marchetti, Claudio Frigerio and Antonia Torchi.) However, some people persisted in thinking that outside agitators explained everything. A press conference organized by right-wing students at the Cattolica claimed that the agitation in nearly every university in Europe was coordinated, by 'a Leninist type organization operating from Basle'; *Corriere della Sera*, 2 June 1968.
14. There was a protest against the Concordat by upper secondary school students (radicals, dissident Catholics and anarchists) who invaded Milan Cathedral, writing slogans on the wall like 'If God exists he must be abolished' and '1929–45 = DUCE/1945–69 = DC'; Report in *Corriere della Sera*, 12 February 1969.
15. 'Look at the gospel. The choosing of the poor and oppressed is made clear from the first page.' *Catechismo dell'Isotto*, quoted in document of the Comitato Assemblea Ecclesiale, 23 January 1969.
16 A survey of religious attendance among students in Milan for 1968 found that half of them went to church. In the Catholic University 65% were regular communicants, whilst only 5% were non-practising. At the State University, by contrast, only 30% of students were regular church-goers; C. Testa: *Giovani '70 inchiesta sulla condizione giovanile in Italia*, Rome 1969; quoted by Tomasi, pp. 77–9. Although opinion surveys are notoriously inaccurate, this survey suggests a picture of a relative continuity; there is a marginal decline in church attendance compared with 1966. Oral testimonies of activists suggests that for a sizeable minority there was an abandonment of habitual church-going.
17. Report of a conference on don Milani, *Lotta Continua*, 6 January 1982.
18. Scuola di Barbiana, *Lettera di una professoressa*, Florence 1967, pp. 18–19.
19. For example, the problem is central to the work of Francesco Alberoni, who tends to underline the parallels and convergences of religious and political protest movements. Indeed, it can be said that Alberoni himself helped create a dialogue between Catholic and Marxist approaches.
20. See Horowitz, *Italian Labour Movement*, Cambridge Mass. 1963, pp. 46–7; for an interesting discussion of this theme, Stephen Yeo, 'A New Life: The Religion of Socialism in Britain 1883–1896', *History Workshop Journal*, 4, Autumn 1977, pp. 5–57.
21. Luigi Manconi, 'Comunione e Liberazione: e che fare di 90,000 scouts?' *Ombre Rosse*, 11–12, November 1975, pp. 92–108; F. Garelli, pp. 275–321. Both Manconi and Garelli argue that Comunione e Liberazione created structures which valorized personal and recreational activities ignored by a more traditional left-wing politics.

7

the spread of student protest the state university, schools and institutes

Politics as Entertainment

The student movement at the State University ('La Statale') formed in the wake of the occupations at the Catholic University. It did not play a leading role nationally, nor did events at the Statale have a resonance within a specific cultural orbit equivalent to the *mondo cattolico*. However, this section of the movement rapidly dominated student politics within Milan. Its influence grew when the national movement was in crisis in the summer of 1968. The particular interest of this case lies in examining how the Statale became so central to the social life of the student movement.

The medical students were the first to occupy their faculty when, in mid February 1968, they took action in protest over overcrowding and the high examination failure rate. A few days later science, arts and law faculties were occupied. During March, April and May student occupations and police evictions produced a ding-dong battle. At the Cattolica there were seven occupations in 1968–9, and the students at the Statale took action with equal regularity. Moreover, as will be seen below, schools too were swept into the fray. There was no let-up in hostilities in 1968 until the June examinations, which at the Cattolica were presided over by the police. Each confrontation led to an escalation. Fascist attacks and the arrival of students at the gates with police escorts demanding the 'right to study' led to a militarization of conflict, especially following the battle of Valle Giulia.[1] On 25 March 1968 street battles broke out involving over a thousand students, when police evicted the occupiers from both the Catholic and State universities. Repression, expulsions and legal action against students provoked campaigns against victimization, and hardened feelings towards the authorities. Students responded by locking up the rectors of the two universities, and by putting 'reactionary' lecturers on trial. Writing on the walls pointed the accusing finger. For example, a certain Bonicalzi was addressed: 'Bonicalzi, you who love prefabrication, tell us about building speculation.' Graffiti also contained ironic advice to workers on how to go to university: 'Workers, you too can go to university – join the police.'

Whilst the struggle for the control of space was lost at the Cattolica, the students at the Statale managed to assert their hold over their territory. The Cattolica activists were relatively isolated from the bulk of the student body by the time confrontation took a more violent turn. Their most effective and popular methods of struggle involved passive resistance, and they were not sufficiently prepared to do battle for a political autonomy which required the free use of institutional space. Moreover, the authorities at the Cattolica held firm. At the Statale the student movement could count on a broader area of support, and had fewer scruples about violent action. It was already more politicized in the early stages, due to a history of organization and activism that was lacking at the Cattolica. Then, the authorities of the Statale were more ready to accept incursions on their prerogatives rather than have more conflict. The students at the Statale effectively made the university into a base for the movement, but their success needs also to be related to their exploitation of its topographical centrality. The Ospedale Maggiore site, which has formed the core of the university since its foundation in 1924, is in the centre of Milan. It is a five-minute walk from Piazza Duomo, where political and trade-union rallies historically follow on from marches through the city streets. The student movement quickly transformed the nearby Piazza San Stefano into its place for meetings and rallies. Students from all the educational institutions came to the Piazza, and to the university for city-wide demonstrations, debates or to coordinate strikes and protest action. When the Statale students occupied the buildings others joined them and helped repel attacks.

However, the attractions of the State University were not only political in a narrow sense. Occupations provided excellent opportunities for an exciting social life including free rock and jazz concerts. A *Corriere della Sera* report entitled the 'Nights of Mao' gave a voyeuristic insight into the carnival atmosphere which reigned during an occupation of the Statale:

> this is how the pro-Chinese (*filo-cinesi*) elements pass the hours of the cultural revolution – they play poker, dress up in lecturers' robes, use crucifixes as weapons, listen to Bach and make toasts with wine from Puglia.[2]

Indeed, an important part of the new politics was precisely these sorts of taboo-breaking acts. Hardly a statue escaped mockery – white marble was desecrated by colourful daubs, heads acquired hats and inscriptions were 'corrected'. And, unfortunately, students also left their mark on their surroundings by destroying and vandalizing them. The fine Renaissance courtyards and Della Robbia sculptures suffered considerable damage.

The State University, at the height of the student movement, afforded numerous opportunities for entertainment, and drew crowds of young people looking for excitement and wanting to see for themselves what the press had made so notorious.[3] The buildings and courtyards, which had been taken over for educational purposes, once again teemed with a sort of life they had known in previous centuries. The university took on some of the features of a market-place and hostel. Student control over the entrance halls, combined with the free flow of persons in and out of the buildings, made them ideal spots for trading and illicit dealing. Most of the goods on sale consisted of books, newspapers and other political paraphenalia, but itinerant street-vendors, mostly Southerners, also came to sell their contraband cigarettes, watches and other things, whilst students themselves made and sold jewellery and leather articles. Sometimes the vendors showed a rare eye for a captive market; before each clash with the police, a small cart would suddenly appear loaded with lemons, which students would use to diminish the effects of the tear-gas. Students turned the university into a hostel for the poor and needy, who spontaneously gravitated to a place where they would not only get free meals at the canteen and a roof for the night, but where they would be humoured by their hosts. Well-known city drunks and even patients escaping from mental asylums drifted around the university.[4]

For students the cobbled streets adjoining the university contained good-quality cheap restaurants and several bars, which they continuously frequented. One of the favourite student places was the 'Strippoli' in Piazza San Stefano, which had excellent food and wine from Puglia. But it was the atmosphere that gave it life, and made it like one of the old fashioned *osterie*, which had all but disappeared from Milan. In fact, the whole area around the university was transformed by the presence of the student movement. Expectation hung in the air. News concerning the movement travelled down the wires of a bush-telegraph run by networks of activists. Bits of information would be exchanged in the entrance hall to the university, whilst posters on the walls just outside announced the next demonstration or meeting. At the 'Strippoli' there would perhaps be discussion of recent events. All in all, there was a feeling that to be at the Statale was to be at the centre of action, even when the air was clear of teargas and the scream of sirens.

Changing Social Relations

The State University in Milan became a centre of a new form of sociality. The idea of fraternity was no doubt idealized within the movement, but it nonetheless pointed to an aspiration which tended to broaden the possibilities for social exchange.[5] This has already been suggested in relation to the changes in dress and appearance – changes which facilitated social and political identification. It was also indexed by changes in linguistic usage.[6] The familiar *tu* form of address was widely adopted within the movement for all exchanges, whereas previously it would not have been used except when addressing a friend, close acquaintance or member of family. This deliberate informality, which was associated with popular traditions, served to dispense with what were regarded as bourgeois distinctions between people, while the withdrawal of courteous forms of address such as the use of titles (*Dottore*, etc.) was a way of snubbing figures of authority. The movement, moreover, created its own peculiar slang (*gergo*), a strange mixture of swear-words and political jargon, which was later dubbed *sinistrese* (left-talk).[7] It had none of the richness of an *argot*, and it bore the imprint of educational institutions in which it was formed, especially in its more verbose and sententious manifestations. However, like the slogan shouted on the demonstration, this slang gave a sense of group identity, but was not exclusive in that it was easily picked up.[8] Thus, joining the movement was made easy even for outsiders; it was sufficient that they learnt a smattering of its terminology for them to be able to engage others in conversation. Above all, it was a sociality based in political activity and discussion, and relied on the most public of vocabularies.

The new sociality produced through the student movement was more extensive than that which preceded it. The activist was at the centre of an intricate web of social relations. A student who was at the State University in 1969 recalls that her diary contained the numbers and addresses of some three hundred people she had met through the movement, the great majority of whom she thought of as her friends. For her it was a period of happiness because 'you were at home everywhere in the city'. Moreover, activists travelled frequently from city to city to attend conferences and demonstrations, and went to Paris, Berlin and other centres of the student movement. Telephone calls through the interfaculty information centres maintained regular contacts. It was a sociality that was made possible by the time and freedoms enjoyed by students, but in turn that time was organized into a relentless timetable of commitments. The interests of the collectivity were made to prevail over those of individual. Above all there was an idea of 'solidarity' informing social relations. This meant that demonstrations could be organized with lightning speed. A series of telephone calls, a roneoed leaflet and a crowd of several thousand could be gathered to protest outside the San Vittorio prison against arrests which had occurred a couple of hours previously.[9]

The student movement made sociality more public by channelling it through political activity, and in the process deeply affected the private and personal lives of its protagonists. Its ideal of how a comrade should aspire to live was represented in the oft-quoted words of Che Guevara:

> Marxists must be the most courageous and the most complete human beings, but always, and above all, they ... must live and pulsate with the masses.... They must be tireless workers, who give themselves utterly to the people, and sacrifice their hours of rest, their families and even their lives for the revolution, yet who are never indifferent to the warmth of human contact.[10]

This heroic model, which closely resembles Christ's conception of the apostolic mission, had a considerable resonance in the student movement. There was a streak of fanaticism about the militant's lifestyle. People were judged according to their political identities or their degree of commitment to the movement. A person was either a comrade or not; and if not, was excluded or marginalized from the activist's social circles, which were constructed largely on the basis of political activity. Thus, during 1968–9 many friendships which antedated the movement, and many family relationships, went into crisis. It was an embarrassment to have a relationship with a revisionist (a member of the Communist Party), and there was a reaction against parents, especially when they were wealthy or held conservative views. Although there was a variety of factors involved, such as teenage rebellion against fathers, it is notable that these conflicts were thought of in a political framework.[11]

The student movement not only rejected certain traditional forms of sociality (mostly those premised on hierarchy and authority), but it gave rise to alternative models and experiments, which liberally interpreted Che Guevara's injunctions. The examples of the commune and of attitudes to sexual liberation offer some insights into these developments.

The most celebrated commune to be established in Milan came out of the occupation of the State University's student hostel (Casa dello Studente) in May 1969. A meeting called for free beds, the extension of services for women students, the evaluation of requests for lodging on the basis of need rather than merit, and job security for all staff. The action led to almost total student control over the premises.[12] However, most students lived with their parents in Milan, so communal living was a marginal experience, especially for those attending the Cattolica. There was no equivalent to the US or British campuses. Moreover, by contrast with the North American movements, the few communal houses shared by activists served mainly as bases for other activities.[13] Little time was spent at home, little space was left for private, personal relationships. The prevalent idea was that everything had to be shared.

Sex too was thought to be something to be shared among comrades. Free love and sexual liberation were facets of the student movement in Italy as in other countries. It was, likewise, a contradictory freedom. A leaflet written by education students at the Statale gives a slightly confused picture of this:

> talking about freedom and revolution without living them in our everyday lives leads to fascism.... That means to say, that for women, if they don't 'masculinize' themselves along authoritarian lines, nothing remains but the task of duplicating, of being the 'duplicating angel' (*angelo del ciclostile*).... The system wants us not to make love.... The bourgeoisie is not interested in the creation of a new relationship between men and women because it would lead to its self-immolation.[14]

Criticism was also directed against the authoritarian and repressive aspects of the Chinese Revolution such as 'the repeated invitations to marriage, maternity and chastity, that is to the prohibition on the rational self-management of one's life'. The leaflet celebrates love-making as anti-authoritarian and anti-bourgeois, but it also suggests that women were being squeezed between older and newer forms of oppression. The vogue for Reichian ideas reinforced those tendencies within a student way of life which exalted self-expressivity.

The idea of sexual liberation was spoken of positively by both men and women in the student movement, but it was often experienced at the time as unpleasant, especially by the women.[15] They were obliged by social pressures to give freely of themselves. During occupations sexual intercourse was actively canvassed, and the women, who were always in a minority, found it difficult to say 'no' for fear of appearing 'repressed'. Within the movement, masculine values, such as the courage and daring of a Mario Capanna in the face of the police, and the masculine image, exemplified by the virile, bearded look, were hegemonic among men.[16] It was the men who were the leaders, and women students were required to dress and behave like them in order to win respect; otherwise they tended to be glamorous appendages of the male leaders (*la donna del leader*). The women activists continued to do the humbler tasks of duplicating and preparing meals. Their role in the movement was subordinate and invisible. The specific nature of women's oppression remained unrecognized; so whilst students were intensely aware of class discrimination and inequalities in education, they were largely oblivious to both the public and private humiliations endured by women as a social group.[17]

The new sociality brought into existence by the student movement was, therefore, a contradictory mixture of freedoms and oppressions. Participation involved extending circles of friendship and breaking down the barriers between people of different ages and classes; at the same time, friendships were circumscribed by political definitions and confused with the category 'comrade'. Public life became more intense, but at the expense of personal concerns. Interpretations of freedom, fraternity and equality claimed to be in the interests of all, but they reaffirmed male powers to define social relations. The repressive and moralistic elements of the new sociality came to the fore when the movement went into decline.

At the Statale the student movement succeeded in maintaining its grip on the institution, which functioned as the headquarters for the movement as a whole. However, at the end of 1969, the movement was subordinated to the newly founded political organizations of the extraparliamentary Left, which replaced the loose structures of grassroots democracy with their versions of Leninist democratic centralism. The most regressive and repressive elements of the new sociality were formalized and institutionalized by the political sects. At the Statale the Movimento Studentesco (now a party) fought tooth and nail to drive out rivals, and to establish the supremacy of Marxist–Leninist dogma and organization; the *statalini* even resurrected Stalin as 'the symbol of intransigent struggle against the bourgeoisie and fascism, as the rejection of the line of the Western Communist parties, and as part of the fight against Trotskyism'.[18]

Although the Movimento Studentesco was perhaps an extreme example of political puritanism, it nonetheless represented wider tendencies that developed out of the movements of 1968–9. Above all, it entailed the construction of a closed political subculture in which narrow political definitions governed the social existence of its members. A Movimento Studentesco document makes this clear, by posing an alternative for school students between a life of militancy and the escapism of bohemianism:

it is not surprising that the bourgeoisie favours a false anti-conformism … comics, detective stories, television, the guitar and long hair are for many young people the only form of social and cultural existence. Through these instruments, the bourgeois ideology of violence … pansexualism and escapism is transmitted.[19]

However, in the wake of the movements there was also a reaction to this new conformism, especially among women and youth, who struggled to assert identities which the Left and student politics had repressed or refused to recognize. Tiny minorities anticipated these developments in a confused way in 1968–9, but they were isolated and marginalized. As will be shown in part IV, it was not until the development of the new social movements in the 1970s that the themes of personal and sexual identities were explored and used to redefine politics itself.

Revolt in the Upper Secondary Schools

On 26 January 1968 the students of the Liceo Berchet occupied their school with the help of city-wide support from university and secondary school students. A month later the Liceo Parini was occupied and the structures were set up, through meetings at the Statale, of a Milanese 'coordination' for the Movimento delle Scuole Medie. The movement spread to all the main upper secondary schools, firstly to the liceo classico and liceo scientifico, and subsequently to the technical institutes and vocational training schools. The movement started in Milan, but quickly assumed national proportions with a wave of occupations, demonstrations, strikes in the spring and then in the autumn. It was very much an offshoot involving teenagers who quickly learnt the political language of their elder brothers and sisters, but while the student movement in the universities went into eclipse, it put down its roots in the schools.

Unlike in the universities, where students were recognized to be citizens with the right to speak, meet and organize politically, in the secondary schools there were heavy restrictions on such activities. Some student associations and publications existed, but under close supervision. An authoritarian regime prevailed in the majority of schools. One of the movement's central objectives was precisely the recognition of school students' adulthood and citizenship. This was true not only in the earlier stages of mobilization, but throughout the struggle with the rigid and intransigent authorities.

Even before the student movement gathered momentum in the universities, a major scandal blew up in a Milanese *liceo* over the issue of freedom of speech, and provoked a national debate. Students at the Liceo Parini published an article in their paper, *La Zanzara*, on changing attitudes towards sex among their fellow pupils which provoked protests from some parents. A police inquiry resulted in arrests.[20] The article itself was in the form of a report on the findings of a questionnaire asking about sex before marriage, contraception and divorce. It reflected tendencies in favour of women's equality in sexual relations and careers. It criticized the Church's role in defining social relations in terms of the 'natural' and 'unnatural', and for causing a sense of guilt about sex. One reply called for 'total sexual freedom and a total change of attitudes', but the overall perspective was one of bringing Italian education in line with the 'majority of civilized countries' and forwarding 'democratic development'.[21] The reaction it provoked was one of moral panic, especially in the Catholic establishment and in the public prosecutor's office; the prosecution evoked the spectre of an Americanization of Italian youth:

> The sexual problem must be scientifically dealt with or we will reach a situation in which the girls will go around with contraceptives in their pockets and a sleeping-bag under their arms ... I am speaking on the behalf of the sane society, the healthy society.[22]

In response to the threat, the article in the Fascist penal code on crimes of opinion (reato d'opinione) was used against the editors of La Zanzara. Camilla Cederna, writing in the enlightened middle-class weekly L'Espresso, observed how in Italian society 'the mechanisms of repression are unloosed when the taboo areas – sex and family, hierarchy and army – are touched.'[23]

What emerges clearly from the Zanzara case is the rigidity of the institutions when faced with criticism. The authorities did their best to keep schools free of what they saw as the dangerous influences at large in society. For them, the school was a bastion of civilized values against the onslaught of a new barbarism. When there were strikes by students at the Liceo Galvani in 1966, the headmaster issued a statement:

> Absenteeism from lessons is a painful business which is neither justified nor acceptable. In school there must be a relationship of trust, respect and confidence, a dialogue between pupils and teachers. These conditions enable the young freely to inform their superiors of the wants, hopes, doubts and difficulties which they come across in their school life.[24]

But it was just this paternalism which the students found repugnant. Attempts to punish and repress in cases where dialogue broke down only provoked further disaffection. The Zanzara incident, for example, led to petitions, demonstrations and mass attendance at the trial. The school was made into a political battleground. Students demanded that:

> the school be thought of and organized not as preparation for society, but as part of society. The school should not be a place for listening but for active participation.[25]

The language of a student report denouncing censorship in schools published in 1967 is full of words and phrases like 'growth', 'maturity', 'democracy', 'participation in civil life'; these indicate a commitment to rights and responsibilities, showing the extent to which students were influenced by the political culture from which this vocabulary derived. But the cultural life inside the upper secondary schools was not always so respectable.

During the mid to late 1960s *liceo* students were reading existentialist literature (Sartre, Camus) and Pavese novels. There was a cultural climate in which the rebel, the outsider, and the loner were the heroes who rejected respectable and bourgeois society. Well before 1968, radicals and anarchists organized meetings against the Concordat and the Vietnam War. Anti-authoritarian ideas and behaviour, stimulated by the youth culture imported from Britain and the United States, were fashionable before they became aspects of the student movement. Students wore long hair and baited the authorities with disrespectful behaviour.[26]

In January 1968 students of Milan's upper secondary schools and institutes occupied their buildings and carried on a struggle against authoritarianism just as did the university students. Often strikes were coordinated throughout the city's educational institutions. Formal structures to organize the movement's activities were created in the wake of spontaneous sympathetic action. When on 7 March 1968 police evicted students occupying six schools, the next day 10,000 students struck in protest.[27] However, it was not until the autumn that the movement spread from the most active schools to involve the majority of institutions. On 28 November 10,000 school students demonstrated for political rights, and every day brought news of an occupation or picket.[28]

The movement's objectives were summed up in a leaflet of the action committee of the Liceo Berchet as follows:

the control and eventual elimination of marks and failures, and therefore the abolition of selection in school; the right of everyone to education and to a guaranteed student grant; freedom to hold meetings; a general meeting in the morning; accountability of teachers to students; removal of all reactionary and authoritarian teachers; setting of the curriculum from below.[29]

To gain these objectives, the leaflet concluded that it was necessary to unite with the working class, since to 'change the school, society must be changed'. The demands that were felt to be the most important, and around which students mobilized, concerned political rights and the autonomy of the movement within the institutions. They were also the questions which could be acted on directly; thus meetings were held in school hours, papers were produced and students came and went from school and class when they wanted to – all without prior permission. Mass disobedience unhinged the normal methods of exercizing authority in the classroom and school. In the celebrated case of the Liceo Parini, the head, Mattalia, tried to open a dialogue with the students who had occupied the school in March 1968. For his pains, he was suspended by the minister of education, who ordered the police to repossess the premises. The resort to police intervention in response to 'illegal' student meetings, the suspension and expulsion of activists and attempts to evoke parental support for the restoration of order – all these measures intensified the students' campaign for political rights.[30] When in October 1968 students at the Liceo Einstein were suspended, 1,300 out of the 1,700 students went on protest strike.[31]

The movement in the schools rapidly developed its own organization, which started in the class and extended to the city-wide coordinating body. As in the universities, the key unit was the general meeting. A statute of the Cattaneo technical institute sets out the standard organizational structure; the general meeting was the sovereign body, and from it were elected commissions and study groups with special functions. Thus, there was a press commission, an administrative commission and so on, and study groups on subjects decided by the general meeting. Each class had a monthly meeting to plan and decide on teaching questions. There was also a paper, which was directly accountable to the general meeting.[32] So, far from being an echo of the university movement or a temporary revolt, the school students' movement established a permanent presence in its own right. The tasks of holding meetings and demonstrations, and of producing leaflets and distributing them, entailed a whole process of political education that pushed formal education to the margins of many teenage lives. At the same time, the ostensible seriousness of the political literature hid the theatrical and entertainment aspects of student politics. A rare report from a study group admonishes fellow students for their very lack of seriousness about themselves:

> it is a paradoxical fact affecting all students that they know how to talk about Dante and Cicero, about Milan and Inter, but they don't know how to talk about their own situation and work. The proof of this is that in certain moments meetings are made into a hell-hole. People shout and clap as if in a stadium.[33]

The ideas of anti-authoritarianism and student power gave legitimacy and new meaning to a whole traditional repertoire of informal resistances in the classroom. Thus absenteeism or the playing up of teachers took political forms and came to signify the refusal of bourgeois ideas.

Although the school student movement privileged the fight for political rights, and was obliged to by the recalcitrance of the authorities, it also thought in terms of alternative methods of learning. A report to the general meeting of the Giorgi technical institute, for example, made four proposals. It called for group work, greater student–teacher cooperation, joint meetings and group meetings with teachers to decide the assessment of marks. As in the case of the universities, great importance was attached to collective work as opposed to individual competitiveness, and cooperation was seen as an end, and not just as a means. Marks were therefore regarded as a divisive instrument of social control from above that had to be neutralized by collective pressure, and then dispensed with.[34] In part, this strategy complemented the fight for political rights because it sought to protect the individual and the group from discrimination in the classroom, and to prevent reprisals against those dedicating time to the movement instead of to their own studies. But it also sprang from a desire to put useful knowledge and real learning before institutional requirements. There was widespread opposition to compulsory Latin and religious studies, and interest in making other subjects 'relevant'.

The idea of alternative learning was especially significant in the *liceo* and technical institutes in 1968–9, because education was regarded as potentially positive and liberating. Hence students campaigned to make the institutions accessible and relevant to everyone. These relatively privileged students looked ahead to further study in the university and could expect to get work without too much difficulty. In other words, there was not yet that pessimism about the point of studying because of lack of job prospects. The late sixties was a prosperous period. However, attempts to develop alternative educational practices foundered in difficult institutional circumstances. Apart from the hostility of the authorities, students lacked the support of sympathetic teachers, who were indispensable to any viable strategy for transforming the educational process within schools. Such teachers were usually isolated individuals. There was little unionization (not counting the professional associations), and no strong network of radical teachers. In fact, it took the student movement to create a generation of teachers committed to more democratic and egalitarian methods.[35] As a consequence, alternative study proved delusory and students adopted a cynical, instrumental approach to their studies; activists channelled their energies into political mobilization outside the classroom. These tendencies were aggravated by the university movement's decline in late 1968, and the domination of the movement by the organizations of the New Left.

Notes

1. The phenomenon of the right-wing reaction among students to the student movement has not been studied, but was an important ingredient of events. Fascists used a range of violent methods to provoke police intervention and to discredit the Left. They invented their own small scale 'strategy of tension'.

2. *Corriere della Sera*, 10 March 1968.
3. For an analysis of student protest as carnival, see Gobbi, pp. 31–47; Passerini, *Autoritratto di gruppo*, pp. 109–15.
4. Lists of those arrested in clashes include a sprinkling of the 'outside agitators' beloved of the *Corriere della Sera*; on one occasion these included 'an actor from Turin, a worker and a designer', *Corriere della Sera*, 2 June 1968.
5. Social movements create the conditions for a more 'disorderly life', which Richard Sennett has described as a positive feature of the sixties experiences: 'I believe the freedom to accept and live in disorder represents the goal which this generation has aimed for, vaguely and inchoately, in its search for community'; Richard Sennett, *The Uses of Disorder*, London 1971, p. 12.
6. For a discussion of how language in Italy has historically been a field of political and cultural conflicts, see Anna Laura Lepschy and Giulio Lepschy, *The Italian Language Today*, London 1979, pp. 19–40.
7. For example: *Angelo del ciclostile, autocritica, cazzate, corretto, gestione, illuministico, impegno, livello di scontro, militanza, obiettivamente, opportunismo, struttura e sovrastruttura, Verità è rivoluzionaria*; see Paolo Flores d'Arcais, *Sinistrese: dizionario dei luoghi comuni della sinistra*, Milan 1978. It is, however, important to distinguish between the moment when the language was invented (i.e. an aspect of the identity-formation of the social movement), and its subsequent degeneration into a new conformism.
8. Patrizia Violi, *I giornali dell'estrema sinistra*, Milan 1977, pp. 1–17.
9. To map and work out the dynamics of the social exchanges it would be interesting to apply the 'network analysis' of social anthropologists; see A.R. Radcliffe-Brown, *Structure and Function in Primitive Society*, London 1952; and J. Barnes, 'Class and Communities in a Norwegian Parish', *Human Relations*, 1, 1954. For a fascinating use of these approaches, see E. Beltrami et al, *Relazioni sociali e strategie individuali in ambiente urbano: Torino nel novecento*, Turin 1982.
10. Luciano Aguzzi, *Un liceo: un luogo di lotta*, Milan 1976, p. 295.
11. Richard Sennett deals interestingly with what he calls, the problem of constructing a 'theory of expression in public', asking such questions as 'is there a difference in the expression appropriate for public relations and that appropriate for intimate relations?' He traces the history of how the balance between public and private spheres and the concomitant importance of 'acting' was destroyed in the nineteenth century; how, that is, the public (including the political) was invested with 'expressive meaning' and people's actions were thereby judged to show their inner characteristics. This in turn produced a puritan desire to authenticate the self. Sennett, *The Fall of Public Man*, especially pp. 10–24. Whereas Sennett addresses the American crisis in which public interactions were converted into a reflection of the individual psyche, this crisis in Italy appeared in reverse. However, in both instances, social identities were spoken of as 'expressions' of the self, and the search to 'authenticate' the self left little room for acceptance of diversities.
12. *L'Unità*, 10 May 1969.
13. Colin Webster, 'Communes', in S. Hall and T. Jefferson, *Resistance through Rituals*, London 1976.
14. Lettere, documenti studenti insegnanti, February 1968.
15. The exchanges between Clara Zetkin, Alexandra Kollontai and Lenin on the subject of free love were obligatory reading. Lenin's puritanism was much mocked.
16. An index of this is the way homosexual behaviour was regarded as unmanly and incurred social disapproval. Reichian ideas served to reinforce traditional heterosexuality, and to uphold the definition of homosexuality as a sickness; see 'Contro Reich', in Angelo Pezzana, ed., *Fuori: politica del corpo*, Rome 1976.
17. Mariella Gramaglia, '1968: il venir dopo e l'andar oltre il movimento femminista', *Problemi del socialismo*, 4, 1976, p. 196. See part IV chapter 21 pp. 313–14.
18. Luisa Cortese, *Il movimento studentesco – storia e documenti: 1968–73*, Milan 1973, p. 156. Marxist–Leninist currents had been present in the student movement since its early days along with other Marxist heresies. When the *Corriere della Sera* saw *cinesi*

under every bed, it was representing a whole movement in caricature. There were, however, some student groupings who lived up to this image. L'Unione dei Comunisti, for example, held 'red weddings', and aped much of the ethico-religious language of Counter-Reformation Catholicism; for an analysis of its paper *Servire il Popolo*, see Violi, *I giornali della sinistra*, pp. 45–67.

19. Ibid., pp. 96–7.
20. G. Nozzoli and P.M. Paoletti, *La Zanzara*, Milan 1966, p. 11.
21. Ibid., pp. 159–67.
22. Ibid., p. 72.
23. Ibid., pp. 71–2. In January 1968 there was renewed trouble over school student papers when the headmaster of the Liceo Berchet took disciplinary action against students for articles they had written; *Corriere della Sera*, 27 January 1968.
24. *Libro bianco sulle associazioni e i giornali studenteschi medi di Milano*, Milan 1966, p. 81.
25. Ibid., this is a quotation from Franco Salvo, *Dalla Magna Carta Alla Costituzione Italiano*.
26. Luciano Aguzzi, *Un liceo: un luogo di lotta*, Milan 1976, p. 63.
27. *L'Unità*, 9 March 1968.
28. *L'Unità*, 30 November 1968.
29. Comitato d'Azione, Il Berchet, 30 October 1968.
30. Viale, *Il sessantotto*, p. 64; and Emilio Samek Ludovici, 'Il movimento insegnanti a Milano', *Inchiesta*, 3, Summer 1971, p. 39.
31. *L'Unità*, 11 October 1968.
32. Cattaneo, Statuto per l'Assemblea, January 1969.
33. Liceo Volta leaflet, undated.
34. *Relazione Riguardante gli Argomenti Discussi nella Prima Assemblea*, ITI G. Giorgi, undated.
35. It has been written that the Italian school movement was much weaker than that in France in the same period because of the relative absence of radical teachers. A movement grew up among teachers (especially among young Catholics in Milan) and established several hundred adherents in 1969, but it did not succeed in introducing a viable strategy for change within the classroom; see Ludovici, 'Il movimento insegnanti a Milano', pp. 38–53.

8

a lost opportunity? the education system after '68

The student movement's impact on Italian society was considerable. It 'showed the country a different image of itself and socialized knowledge of how that society worked'. [1] But the effects were most deeply felt in the social groups and institutions with which students were in closest contact. It was not factory workers so much as teachers, the liberal professions, publishers and researchers who were directly challenged by the movement, and whose ranks were subsequently joined by ex-student activists. But first of all it was the education system which felt the impact of the student movement.

The student movement's effects on the educational system can be judged by asking the questions: 'Did it make education more democratic and egalitarian?'; 'did the movement change who entered further educational institutions, what students did inside them, and what qualifications they got on completing their studies?'. Finally, it will be asked whether the movement changed how the very concepts of education and schooling were understood. The effects will be considered, in other words, in relation to access to further education, the nature and control of the learning process, and to the forms of qualification obtained in the institutions. The more general question about changing conceptions of intellectuality will be examined in chapter 10 in terms of the student movement's impact on intellectual and cultural roles in society. [2]

The student movement's first important campaign was over access to the universities. It proclaimed everyone's right to study and symbolically opened the gates of the faculties to all-comers, and welcomed workers to participate in seminars, discussions and meetings. Students demanded the establishment of the 'mass university', meaning a university open to the 'masses'. In their campaign they won the propaganda war against a government which held out the promise of education as a right, but then reneged on it. The PCI and the unions were persuaded to oppose the Gui reforms, but ultimately the wave of student occupations made it impossible for the government to limit the numbers entering the universities. However, the student victory was limited. Students exercised a veto in the name of a general principle, but they did not address some of the immediate and resolvable social and economic problems behind inequalities of access. Firstly, although the movement resisted increases in fees, it did not campaign systematically for student grants. The winning of a living grant would have allowed poorer students to study full-time without having to do other jobs, and would have allowed access to those whose families could not afford to support their children's further education. In addition, financial independence could have released students from dependency on the family. However, the movement did not take up the issue seriously because, in its eyes, the demand smacked of a narrow economic corporativism (perhaps because the leading activists were mainly drawn from middle-class families they were less concerned about financial difficulties).

Secondly, the movement did not propose legislative reforms that would facilitate access to the universities. Its anti-reformism and anti-parliamentary politics precluded such a strategy. In other words, the movement rejected a statist orientation that was a necessary part of any moves to make what were state institutions more accessible. This rejection also had negative effects on the attempt to democratize the upper secondary school. A reform bill of 1967 which proposed to open these schools to everyone and to raise the school-leaving age to sixteen was brushed aside by the student movement.[3]

The movement therefore managed to win tactical victories, but not to open up further education to the working class. Although the elite university was transformed into a mass university in that student numbers increased fivefold from 1965 to 1979, to reach nearly a million, the percentage of students from working-class backgrounds increased by only a small amount, and remained lower than in other industrialized countries with quota systems. Moreover, the privileged route to the university via the upper secondary school remained intact.[4]

The impact of the student movement was more dramatic in relation to life inside the educational institutions. There was no return to a pre-1968 situation, either in the teaching and studying methods, or in the political relations between the students and authorities. Not that there were no attempts to put the clock back. A right-wing government in 1972 carried out a harsh law and order campaign; in an interview Giovanni Gozzer estimated that in a period of three months, 1,200 schools, institutes and universities had been occupied, and that the conflict resulted in ten thousand disciplinary proceedings, three hundred arrests and the resignation of thirty-eight headmasters.[5] However, most of the demands for a new pedagogy made by the movement in the universities were conceded. Examinations were adapted to student needs rather than vice versa; written (as opposed to oral) examinations and certain subjects were no longer compulsory; attendance was no longer checked; seminars and collective study were introduced. The education process was liberalized to allow greater student participation. Similarly, students in the upper secondary schools as well as in the universities were conceded political rights. At first these were informal, but in 1974 they were written into a charter of rights, which created elected representative bodies in the schools.

The students' successes in undermining traditional authority structures and in establishing grassroots democracy within the institutions were remarkable. They showed the power of a substitutionalist strategy in action. Students set up counter-courses involving collective and interdisciplinary study, and then called for them to be recognized. They held meetings and opened the doors to outsiders without requesting permission from above. In doing so they questioned the whole nature of the educational process as it was constituted within the institutions. The movement challenged divisions created or sanctioned by past statist educational practices, such as those which induced competitive relationships between students or those which separated schooling from other social and political activities. However, the movement's substitutionalism also carried severe limitations.

Firstly, the enormous energy expended by the movement in encouraging educational 'self-activity' by students could not last indefinitely. It could not make up for the structural problems arising from overcrowding, lack of investment and absence of postgraduate research possibilities. If anything, these difficulties were aggravated by the increase of student numbers and the resistance to change on the part of powerful vested interests. Secondly, the movement's substitutionalism rapidly led to a narrow and instrumental politicization of educational processes. This was evident in the movement's fascination with the ideas of the Chinese Cultural Revolution which drew sharp distinctions between bourgeois and proletarian culture. Luciano Aguzzi cites a case when subjects were divided into three categories according to political criteria. Greek and Latin were classed as 'pre-bourgeois remnants'; History was 'purely ideological'; physics, chemistry, mathematics and philosophy were 'indirectly ideological'. The abolition of history was proposed as it was of less importance than the study of the present.[6] This is an example of especially crude thinking, but most analyses assumed that the educational institutions were functional to the capitalist system in some simple sense.

Ideological certainties substituted empirical inquiry. Students fought a propaganda battle in which slogans substituted for study, or they left further education in search of 'real knowledge' learnt in general political struggles.

The liberalization of studies within the universities and schools produced interesting experiments, especially where genuine cooperation was developed between students and teachers. In Milan, the architecture faculty of the Polytechnic was a good example of this, as was the political science faculty of the State University.[7] However, the potential of alternative courses and methods of study remained largely unrealized. An account by a teacher in Milan gives a dismal picture of developments in upper secondary schools:

> the slogan we all shouted in '68 'Smash, don't change the bourgeois school' has done the student movement more harm than even the Christian Democrat Ministers of Education themselves.[8]

Too often student demands concerning education served short-term laziness rather than radical objectives. Or rather, a refusal to be educated was interpreted simplistically as a radical political act in itself. An account from a student journal, Le Formiche Rosse (The Red Ants), celebrates this form of insubordination:

> It's when you prefer to go out and smoke a cigarette and talk about your problems that you discover that all the other students are there too .... Occasionally the headmaster passes and sends everyone back into the classroom .... Do you then have to follow the lesson? No. You only need to enter the room to see that only a few arse-lickers are paying attention and ... that the rest are reading the paper or talking about sport.[9]

The effect of this sort of action, according to Aguzzi, was to make the school an 'empty box' which served only to waste time in. Far from having radical political consequences, this student resistance reinforced social inequalities in the distribution of cultural capital.

Although different because of its political language, this attitude to school (and to the hard-working student) closely parallels the pupil resistance in British schools observed by Paul Willis. Similarly, the opposition of the students to mental work expresses a class antagonism and critique of relations of authority, which simultaneously reproduces relations of subordination. Willis writes:

> Mental work demands too much, and encroaches ... too much [on] those areas which are increasingly adopted as their own, as private and independent. 'The

lads' have learned only too well the specific form of mental labour is an unfair 'equivalent' in an exchange about control of those parts of themselves which they want to be free .... Resistance to mental work becomes resistance to authority learnt in school. The specific conjunction in contemporary capitalism of class antagonism and the educational paradigm turns education into control, (social) class resistance into educational refusal and human difference into class division.[10]

Aguzzi treats this educational refusal as an aberration resulting from a 'bad' politics, but it needs also to be understood in Willis' terms. It was a refusal which in the mid and late seventies connected up with a refusal of work and the development of a youth movement.[11]

Finally the student movement's effects on the educational system need to be related to the forms of qualification obtained in the institutions. Again, the movement's successes were double-edged. In the upper secondary schools it played a major role in making it difficult for teachers to fail students. The struggle against selection processes ended in the virtual elimination of examinations, which became mere formalities. The failure rate dropped dramatically.[12] This had the positive result of making it possible for more students to go on to university, but was negative in that no new forms of assessment were established to enable students and teachers to evaluate performance and aid learning without resorting to discrimination. In the universities, it also became easier for students to acquire a degree, but these steadily lost their value both in the eyes of employers and of the students themselves.[13]

The overall impact of the student movement on the education system in Italy turned out to be negative in as far as the institutions showed themselves incapable of responding positively. On the surface it appeared more democratic and egalitarian due to the destruction of authoritarian forms of selection and social control, and the absence of a quota system. Yet the class inequalities survived. For example, only the children of the middle classes could afford the years of study needed to become a doctor or engineer. So far, attention has been drawn particularly to the short-comings of the movement itself in developing an adequate strategy for transforming education. Above all, it has been pointed out that its refusal to make demands and campaign for substantial reforms had debilitating consequences. It entailed isolating other social groups from participation in changing education and it enabled the government and educational authorities to avoid taking action, thereby protecting vested interests. The movement's creative substitutionalism was defeated by the sheer weight of structural obstacles and because it did not connect up with wider educational transformations. However, to attribute responsibility to the student movement for not reforming the educational system would be to overlook the role played by those with the power to make such changes. Giorgio Ruffolo writes that:

> the Italian ruling classes' response to the students' revolt accorded with a time-honoured and happy-go-lucky tradition of making paltry concessions rather than genuine changes; instead of building more schools and extending participation, the government offered some more grants and easier examinations.[14]

The concession of the 150-Hours Scheme, which facilitated paid study leave for workers lacking in basic educational qualifications, was perhaps a partial exception; it was the most innovative reform in the education field of the 1970s. It demonstrated what possibilities for change were open if the intelligence and organization of social movements were given space, time and money to develop.[15] The scheme promised to release educational practices from their imprisonment in the formal schooling system, and to create an alternative to the either/or between statist and substitutionalist options. The roles of student and teacher too were put in question.[16] However, the scheme also served less idealistic purposes. It was designed to make up for the inadequacies of the schooling system, and this was a way of doing it cheaply (especially via employment of part-time teachers). Furthermore, the scheme was isolated and marginalized rather than used as a spring-board for changing the educational system.[17] Otherwise, during the 1970s the schools and universities were mainly left to rot.

Attempts at reform were swallowed up in the quicksands of corporate interests. The *impasse* of the political system was paralleled in the place-seeking and time-serving of academia. The average student in the universities rarely attended courses, and the notion that further education was a 'parking-area' for the future unemployed signalled a cynical awareness of the devaluation of qualifications on the labour market. The student movement of 1968 perhaps created a unique opportunity to carry out systematic reforms against the interests of university barons, backward-looking headmasters and teaching staff, and a hundred-and-one petty feudalities. Its defeat meant that the situation which generated the social conflicts in the 1960s got worse. The figure of the unemployed, casually employed or unemployable student became emblematic of the political and cultural crisis of the late 1970s.

Notes

1. G. Bechelloni, L'Università introvabile', *Rassegna Italiana di Sociologia*, 1, 1977, p. 9.
2. See Johnson, *The State and the Politics of Education*, pp. 28–9.

3. L. Aguzzi, *Scuola, studenti e lotta di classe*, Milan 1976, pp. 56–60.
4. G. Bechelloni, 'L'Università introvabile', pp. 9–18.
5. Giovanni Bianchi, ed., *Giovani tra classe e generazione*, Milan 1973, p. 27.
6. L. Aguzzi, *Scuola, studenti e lotta di classe*, Milan 1976, p. 164.
7. In both instances there was a teaching staff that was sympathetic to the objectives of the student movement, and saw the opportunity to integrate a radical politics with empirical study and research. The case of the sociologists has already been discussed above. The architects played an important role in the early 1970s by working with the tenants' movement and opposition to certain urban development schemes; see Ettore Pasculli, *Analisi politica delle lotte per la casa a Milano*, mimeograph, Faculty of Architecture, 1976–7.
8. Aguzzi, *Un liceo: un luogo di lotta*. p. 206. Whilst Luciano Aguzzi was writing as a teacher committed to radical reforms and student participation, the mid seventies saw the emergence of a 'school-life' literary sub-genre which celebrated or denigrated anti-educational attitudes; for a bad example see Vittoria Ronchey, *Figlioli miei, marxisti immaginari*, Milan 1975.
9. Quoted in *Rosso*, December 1973.
10. Paul Willis, *Learning to Labour*, London 1977. p. 103.
11. See chapter 20.
12. Luciano Aguzzi writes of a *liceo scientifico* in Milan where the failure rate dropped from 29% in 1968–9 to 2% in 1974–5; *Un liceo: un luogo di lotta*, pp. 44–6.
13. Above all, there was a devaluation of educational qualifications because of the excess of supply over demand. The number of graduates required by industry in 1970 was the same as in 1963, although there were many more graduates; Barbagli, *Disoccupazione intellettuale*, pp. 345–6.
14. Ruffolo, *Riforme e controriforme*, p. 112.
15. For further analysis of the 150-Hours Scheme, see chapter 10.
16. Giovanni Gozzer, *Rapporto sulla secondaria*, Rome 1973, pp. 5–21.
17. Massimo Negri, *Scuola di massa in Europe*, Florence 1975, p. 28; Aguzzi, *Scuola, studenti e lotta di classe*, pp. 86–90.

9

going to the people: students and workers

The theme of worker–student unity recurred throughout the development of the student movement. Students participated in the vast demonstrations that accompanied the strikes of the early sixties and student politics was predominantly shaped by the organizations and ideologies of the Left. However, the idea of unity was interpreted and acted on in different ways. Three phases can be identified. First, in the early and mid sixties student unity with the working class was mediated through institutions, namely the parties and trade unions, and was conceived as an alliance between different social groups. In the second phase, unity was theorized in terms of a direct, unmediated relationship between the student movement and workers. The notion of alliance was discarded, since it implied differences of interest, and was replaced by an idea of unity based on shared oppressions. Student struggles against educational and state authoritarianism were perceived as parallel to those of workers and against a common enemy. In the third phase, unity came to be interpreted as student mobilization and organization against the exploitation and oppression in the factories and workplaces rather than in the universities and schools. This chapter will deal with the theory and practice of student–worker unity in the second and third phases. The focus will be on the student movement and its development, and not on its influence on workers' struggles, which will be considered in Part 3.

During the waves of student occupations at the beginning of 1968, the idea of unity with the working class was continuously reiterated. As has already been written, not only Marxist ideas, but emblems and symbols such as red flags were borrowed from the workers' movement. Students' assertion of their identity through their dress, participation in collective action and pursuit of new social and moral values was done in opposition to bourgeois norms and in the name of working-class ideals. Student perceptions of their objective class position also changed. Either they rejected their privileged backgrounds out of choice, and conceived of a future among the ranks of the wage-earners. Or, alternatively, they interpreted their professional work as a means of destroying privilege from within.

Student documents from the March 1968 occupation of the Statale make frequent reference to the change in students' economic prospects. This feeling was perhaps strongest in the movement in the humanities faculty, which was one of the least career oriented; its programmatic statement read:

> Students know that the jobs they will get when they graduate will not be ones of power, but will mean obeying other people's orders.[1]

A law faculty leaflet claimed that only 6 per cent of graduates acceded to the profession, and the rest 'are absorbed by the labour market as lowly paid clerical workers'. Among engineering students only one-fifth were thought to be likely to get jobs in the profession. A document called the department a 'dream factory'.[2] Fear of unemployment does not appear much in the student publications, though there is an acute awareness that students were no longer a protected and privileged elite, and a supposition that their futures lay more with a working-class than a middle-class destiny.[3] Thus unity with workers was not thought to be a purely ideological question, though few seriously considered material and social consequences of proletarianization. In the heady days of student activism this did not create much anxiety about personal prospects. Calculations about career opportunities were thrown to the winds in preference for living for the moment and for a utopian future.

However, some groups of students looked at their training as a means of putting special skills to the service of the working class. The medical students are an especially interesting example in this respect. They were the first to occupy their faculty at the Statale, which was especially surprising given its predominantly middle-class and conservative nature. The action committee raised issues concerning students' own situation – it denounced the baronial power structure, the high student–teacher ratio, inadequate facilities and ruthless selection – but it also criticized the organization of medicine as a social practice. They published a pamphlet, translated from French, which questioned the Left's quantitative approach to health, which consisted of demands for more medicine and more hospitals. Such demands, it claimed, were based on the acceptance of rigid hierarchies, narrow definitions of health and on an ideology of scientificity. The pamphlet called instead for an attack on the causes of ill-health (for example, industrial accidents), for a decentralization of services into the community and a diminution of the divisions of labour among health workers.[4] *L'Unità* reported nearly a year later that, during a subsequent occupation of the medical faculty, open seminars were held on the theme 'Medicine and Society'. It involved 'study groups with the direct participation of factory workers and the inhabitants of *quartieri* in Milan', and the discussion of health at work and preventative medicine.[5] The challenge, which started in the university, had extended outwards.

A key notion among medical students was the idea of putting themselves 'at the service of working class'. This entailed providing a service which was not only free but given without the expectation of prestige or honour in return. The idea of 'service' stemmed from the Chinese model of the 'barefoot doctor' and of the intellectual who worked in the fields and learnt from the peasants. According to this approach, it was the workers who had the collective power to improve health conditions by fighting the causes ill-health, which were rooted in the capitalist organization of society. The task of the radical doctor was to increase awareness of the class dimensions of health, and to help people be confident of their judgements. In Turin at the Molinette hospital students gave leaflets to visitors explaining how 'the bosses destroy our health and then try to patch us up'. Together with some of the doctors, they organized meetings to which Fiat workers were invited. In April 1969 one meeting drew some two hundred workers and four hundred students and set a precedent for the impressive worker–student assemblies which met during the Hot Autumn.[6] The student movement's ideas about democracy, accountability and participation were being applied to break down the corporative privileges of student and doctor in the interests of a general social transformation.

The movement in the engineering faculty at the Statale made similar critiques of the role of engineers in sustaining the dominant ideology. A document produced during the occupation of the faculty in March 1968 made no concessions to the ideals of the liberal professions:

> the nucleus of bourgeois ideology is the concept of technical rationality and efficiency. This means the conditioning of the student's mind to the conception of the engineer as God, presiding over every cog in the productive process. The idea is also reinforced by other incentives such as grades, degrees, the profession, social status and wealth.[7]

As in the case of the medical students' critique of medicine, the role itself was being attacked. It was not a question of appealing to the social conscience of doctors and engineers, or of winning them over to the side of the working class, but of prefiguring their supercession as professions set above other forms of work and other workers. The vision involved both self-abasement and the learning of humility in the existing society, and the anticipation of the utopian unity of the future society. Again, the Chinese model was the source of inspiration, which was counterposed to the modern capitalist factory. In China, according to one student document:

> the factory ... is not a purely economic unit.... It is the place where illiterate workers learn to read and write, and where the workers can perfect and extend their skills.... Often houses, schools and recreational facilities are built around the factory by them.[8]

The document went on to describe how inside the factory there were no bureaucracies, nor systems of material incentivization, such as piece-rates. Leaders were elected and there was a high degree of equality in society. In this framework, the machinery, which in capitalist factories was used to subordinate workers, was subordinated instead to their needs. This vision provided the means to judge the contemporary divisions of mental and manual labour, which the student movement identified as the fundamental barrier to unity between workers and the future technicians, lawyers, doctors and engineers in the universities. When students put themselves 'at the service' of the workers, they were therefore negating their assigned role as the agents of domination.

From the summer of 1968, the student movement in the universities ceased to concentrate on political activity within the educational institutions. The movement continued, but many activists looked to the industrial struggles for a lead. The national conferences were dominated by discussion of worker–student unity, and the 'worker commissions' at the universities became the main locus of activity. Guido Viale recalled that:

> after the struggles of '68 a large number of students were no longer interested in the university ... it was no longer where they socialized and its struggles appeared to them to be futile and folkloristic.[9]

Instead, according to Viale, student militants were following one of three paths: Firstly, they were leaving their studies to take up jobs in factories; secondly, they were becoming 'professional militants' in the student movement; and thirdly, students were addressing the question of student–worker unity by working with clerical as well as manual workers, and by examination of their own material situation as part of the proletariat. Each of these options is worth examining to see the way the student movement related to the working class outside its own institutional context.

The decision to take a factory job is more interesting for its symbolic significance than for its political effects. Very few students decided to become workers, but these few realised a fantasy that was entertained by thousands of others. They were literally stripping themselves of their class privileges and plunging themselves into the exploited class. It was an act of total negation of the student identity, and a crossing of the frontier between mental and manual labour at the point where the divide seemed deepest. The case of Andrea Banfi, a student from the Statale who left his studies to take a job at Alfa Romeo, gives a glimpse of this unusual interpretation of student–worker unity. Andrea Banfi created a storm, however, when it was discovered that he was not a semi-educated son of a peasant as he had declared, but an ex-student and, furthermore, the son of a PSI senator. The company promptly promoted him to a white collar job, and then sacked him. A fellow worker commented:

> We immediately went on strike and the whole of the second shift stopped in protest. If a bourgeois wants to renounce his class privileges to fight and pay in person, it's not that he thinks like one of us, he is one of us.[10]

At the opposite end of the spectrum, there were student activists who concentrated on developing alternative educational practices. The movement at the Statale, which established its hegemony over most of the Milanese movement, worked to build up links with the unions. However, this orientation towards the official workers' movement was not acceptable to many students who regarded the unions, along with the traditional Left, as reformist and revisionist; they sought direct links with workers.

The events at Pirelli, where workers had formed a 'rank-and-file committee' independent of the union, and the mobilization of white-collar workers in Milan during the autumn of 1968 created a favourable atmosphere for student–worker unity.[11] Students provided a service for workers by making available facilities for meetings and helping distribute leaflets, and they joined picket-lines and demonstrations. Students from the Catholic University worked through the FIM–CISL, with the help of Bruno Manghi and other radical lecturers who collaborated with the union. The idea that students should put themselves at the service of the working class predominated, especially in 1968.

Statements by students exuded humility and a willingness to learn:

> we students refuse to be either tomorrow's agents of exploitation in the hands of the bosses, or to be exploiters ourselves .... In the struggle against exploitation the most important role will be played by the working class ... we want to know and discuss your problems so as to learn how to struggle against capitalism and to teach the lessons to younger students.[12]

However, students also played a more active and interventionist role, which was implicitly vanguardist. Student activists felt that they were qualified to be teachers and educators. The student movement had acquired considerable prestige, especially in the eyes of younger workers. Its activists were skilled organizers, public speakers and leaflet-writers, and some had the advantage of having studied the Marxist classics. After a year of frenetic political agitation involving occupations, demonstrations and clashes with the police, such individuals could claim to have taken risks and made sacrifices for the movement. Moreover, it seemed that in many respects students had anticipated the demands, forms of action and organization that were being learned by a workers' movement in the early stages of mobilization. Students had been the first to insist on grassroots democracy based on general meetings, and on the effectiveness of direct action. They had organized themselves to deal with police attacks.

To what extent student interventions influenced the workers' movement will be considered in later chapters, but it is important here to point out that students and agitators could not help but think that they had had a significant part in setting the ball of mobilization rolling. Throughout 1969 students and workers participated together in vast demonstrations and mingled their collective enthusiasm in meetings held in schools and universities. In the excitement, groupings of workers and students were formed in the main Milanese factories. Political fantasies took flight. A document produced by students at the Statale, for example, spoke of the rise of urban guerrilla warfare in the metropolitan countries, where the complexity and precision required by capitalist organization laid the system open to attack. The student movement was described as the guerrilla force:

> only the working class can make the revolution, but whilst capital has its police . . . the student movement is the guerrilla force of the working class in as far as it creates disorganization and disorder.[13]

Student activists perceived of themselves in a variety of ways – as detonators, ideologues, leaders, and even as guerrillas, but less than ever as students. After the dramatic events at Fiat during the industrial dispute of June–July 1969 when mass meetings involved thousands of workers and students, it seemed that the overthrow of capitalism was a real possibility.

Through the rebel factory workers students lived out their fantasies and their dreams of revolt. And, vice versa, workers were attracted by the outside agitators who handed them leaflets at the works entrance and engaged them in conversations about revolution, China and Marxist theory. It was a strange encounter. For the most part, the students were from middle-class backgrounds and enjoyed the educational and other privileges of their class. If it had not been for politics, these social groups would have scarcely have come in contact with one another socially.[14] Through politics there was an exchange which involved much more than conversations about Marx. It was not simply that the agitators were preaching the gospel; they themselves had come to learn 'what it was really like' to be a worker. It was a situation not unlike that analysed by Jacques Rancière in terms of the 'thoroughgoing reciprocity in which workers and intellectuals figure in each others' imaginations in endless circularity'.[15]

Unfortunately these reciprocal fantasies have not been investigated; it can be guessed that they were filled with images and ideas stranger than anything hinted at in contemporary political discourses. Not least, meetings between students and workers had distinct sexual as well as class connotations.[16] This desire on both sides to make a new social identity – to imagine 'the self' as different through 'the other' – was in many ways liberatory and positive. It meant escaping from the prison of a preconstructed social identity. It meant conceiving of a life that was free from the seemingly inevitable constraints of the existing society. And, in practice, the meeting of workers and students entailed a crossing of social and cultural frontiers. New possibilities were opened up for living a life in which every sort of person met socially. The promise was there of rich and diverse experiences which a class society prohibited.

The coming together of outside agitators and workers had its positive, utopian moments – moments which prefigured an egalitarian society. The relationship, however, was not always reciprocal in an egalitarian sense. The students were often more fascinated by their image of the working class than interested in getting to know workers as individuals. They thrust them back into a class identity which was imprisoning in so far as it denied individuality and disqualified dreams and ambitions which deviated from proscribed notions of class consciousness. Thus, student activists, who had started by demanding education as everyone's right, ended by telling workers that the pursuit of learning and culture was an illusion. Vittorio Foa wrote of this attitude:

> that workers' dream and desire for books is rightful even when the books themselves are full of lies. Culture and books can be criticized when they have been mastered, not by rejecting them *a priori*, and then delegating the leadership of one's struggles to the offspring of the capitalists.[17]

The middle-class utopian thinkers who went to preach to Rancière's proletarians looked forward to guiding a working class which was industrious and disciplined. A class that was above all productive. By contrast, many Marxist intellectuals and students in Italy in 1969 admired workers' disruptiveness. Although their situations were very different, they saw a common enemy in 'the system' and authority.[18]

In Italy, the interaction and joint action between students and workers in 1968–9 reached levels unique in Western Europe, and the subsequent development of social movements in the seventies bore this imprint.[19] Indeed, the Italian movements acquired aura and status internationally for their working-class involvement. However, this did not result just from the influence of the agitators, though it seemed so at the time.

An understanding of the Italian case needs to take into account two important historical considerations.[20] Firstly, the fact that one cannot talk about a consolidated working class and working-class culture in Italy in the way that has been done for Britain, France or Germany. As Maurizio Gribaudi has shown in his study of Turin, social mobility meant that many families experienced a working-class condition as a 'stage' rather than as the basis for a fixed identity.[21] There have been virtually no cores of heavy industry where strong *ouvrièreisme* has developed, meaning a working-class identity counterposed to the influence of other social groups. Secondly, the development of Italian trade unionism and socialism has been characterized by the unusually high degree of participation by middle-class activists, and this remained the case in the postwar period. The openness to 'outside' ideas and organization therefore has historical and structural explanations. In the 1968–9 hiatus this was given a new twist by the simultaneity of the crisis in relations in the education system and in workplaces, which meant an encounter not just between individual members of the middle class and workers but between students and workers as two groups sharing homologous situations. However, the student movement was superceded by a number of political organizations which claimed to represent the working class. Political groups such as Lotta Continua, Avanguardia Operaia, Potere Operaio, Il Manifesto and the archipelago of other organizations came into existence because of the students' movements.[22] Not that a New Left did not predate 1968, as has been seen, but it was isolated. The movement not only popularized the ideas of its forerunners, but provided the leadership, cadres and the bulk of the membership of the groups. At the same time, the political groups put an end to the student movement as an autonomous force; student issues were subordinated to strategies relating to the industrial working class; the ideas of the party and political leadership, which the student movement had criticized, were re-established as orthodoxies. The new organizations claimed to represent the working class. The worker-student unity developed by the movements of 1968–9 gave way to a hierarchical relationship in which the ex-student activists were usually the leaders. For a large part of the movement (though not all if it) the liberatory utopianism it generated was destined to collapse under the weight of a new orthodoxy.

Notes

1. *Carta Programmatica – Facoltà Umanistiche Presentata all 'Assemblea Occupante*, 19 March 1968.
2. Comitato di Lotta, Statale-Ingegneria.
3. The reference to further education as a 'parking area' (*area di parcheggio*) – that is a place for temporarily absorbing unemployment – appears in student documents in late 1968 and early 1969, but does not become a central theme until the 1970s.
4. Movimento Studentesco-Medicina, leaflet of Comitato d'azione salute, undated.
5. *L'Unità*, 17 January 1969.
6. 'The Worker: Student Assemblies in Turin' in Red Notes, *Working Class Autonomy*, p. 187.
7. *Documenti Conclusivi dei Lavori Dell'Assemblea degli Studenti della Facoltà di Ingegneria*, 8–14 March 1968.
8. Engineering Faculty, Comitato di Lotta, leaflet, undated. For a sophisticated example of enthusiasm for the Chinese factory, see Emilio Reyneri, 'La lotta per la produzione e l'organizzazione del lavoro nelle fabbriche cinesi', *Vento dell 'Este*, 23, 1971.
9. Guido Viale, *Sessantotto*, p. 75–9. The killings of workers at Avola in December 1968, and at Battipaglia in April 1969, were important turning-points in this respect. The massive protest demonstrations and sense of moral outrage in leaflets etc. point to a feeling that the important things happened in the streets not in the classroom.
10. *Re Nudo*, November 1970.
11. See part III, chapter 15.
12. Borletti Gruppo Operai, *Studenti*, leaflet, 7 October 1968.
13. Leaflet entitled: *Guerriglia urbana e rivoluzione operaia*, unsigned and undated, but likely to have been written in 1969 because of the way it references the student movement; this leaflet can be read as evidence of a fascination with political violence which was common in the student movement. However, it can also be read as a gesture of the 'lunatic fringe'. Situationists and anarchists delighted in horrifying everyone who picked up one of their leaflets. One headed: *Andate e mercificatevi* (Go sell yourselves), was handed out at the Milan Trade fair in 1969. It began: 'You – have a house, have a TV, have (perhaps) a car – but you have a shit life', in *I dieci anni che sconvolsero il mondo*, Rome 1978, pp. 104–5.
14. The image of the student was still that of a *figlio di papa* for many workers. And diffidence and suspicion did not evaporate when students declared themselves pro-worker. Nanni Balestrini writes about the students at the Fiat factory gates 'in the end I thought they were mad, silly buggers, missionaries'; *Vogliamo tutto*, p. 53.
15. J. Rancière, *Preface to Proletarian Nights*, p. 10.
16. Students acquired a reputation for bohemianism which was reinforced by press stories of their outrageous behaviour. Free love, drugs, and every sort of excess and transgression was associated with students. The other side of the coin to prejudice against students was a fascination with their lifestyle. Young workers, especially, were attracted to it, and the idea of picking up a woman student must explain many cases of otherwise inexplicable interest in Marxist theory.
17. Vittorio Foa, 'Introduction', pp. 41–3. There were students, especially in the education faculty of the Catholic University, who undertook voluntary teaching in poor areas (the so-called *università popolare*), but it was not until the setting-up of the 150-Hours Scheme in 1973 that this sort of initiative gained political credibility.
18. The relationship between students/intellectuals and workers can be analysed in terms of homology of position. Bourdieu proposes a homology in the position between the 'scientific Marxists' and the organized, skilled working class, and between the

subordinate intellectuals/artists and unskilled, non-organized workers. The latter arises in the case of Lotta Continua agitators and immigrant factory workers in Turin. Bourdieu suggests, moreover, that 'alliances have greater chance of materializing, and lasting, if the partners ... have less opportunity to enter into direct interaction; encounters bring together not abstract individuals but total persons, all of whose practices, discourse, and even simple bodily appearance express divergent and, at least potentially, antagonistic disposition'; *Homo Academicus*, pp. 179–80.

19. See chapter 21 for the relationship between the women's movement and industrial workers in Italy.

20. I owe these observations to a paper given by Bruno Manghi at the conference: 'Le culture e i luoghi del '68' held in Turin, 3–5 November 1988.

21. Maurizio Gribaudi, *Mondo operaio e mito operaio*, Turin 1987.

22 Lotta Continua was perhaps the most important organization to come out of the student movement. Precisely because it did not have a Leninist conception of the party like most of the other extraparliamentary groups, it was most responsive to grassroots movements; see Luigi Bobbio, *Lotta Continua: storia di una organizzazione revoluzionaria*, Rome, 1979. Whilst Lotta Continua began as a mainly Turin-based organization, Avanguardia Operaia was largely Milan-based. It had members in industry who had been active in the CUB's in 1968–9 and students, mainly from the science faculties of the State University. Its politics were much more orthodoxly Leninist; early documents speak of students bringing 'consciousness' to workers who would otherwise be stuck in trade-unionism; see *Avanguardia Operaia*, November–December 1969; and March–April 1970.

10

dreaming of a cultural
revolution

The student movement's critiques of the educational system, for its exclusivist and hierarchical structures of access and control, extended beyond the institutions themselves. The movement had always insisted that schooling was not so much a means of changing society as of legitimating existing inequalities, and that therefore the forms of knowledge that it passed on to students were partial and limiting. Instead, it proposed a strategy of 'education through struggle' that connected the different spheres of society through a political movement. As has been seen, students of medicine at the State University in Milan linked their struggles over course contents and teaching methods to the organization of health in society. Architecture students related their studies to the politics of housing, and the movement at the Catholic University questioned the role of the Church in supporting the status quo. The student movement created an acute awareness of how knowledge and skills were socially constructed and transmitted, and how they were made to serve class interests in the hands of the doctor, engineer or teacher. Students, moreover, represented a pole of attraction for those involved in cultural production.

Pierre Bourdieu has commented interestingly on the role of youth within modern European culture:

> It is clear that the primacy the field of cultural production gives to youth can, once again, be traced back to the basis of the field in the rejection of power and of the 'economy'. The reason why 'intellectuals' and artists always tend to align themselves with 'youth' in their manner of dress and in their whole bodily hexis is that, in representations as in reality, the opposition between the 'old' and the 'young' is homologous with the opposition between power and 'bourgeois'

seriousness on the one hand, and indifference to power or money and the 'intellectual' refusal of the 'spirit of seriousness', on the other hand. The 'bourgeois' world-view, which measures age by power or by the corresponding relation to power, endorses this opposition when it identifies the 'intellectual' with the young 'bourgeois' by virtue of their common status as dominated fractions of the dominant group, from whom money and power are temporarily withheld.[1]

This observation does not perhaps apply to all intellectuals and artists in the wake of 1968; Pasolini for example had little time for the student rebels. But at a European level it is possible to see cultural alignments crystallizing out along these lines. This was particularly apparent in France, a country in which intellectuals were historically prominent in revolutionary upheavals, but in Italy too, film-makers and others rallied around the forces of opposition to the status quo. The idea of cultural revolution galvanized the left-wing intelligentsia.

The cultural challenge represented by the student movement was central to the development of a counter-culture in the 1970s. In every Italian city (and perhaps more so in Milan than elsewhere) bookshops, cultural centres, political centres, bars and eating places testified to the existence of a world separate from and in conflict with the dominant urban institutions. Its boundaries were often marked out by graffiti. But the cultural revolution also penetrated the practices of those working within the dominant institutions, especially the professions. As will be seen, it was an experience which was both positive and negative. In the 1970s the contradictions of the 1968–9 years were lived out in the cultural and intellectual field.

Counter-Information

The idea of counter-information has a long history which antedates the student movement. It was at the heart of struggles for freedoms of speech and opinion which in Italy were closely associated with the radical wing of the movement for national unification. Then the workers' movement from the time of the early Socialist Party put great energy into producing party, union and other papers. The movements of 1968–9 revived the campaigning spirit of more heroic times. But counter-information was seen as more significant and was more self-consciously undertaken than at any time since the Resistance. (The word *controinformazione* itself was coined in the late sixties.) The new importance of the mass media in society was highlighted by its role in representing contemporary conflicts, whilst the student movement led the way in exposing and counteracting their disinformation (*disinformazione*).

The student movement was hostile to the national press. Students read the papers voraciously to see what was happening in the world (it was a period of dramatic advances by the North Vietnamese, of street insurrections in Paris and so on), and also to read accounts of events in which they themselves had participated. They were, therefore, unusually media-conscious and aware of how they themselves and the movements with which they identified were being reported. They were in a position to make 'oppositional readings' of the newspapers not only on the basis of ideological positions, but through personal experience and oral accounts of demonstrations and occupations.[2] The formation of a collective identity through the movement created a heightened sensibility as to how that identity was represented by the dominant groups. Thus the reports in the *Corriere della Sera*, which spoke of the students as 'Chinese' (*cinesi*) and which constructed a stereotype of the movement activists as alien and threatening, provoked anger, scorn and, on one occasion, petrol-bombs.[3] At the information centres in the universities there were boards with the day's press cuttings concerning the movement, where students wrote up their opinions and comments.

Two of the movements' graffiti about the press give an insight into its critique of the mass media. Firstly, some writing on a Milanese wall explained: 'The difference between balls and pillocks is as follows: the balls are written by the *Corriere* and it's the pillocks that read and believe it.' A second piece of graffiti examined the difference between two papers: 'For a falsely objective version read the *Giorno*, and for an objectively false one read the *Corriere*.'[4] These comments are interesting for their very format and style. They are sprayed on to the wall for all to see, and address the passer-by directly and succinctly. They involve the reader in a little puzzle or play with sexual swear-words in ways that make the reader appear cleverer than the pretentious readership of the *Corriere*. Then, because they are memorable, the graffiti are likely to be copied and recounted. As for their message, these graffiti spell out the movement's total opposition to the press. It does not call for fairer reportage or more objectivity, but seeks to destroy the myth of objectivity and disinterestedness.

The movement attacked what it regarded as the inevitable disinformation coming from papers like *La Stampa*, owned by Fiat and other corporations. These were thought to black-out news or to distort and manipulate information according to the needs of the owners and the capitalist class in general. This power resulted from economic leverage (the ownership of the means of communication), and from the servility of the journalists, the 'bosses' lackeys' (*servi del padrone*). This model of media manipulation fitted with the complementary notion of false consciousness, and with the Marcusean analysis of the 'one-dimensional society', according to which consensus was achieved by the ruling class through its control and manipulation of various private and state apparatuses, (for example, the Church, the media and educational institutions).[5] Symptomatically, Marcuse's book *One-Dimensional Man*, published in 1967, sold 150,000 copies within a year.

This model of total social control from above did not, however, induce a sense of pessimism or hopelessness among its promulgators in the movement. Rather, it heightened awareness that every aspect of life was affected by cultural domination, and of the need 'to get rid of the policeman in our heads' (*eliminiamo il poliziotto che è nel nostro cervello*), as one slogan put it. The movement's responses set the agenda for the creation of communicative strategies from below in the following decade. These can be considered under two headings: counter-information and counter-culture.

The counter-information developed by the movement ranged from individual, improvized acts to more collective and long-term action. The most common forms of counter-information used the walls of the city and the roneo machine to communicate messages. Graffiti appeared everywhere; a survey carried out in 1969 in the university and polytechnic areas of Milan counted 868 examples; in the hottest months of student revolt, the signposts near the university had to be replaced every fortnight because of graffiti; in January 1971 the prefect of Milan called for action against graffiti, which according to a municipal estimate, totalled thirty-one thousand in number.[6] The graffiti about the press, which have already been mentioned, were perhaps more subtle than the majority of examples, but even the crudest and simplest ones expressed the desire to have a say. Instead of passively reading the publicity in the underground trains and stations, young passengers added their own 'bubbles' with comments, carrying on a conversation in graffiti with a previous wall-writer. The roneoed leaflet was another form of counter-information developed in 1968, which had a democratizing potential in that it was cheap and easily produced, though it seems that often the sheer ease of reproduction resulted in overkill.

The leaflets *dazibao*, slogans and graffiti of the movement enabled the collective and individual expression of feelings and opinions on a massive scale. However, it was the weekly newspaper which became the preferred vehicle for the movement's propaganda. It represented a more durable challenge and the first step in the construction of an alternative circuit of information to that constituted by the national press. The most successful of these was *Lotta Continua*, which first came out in November 1969, but it was joined by *Il Manifesto* and others at local and national levels.[7] They were the organs of the extraparliamentary political groups which were mostly formed in 1969.

Their most important campaign of counter-information concerned the events of late December 1969 – the Piazza Fontana bombing, the so-called suicide of Pinelli, and the witch-hunt that put Pietro Valpreda behind bars. Whilst the *Corriere della Sera* and the national press blamed the anarchists and the Left for the terrorism and supported police action against them, *Lotta Continua* in particular played a crucial role in telling a different story.[8] A group of journalists wrote a book called *The State Massacre* (*La Strage di Stato*) in which they exposed the fascist nature of the bombing, and the connections between its perpetrators and high state officials. A remarkable feat of investigative journalism, selling over 100,000 copies in two years, it established the importance of the development of alternative sources of information, and hence of papers written from within the movement. It set in motion grassroots investigations in factories, schools and neighbourhoods into local Fascists, whose names were then published in papers and leaflets.

Radical journalists working within the commercial press were also encouraged to investigate corruption and the abuse of power. They organized the Committee Against Repression to defend freedom of opinion when editors of the minority press were charged under the surviving articles of the Fascist penal code, which included the 'crime of opinion' (*reato d'opinione*) and 'criminal incitement' (*instigazione a delinquere*). In a country in which the press had been traditionally tied to the interests of the state and to political parties, the growth of radical journalism under the impact of the new counter-information campaigns was an important change.[9]

The growth of counter-information was not without its negative aspects. The tactics of exposure and denunciation sometimes bordered on symbolic lynching in which moral outrage was whipped up at the expense of rational criticism and understanding. The hounding of the police chief thought (erroneously) to be responsible for Pinelli's death is a case in point,[10] while aspects of Red Brigades' propaganda fit this model,[11] and an instrumental Zdanovite conception of cultural action gained an unfortunate ascendancy within much of the extraparliamentary Left. However, counter-information also gave a fillip to the critical study of the media which Umberto Eco pioneered in Italy. His *Towards a Semiotic Guerrilla Warfare*, published in 1967, anticipated developments, while his institute at the University of Bologna produced a number of studies concerned with critiques of the dominant media and the means of developing alternatives.[12]

Refounding a Popular Culture: The Case of Radical Theatre

The campaign in the defence of Pietro Valpreda, which lasted several years, saw some inspired acts of counter-information, including the adoption of the prisoner as a parliamentary candidate. A memorable song told the story of Pinelli's death and the tragic episode was the subject of Dario Fo's play *Accidental Death of an Anarchist*. In this period, counter-information linked up with the development of a wider counter-culture based on the movements of opposition. Playwrights, actors and actresses, film-makers, cartoonists and others channelled their energies into political work.[13] In the light of the student movement's critiques of the traditional role of the artist and intellectual, their commitment was not restricted to signing petitions and fund-raising.[14] Goffredo Fofi outlined their new role within the movement;

> no cultural revolution is possible without a direct relationship with the masses, and the only real relationship is through political militancy, even if today ... this must be mainly an individual connection with particular struggles given that there does not as yet exist a party to unify the different activities.[15]

The new role can be seen at its most creative in the theatre of Dario Fo.

Dario Fo and Franca Rame had been performing an experimental theatre which dealt with political issues since the early 1960s; on one occasion Fo was even challenged to a duel by an artillery officer for slighting the honour of the Italian army, and he was also arrested in Siena for abusing President Johnson in a play. However, they were working within traditional theatre and therefore to privileged middle-class audiences. In 1968 they decided to leave it, 'because', writes Franca Rama, 'we had realized that, despite the hostility of a few, obtuse reactionaries, the upper middle class reacted to our "spankings" almost with pleasure'. The mass movements of 1968–9 put their political integrity in question. According to Franca Rame:

> You are allowed to mock authority, but if you do it from the outside, you will burn. This is what we understood. In order to feel at one with our political commitment, it was no longer enough to consider ourselves democratic, left-wing artists full of sympathy for the working class and the exploited.... The lesson came to us directly from the extraordinary struggles of working people, from the young people's fight against authoritarianism and injustice in the schools, and from their struggle for a new culture and relationship with the exploited classes.... We had to place ourselves entirely at the service of the exploited, and to become their minstrels.[16]

The decision to take theatre to the workers and make it part of the movements of opposition meant changing that theatre. Firstly, the plays had to be performed wherever people met socially; to begin with, the locations were workers' clubs, bowling alleys, occupied factories, suburban cinemas, and only rarely theatres. In their first year they performed to over 200,000 spectators, of whom 70 per cent had never previously seen a play. Secondly, the plays were written and performed as political interventions. (And they were very much the product of collective decision-making, even if Fo was the charismatic leader.) This was the case with *Accidental Death of an Anarchist*, put on in Milan during the trial of *Lotta Continua* for its part in blaming the chief-of-police for Pinelli's death. But many other performances were adapted to take account of the particular local struggles. Thirdly, Dario Fo and his company, Il Comune, developed a special relationship to the audience. During performances of the plays, which were mainly farces, the audience was invited to participate as in an English pantomime, and afterwards there were discussions about the issues being dealt with. Moreover, the takings would often be contributed to solidarity campaigns and strike funds.[17]

The work of Dario Fo and Il Comune was especially important because it represented a developed cultural politics – a cultural politics which predominated in the social movements in the first half of the 1970s. It was not merely an example of agitprop theatre used as a tactic; it was an expression of a more ambitious project of refounding a popular culture. Fo himself was an exceptionally brilliant and lucid spokesman for a conception of theatre and art which Il Comune attempted to enact through its performances. Speaking at an event in France, he outlined the origins and history of popular theatrical forms. For Fo, the heyday of popular theatre was during the Middle Ages (in Paris in the fifteenth century, he told his audience, there was one juggler to sixty inhabitants), and it was this tradition which provided the raw materials for the reconstruction of a living theatre. This popular theatre had, according to Fo, been killed off by the bourgeoisie and the problem was to undermine bourgeois artistic norms in their turn. Brecht had argued along similar lines, said Fo:

> You always go back to Brecht; he explained it well, but it's a little difficult to understand. He said that you must always act in the third person, escape from individualism and egoism ... be someone who is on the outside, and who presents the person as a chorus. The comedian must destroy the figure of the comedian himself, and then recompose it in front of the spectators.[18]

But Fo argued that epic theatre was not Brecht's invention; it was part of popular tradition which needed to be resurrected:

> Really to understand epic theatre, it is enough to see the people. The people
> always hold to a different ideology from the bourgeoisie. There is a collective
> spirit: we talk about ourselves, our problems, the problems of the community.
> We aim to create a community like the community of the theatre in the Middle
> Ages.... You must act with the public, listen to its rhythms, improvize ... you
> must change at the drop of a hat, cut, and alter your timing.[19]

In the Middle Ages, according to Fo, 'the people's culture' was
autonomous from that of their rulers, and this is what modern theatre has
to recreate – an autonomous culture. The intellectuals' task was to help
rediscover popular history, language and culture, and to free it of
'bourgeois baubles'.

To make his case, Dario Fo refers to Mao Tse-tung's and Gramsci's
ideas, thereby claiming legitimacy for his theories within the Communist
tradition. Yet it is Rabelais who inspires him:

> When Rabelais speaks French he carries out an operation which has been lost
> to us. He takes up several expressions from dialects and enriches his own
> language, thereby making something un-bourgeois. He sought to make a sort
> of lexical revolution, and that's an example we must follow.[20]

But more often Fo refers directly to contemporary events as a source of
ideas and a context for creating a new set of relations with the audience,
giving back to 'the people' what he has learnt from them:

> I feel myself part of the people, and when I'm going to write a play, I go to the
> people, not to flatter but to learn.... When the movement calls us because
> there is a trial, we turn up the day beforehand and reconstruct the event. I play
> the judge, the lawyer plays the lawyer, the workers play the workers, some
> comrades play the police, and the show is on. And when the real spectacle is on
> – that's to say the moment of judgement – there are some cracking jokes
> because the public understands the hypocrisy of power.[21]

The test of this idea of theatre was measured by its capacity to generate
audience involvement, and its power to entertain and educate at the same
time. This was a test in which Il Comune and Fo triumphantly succeeded.
What is more problematic is whether this theatre contributed to a transformation of the cultural situation over a longer term.

The role of Fo's theatre can be compared to the role played by don
Milani in providing a critique of the dominant culture and a model for a
popular culture. Although they belong to different worlds – don Milani to
a Catholic world and Fo to a secular, socialist tradition – there are close
parallels in their work. Both see 'the people' as the creators of language,
which the rulers then formalize, suck dry and use as an instrument of

domination (in the shape of the bourgeois school or theatre). The people use words in a simple, concrete and direct way which describes reality truthfully and with beauty, but they are made to distrust their own sensibilities by cultured elites. Those that work the soil or work in the factories are somehow closer to Nature (to the 'nature of things') than those who rule over them, and the rhythms of their labour resonate in the deeper structural movements of the culture, which, however, are hidden from them by the cleverness and artifice of those who do no work. Popular culture is without boundaries (or rather it is potentially universal) because it springs out of everyday life, whilst Culture with a capital 'C' is closed within the walls of museums and theatres or within library tomes. As the originators of language and the 'rooted' members of society, the ordinary people bear within them the traces of earlier cultures; they have a history which makes the history of the ruling group into the fabrication of *parvenus*. All these elements, (albeit with different stresses and combinations), underpin Dario Fo's and don Milani's visions of how to change the order of things. Whilst it gave them great strengths, it also entailed severe weaknesses.

The strengths can be seen in the degree of influence exercised by the work of don Milani and Dario Fo within the social movements, and in the mobilizing qualities of the ideas of popular creativity, autonomy and self-activity. Labour was invested with dignity and culture was divested of mystique. A widespread desire by factory workers and others to have their say brought the sound of unheard voices into a cultural world built on their exclusion. The ideas of popular culture celebrated not the enfranchisement of the masses and their inclusion within the formal domain of the cultural (the schools, universities, and so on), but the destruction of the frontiers of knowledge policed by academics, doctors, lawyers and politicians. They envisaged the return of distinctively cultural practices to the fields and workplaces, and the re-establishment of a new harmony of head and hand. It was a utopian vision of considerable appeal, which went eyond the immediate situation. It drew on a rich vein of radicalism in Western European culture, which can be identified in writers as various as Rousseau, Marx and Bergson.

The weaknesses of this project of cultural revolution are intertwined with its strengths. Its appeal to myths inspired enthusiasm by providing epic narratives for class struggle in culture. But the evocation of a golden age and of an image of a pure popular culture served also to limit and even stultify cultural innovation. Just as the notions of reliving the Bolshevik or Chinese Cultural Revolutions blinded activists to social changes and complexities, so myths of a past popular culture made it difficult to work within a contemporary environment.

The particular predilection for myths is clearly manifested in the fascination for China. China acted as a sort of spiritual homeland for a generation which could no longer believe in the USSR. Much of the young Italian intelligentsia of the period greatly admired the Chinese Cultural Revolution; China represented a model of how intellectuals could work with and among the people (the students who worked in the fields whilst the peasants studied; the 'barefoot doctor'; the poet or painter whose art 'served the people'). At the same time, Chinese culture was presented as the combination of popular wisdom and a sophisticated but simple Marxism. Brecht's poems, inspired by Chinese subjects and the writings of Lu Hsun, became enormously popular. Above all, there was an image of Chinese people as hard-working but happy. Intellectuals who travelled there (especially women, it seems), wrote about this:

> In China there are no signs of alienation, nervous disorders or of the fragmentation within the individual that you find in consumer society. The world of the Chinese is compact, integrated and absolutely whole.[22]

What is significant, of course, is not what this tells us about China, but what it tells us about the writers and readers of this literature. Umberto Melotti draws attention to the historical precedents:

> It is worth recalling how this mythology of 'Socialist China' has emerged historically. In many respects, it is reminiscent of the eighteenth-century mythology of 'good and just government in China', which was spread on the basis of similarly insufficient evidence among the enlightenment philosophers and men of letters.[23]

The Chinese myth was believed in by those who wanted to create a simple, humane egalitarian society in the place of the divided and competitive society in which they lived. It made it possible to criticize the existing order of things with reference to an ideal just as Montesquieu, Rousseau, and others had done in the past. However, the dream of a unified popular culture was backward-looking. It harked back to Communist and Socialist traditions at a time when they no longer connected up with the everyday experience of the majority of people. The ideal of a class-based, autonomous culture did not help make sense of a situation of cultural diversification in which identities were constructed across classes and across national frontiers. The Chinese myth was more a throw-back to a golden age than a future-oriented utopia.

The idea of remaking a popular culture entailed celebrating older technologies and the close relationship between producer, product and consumer which they realized (Fo's theatre was typical in this respect). This was regarded as authentic by contrast with the mass culture produced by the modern media which, however, had effectively marginalized older cultural forms. This New Left, like the traditional Left, dismissed mass culture as part of the capitalist 'consciousness-industry'.[24]

There were intellectuals who took a more critical view and refused the either/or choice between being apocalyptic or conformist (to borrow the terms of Eco's famous study *Apocalittici e integrati*) in their attitude to mass culture.[25] Apart from Eco himself, Francesco Alberoni stressed the way mass culture promoted change, rather than simply confirming the status quo.[26] However, their rationalism and cosmopolitan outlook was marginalized in the wake of the movements. Far more representative of the general rejection of 'mass culture' and espousal of 'popular culture' was the charismatic figure of Pier Paolo Pasolini. Through his writing, films and journalism, Pasolini gave passionate expression to his disgust for consumer society and all its works.[27]

However, whereas Pasolini's vision was fundamentally at odds with the imposition of any kind of uniformity, for the most part the search for a 'genuine' popular culture was strangely provincial and backward-looking. When cultural exchanges across frontiers were multiplying as never before, and when the plurality of signs and images defied simple categorizations according to class origin, there was a longing for cultural purity – for the 'compact, integrated society' in which community appeared as a simple, organic set of relations between people. The disorder of the city was rejected in the name of an ideal, organic society which was rural in its inspiration. It was utopian, therefore, in the pejorative sense, because it attempted to deny the complexity, diversity and conflict of modern societies. Moreover, it conjured up a relationship between intellectuals and 'the masses' which was untenable.

A Culture of Guilt

The student movement of '68 did not by itself produce a radicalization within the professions and the development of an extensive counter-culture; its impact must be taken in conjunction with that of the workers' movement, and its importance needs to be understood as symbolic. ''68' is used here as a shorthand way of referring to all the various radical currents which surfaced in the late sixties and early seventies. It is a term which covers a considerable range of strategies for change – a range which resulted from the reactivation of older civil-libertarian as well as the creation of new forms of resistance. '68 brought into the open a plurality of politico-cultural positions, and marked a break with the clear demarcations into 'camps' that had been inherited from the Cold War period. If the old alignments were still visible, they were now criss-crossed by differences within both the Communist and Catholic 'worlds'. Moreover, a radicalism which was more typical of the United States was beginning to get a foothold in Italian society, as the development of a sexual politics in the early seventies was to show. However, it was not until the mid seventies that the richness and diversity of cultural changes became fully visible.

In many respects, the cultural changes immediately following on from the social movements were not as innovative as they seemed at the time. Or, rather, there was a widespread misrecognition of what was 'old' and what was 'new'. The first stirrings of a post-'68 feminism and youth politics (which are dealt with at greater length in part IV) were frequently ignored or regarded as a sixties hangover, whilst the rediscovery of Marxism was seen as something quite novel. A description of the rebirth of Marxism written by Perry Anderson in 1974 sums up a perspective common to the New Left in Western Europe:

> The advent of a new period in the workers' movement, bringing to an end the long class pause that divided theory from practice, is now however visible.... The chance of a revolutionary circuit between Marxist theory and mass practice, looped through real struggles of the industrial working class, has now become steadily greater. The consequences of such a reunification of theory and practice would be to transform Marxism itself – recreating conditions which, in their own time, produced the founders of historical materialism.[28]

It was a perspective which recapitulated the historical model. All the heresies of the New Left, from the Trotskyisms, which were stronger in France and Britain, to the Marxist–Leninisms which dominated in Italy, proclaimed that the moment had come for the refounding of the Communist project and the establishment of a new and fruitful relationship between theory and practice, between intellectuals and masses.

How the relationship between Marxist intellectuals and the working class was to be changed was a matter for debate. There was no uniform position. But it Italy, where the Chinese model of cultural revolution was so influential, there was little space for the intellectual mandarin. As has been seen in relation to the student movement, populist evocations of 'mass practice' tended to prevail over theoretical concerns. Discourses were above all moral.

A number of positive consequences flowed from this orientation. Intellectuals and professional people turned their backs on the privileges and status accorded to them in society, and sought to redefine their roles in terms of social cooperation among equals rather than of competition between individuals and corporate interests. They sought to undermine the culture which exalted mental labour and despised those who worked with their hands. However, the search for what Goffredo Fofi called a 'direct relationship with the masses' was a contradictory phenomenon with some decidedly negative features. It was caught between a desire to lose a class identity and yet to preserve the intellectual's special mission in society.

The contradiction in the left-wing intellectual's self-image following '68 is interestingly dealt with by Richard Sennett in relation to Jean-Paul Sartre. Although the analysis focuses on him, it deals interestingly with the relationship of culture and radical politics:

> What then is the role of the intellectual *gauchiste*? Gerassi asks Sartre, and the philosopher gives a peculiar answer. The only writing worth doing, he says, is the political tract, because the position of the intellectual has changed: 'He must now write with the masses, and through them, and therefore put his technical knowledge at their disposal. In other words, his privileged status is over. Today it is sheer bad faith, hence counter-revolutionary, for the intellectual to dwell on his own problems.' Sartre now believed the intellectual must sacrifice himself for the workers; 'he must be dedicated to work for their problems, not his own.'[29]

When asked why he had just finished a two-thousand-page book on Flaubert, Sartre accused himself of 'petty-bourgeois escapism'. And when asked about his support for a Cuban poet imprisoned for counter-revolution, he explained that all genuinely revolutionary governments honour creative freedom. He contradicted himself. Sennett comments:

> In his guilty confusion, Sartre shows himself to share ... two assumptions about workers.... First, that the man of culture – the poet, philosopher, social visionary – inhabits a world that cannot be assimilated to the realities of working-class life. Sartre apologises for thinking about Flaubert. He respects the work workers do, indeed he idolises it; he is afraid he will alienate them by his work. Yet at the same time he is afraid his work is innately privileged ... and may have rights against the revolution ... culture and the masses, if not necessarily enemies, have at best few interests in common.... Second the basis of rebellion is still a calculation of material interest. Material hardship caused by the system makes people rebel, material reward makes them defend ... [he] does not really believe that the aphorism, Man lives not be bread alone, applies to workers.[30]

In the post-1968 period in Italy the idea of cultural revolution was heavily impregnated with the attitudes implicit in Sartre's answers. Intellectuals did indeed 'sacrifice themselves for the workers', and the political tract became the privileged vehicle for cultural and political writings. They felt anxious about petty bourgeois pursuits and signs of individualism. Intellectuals wanted to abolish themselves as a caste and to become honorary members of the working class which they sought to serve. When in 1973 the 150-Hours Scheme was established, giving workers the right to study-leave, it was welcomed as a chance to do just this:

> The presence of the working class and its struggles has really made itself felt. If until now it only affected a few more class-conscious intellectuals, now there is a refusal to delegate even in this sphere, (i.e. the workers are taking over education themselves). The struggles are also invading the cultural field and transforming interpretations of reality into a social need to be put alongside other needs (housing, services, etc.).[31]

The intellectual, in the old sense, would be replaced by a new 'collective intellectual' combining the 'intellectuals, technicians and workers'.

This vision of the transcendence of divisions of mental and manual labour appears to subvert the Sartrean dichotomy. However, the initial 150-hours courses reproduced it in another guise. The project of creating a 'working-class culture', and criticizing culture 'from a workers' point of view' was approached in such a way that courses dealt almost exclusively with the factory. The preferred themes included health hazards, the labour process and trade union history.[32] In other words, worker-students did not study philosophy, literature, languages or other subjects which were usually regarded as Culture with a capital 'C'. Those organizing the courses (the trade unions, teachers and political activists) either assumed that workers would not be interested, or that they would be alienated by such things. Instead, they applied their *operaist* version of materialism to return the workers 'in theory' to the factories they had escaped from for a few hours. While the 150-hours courses were often useful to political militants and factory delegates, they often did not respond to the needs and secret desires of the majority. Instead of liberating workers from the thrall of intellectuals, the scheme in its initial years fulfilled the fantasies of *operaist* theorists rather than those of the *operai* and *operaie* themselves. The old divisions between the educators and the uneducated were far from abolished.[33]

This narrow materialist conception of culture infected not just those working in education, but artists, writers and film-makers who associated themselves with the social movements. Notions of 'political relevance' pressed down on them, and it became difficult to do work without an explicit political theme. Content was considered all-important and form was treated as secondary – indeed, any formal experimentation was regarded with suspicion. It was thought that the workers would not understand or like cultural products which were 'difficult'. Intellectuals and artists should, in other words, give up self-indulgence and the preoccupations of their subculture and class, and put themselves at the service of the masses who did not want to read Dante or see Godard films. Both the bourgeois culture learnt at the *liceo*, and the culture of the avant garde were to be rejected in the name of 'cultural revolution'.

In a survey of cultural production in the wake of '68–9, Luigi Manconi describes the period from 1967 to 1974 as the 'dark years'; whilst there was some ferment in the fields of music, theatre, poetry, reviews and publishing, there was little of significance produced; the results of work in photography, cinema and the novel were 'undoubtedly modest':

> The reasons for this: the years 1967–9 effectively represented an unprecedented break with the previous thirty years in terms of ideologies and culture. And this was a good thing; but it also drained the expressive energies of the future generations for a five-year period. From this resulted a condition of 'memory-lack' for a whole stratum of young people, especially in relation to their own historical/social identity.... Moreover, the culture industry was hostile to innovation.[34]

This explanation for the cultural poverty of the '68 generation is not adequate, however. It is necessary to show how a certain conception of politics and of the relationship between intellectuals and the working class paralysed or hampered creative activity. Whilst someone of the independence and inventiveness of Dario Fo could still work well, a younger generation found itself merely imitating him. Above all, it was caught in the impossible contradiction of Sartre's position. Intellectuals felt that they only had a right to exist in so far as they were being useful, and usefulness was defined narrowly. Cultural practices had to produce political messages. Pedagogic modes prevailed, and a moral universe was created with its good and bad characters. Thus, Goffredo Fofi, who was an important critic and spokesperson on the cultural politics of the Left, wrote a book on Italian cinema in 1971 in which he judged film-makers according to a grid of political correctness.[35] The cinema journal which he edited, *Ombre Rosse*, actually ceased to talk about films and dealt instead with directly political issues. This was symptomatic of the way in which the specificity of the cultural was reduced in this period to a notion of class struggle which allowed little space for fiction. Whether in film or writing, a narrow realist interpretation of 'documentary' held sway.

The 'dark years', however, hid undercurrents within Italian cultural life which were to break the surface in the mid seventies. The Sartrean position was extremely fragile. Manconi has written that behind the screen of the 'monoculture' many 'cultivated their own secret vices in clandestinity' or sought to infiltrate them into the dominant political discourses. When the hold of the narrow notions of the political was put in crisis (the so-called 'crisis of militancy'), it was through appeals to those things which had been sacrificed in the past – personal and private life, poetic and literary forms, notions of creativity.[36] Furthermore, it was discovered that the young workers, who were said not to be interested in such things but only in working conditions and factory struggles, were much more attracted to the world of youth subcultures and, in the case of women, to the feminist movement, than to the extraparliamentary Left. Whilst '68 did represent a break within Italian culture, its full implications did not become apparent before the emergence of the new social movements in the 1970s.

Looking back over the 1970s it is possible to offer a tentative evaluation of the cultural changes brought about by or through the social movements which dominated the horizons of a generation. Goffredo Fofi has commented that it was a decade in which there were lively experiments, but that many opportunities were lost and that little of lasting cultural significance was produced. The revival of cultural activities in the mid seventies and the proliferation of small publishers gave rise to

> a production which was very immediate, tied to the ideas of the moment and lacking in reflection … it was partly a pursuit of fashion and partly a response to real needs.[37]

The lack of a major film or written piece should be explained in terms of the preference for producing the ephemeral (whether in the shape of radio, music or theatre):

> The 'cultural product' of the movement was directed towards the immediate. It sprang from the desire for direct participation in making culture … so that the result was fragmentary, uneven, instantaneous, inconclusive and without respect for canons governing writing or performance.[38]

While this approach to cultural life and activity had its moments of genuine innovation (as in Dario Fo's theatre), it was vitiated by assumptions about the relationship of culture to class politics and the role of the intellectual or artist in this relationship. This weakness in the foundations of the counter-cultural project has made it an easy target for the critical attack by members of the cultural establishment, and has led to its abandonment by many of its leading proponents.[39] But whether this crisis and re-evaluation leads to important contributions in the future by the generations of the '68 and '77 movements in the scientific and cultural fields, as Fofi hypothesises, is an open question.

Radicalization within the Professions

The concept of 'cultural revolution' was important in post '68 oppositional politics in Italy because it stood for total change. It embodied the
aspiration to transform daily life in all its aspects, so that politics was no
longer separated from ordinary decision-making. Some of the strategies
for making a cultural revolution centred on the construction of alternative
and oppositional areas; creating counter-information and popular culture
were both projects designed to autonomize the production and consumption of cultural goods from the laws and ideas of the market. They were,
above all, extra-institutional. However, other strategies involved the 'long
march through the institutions'. They entailed taking the struggles of
'outside society' inside the corridors, courtrooms and classrooms of the
powerful. This other aspect of the cultural revolution was especially
significant for radicals working within the professions.

The movements of 1968–9 swept the professions into the political fray.
Doctors, lawyers and teachers as well as journalists and film-makers were
drawn into the social conflicts, and new conflicts erupted within their
ranks. Not that they had previously been detached from politics. On the
contrary, different tendencies jockeyed for power in their representative
bodies. The Left had its advocates, even though they had none of the
influence of groups like the Freemasons. However, the movements not
only aggravated existing divisions; they created new ones by questioning
the privileges, lifestyles and mystiques cultivated in the professions. They
attacked the professional ideologies (for example the journalist's concept
of impartiality or news values), which the traditional Left had by and large
respected.

The new wave of radicalism driven on by the student movement was
radical in a root-and-branch sense. It reiterated themes with a longer
history such as secularizing calls for the use of vernacular and the
elimination of mystifying rites and rituals. But it framed these in a new
way; for example, in terms of the abolition of the hierarchies of mental
and manual labour.[40] There was the emergence of a new conception of the
relationship between intellectuals and 'the masses' which was founded on
particular competencies. As Michel Foucault has written:

> A new mode of 'connection between theory and practice' has been established.
> Intellectuals have become accustomed to working not in the character of the
> 'universal' and the 'exemplary' ... but in specific sectors where they are
> situated by their professional conditions of work or their conditions of life....
> And yet I believe they have become closer to the proletariat for two reasons:
> because it has been a matter of real, material, everyday struggles, and because
> they often came up against the same adversary, even though in a different
> form.[41]

This change in the role of the intellectual can be seen in a number of fields. Most obviously, radicalized teachers in schools and universities found themselves having to work in new ways not only with students, but with parents and in the community.[42] A massive number of ex-students went into the profession in the early 1970s (the education system above all produced teachers) and took with them the ideas which they had fought for in the movement. The profession which, more than any other, had had the historical mission of creating generations of loyal Italians was joined by an army of subversives with very different intentions. But other professions were similarly if less dramatically affected.

Radical doctors, for example, played a vital role in struggles over health and safety at work.[43] They put their specialized knowledge at the disposition of workers who were already defining health as a psychic and social as well as physical condition. Then in the mid 1970s doctors participated in and supported the campaign for abortion. The women's movement, by developing a politics of the body, made medicine a key arena of social conflict, and had far more profound implications for how medicine was conceived as a system of knowledge and power than any previous movement.[44] But this was also an aspect of the fact that medicine had become a crucial metaphor for the exercise of power in modern capitalist societies. The conflicts over the control of the body and over definitions of normality and deviancy suddenly grew in importance. The struggles of the 1960s such as those over psychiatry (which in Italy were associated with the work of Giovanni Jervis) were merely the anticipation of this.[45]

However, this section will focus on the battles in the legal profession. Law Students, like medical students, were traditionally conservative in their lifestyle and politics. They were almost exclusively from middle-class backgrounds, and a large percentage had fathers in the profession.[46] They were, in other words *figli di papa* – though rarely his daughters. Nonetheless, law students too were active in the movement (though it should be noted that a large number opposed it). At the State University of Milan they occupied the faculty, and were responsible for the kidnapping (*sequestro*) of a law professor, who was put on trial for his allegedly reactionary behaviour.[47] At both the Catholic and State Universities, law lecturers broke ranks and supported student occupations. As the mock celebration of the beginning of the legal year in 1969 showed, the pomp and circumstance of the law did not go unquestioned. On the contrary, the law was in the eye of the political storms of 1968–9.

To understand this development, it is worth putting it briefly into historical context. More so than in many countries, the legal system of the Italian state was an object of suspicion rather than veneration for wide sections of the population. Liberal-progressive intellectuals looked back to

Beccaria to ground their arguments against the persistence of Fascist penal codes, while popular antagonism to the law and its representatives could draw on a rich store of sayings and proverbs. There were divisions within the *paese legale*, but above all there was the divide between the *paese legale* and the *paese reale*. The events of 1968–9 brought these divisions into the open.[48]

The clashes between students and workers and the police were also clashes between different conceptions of law and order. Implicitly, the former made recourse to notions of 'natural justice' as embodied in the popular maxim of the time: 'It is right to rebel' (*E giusto ribellarsi*), or even to justifications for revolt based on the rights of the poor to steal rather than suffer hunger contained in Catholic theology. On the other side, the police were given the task of upholding the law, although in 1968–9 this frequently involved administering punishment in the street. In other words, mass social conflict brought the question of the law out of the court-room and into the *piazza*; and, vice versa, the passions and disputes of the streets were taken into the seats of judgement. The law did not stand above conflicts but was invested by them. Indeed, the drama of social conflict in 1968 was marked by the trial of leading militants.[49]

It is an important feature of social movements that they seek to right wrongs in society as a whole. The idea of injustice is intimately bound up with how the social contract is defined, as much informally as formally. The ordinary subject is also a legislator, and never more so than when participating in a social movement.[50] Nonetheless, a movement has to face the law as an institution which imposes codes and practices. Movements, in brief, need lawyers.

The necessity of using the law as well as fighting against it was made apparent in 1968–9 when charges were brought against tens of thousands of students and workers who had been involved in demonstrations, occupations and strikes. Lawyers were required to defend them, and to block attempts by employers and others to have certain forms of protest declared illegal. By the end of 1969 the 'campaign against repression' (as it was called) became a political priority. After the Piazza Fontana bombing there were widespread fears that civil liberties would be suspended and that the conditions would be prepared for a coup d'état (see chapter 15). It was recognized that there were laws which had to be defended and extended so that the conditions favourable to political activity could be created. There were, therefore, ambiguities in the attitude of the social movements towards the law as an institution. It appeared, on the one hand, as an instrument of capitalist rule, and on the other as civil rights. Whilst the radical lawyer or magistrate could only function because of the second conception, this was not automatically the assumption which informed his or her way of working. In fact, two organizations – Soccorso Rosso and Magistratura Democratica – were set up in the early 1970s which expressed the different political approaches to the problem. It was a difference with far-reaching implications.

Soccorso Rosso (Red Aid) was an organization of professional people (lawyers, doctors and others) who gave their time and specialized skills to help victims of repression and oppression.[51] Its name, which was the same as that of an organization founded in 1922 by the Third International to aid victims of reaction, points to its general political alignment. Although Soccorso Rosso combined different outlooks (much more so than a political party), it was primarily oriented towards using the law in whatever way possible to defend the factory militant or political activists. It did not concern itself with changing the law nor with campaigning around civil rights as a general political issue. Such an approach was regarded as basically reformist. The legal system could, it was thought, only be changed by exposing it as the embodiment of class rule. The defence of the individual offered the opportunity to denounce class injustice. The only real justice was popular justice carried out in the class war. A number of activists in Soccorso Rosso saw their role as 'serving the people' in two senses; firstly, as the partial, limited and, in the long term, inconsequential defence of the accused; and secondly, in the construction of a 'people's justice', which entailed making the accused into the accuser. Between bourgeois justice and proletarian justice there could be no meeting point. The idea of the law as independent from politics was a fiction which could only be unmasked by openly subordinating it to politics with the dictatorship of the proletariat.[52]

Magistratura Democratica (Democratic Magistrature) represented an approach which Soccorso Rosso deemed reformist. It was an organization within the legal profession which sought change through and in the institutions.[53] It meant making the law, as an institution, more responsive to the interests and the values expressed by the social movements. In other words, the law had to be brought closer to the needs and aspirations of the *paese reale* and, therefore, detached from its associations with the ruling order. Magistratura Democratica organized a current of opinion which encouraged a more liberal interpretation of the law, and which canvassed legal reform. Among its successes can be counted the implementation of the 1970 Labour charter; whilst in the postwar period managements had enjoyed legal advantages and cooperation from judges, in the 1970s the legislation was successfully used by unions to protect workers' rights.[54] More generally, Magistratura Democratica played an important part in arguing the case for civil rights in the mid to late 1970s, when they came increasingly under attack from both Left and Right. It argued, moreover, that the law as an autonomous institution was a necessary part of any strategy for radical social transformation of the state if it was not to end up in totalitarianism.[55]

The experience of radicals working in the law in the years following 1968 seem to bear out Foucault's general observation about the changed role of intellectuals: namely, that they had more to gain and more to offer in the struggle against the dominant power structures in so far as they worked radically in their specific situations. It can perhaps be judged one of the more positive aspects of the cultural revolution. The influence of radical teachers, lawyers, doctors, social workers and others increased knowledge and awareness of the new complexities and forms of power within society.

The idea of cultural revolution inspired by Chinese examples went into eclipse by the mid-1970s. The notions of popular culture, of the relationship of intellectuals to masses, and of what a utopian society would look like, had become barriers to understanding an action. It would be wrong, however, simply to dismiss them as irrelevant. The negative and guilt-creating experiences, as well as those which were positive and liberating, taught activists a great deal. The answers proposed along Chinese lines resulted in a moralistic and dogmatic cultural politics, but the questions raised about how to change society remained crucial.

Notes

1. Pierre Bourdieu, 'The production of belief; contribution to an economy of symbolic goods', *Media, Culture and Society* 2, 1980, p. 288.
2. The student movement along with the other movements of the 1960s was important for how the mass media were studied. New approaches to media analysis were developed by radicals; see Giovanni Bechelloni, *La Macchina Culturale in Italia*, Bologna 1974.
3. Students, inspired by the German movement's attacks on the Springer press buildings in Berlin, demonstrated against the *Corriere della Sera*. A student leaflet noted that the 'picket against disinformation' ended in 252 arrests. It claimed that student violence was a response to the violence of the system as manifested in the schools, factories and media. Calling students 'hooligans' is described as a form of violence; State University leaflet, undated.
4. *La contestazione murale* pp. 105–25.
5. For an account of the influence of Marcusean ideas within the student movement see S. Sidotti, 'Emancipazione e politiche culturali negli anni 60: Marcuse in Italia', *Rassegna Italiana di Sociologia*, 2, April–June 1974.
6. See Tiberi, *La contestazione murale*, pp. 105–25; and *Corriere della Sera*, 10 January 1971.
7. See Violi, *I giornali dell'estrema sinistra*.
8. For an account of events, see Camilla Cederna, *Una finestra sulla strage*, Milan 1971 and Piero Scaramucci, *Licia Pinella: una storia quasi soltanto mia*, Milan 1982.
9. G. Bechelloni, 'The journalist as political client in Italy', in A. Smith, ed., *Newspapers and Democracy*, London 1980.
10. 'The paper *Lotta Continua* said one thing alone: Calabresi, murderer. I remember a blood-curdling cartoon with a toy guillotine and Calabresi showing his daughter how to chop the head off a doll wearing an anarchist "A" on its dress. On marches people

used to shout: "Calabresi, you'll be suicided too"'; Giampaolo Pansa, *Panorama*, 17 August 1988.

11. See chapter 19, pp. 281–2.
12. See Umberto Eco and Patrizia Violi, 'La controinformazione', in Paolo Murialdi and Nicola Tranfaglia, *La stampa italiana del neocapitalismo*, Bari 1976; 'Towards a Semiological Guerrilla Warfare' is available in English in Eco's *Faith in Fakes*, 1987; see also the work of the Isituto Gemelli at the Catholic University of Milan: its publication IKON, and the work of Franco Rositi.
13. For example, Licia Pinelli recalls that Pasolini approached her about making a film about her husband's death, and how she was 'adopted' by liberal-progressive circles in Milan; Scaramucci, p. 125.
14. Students invaded the Pesaro film festival and issued manifestos on what radical film-making should involve; see G. Fofi, *Il cinema italiano: servi e padroni*, Milan 1971, pp. 81–6. The Venice Biennale and few of lesser events were also targets of attack by art students and radical artists. The French led the way, and in France the debate on film and culture was richer than in Italy; for an account, see Sylvia Harvey, *May '68 and Film Culture*, London 1978.
15. Fofi, *Il cinema italiano*, p. 12.
16. Franca Rame, Introduction to Dario Fo, *Can't Pay? Won't Pay!*, London 1978, p. vi.
17. Ibid., pp. vii–xii.
18. 'Dario Fo à Vincennes', *Cahiers du Cinema*, 250, May 1974, p. 20.
19. Ibid., pp. 20–1. Dario Fo's *Mistero Buffo* is a daring example of his ideas in practice; the play invents a language out of the dialects of the Po valley. For a critical assessment of Fo, see Lino Pertile, 'Dario Fo', in M. Caesar and P. Hainsworth, *Writers and Society in Contemporary Italy*, Leamington Spa 1984.
20. Ibid., p. 22.
21. Ibid., p. 24.
22. This was written by Maria Antonietta Macciocchi. Others who studied and visited China, writing about their experiences include Edoarda Masi, Rossana Rossanda and Lisa Foa. Pier Paolo Pasolini and Dario Fo were among those in the world of culture who were especially attracted by the Chinese myth. Umberto Melotti, 'La vera natura della societa cinese e le contraddizioni della nuova sinistra italiana', *Terzo Mondo*, December 1975, p. 60.
23. Ibid.
24. See Hans-Magnus Enzensberger, 'Constituents of a Theory of the Media' in Dennis McQuail, ed., *Sociology of Mass Communications*, London 1972. Gian Carlo Ferretti has written how the battle of the 'organized workers' movement' '*per una cultura popolare*' was lost. The mass market continued to be dominated by literary genres such as romance, crime and thriller stories produced by the major publishers. Communist Party intellectuals competed within the terms of the divide between the 'two cultures' which they did not substantially attack. The publishers of the New Left likewise made no inroads into the mass market, and remained in a ghetto. The cultural divides were even greater if it is borne in mind that relatively few Italians read books or newspapers at all; see Gian Carlo Ferretti, *Il mercato delle lettere*, Turin 1979, especially pp. 19–50. But antagonism towards pop culture (as opposed to popular culture) was common to working-class militants in the post '68 years. An article entitled 'Let's talk about culture' in a factory paper contrasts a song of the rice pickers (*mondine*) with the pop song of Celentano called 'Who doesn't work, doesn't make love' (*Chi non lavora, non fa l'amore*): 'Whilst the first song is characterized by concreteness, truth and humanity, the second is evidence only of a defeatist and couldn't-care-less (*qualunquista*) mentality'; in *Voce del Lavoratore*, Bolletino unitario del Consiglio di Fabbrica: Sit Siemens, 1970.
25. For a more extended discussion of the issue of mass and popular culture, see Zymunt Baranski and Robert Lumley, *Culture and Conflict in Postwar Italy*, London 1990, and Stephen Gundle, 'L'americanizzazione del quotidiano. Televisione e consumo nell' Italia degli anni cinquanta', *Quaderni Storici*, 62, 1986.
26. Francesco Alberoni, 'Società, cultura e comunicazioni di massa', *Annali della Scuola*

Superiore delle Comunicazioni Sociali in Bergamo, Università Cattolica del Sacro Cuore, no. 2, 1966.

27. The 'Pasolinian approach' is 'the one that maintains that mass culture is responsible for the so-called process of homologization; the progressive loss, that is, of every distinctive characteristic, every specific or particular tradition, even the cancellation of memory itself, leading to the complete substitution of a traditional cultural heritage by prefabricated conception of life and the world imposed from above'; Amalia Signorelli, 'Cultura popolare e cultura di massa; note per un dibattito', *La Ricerca Folklorica*, 7, 1983, p. 3; for a more complex analysis of Pasolini's own work, see Zygmunt Baranski, 'Pier Paolo Pasolini: Culture, Croce, Gramsci', in *Culture and Conflict in Postwar Italy*.

28. Perry Anderson, *Considerations on Western Marxism*, London 1976, pp. 95–6.

29. Richard Sennett and Jonathan Cobb. *The Hidden Injuries of Class*, Cambridge 1972, p. 5.

30. Ibid., pp. 6–7.

31. Stefano Merli, 'Per un nuovo modo di fare ricerca storica', *Fabbrica e Stato*, July–August 1973, p. 82. For further explanation of the 150-Hours Scheme, see part II, chapter 17, pp. 265–6.

32. Interview with Giuseppe Magni, a course organizer in Milan from the inception of the 150-Hours Scheme, April, 1978.

33. The hidden history of the 150-Hours Scheme is very different from its official version. Like much of what goes on in classrooms it remains a private affair between students and teachers. But unlike the school situation, the workers were halfway between being students and themselves being the teachers of the teachers. It created a confusion of roles and a meeting of cultures which opened up great possibilities for experimentation, but which often led to disillusionment.

34. Luigi Manconi, *Nuovo, difficile: una proposta bibliografica sulla produzione culturale delle ultime generazioni*, a reading guide published by Feltrinelli, June 1979, p. 22.

35. For example, Goffredo Fofi writes of late Rossellini films: 'Rossellini passes from the estatic flowers where a half-wit St Francis raises his hymn to God and the DC, to Mediterranean locations where Ingrid Bergman finds him (God, that is) in the mouths of volcanoes or in the lava at Pompeii'; *Il cinema italiano*, p. 72.

36. Manconi, *Nuovo, difficile*, pp. 22–3.

37. Fofi, '*Piccola editoria*', p. 77.

38. Ibid., p. 78.

39. In the late 1970s and early eighties a number of episodes from the momentous to the banal signalled the subtle shifts and the jolts in opinion which brought the 'generation of '68' to turn their backs on their own history. The ascendancy of red terrorism was the most important single development, but analyses need also to note how the tone of articles in *L' Espresso* changes: For example, the coining of the word '*sinistrese*' to describe a certain left-wing vocabulary and style of speech and then its rapid adoption indexed a significant change in attitudes; see Paolo Flores d'Arcais, 'Dizionario dei luoghi comuni della sinistra' *L' Espresso*, 19 December 1976.

40. This theme recurs throughout the debates during and following the movements of 1968–9. The Chinese model played a crucial role in 'proving' that divisions of labour could be broken down if politics was put 'in command'. The review *Vento dell'Este*, for example, published Mao's *Charter for the Anshan steelworks* and other documents to show this; see E. Reyneri, 'La lotta per la produzione e l'organizzazione del lavoro nelle fabbriche cinesi', *Vento dell'Este*, 23, 1971. Some on the Left thought that the Chinese model was not applicable in the West, but nonetheless regarded divisions of labour as the most significant definers of class society. Michele Salvati and Bianca Beccalli proposed a socialist strategy which involved: i) elimination of forms of work; ii) job rotation where possible; iii) expansion of the technical/scientific sector subject to democratic controls; iv) recomposition of jobs. They suggested that society had a choice between prioritizing how work was done or how much was produced. This was a sober version of utopianism; see M. Salvati and B. Beccalli, 'Divisione del Lavoro: capitalismo, socialismo, utopia', *Quaderni Piacentini*, 40, 1970.

41. Michel Foucault, 'Truth and Power', in Meagan Morris, ed., *Power, Truth, Strategy*, Darlington, Australia 1979, p. 42.

42. See the reflections and initiatives of the Erba Voglio collective in Milan, Elvio Fachinelli, ed., *L' Erba Voglio – pratica non autoritaria nella sculoa*, Turin 1971.

43. See Vito Foa, 'La tutela della salute nell'ambiente di lavoro', in *Fabbrica a Salute: atti della conferenza nazionale CGIL–CSIL–UIL*, Rome 1972, pp. 207–9; Giovanni Jervis, 'Condizione operaia e nervosi', *Inchiesta*, 10, 1973. Giulio Maccacaro, *Per una medicina da rinnovare. Scritti 1966–76*, Milan 1976.

44. A landmark was the translation and publication by Feltrinelli of the Boston women's Health Collective's *Our Bodies Ourselves* in 1974. A women's catalogue of 1980 listed over eighty books under the heading 'Our Body'; *Librellula Liberia delle Donne Catalogo*, Bologna 1980. Women had been largely excluded from the most prestigious professions, so the 1970s were also important as a period in which women were becoming doctors and lawyers.

45. For an assessment of Giovani Jervis' important work in the field of psychiatric care, see Paolo Crepet and Agostino Pirella, 'The Transformation of Psychiatric Care in Italy', *International Journal of Mental Health*, 14, 1985; pp. 155–73.

46. Martinotti, *Gli studenti universitari*, p. 55.

47. The Trimarchi affair is interesting as an example of the student movement's application of Chinese-style Cultural Revolution in Italy. The idea was to elicit public confessions from reactionaries and wrong-doers, making them reply to accusations coming from their victims. Thus the peasant would enumerate the landlord's cruelties. Trimarchi, however, did not play according to the rules and argued his case. Subsequently students were brought to trial in the 'normal' way. See *Corriere della Sera* 10 March 1969, 22 March 1969.

48. 'The underlying issues, as always, were: whose law, whose order? The tensions were vividly captured in the distinction which was frequently made in the early nineteenth century between the "social order" and the "political order" the first was seen to represent the political elite the second did not'; John A. Davis, *Conflict and Control. Law and Order in Nineteenth-Century Italy*, London 1988, p. 11.

49. In the memoirs of Milan student leader, Mario Capanna, there is a description of the mobilization in defence of students on trial which reveals the intensity of feeling against the legal system as well as a decision to use the courtroom as a political forum; Capanna, *Formidabili quegli anni*, pp. 72–3.

50. Antonio Gramsci wrote perceptively of this broad conception of the law; A. Gramsci, *Prison Notebooks*, pp. 265–6.

51. Rocco Ventre, a noted lawyer and member of Soccorso Rosso, defined its role: 'it helps the accused in plain daylight (*alla luce del sole*), in the context of the rights guaranteed by the penal code which is their only protection from physical harm'; *La Repubblica*, 21 May 1980.

52. Although it should be made clear that Soccorso Rosso contained a range of political opinions, among these there was a current favourable to the armed organizations on the Left. In 1976 Soccorso Rosso was responsible for editing a collection of Red Brigades documents, which it introduced as a contribution to dispassionate debate, whilst making clear: 'For their origins, their political practice and for what they have written we recognize them as comrades, and when reaction attacks them we are at their side ... which means offering them militant help including, though it is the least important, legal aid'; Soccorso Rosso, *Brigate Rosse*, Milan 1976, p. 5. Whatever the organizational connections a 'red thread' of shared beliefs ran between some members of Soccorso Rosso and the Red Brigades. Above all, they shared a conception of popular justice which modelled itself on Chinese practices but did not stop at applying the ruthlessness of a Stalinist show-trial. See part IV, chapter 19, pp. 283–4.

53. Alberto Melucci, 'Vers un système de relations professionnelles en Italie', *Sociologie de travail*, 1, 1976, pp. 397–400.

54. *Statuto dei lavoratori: un bilancio politico*, Bari 1977, pp. 30–33.

55. Luigi Ferrajoli and Danilo Zolo, *Democrazia autoritoria e capitalismo maturo*, Milan 1978.

the story in pictures

the writing on the wall . . .

Be realistic, demand the impossible

Christian Democracy and bosses . . . Occupations

Against academic authoritarianism – Student Power

OCCUPAZIONE DI
PALAZZO CAMPANA
UNIVERSITA' DI TORINO
NOVEMBRE · DICEMBRE 1967

CONTRO L'AUTORITARISMO ACCADEMICO

POTERE AGLI STUDENTI

Smash the bourgeois state, don't change it

'68 and the cartoon strip . . .

In the commune it'll be from each according to his abilities, to each according to his needs

But everyone'll have to renounce all forms of private property

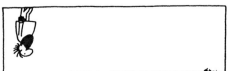

BEGINNING WITH YOUR WOMAN!

Calm down! It's just a bottle of Lambrusco, not a Molotov!

EXACTLY!

Culture must be defended

GODARD

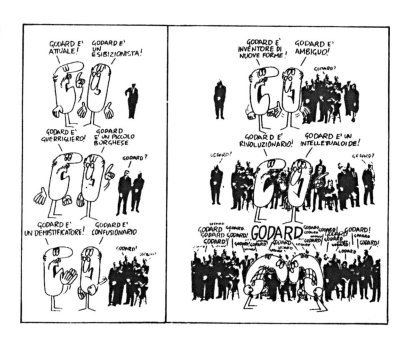

the worker . . .

South – 2,000 kilometres

Gasparazzo and . . . The Big City

I am labour power but I'm variable

The cost of living, Cipputi? It depends if you're buying or selling

fashion and politics . . .

Dress lengths

Hello, what are you called?
You think if I knew that I'd dress like this?

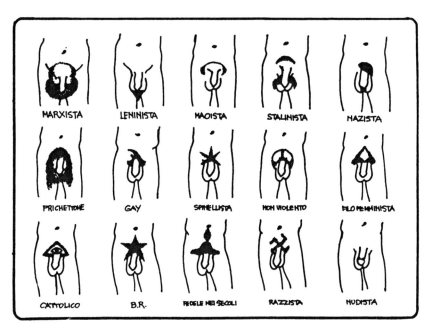

Marxist	Leninist	Maoist	Stalinist	Nazi
Freak	Gay	Dope-smoker	Pacifist	Feminist
Catholic	Red Brigade	Loyalist	Racist	Nudist

I was white, then red, now I'm green. White, red, green . . . I'm the typical clapped-out Italian Left intellectual

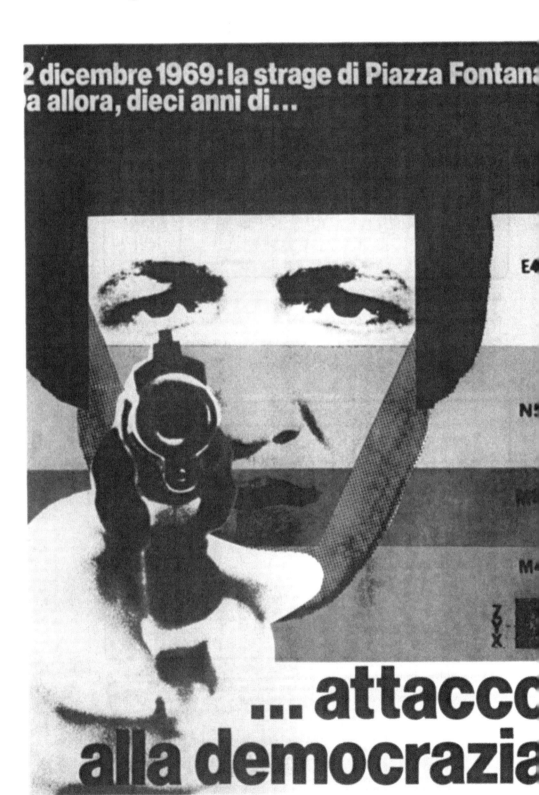

**Your mother and I are terribly worried . . . Andrea . . . give us your word
that you don't take drugs**

maps of the past . . .

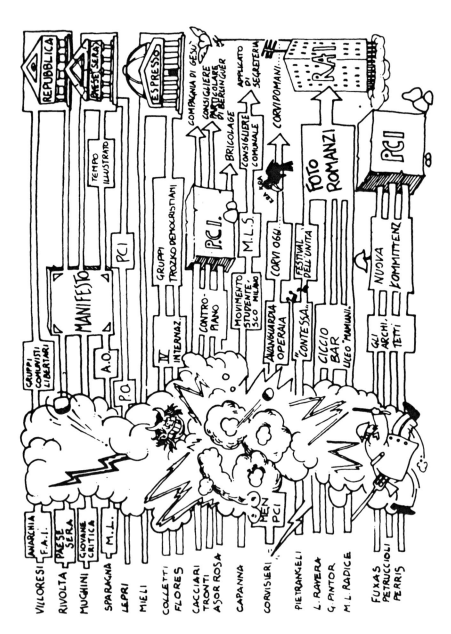

The careers of . . .

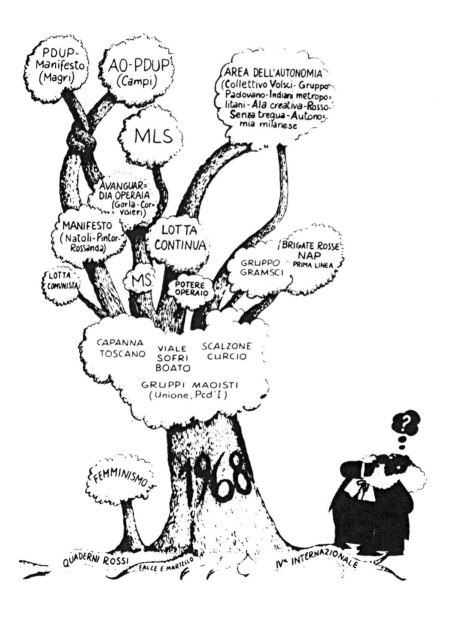

The genealogy of revolt

society of the spectacle . . .

MILAN THE SENIGALLIA FAIR SATURDAY AFTERNOON

JEANS ARMY-SURPLUS SHIRTS
CONTRABAND CIGARETTE DEALERS

CARDSHARPS
CORD TROUSERS   DESERT BOOTS

NAVY PULLOVER   POSTER

LONG RED SCARF   DUFFLECOAT

HAND PICKING UP A STONE

CITY AT NIGHT   EMPTY

EVENING DEMO   TENSION   NOISE   SLOGAN   BANNERS

FAMILY WITH THE NEWS

RAI LOGO IN BLACK & WHITE

THE STATE UNIVERSITY DAZIBAO

OLD MAN IN THE HALL SELLING ANTI-TEAR GAS LEMONS

POLICE CHARGE PRECEDED BY THREE BLASTS ON A HORN

EYES RED AND SWOLLEN THUDS SIRENS EXPLOSIONS

BARRICADE IN VIA LAGHETTO SMOKE PEOPLE RUNNING

CLASS PHOTO WITH TEACHER · GIRLS IN SMOCKS
MANZONI GRAMMAR SCHOOL CLASS III D YEAR 1969-70

FIRST-YEAR GIRLS

FEET IN WOMEN'S SHOES

PIAZZA SANT'AMBROGIO GIRL BOOKS STRAPPED WITH BELT

LEAFLETTING AT THE ENTRANCE — COLD FINGERS

CORRIDOR-BASED COLLECTIVE MORNING — STRIKE MEETING

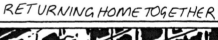

RETURNING HOME TOGETHER

SCHOOL OCCUPATION ON THE OUTSKIRTS — TRAM

163

DEMONSTRATION IN THE USA AGAINST THE VIETNAM WAR

CLASHES OUTSIDE THE US CONSULATE
STUDENTS ARRESTED BY POLICE

LINE OF DEMONSTRATORS RUNNING
HO HO HO CHI MINH HO HO HO

SCHOOL STUDENT STEWARDS BALACLAVAS HELMETS

LOVERS AND COUNCIL ESTATE

GIRL DOESN'T SPEAK AT MEETING

COUPLE HAND-IN-HAND PIAZZA WITH TREES SPRINGTIME SUNSHINE

GUY SPEAKING AT A MEETING

THIS IS NOT A LOVE STORY

PART III

the workers' movement

After a period of relative quiescence in the workplace, the years 1968–9 were turbulent. The scale of industrial conflict during the Hot Autumn of 1969 made it the third largest strike movement recorded in history in terms of lost working time (after, that is, the May 1968 general strike in France, and the British 1926 general strike). However, Italian workers not only withdrew their labour on a massive scale, but challenged the organization of work and the system of authority within the factory. In some cases, workers rebelled against the factory system itself and its hold over their lives. Industrial workers created a movement which overturned many of the rules and assumptions governing everyday behaviour and the regulation of conflict.

The following chapters will attempt to explain why it was that in Italy industrial conflict took on such radical forms; why it was that workers defied managements and rejected negotiation; why questions of pay and conditions turned into sources of a more general attack on social injustices. Some of the answers, as has been seen, lie in the longer history of class conflict in Italy, which made the factory a site of political and social antagonisms.[1] However, the social movement itself drew on and intepreted those traditional antagonisms in new ways. It is necessary to see how the movement developed in its early stages to understand its most dramatic manifestations during the Hot Autumn. Although description and analysis will focus on the struggles of autumn 1969, the first chapters will deal with the mobilizations, starting in early 1968.

The movement's development can be roughly divided into four phases, and the chapters are organized accordingly.[2] In the first phase of mobilizations, which was given a fillip by the turn-out for the general strike over pensions in March 1968, workers took action and made demands along fairly normal lines. In the second phase, which covered the period from autumn 1968 to spring 1969, industrial conflict took an unprecedented turn when workers organized themselves independently of the unions and resorted to forms of direct action. However, the conflicts tended to be localized until the Hot Autumn of 1969 when different struggles converged in action over national contracts. After the signing of the agreements, a fourth phase followed. It is more difficult to date, but can be characterized as the period of the movement's institutionalization.

The chapters are organized chronologically to chart the phases of the movement's development. Thus, chapter 11 deals with the first signs of revolt in the workplaces, whilst chapter 17 outlines the processes of institutionalization. However, they also examine certain exemplary cases of industrial militancy such as the Pirelli company's disputes in Milan (chapter 12), white collar agitation (chapter 13), and the Turin events (chapter 14). These respectively raise the issues of the development of grassroots organizations, the role of the so-called 'new working class', and the 'refusal' of the factory system. While the focus is on Milanese developments, these are put in a national context, and the workers' movement is assessed more generally in terms of its role in representing oppositional forces in society.

11

breaking the ice:
spring–summer 1968

The term '*maggio strisciante*' was coined to describe the development of social and industrial conflict in Italy in 1968–9. Literally translated as the 'drawn-out May', it points to how the movement in the workplaces was a process stretching over months, rather than a phenomenon identifiable with a major event. Whereas in France a massive general strike followed a student insurrection, in Italy the social crisis was more diffused and prolonged; a series of conflicts, from the *jacquerie* of the Marzotta factories of Valdagno in late March, to the street battles between Fiat workers and police in Turin in July 1969 (episodes which will be dealt with in the following chapters), marked important shifts in the development of industrial and social conflict. The student movement had important consequences for setting the stage and heightening social expectations, but these resulted from the continuous mobilizations rather than from any particular confrontation.

The most significant single event in the early stages of the movement was not a spontaneous revolt, but the general strike on 7 March over pension reform organized by the CGIL. It coincided with the parliamentary debate on the subject, and followed the breakdown of the negotiations with the government that had initially justified the postponement of the strike in November 1967. The other confederations withdrew from strike action at the last minute, but participation was not limited to CGIL members. Mobilization in Milan involved three hundred thousand engineering workers alone. It signalled a radical change of mood in the workplaces; Rina Barbieri recalls:

There was something in the air that encouraged workers to take back what they had lost in the previous few years ... the strike for pensions, that's what happened in 1968 that really changed things. . . . There was huge participation, far beyond our expectations, including that of the white-collar workers . . . it was an issue that affected everyone.[3]

The strike had a special significance because it expressed a surge of unity from below, and protest against the Centre–Left government. It was also a sign of general moral outrage at the treatment of pensioners. Despite the recalcitrance of the CISL and the UIL, workers belonging to those confederations joined the action. In Milan the FIM–CISL defiantly called for participation, and, in addition, many non-unionized workers took part. The ideological differences that divided the official organizations were shown to count for less among ordinary workers than they did among their representatives. Disillusionment with the government's capacity to introduce reforms made strike action the only alternative. At this point, it was still largely conceived of in terms of applying pressure on the state from below, but the scale of mobilization revealed a newfound strength which militants channelled into collective bargaining. The expansion of the welfare sector, which was meagre in Italy by comparison with other Western European countries, remained an objective of the movement. However, industrial action in the workplace had the advantage of giving quick and tangible results, which could not be expected from Italian governments.

Company Collective Bargaining

The early months of 1968 saw the development of collective bargaining to a degree not experienced since 1960–1, reaching the highest level in the postwar period.[4] The phenomenon of 'wage drift' – the difference between nationally fixed wages and those won through company and plant bargaining – was a normal feature of most other advanced capitalist economies, but it was new in the Italian situation. Here national contracts for each sector and a highly centralized bargaining apparatus set limits to local agreements. Traditionally, industrial conflict coincided with the calendar of contract renewals, which were usually every three years. The movement of decentralized bargaining, which sprang up mainly in the larger factories of the manufacturing sector on rank-and-file initiatives, therefore had a peculiarly destabilizing impact on industrial relations, causing problems for the unions as well as for managements. In 1968 a conjunction of factors combined to produce the first signs of a movement of shopfloor rebellion, which gathered momentum in the course of the year.

The first conflicts developed around traditional issues; the key demand coming from workers was for wage increases. Since 1963 real wages had been in decline. Although no formal incomes policy had been implemented in Italy, governments' deflationary policies had effectively curtailed wages by weakening bargaining power. Firstly, the postponement of the engineering workers' contract (the pace-setter for other sectors) from 1965 to 1966, and then the meagreness of the 5 per cent increase stretched over 3 years (conceded in 1966) lowered living standards.[5] Production rose steadily after 1964 but without proportionally reducing unemployment, and profits recovered dramatically. In particular, companies were able to raise prices because of favourable international conditions, and to benefit from an inflation which reduced real wages. Then, payment systems within factories were changed to remove or lessen wage-linking to productivity.[6]

Resentment over wages had already shown itself in 1966 during the struggle for the renewal of the engineering workers' contract. In the aftermath, there was considerable bitterness at the way unions had signed the contract prematurely (it was labelled a *contratto bidone*, a 'rubbish agreement'). The disproportion between the scale of mobilization and the paltry results was especially great because of the cost of strikes to the workers themselves. There was no system of strike pay or state benefits for strikers' families in Italy.

In 1967 there was widespread discouragement and loss of confidence, especially among activists on the shopfloor. This was not dispelled until the general strike in March, which showed the growth of a new awareness of bargaining power among workers. Explanations of this change point to two developments: to the consequences of a spurt in production because of a buoyant international market; and to the changed position of workers in relation to the labour market.

Until the beginning of 1968 production increased without significant recourse to additional labour. Then for two years 'manning' levels rose, especially in the engineering sector. Fears over job security subsided, and workers found themselves in a position to ask for wage increases, taking advantage of changes in the production process to press their case. At Alfa Romeo, which had two car plants in the Milan area, the lively commercial boom began in 1968; in the first nine months sales increased by 36.6 per cent with respect to 1967. The increase was determined by and, in turn, determined a continuous reorganization of the labour process; the intensification of line-speeds and continuous technological innovations provoked stoppages and strikes. But the company, in its concern to maintain continuity of production, was prepared to make concessions to prevent strikes.[7]

Although employment rose in 1968, employment in industry over the year did not increase much above its 1964 level. In other words, explanations linking bargaining directly to employment levels are inadequate. It was not the removal of a 'reserve army of unemployed' that unleashed industrial militancy, as in 1959–60. Rather, it was the blocking of that mechanism due to the 'compartmentalization' of the labour market. Industry no longer required raw recruits from the countryside, as it had done in the 1950s. From 1963 Italian capitalism entered a phase of 'precocious maturity' characterized by the demand for a new type of labour power: Massimo Paci has written:

> the workers required are those who possess certain qualities: they must be men, not too young and not too old; preferably they are married, have a certificate from the lower secondary school and have already been socialized into an urban-industrial environment.[8]

Those made redundant in the mid sixties – the young, women and older workers – were not therefore the type of labour needed to sustain the heavier workloads and speed-up of production. Furthermore, the limited movement of labour between the sectors and the tendency to stay on at school in order to escape the prospect of manual work increased the difficulties of the employers in finding the right kind of new employee. In Milan and the industrial triangle the difficulties were especially great.[9]

The change in the market position of semi-skilled workers explains the spread of collective wage bargaining. The unions pursued increases in production bonuses and piece rates. The Milan area had a leading role in clocking up agreements. *L'Unità* reported in late April that in three months sixty engineering companies had been in dispute in the Province of Milan, and that in four to five months one hundred agreements had been signed, covering seventy thousand workers, mainly in the large factories.[10] *L'Unità* reports in April and May speak regularly of thousands of workers in dispute and of the 'leapfrog' effect of agreements. They give the impression of a harmonious relationship between workers and unions going forward together; 'the agreements are the fruit of constant and massive pressure by the workers and exemplary organization and guidance by the unions.'[11] The unions did show flexibility; they promoted strike action during negotiations in the wake of workers' spontaneous refusal to abide by the traditional truce for talks. Where the unions were strong (in the Milanese area unionism had survived the worst effects of management repression and the CGIL had kept its majority position), bargaining was orderly, and often did not go beyond the threat of action, as in the case of Alfa Romeo.[12] Moreover, the demand for more money was a traditional demand that could be channelled without difficulty.

However, the most significant industrial conflicts for the future development of the workers' movement took place where unions were weak or unable to articulate the demands of the workers, and where continuities with the paternalist/repressive industrial relations of the

1950s were greatest. In these instances, wider issues concerning management powers and authority were at stake. Nationally, the struggles at Marzotto, at Fiat in Turin, and at Montedison of Porto Marghera were particularly important. Within the Milan area there were no equivalent rebellions, but an examination of particular factories is useful in showing the dynamic of the shopfloor movement.

Rebellion at Marzotto, Fiat and Montedison

On 19 April workers from the textile factories of Valdagno in the Veneto pulled down the statue of Gaetano Marzotto from its pedestal in the town square. Throughout April and May Fiat workers in Turin took industrial action in pursuit of a company agreement for the first time since 1954. At Montedison's Porto Marghera petrochemical plant wildcat strikes in the spring led up to months of confrontations in which workers showed themselves ready to destroy plant by totally withdrawing their labour. Each of these moments of conflict made headline news and were symptomatic of a radicalization among workers that went beyond the demand for wage increases alone.

The insurrection of Valdagno had many of the characteristics of a *jac-querie*.[13] What started as a series of stoppages over work conditions beginning in late 1967, escalated into a total strike which was followed by a lock-out in April. In the street battles which followed the workers were joined by students from Padua and Trento and police reinforcements had to be called in from Padua. It was an exemplary case of a struggle against a paternalist system in a company town. Resentment over exploitation in the factory rapidly grew into a rebellion against a virtual 'truck-shop' system, and against the symbols of the Marzotto family's dynastic rule. Although the particular form of the rebellion was isolated, and had parallels in the assault on municipal buildings in the South rather than in the conflicts of the industrialised North, its significance was more than picturesque and symbolic.

Firstly, the paternalism at Marzotto was an extreme case of a type of régime that continued to be more than a residual form of industrial relations in Italy, especially in the 'white' areas (areas of strong Catholic traditions and support for the Christian Democrat Party). Secondly, the rebellion had also been against the local moderate CISL union, and became a point of reference for radical elements in that union. And finally, the events of Valdagno came a fortnight after the Valle Giulia street fighting between students and police in Rome. They highlighted the repressive intervention of the state in industrial disputes, and underlined the new unity between students and workers. It was the period when the

173

theme of the legitimacy and political value of proletarian violence was much debated.

The strikes at Fiat over piece-rates were not marked by particular innovations in either the demands or forms of action. Their importance lay rather in the fact that a long period of inaction had ended. Events at Fiat had great symbolic importance. In the postwar period, the elections to the internal commissions at Fiat were reported as if they had been general elections, and the clashes of Piazza Statuto in 1962 had been interpreted as the first sign of a new type of working-class insubordination. Sections of the student movement and political groupings in Turin took the strikes in the spring of 1968 as a cue for intervention in support of workers' struggles.[14]

At Porto Marghera, an industrial estate at Mestre where the Montedison petrochemical plants employed fifteen thousand people, disputes over grading in the spring, and then over a production bonus in July, led to exemplary instances of industrial action in the most advanced technological sectors. The high capital intensity and the continuous production process at the plants made them particularly vulnerable to disruption. Against the wishes of the unions, which felt obliged to honour the 'peace formula' in the 1966 contract, independent mass meetings called strikes on alternate days. In July pickets prevented maintenance men from entering, thereby risking the destruction of the plant by their refusal to identify with the interests of the company. Throughout the disputes decisions were taken by open meetings, which shortcircuited the unions. More heed was paid to proposals coming from the political group Potere Operaio and from students than to union officials. In response to a management offer of a 1.5 per cent production bonus increase, workers took up Potere Operaio's call for a 5,000 *lire* increase for all. The ideas of workers' autonomy theorized by the *operaist* groups, seemed to have its practical demonstration. According to these, the struggles exemplified the autonomy of self-organization and the autonomy of workers' forms of action and objectives from the cycle of capital. In other words, workers' action was not thought to be recuperable either by unions or by the company. This version of 'workers' autonomy' (*autonomia operaia*), which was first theorized by Mario Tronti and others in the mid sixties, gained credibility and influence. Its promulgators canvassed action that escaped union control and introduced a revolutionary perspective into industrial disputes.[15]

Milan Area

A correlation of the degree of conflict in industrial disputes in twenty-four engineering companies in the Milan area with the presence of the FIOM, shows a correspondence between relatively weak unionization and high levels of conflict. In these cases, the discontent over the erosion of real wages was particularly great because managements had minimized bargaining and cut down piece-rates whilst increasing workloads, thereby taking advantage of the weak organization and division of the workforce. In the more favourable bargaining situation of early 1968 there were outbreaks of often violent action.[16] A brief outline of events in some of the Province of Milan's main engineering factories during the spring of 1968 will give a picture of the early mobilizations.

The Magneti Marelli light engineering factories at Crescenzago had a workforce of four thousand in 1968.[17] A fifth was composed of skilled fitters, checkers and maintenance men, whilst the majority of workers, 40 per cent of whom were women in the lowest two grades, did 'parcellized' and repetitive jobs on automated and semi-automated machines on production lines. In 1960–62 the workers of Magneti Marelli played a leading role in the strike movement, but the management had used the recession to reimpose hierarchical control from above. A measure of its success was the fact that heavy overtime was being worked at a time when workers were being temporarily laid off (*cassa integrazione*). Attempts at industrial action were met with lockouts, and wages were held down through failures to honour agreements, aided and abetted by the only recognized union, the UILM.

The end of layoffs, the take-on of workers and the success of the pension reform strike put new heart into both workers and unions, but the radical impetus to the strikes for wages and bilateral assessment of payments came from the newly employed young male workers. This group had no fear of management and was angry over the disparity between their qualifications and the de-skilled nature of the jobs they found themselves in. Moreover they suffered from discrimination; because of their age they received lower wages for the same work as done by older workers. When students at the factory gates called for a march to the city centre, the young workers took up the idea and made the unions accept it at an open meeting. It was the students with their experience of demonstrations rather than the unions who organized the march from Magneti Marelli, which was the first since 1949. However, the formation of an 'autonomous grouping' outside the unions was too weak to promote alternative initiatives. The twenty days of strikes ending in an agreement in May did not drastically alter the balance of forces in the workplace, though they led to greater bargaining activity, and hence the recognition of the unions.

The Innocenti company at Lambrate was divided into three separate factories; one heavy engineering (with just over 1,000 manual workers and 700 white-collar); the Lambretta motor vehicle plant (with 1,400 workers); and the car factory (with 1,500 workers).[18] Each factory was different in terms of economic situation, labour processes, the composition and traditions of the workforce, and these provided the conditions for the diverse timing and trajectories of mobilizations. In early 1968 it was the heavy engineering factory with its highly skilled male workers, who averaged forty years of age and were of northern origin, who took action rather than the young, semi-skilled southern workers of the car factory. Traditionally the former had not been militant. They had enjoyed some of the benefits of the paternalist/repressive system at Innocenti (such as high overtime rates and 'merit awards'), because of the relative scarcity of their skills. They were proud of being skilled. The turn to industrial action in 1968 was provoked by attacks on their privileges. Production increases were sought by management through the intro-duction of night shifts and the employment of additional skilled workers at higher rates. During an episode of drunken bravura a worker told a manager that they wanted 100 *lire* an hour more, and instantly, 'like a spark in straw' (*una scintilla in un pagliaio*), the word spread, bringing the heavy engineering factory to a stop. In the ensuing dispute the workers responded to a breakdown in negotiations with spontaneous acts of violence; internal marches within the factory and offices drove out the white-collar workers, the majority of whom opposed the strike, smashed windows and organized mass pickets. Finally they went on all-out strike (*sciopero ad oltranza*) until the signing of an agreement. From the begin-ning to the end, the timing and forms of action and the main demands came about 'spontaneously', in the sense that the unions followed the decisions which had already been taken. However, the 'autonomy' shown by the workers of the heavy engineering factory was of a limited kind. Above all it showed a power based on the solidarity bargaining position and sense of independence of the skilled workers. The intervention of political groups from outside (Potere Operaio) met with no response, and the strikes did not break the repressive climate in the car factory where most workers were not skilled.

The Autobianchi car factory at Desio had about 2,600 employees.[19] An unusually low percentage of these were skilled due to the importation of 'kits' for the Mini from Britain, which meant that there was mainly a requirement for assembly work. The siting of the factory in a 'white area' was part of a deliberate policy of excluding trade unions from the plants, and in the 1960s a paternalist regime prevailed. The level of conflict remained low and there was little bargaining activity since management preferred to take decisions unilaterally. In 1968 a big expansion of production, intolerable speed-ups of the line and grievances over hours (which were longer than in other companies in the sector and did not include the payment of lunch breaks) fuelled shopfloor discontent.

However, the crucial change in the situation resulted from the takeover of Autobianchi by Fiat, since workers took the opportunity to demand parity of conditions with their other factories.

In mid February 1968, after the refusal of parity with Fiat, the internal commission organized strike action. The workers' response was unprecedented in terms of participation and militancy. In March there were lightning strikes instead of the traditional twenty-four-hour stoppage; mass pickets prevented entry to the factory and the cars of two scabs (*crumiri*), who climbed over the wall, were set on fire. Anger over the white-collar workers' refusal to join the strike ended in the invasion of the offices and destruction of office equipment. On one occasion, the personnel manager, who had a reputation for terrorizing employees, was dragged into a field. A worker recalls: 'He stayed in the rain for two hours whilst workers threw insults and punches at him; it was unbelievable.' Violent incidents followed the breakdown of talks and attempted lockouts but the agitation otherwise remained under union control. The leading activists within the factory were the skilled workers of the fitting shops (*reparti di preparazione*) and their concern for wages rather than for conditions prevailed in the formulation of demands, which were mostly met in an agreement drawn up in April.

Sit Siemens, a partly state-controlled company, was the biggest Italian enterprise in the telecommunications sector and enjoyed a monopoly position in the market.[20] Unlike most engineering companies, it had been in continuous expansion during the recession of the mid sixties and had almost doubled its output between 1960 and 1968 due to the telephone boom and switch to STD. The number of employees rose by 600 between 1967 and 1968 to reach 7,900. In 1969 there were 8,550 employed at factories in Milan and Castelletto. 51 per cent were women workers who were engaged in mass production and assembly work, 30 per cent were skilled male workers with jobs in fitting maintenance and testing, and there was a section of semi-skilled men engaged in heavier production work. There were technicians in the laboratories at Castelletto, while the majority of clerical workers were in Milan. The workforce was highly stratified according to the organization of the labour process, and this was reflected in its relationship to the unions. Among the women workers there were high turnover rates and low levels of unionization, whilst the core of the union membership and leadership was found among the securely employed skilled men.

Unlike the other engineering factories which experienced outbursts of militancy in the early months of 1968, Sit Siemens management was not known for repressive and paternalistic practices. However, the gap in representation between the union and the shopfloor meant that mobilization took uncontrolled forms, especially through the autonomous action of different shopfloors. Already in 1966 a strike committee had been organized independently of the union during the national contract dispute and had managed to promote an embarrassing demonstration at the Milan Trade Fair. Although this grouping disintegrated after the signing of the contract, it had effectively identified the main grievances, especially those of the women workers; these resulted from speed-ups which provoked exhaustion and even hysteria, and worsening conditions of work. The cuts in the piece-rates (by an average 6 per cent over 1967) aggravated resentment over the poor 1966 agreement, which had allowed productivity increases without doing much to improve wages.

The failure of a strike call over production bonuses in November 1967 showed that the majority of workers were concerned about conditions rather than the question of pay in itself. A member of the internal commission explained: '[the workers] told us: what we take with the right hand is taken away from the left by the bosses who cut the time on the piece-rate.' Demands drawn up and presented to management in February 1968 were the first attempt by the unions to confront the different conditions of work in the various sections of the factories. Upgrading for workers in the lowest grades, the elimination of health hazards and bargaining over the fixing of piece-rates were all issues that evoked a crescendo of participation in strikes. These were organised at shop level and included internal marches and invasions of the offices. Particularly surprising was the participation of about 30 per cent of the white-collar workers, despite their exclusions from drafting the demands. Although the agreement reached between management and the unions was considered inadequate ('extra money from piece-rate changes can only buy another cup of coffee a day'), no effective proposition emerged because the internal commission's bargaining position and prestige among the mass of workers was greatly reinforced.

From developments in Milan and elsewhere it is possible to make some observations on the first phase of workers' mobilizations. These can be grouped in terms of the demands, forms of struggle and organization, and leading protagonists involved.

The main demand in this period was for greater production bonuses and revised piece-rates; demands for union rights and better working conditions remained secondary. In other words, workers sought to improve their situation within the existing pay structures and working arrangements. The only new element was the demand for across-the-board lump sum pay increases. To begin with, it was put forward without any particular gloss, but it quickly acquired anti-capitalist connotations, especially in the eyes of *operaist* theorists. Its great advantages were seen to be its egalitarian effect of benefiting all workers whilst reducing differentials, and the fact that it was easily understood by everyone, not requiring the mathematical expertise needed to work out percentage wage increases.

The forms of industrial action in this first phase showed a continuity with past practices. Workers left the workplace during stoppages and carried on the dispute from the outside. However, some things had changed: picketing had become more violent; there was an increase in the number of demonstrations, and these often involved student participation; there were no more truces for negotiations. In this period, the workers acted through the unions, the most dramatic exception being the independent mass meetings at Porto Marghera. However, there were straws in the wind which suggested that workers were dissatisfied with their representatives. The feeble implantation of the unions in many factories, and the relative isolation of the internal commissions, meant that they had inadequate channels through which to feel the pulse of the workplace. This was especially debilitating when many union officials were frightened of the risks of defeat, and sceptical about the spirit of militancy.

The leading protagonists in the mobilizations tended to be the skilled workers, who were often also the more politicized and unionized. Certainly, they enjoyed more bargaining power than other groups. In certain instances, as at Innocenti, they used their advantages to benefit themselves alone, but skilled workers were among the radical leaders at Porto Marghera. However, the prominence of these workers was related to the timidity of the semi-skilled, who were less experienced and confident, and whose interests were inadequately represented by the unions. It was not until the autumn and spring of 1968–9 that these workers acted independently in pursuit of their own interests.

Notes

1. See chapter 2.
2. This periodization is based on that found in Ida Regalia, Marino Regini and Emilio Reyneri, 'Conflitti di lavoro e relazioni industriali in Italia, 1968–75', in Colin Crouch and Alessandro Pizzorno, *Conflitti in Europa*, Milan 1977.
3. Rina Barbieri interview.
4. Michele Salvati, 'Slittamento salariale e sindacato con riferimenti all'industria metalmeccanica, 1954–69', *Rassegna Economica*, 6, 1970, pp. 1397–1442.
5. D. Soskice, Le relazioni industriali nelle società occidentali', in Colin Crouch and Alessandro Pizzorno, *Conflitti in Europa*, pp. 394–96.
6. M. Salvati, *Il sistema economico italiano*, pp. 40–41.
7. A. Sandretti, *Lotte all'Alfa Romeo, 1970–73*, Tesi di Laurea, Università degli Studi di Milano, Facoltà di Scienze Politiche, 1973, p. 31.
8. Paci, *Mercato di lavoro*, p. 275.
9. M. Paci, *L'evoluzione dell'occupazione in Lombardia e la mobilità delle forze di lavoro*, Milan 1968, pp. 15–61.
10. *L'Unità*, 23 April 1968.
11. *L'Unità*, 10 May 1968.

12. Emilio Reyneri, 'Maggio strisciante: l'inizio della mobilitazione operaia', in A. Pizzorno et al., '*Lotta operaie e sindacato, il ciclo 1968–72 in Italia*, Bologna 1978, p. 85.
13. E. Reyneri, 'Comportamento di classe e nuovo ciclo di ciclo di lotte', *Annali della Fondazione Feltrinelli*, 1974/5, pp. 850–60; Viale, *Il sessantotto*, pp. 148–9; Foa, *Sindacati e lotte operaie*, pp. 164–6.
14. For interesting autobiographical accounts, see Red Notes, *Working Class Autonomy*, pp. 167–203.
15. E. Pasetto and G. Pupillo, 'Il gruppo "Potere Operaio" nelle lotte di Porto Marghera', *Classe*, 3, 1970, pp. 93–115.
16. E. Reyneri, 'Maggio Strisciante', pp. 84–92.
17. This account is drawn from L. Dolci and E. Reyneri, *Lotte operaie e sindacato*, vol. 3, pp. 23–48.
18. This account is drawn from L. Luppi and E. Reyneri, *Lotte operaie e sindacato*, vol. 1, pp. 115–44.
19. Ibid., pp. 31–52.
20. This account is drawn from I. Regalia and M. Regini, *Lotte operaie e sindacato*, vol. 4, pp. 25–58.

12

Pirelli: a case of permanent conflict

The period from autumn 1968 to the opening of the 'contract season' a year later has been described as one of structural crisis for the industrial relations system in Italy, and for the relationship between the unions and the mass of workers.[1] This crisis was most dramatically experienced at the Pirelli rubber factory in Milan, which was torn by disputes from September 1968 to December 1969, and at the Fiat plants in Turin, which were hit by wildcat disputes in April 1969. The emergence of the semi-skilled workers of the large factories of the manufacturing sector as a leading protagonist of industrial action, and the generalization of conflict to groups of workers previously little involved in disputes, like white-collar workers, radically transformed industrial and social conflict in Italy.

This chapter will focus on the conflict at the Pirelli company which became a *cause célèbre* in late 1968, and will be followed by a chapter on white-collar and technicians' struggles. However, it is necessary first to put these developments into a general political and economic context.

In the last quarter of 1968 and throughout 1969 output in the economy continued to increase, and new workers were taken on in large numbers. The multiplication of company agreements signalled an accentuation in the wage drift; at Alfa Romeo the number of agreements tripled in 1968.[2] At Sit Siemens the 130 agreements of 1968 rose to 250 in 1969.[3] In the face of this movement, the Confindustria and the government lacked coherent strategies of containment and control. The Confindustria adopted a line of maximum resistance, particularly with regard to incursions on management prerogatives, and called for government support in outlawing wildcat strikes. A traditional suspicion of unions, particularly of the communist-dominated CGIL, vitiated attempts to encourage them to discipline their memberships. The government, however, refused to enter the lists on the side of the employers. Throughout the industrial disputes of 1968–9 it tried to avoid partisanship. It tended to intervene in cases of deadlock in the private sector at the behest of the local authorities, or acted 'indirectly' through the managements of partly state-controlled companies. Its pluralist policy was outlined by Donat-Cattin in a debate on the Labour Charter (*Statuto dei Lavoratori*), which the Socialists in the government keenly supported;

> Our assessment of conflict must change. It is a physiological not pathological aspect of an economy undergoing continuous and accelerated change. Conflict must neither be repressed nor checked; rather it is a good thing that it is openly expressed. Although one should not deny the importance of preventing conflict, more emphasis should be given to its regulation by the parties concerned than to state coercion in the resolution of the differences leading to conflict.[4]

This statement of principle contained a recognition of the *de facto* freedom of collective bargaining won by workers on the shopfloor, and looked forward to an institutionalization of conflict underpinned by the legislative protection of trade unions. Furthermore, the attempts to form governments without Socialist Party support or participation failed, showing the difficulties of the Christian Democrats in obtaining a consensus for more right-wing policies. However, no new reforms were forthcoming from the Centre–Left government. Two general strikes were called by all three union confederations on 14 November 1968, and on 5 February 1969, before the government agreed to index-linked pensions. Without the traditional arm of deflation, government economic policies consisted of riding out the storm.

In the eyes of the majority of the population, the state remained unpopular. The stalemate of the May 1968 elections meant that there was no immediate prospect of new government policies. Then two police attacks on picket lines added to the history of bloodshed that stained labour relations in Italy. At Avola, a town in southern Italy, two farm-workers were killed by police during a demonstration on 2 December; at Battipaglia near Naples in the following April two more people were killed by police during a dispute over a factory closure. The response in the factories in the north was massive and immediate: workers took strike action and held protest meetings. The killings were interpreted as symptomatic of the state's repressive character and of the inherent violence of exploitation. In their aftermath the union confederations adopted the slogan 'Disarm the police'. Importantly, the PCI entered into full opposition to the government and consistently blamed the police for all outbreaks of violence during demonstrations and pickets.[5] Although at ministerial level the aim was to depoliticize labour disputes, at a local level prefects and police acted according to well-established precedents, and managements brought charges that by October 1968 involved a total of ten thousand workers and students.

It was in this setting of escalating political and social tension that industrial conflicts focused issues, linking generalized discontents to the particular disaffections of the workplace. The Pirelli rubber company became emblematic in this respect. Years of pent-up hostilities surfaced in a dispute which riveted local and national attention for months.

An Outline of Events

On 13 February 1968 the three union confederations and the Pirelli management signed a national contract for the rubber sector. The agreement, like those to follow in 1968–9, did not have the support of the mass of Pirelli workers and gave rise to further disputes on unresolved issues. The factories consequently became the sites of what came to be called 'permanent conflict' (*conflittualità permanente*). The causes of frustration and discontent on the shopfloor were similar in many respects to those that troubled the engineering sector, and the unions were similarly out of touch with shopfloor opinions. However, at the Pirelli works in Milan industrial conflict took new forms which set an important example to the movement of opposition in the workplaces.

Firstly, some workers at Pirelli organized an independent rank-and-file grouping calling itself a CUB (*Comitato Unitario di Base* – 'unitary base committee'), which was heralded nationally as a model of workers' autonomy; secondly, their 'output-reduction strikes' (*sciopero di rendimento* and *autoriduzione*), signalled a breakthrough in the invention of new forms of industrial action. These two phenomena will be looked at separately, but first it is necessary to place them in the context of the chronology of events and specific situation of the Pirelli company.

A key source of disaffection at Pirelli was the piece-rate system; 80 per cent of the eight thousand manual workers of the Bicocca factory in Milan did piece-work, and it was responsible for a large proportion of their wage packet. Incentives, combined with fines for bad work, were an important element in the Pirelli management strategy for controlling the workforce. Relatively high wages linked to productivity paved the way for the drastic reductions in the workforce in the postwar period. The number of employees fell from twenty-one thousand in 1948 to a low point of eight thousand employees in the late 1950s, when the company introduced automated and semi-automated labour processes. During the boom of the 'miracle years' young male semi-skilled workers were taken on to replace older, skilled workers. They were attracted by the wages and were recruited as part of a strategy to undermine what remained of a strong Communist and CGIL presence in the factory at Bicocca. They bore the brunt of the massive increases in workloads following even bigger orders for tyres, cables and rubber products coming from Fiat and the engineering industry.[6]

In the mid 1960s Pirelli had firmly established itself as an international company in the rubber sector, second only to Dunlop in the European market. After a slight fall due to the recession, by mid 1966 production had risen 15 per cent over the previous year. From 1964 increases in workloads, rather than investment in new machinery, was the chief means of raising productivity. One worker in the vulcanization section told a researcher that in 1964 he had had eight machines to tend, but as a result of rationalizations the number had increased to seventeen, and he had to produce 390 tyres instead of 15. From 1964 to 1968 production doubled using the same labour and machines.[7] However, because of a change in the payment system, profits rose but not wages. In 1964 Pirelli severed the link between production bonuses and productivity, and reduced piece-rates, by changing from an individual to a collective payment system. The company saved itself 50 *lire* an hour through the latter alone, and cut real wages by an overall 20 per cent.[8]

The agreement which sanctioned the changes in the payment system in 1964 was originally signed by the CISL and UIL alone, but the CGIL conceded the next year, in order to gain the benefits of the check-off system whereby the company deducted union dues directly from the wage packets.[9] This formal recognition of the unions was an aspect of Pirelli's much publicized 'enlightened' approach to industrial relations. Yet union membership for 1966–7 did not exceed 30 per cent of the workforce and management refused to allow shopfloor bargaining.[10]. For the most part, especially among the younger workers, the gap between the unions and the mass of workers widened rather than narrowed as a result of the contract. For the unions had *de facto* agreed to worse conditions and pay, and now had less need to keep in touch with the membership through the simple activity of dues collection. They had also agreed to a two-and-a-half year truce, which effectively postponed bargaining activity until the next contract was negotiated. The CISL and UIL welcomed the truce because they openly recognized the company's need to plan ahead on the basis of the maximum 'predetermination of variable factors such as the wage'. A lament in a CGIL factory report reveals the general distrust of the union among workers:

what's worse is that they haven't learnt that they're the union, and that the union isn't a boss to go to only in times of disputes.

An old militant when asked: 'Do you think that the union can grow?' replied: 'Yes, but only on the eve of the Revolution.'[11]

Although the strikes over the renewal of the contract in early 1968 involved almost all the manual workers and 70 per cent of white-collar workers, the contract that was eventually signed did not reflect this militancy. Instead of the requested three hours reduction in the working week, one hour was agreed to, along with a 5 per cent increase on basic wages. The question of piece-rates was left to 'further talks'. Workers were so angry over the piece-rates that they took industrial action spontaneously without reference to the unions. As was typical in the first phase of mobilization, it was a group of skilled workers who initiated action; the typography section struck in May for the re-establishment of the piece-rates they had had in 1952. For them, the primary concern was to increase wages. However, other workers who followed suit began to open up questions about the relation of piece-work to conditions of work as a whole.[12]

The first sections to take industrial action were those with the worst working conditions, like the tyre and vulcanization sections, which also had a high percentage of newly recruited, young, semi-skilled workers. They were exposed to health hazards such as fumes, skin diseases (eczema and others), exhaustion and nervous disorders resulting from the speeds of the production cycle.[13] Although workers demanded the elimination of poisonous fumes and the slowing-down of work speeds, the issue of the piece-rates was originally tackled in terms of improvements in pay. The action taken, however, implicitly undermined the function of piece-rates in regulating productivity. In the tyre and vulcanization sections before the August break, and then in eighteen sections following the holidays, workers implemented a co-ordinated reduction in output (*autoriduzione*). Without awaiting management permission, they worked at speeds that were less tiring. Whilst the effect on output and profits was considerable, the loss in earnings was relatively little; a 10 per cent reduction of production was costing the workers a mere 150 *lire* a day, the price of two cups of coffee.[14]

Autoriduzione quickly became the preferred form of action, but it was only an option for those on piece-work. Industrial action therefore included lightning strikes and general stoppages. A report in *L'Unità* described how workers decided on action:

> They are spontaneous strikes, decided on directly by the workers in each section during improvized meetings; these are held all over the place – in the canteen during meal-breaks, by the slot-machine, while having a smoke, or even in the street outside.[15]

Such spontaneous sectional stoppages had only happened once before at Pirelli in the previous twenty years. On that occasion, the management successfully defeated the workers by locking them out.[16]

In 1968, however, threats of fines and suspensions, and the attempted lockout in mid December, were counter-productive. The Pirelli management waged a propaganda war on the guerrilla action in the factories through the Assolombarda, the employers' association for Lombardy. A statement in October spoke of the intimidation of white-collar workers and complained more generally that:

this agitation [a group of workers in the tyre plant suddenly took industrial action, thereby stopping work in the plant as a whole] ... is contrary to every trade union practice and is carried out by inadmissable methods.[17]

Yet, far from discouraging workers, such pronouncements were taken as evidence of the effectiveness of their action and were treated as almost welcome publicity.

The Pirelli management took a hard line because it was a test-case in industrial confrontation. The company had an influential voice in the national and regional employers' associations and had a clear policy of maintaining 'management's right to manage'. As a result, the mobilizations at Pirelli took on symbolic significance for the workers' movement too. The pickets of the company office block, the so-called 'Pirellone', became scenes of mass solidarity involving the whole of the Milanese working class. The marches of the Pirelli workers created a particularly vivid image because of their distinctive white overalls, which contrasted with the *tute blu* of the engineering workers. The sheer din coming from the beating of milk cans (a practice started in the struggles of the early sixties), and from the echoing slogans transformed the atmosphere of the city centre. The continuous invasions of streets which had become the preserve of offices and shops, served as a reminder that the wealth was actually produced by some and consumed by others. One account of a march going down the fashionable via Monte Napoleone, which had shopwindows laden with expensive goods, speaks of a worker waving his empty food-box (*schiscetta*) and shouting: 'This is how Pirelli treats us'.

On 2 December 1968 the coincidence of the lockout at Pirelli, the killings of Avola, and the occupation of several schools, created an exceptional mood of tension and anger in Milan. The convergence of struggles around the question of management and state repression represented a moment of general mobilization and solidarity. There were twenty-minute stoppages to remember the dead in all the factories, thousands of posters covered the walls of the city, which became the 'theatre of impassioned demonstrations, marches and meetings, many of them entirely improvised'. The

Pirelli workers demonstrating outside the RAI-TV buildings with a banner calling for the disarming of the police, were joined by hundreds of students on strike.[18]

Under immense political pressure, Pirelli withdrew the lockout notices, and on 22 December agreed to raise payments for piece-work and to establish bargaining procedures in the event of disputes. The company recognized union representative responsible for negotiating piece-rates.[19] Although this marked the first step in allowing the unions a continuous presence on the shopfloor, whereas previously severe limits had been placed on their freedom of movement, the management wanted them to control not represent their membership.

Unfortunately for the Pirelli company the unions could no longer be relied on to channel and control rank-and-file discontent. They showed the same weaknesses resulting from hierarchism and inflexibility as their counterparts at Montedison in Porto Marghera. The CISL and UIL, which had been openly anti-Communist and 'collaborationist', experienced revolts against the old Cold War leaderships; while the CGIL had two-thirds of its branch leadership at Bicocca replaced between October and December, mainly by younger militants. Yet the new leaderships did not have a solid basis on the shopfloor. The desire to keep a centralized hold on decision-making power sprang from fear of shopfloor spontaneity and independent organization. The CUB, for example, represented a threat when it successfully outflanked the official organizations by promoting *autoriduzione*. In reply, the unions proposed factory branches to link the shopfloor and the company organization. But by the end of 1969 the CGIL branch only had about forty active members. The fact that it was a purely organizational proposal coming from above, and that it was based on union loyalty rather than on the common identity of the shopfloor made it a non-starter. The CGIL attacked *autoriduzione* and warned of the dangers of 'sectionalism' (*repartismo*) just at the moment that workers were coming together over shopfloor issues, and was forced to adopt this form of action officially.

The agreement of December 1968 therefore provided only a breathing space. Agitation broke out in some sections over grading and health hazards in early 1969. Workers carried out *autoriduzione* to keep down work speeds, and overtime was banned.[20] In March Pirelli produced what was labelled 'the mini-decree' (*decretone*) in an attempt to outmanoeuvre the unions. In return for six days continuous production a week, the company offered an immediate concession of a forty-hour week with staggered rest days. Women were to work on a part-time basis. The proposal, however, was turned down.[21] There was opposition to Saturday night working, which had previously been eliminated by workers who had simply refused to work that shift. A firm stand was taken against part-time working. This is of interest as one of the rare occasions on which the problem of women's work was directly addressed.

L'Unità reported a discussion with women workers. The journalist in question was careful to give their age and parental status, although the paper did not do so in the case of male workers. Antonietta, 'aged thirty-six and the mother of a child of six', was reported as saying:

> I don't work for pleasure, but because I have to contribute to the household budget, and to make sure that we don't just eat soup. Maybe 'part-time' work is what Pirelli's wife does.[22]

A CUB pamphlet dealing with the *decretone* reiterated this position and pointed out:

> The bosses present us with the problem upside down. Instead of improving women's conditions by providing full-time education, public canteens and nurseries, thereby enabling women to work without being exploited as they are now, they want them to work less and earn less.[23]

The pamphlet goes on to criticize the part-time working scheme as a halfway house to unemployment, and as a way of increasing exploitation during the four hours that would be worked. In its place, the CUB calls for a reduction in working hours for women, without a reduction in pay. Whilst it is interesting to note that the CUB analysis of women's oppression tentatively acknowledges the double nature of women's work, and the need to lessen their burden, its approach does not differ substantially from that of the trade unions and traditional Left parties. It starts from the premise that women should be responsible for housework rather than men, and says nothing about women's particular problems as waged workers.[24]

Whatever the limitations of the opposition to Pirelli's *decretone*, it nevertheless succeeded in defeating the management manoeuvre. Industrial conflict continued unabated. In May 1969 the unions launched a new campaign in response to further sectional stoppages, and to the harryings of the CUB, which called for large wage increases, the abolition of piece-work, parity between manual and white-collar workers, and a reduction in the number of grades. The unions' demands were much less radical. Above all they centred on the issue of union recognition on the shopfloor. However, the Pirelli management maintained its intransigent refusal to extend bargaining rights to the unions over questions of production, which were considered management prerogatives. The dispute continued into the Hot Autumn of 1969 when it became a focal point of Milanese mobilizations. However, before that time the experiences of the

CUB at Pirelli and the example of the *autoriduzione* struggles had become part of the patrimony of the workers' movement as a whole.

Autoriduzione

Autoriduzione – worker-controlled reduction in output – was a form of industrial action that captured the imagination of wide sections of activists on the shopfloor, in the Left, within the trade unions, and in the social movements more generally. Two contemporary accounts give some indication of the enthusiasm for *autoriduzione*:

> The reduction of work speeds is a masterpiece of consciousness (*auto-coscienza*) and technical ability. It is as if an orchestra had managed to play a difficult symphony harmoniously without the conductor and at a tempo agreed upon and regulated by the players of the single instruments.[25]

This is Aniello Coppola writing an article in *Rinascità* entitled 'Pirelli – a victory for workers' inventiveness'. He goes on to say that the feat is even more remarkable given the low educational qualifications and the number of immigrant workers involved. A second account, published a year later in the paper *Il Manifesto*, recorded how the factory

> functioned with the regularity of a clock, but the tick-tock is more spaced out in time; it has a slowness that exasperates the bosses, who protest about the 'irregularities' of this form of struggle. The workers, for their part, acquire consciousness of their power and learn to make the bosses dance to the rhythm of their music.[26]

Initially workers reduced output because it was an effective way of making the company pay without themselves incurring great losses. They turned an iniquitous piece-rate system to their advantage. *Autoriduzione* began 'spontaneously' in so far as the action was initiated in individual sections and without predefined plans or organization. However, as the above accounts underline, *autoriduzione* in an enormous plant like Pirelli's at Biococca required remarkable coordination and discipline. The militants of the CUB acted as a catalyst, but the extensive implementation of *autoriduzione* was only possible because of the network of unofficial representatives on each shopfloor. Many of these were drawn from the ranks of the CGIL, and PCI. One of the protagonists recalls:

> The comrades of the PCI worked day and night to connect one section in dispute with another. There was nothing spontaneous about it, except in the fantasies of distant observers.[27]

Autoriduzione began pragmatically as an effective form of action, but it was quickly invested with more general political and ideological meaning. When workers continued *autoriduzione* after the formal termination of industrial action, they enacted their demand for more human working conditions. It became an end in itself as well as a means to an end. In the words of the student movement it was an example of 'practising the objective'. The self-organization involved put in question the hierarchy of command in the factory. At Pirelli the foremen had exercised control by discouraging communication between groups of workers (especially between the older and younger workers), and by calculating piece-rates and recommending workers for promotion. When workers assumed direct responsibility for production speeds and built an intricate web of contacts between themselves they undermined the foremen's position. Similarly, this direct democracy with its informal delegate structure undercut the vertical and hierarchical structures of the unions. Direct action, moreover, cut out the need for outside organizational mediation, such as that provided by the union.[28]

The political significance of *autoriduzione* also owed something to its opponents, who denounced it as 'illegal and un-trade-unionist'. This 'illegality' was seen as a virtue by activists concerned to raise workers' consciousness. An interview with a worker member of the CISL at Pirelli stresses the positive aspects of these struggles against the organization of work in the factory:

> In my opinion sabotage always takes place in companies with a scientific organization of work, where they are liberatory acts, whether carried out by individuals or groups. The fact that workers develop harder-hitting forms of action against the bosses is a sign of their anti-legalism, and greater awareness of their situation.... The first serious fight over the speeds of the line was a major event .... Ultimately when the speed of assembly work was changed without the agreement of the workers, they just didn't do part of the work ... and that became routine.[29]

When *autoriduzione* was first implemented against Pirelli, there was conflict between its advocates, especially between the CUB and the unions. The latter clung to traditional strike action. During the autumn and winter of 1968 the unions changed their position and consented to *autoriduzione*, but disagreements remained about how and to what ends it should be carried out. The CUB saw it as a disruptive and 'anti-legalitarian' method of struggle which expressed the workers' total opposition to and estrangement from the capitalist system.[30] Meanwhile, radicals within the unions underlined the discipline and organization which it demanded of the workers. For left-wingers inside the PCI, and for PSIUP militants in particular, it prefigured workers' control of production in a socialist society. *Autoriduzione* showed that the workers themselves could do the managing. The use of the vivid imagery of orchestras and clocks to describe the Pirelli action contrasts with the CUB's stress on disruption. The workers' cool, calculated rationalism is counterposed to the confusion and petulance of the bosses.[31]

Which of these interpretations came closest to describing the Pirelli workers' consciousness and aspirations is difficult to say. Each, it seems reflected currents of opinion and attitudes within the workforce, although it should be said that the majority were less politicized than the activists. Participation in general strikes was low and the unions still managed to win majorities for their resolutions during general meetings.[32] The activists were therefore too optimistic in their expectations, but they nonetheless succeeded in making *autoriduzione* symbolic and significant for the workers' movement as a whole. Their example encouraged not only imitation but widespread reflection on creative and inventive methods of industrial action. In the first months of 1969 organizations of this kind sprang up in most of the cities of northern Italy, and in July 1969 they were able to hold a conference in Turin, which was attended by hundreds of workers and students. They were drawn together by a shared antagonism to the reformist politics of the unions and Left parties, and by the feeling that the time was ripe to create alternative organizations. There were considerable differences between the groupings about their methods of work and their relationships to the official labour movement, which surfaced during the autumn, but during the first heady months when the CUB at Pirelli was making the news, the spirit of unity prevailed.

The Pirelli CUB

The CUB at Pirelli was the best known and most influential experiment in workers' self-organization prior to the Hot Autumn. It has been broadly defined as follows:

> The CUBs were informal grassroots groups made up of workers and students. During the crisis of Italy's industrial relations system, when unions and parties were slow to respond to the new spirit of militancy, they took a leadership role in certain factories. They promoted workers' self-activity and gave expression to anti-capitalist feelings.[33]

The CUB at Pirelli was founded in February 1968, directly after the signing of the unsatisfactory national contract for the rubber sector workers. It began as an attack on that agreement. The CUB pressed for industrial action over piece-rates, health hazards and grading, and criticized the unions for their spinelessness. The nucleus of the CUB was composed by militants with considerable experience in the CGIL and left-wing parties. A report of March 1968 refers to its promoters as 'comrades with considerable influence among the workers. In their sections you can feel the unity among workers.... Their meetings, despite the semi-clandestinity, are far more crowded than those held by the unions'.[34]

Prior to the formation of the CUB at Pirelli there had been groupings set up to promote struggles in the workplace, outside and in defiance of the unions, as at Sit Siemens in 1966. However, they had been dissolved after the engineering contract struggles because of lack of support. In early 1968 conditions had changed. Firstly, spontaneous agitation in the factories proved durable rather than sporadic. Secondly, a generation of militants, encouraged by the student movement, saw the possibility of constructing independent organizations on the shopfloor. In Milan a current had formed within the CGIL which promoted 'round-table' discussions and an 'open letter' to militants on the need for action over workers' conditions (*condizione operaia*). It claimed that the unions were incapable of representing shopfloor opinion. This tendency, which identified with the reviews *La Sinistra* and *Falce e Martello*, organized the first meetings of the CUB at Pirelli.[35]

This CUB was very much a child of an orthodox left and trade-union experience. It was at home in a factory with a long political tradition. It came into existence because the unions overlooked the pressing pre-occupations of the mass of workers, whose health as well as wage packets had suffered from the intensification of work. However, the CUB originally saw its function as a pressure group on the union, and rejected ideas of forming an alternative union or of leaving the unions.[36]

The CUB's guiding principle was to 'start directly from the workers' conditions in the factory'.[37] In retrospect, this approach seems rather banal, but it was radical at the time, and reflected the influence of the *Quaderni Rossi*. Since the unions at Pirelli failed to consult the shopfloor and were more concerned with their ideological differences, basic grievances were left to fester. The CUB's first actions were simply designed to reactivate trade unionism. Its demands of June 1968 for the restoration of production bonuses tied to productivity and for increases in piece-rates, showed a respect for the traditional payment system. However, the CUB rapidly assumed more radical positions which challenged management despotism. It called for the total abolition of health hazards, including piece-work, the elimination of the lowest grades and equal wage increases for all workers. Whilst the unions accepted the existing framework governing workers' conditions in the factory and asked for compensation where health was endangered, the CUB started from the premise that workers' needs should determine how the production process was organized.[38]

At no time during 1968–9 did the CUB counter-proposals win majorities and defeat the unions' motions at general meetings. When it came to formal decision-making the workers were diffident about the radical alternatives, but over the two years it was these which dominated agendas. Moreover, workers willingly rebelled against agreements drawn up in their name by the unions, and resorted to forms of industrial action promoted by the CUB, although not always.[39] When in May 1968 it called for workers to follow the example of the Renault occupation in France, the message fell on deaf ears. It was more the product of fantasy, perhaps encouraged by the student participants in the CUB meetings, than a tactic related to the experience at Pirelli.[40] When the CUB propagandized *autoriduzione*, however, it had greater success. In particular its refusal to timetable stoppages or reductions in output made spontaneity the most democratic and incisive method of destroying the discipline imposed by management. The fame of the Pirelli CUB resulted from its remarkable success in making a science of wildcat actions and in promoting them, rather than in its theoretical or political formulations. The unions were forced to follow the CUB's lead to keep control of the situation in the factory. The *Corriere della Sera* reported in September 1969:

> It seems that the unions have despite everything, mounted the tiger – represented by a mere 200 wild activists out of a total of 12,000 workers – and that now they're trying desperately to check its stride.[41]

The fact that such a small minority could have such influence was a sign of the newfound combativity of workers, but also of its ability to interpret and give expression to the imagination of the shopfloor.

The project of the CUB at Pirelli was to construct a new form of political organization and practice. Although it occupied a vacuum left by the unions, its ambitions went beyond the horizons of unionism. According to the CUB the unions acted 'within the logic of the capitalist system by manipulating worker militancy and compressing it between the beginning and end of negotiations'.[42] In key respects the CUB was conceived as an alternative approach to political activity, which adopted some of the analyses popularized by the student movement. The CUB contained not only workers at Pirelli, but outsiders including students activists, several of whom came from the Catholic University. In the collection of documents published by the CUB in early 1969, the opening paragraph deals with worker–student unity:

> The CUB has forged a new kind of link ... from the purely instrumental one in which the students had a service function as the distributors of leaflets and members of the picket line. In the CUB students no longer have a subordinate role, but participate in the first person in the workers' political activity.[43]

Such continuous participation, it was stated, entailed a rejection of 'workerism' (according to which industrial workers were only revolutionary subjects). It surmounted the separation of the activities of the student and workers' movements, which was encouraged by the Communist Party and CGIL. By combining the students' time (for research, and so on) and mobility, and the workers' knowledge of the concrete situation, the CUB offered new possibilities for breaking down the artificial divisions between the social groups.

Another and more fundamental division that the CUB consciously set out to overcome was that between economic and political struggles. A CUB pamphlet stated:

> The economic struggle is fruitful only if it is against the general political plan of the bosses in the factory and in society. Political struggles cannot be separated from the economic struggles. It is workers' consciousness of their own interests and rights in the workplace that leads to general struggle in society, and vice versa.[44]

The CUB was seen to be a means of combining the political and economic struggles by focusing attention on the question of power within the factory. The conflict itself was thought to generate greater consciousness of the need to confront the system of exploitation as a whole. The stress put on violent and disruptive forms of industrial action stemmed from this concept of learning through conflict.

However, the political ambition of the majority of the CUB activists, to found a unitary communist practice in the everyday struggles of the shop-floor, was undermined by the appearance of ideological divisions, which it had originally been set up to overcome. Some attributed this development, which had disastrous consequences, to student influences. A group of Pirelli workers wrote retrospectively:

> In '68 when the slogan was 'workers' power' and 'the proletariat must rule', it is very strange and symptomatic that the student intervention in the factory, even though useful in some respects to the workers, hid the intention of ruling over the proletariat as soon as possible.[45]

Undoubtedly there is some truth in this assertion that outside intervention was to blame; the split in the CUB in June 1969 resulted directly from decisions taken by outsiders, especially by the political group Avanguardia Operaia, which aimed to make it into a 'school of communism' to train political cadres. However, there were factors that allowed the 'takeover' to take place.

The CUB never linked the general affirmations about the need to combine political and economic struggles to the specific issues in the factory. All its literature concentrated on the latter and no mention was made even of questions of education, despite the student involvement. The CUB's analysis of the unions, according to which they were incapable of renewal, made it unaware of its own role in stimulating that renewal. Above all, the assumption that industrial conflict automatically created revolutionary consciousness, and that the factory was the microcosm of the social order produced unwarranted hopes in swift social change. The CUB like the unions before them ignored many of the preoccupations of the mass of workers.

Notes

1. E. Reyneri, 'Maggio Strisciante', pp. 93–107.
2. Sandretti, p. 30.
3. I. Regalia and M. Regini, *Lotte operaie e sindicato*, vol. 4, p. 68.
4. Quoted by Tiziano Treu, 'Lo sciopero nello statuto dei diritti dei lavoratori' in A. Alessandrini, ed., *Conflittualità e aspetti normativi di lavoro*, Bologna 1978, p. 81.
5. For example, *L'Unità* (4 December 1968), the official paper of the PCI, reported that a demonstration by some 10,000 people in Milan over the Avola killings had been attacked by police 'with vicious charges, truncheon-attacks, tear-gas ... the police began a real rounding-up operation, arresting anyone whom they regarded as "suspicious" ... they were greeted by the shout: "Assassins! Assassins!" and by mock fascist salutes.'
6. Valentino Parlato, 'Rapporto sulla Pirelli', *Il Manifesto*, October–November 1969; Bolchini, p. 43; pp. 97–100.
7. Bolchini, pp. 1–29.
8. Gruppo di compagni del consiglio di fabbrica della Pirelli Bicocca, *Le Lotte alla Pirelli: 1968–72*, Milan 1972, p. 8.
9. Vito Basilico, 'Pirelli: un decennio di lotte viste da un protagonista' *Classe*, 12, 1976, pp. 278–9.
10. Bolchini, p. 184.
11. Ibid., p. 188.
12. G. Bianchi et al, *Grande impresa e conflitto industriale*, Rome 1970, pp. 79–82.
13. Bolchini, p. 48; Bianchi et al, *Grande impresa*, p. 74.
14. Bianchi et al, *Grande impresa*, pp. 82–5.
15. *L'Unità*, 20 September 1968.
16. M. Sclavi, *Lotta di classe e organizzazione operaia*, Milan 1974, p. 38.
17. *Corriere della Sera*, 11 October 1968.
18. *L'Unità*, 4 December 1968.
19. Sclavi, pp. 56–7.
20. Bianchi et al, *Grande impresa*, pp. 86–7.
21. V. Basilico, 'Pirelli', pp. 84–285.
22. *L'Unità*, 5 April 1969.
23. CUB–Pirelli–Lotta Continua leaflet, 4 June 1969.
24. Piero Bolchini, whose 1967 book on the Pirelli company identified many of the grievances which subsequently enflamed industrial relations, both recognizes the suffering of women workers, and sees it from the point of view of a male Leftist. He records an interview and comments on it: 'The woman worker, if she is young, aims above all to get married ... or she just looks forward to getting old quickly and having a pension ... It is a desperate situation that proposes escape through petty-bourgeois models of living ... only in very rare cases do women workers participate in the trade union, political and cultural life of the factory.' *La Pirelli*, pp. 49–50.

25. Aniello Coppola, 'Pirelli; una vittoria dell'inventività operaia', *Rinascita*, 20 December 1968.
26. V. Parlato, 'Rapporto sulla Pirelli'.
27. V. Basilico, 'Pirelli', p. 282.
28. M. Regini and E. Reyneri, *Lotte operaie e l'organizzazione del lavoro*, Padua 1971, pp. 31–5.
29. Ibid., p. 170.
30. CUB Pirelli, *Linea di massa – documenti della lotta di classe*, June–December 1968, p. 3.
31. See a comprehensive formulation of this approach in the work of the general secretary of the engineering workers section of the CGIL during the period – Bruno Trentin, *Da sfruttati a produttori*, Bari 1977.
32. Sclavi, pp. 53–4; p. 74.
33. G. Bianchi, *I CUB* Rome 1971, p. 11.
34. *La Sinistra*, 30 March 1968.
35. *La Sinistra*, 8–9 September, 1967.
36. Bianchi, *I CUB*, p. 42.
37. CUB Pirelli, *Linea di Massa*, p. 3.
38. Ibid., pp. 4–5; p. 20.
39. Bianchi, *I CUB*, pp. 46–50.
40. V. Basilico, 'Pirelli', p. 281.
41. *Corriere della Sera*, 5 October 1969.
42. CUB Pirelli, *Linea di massa*, p. 3.
43. Ibid., p. 2.
44. Ibid., p. 2.
45. Gruppo di compagni del consiglio di fabbrica, *Le lotte alla Pirelli*, p. 22.

13

technicians and clerical workers awake

On 8 April 1969 *L'Unità* reported the views of a Philips white-collar worker, one of a thousand who had come out on strike in support of a colleague sacked for attempting to form an Internal Commission:

> If they had sacked me before, I wouldn't have known what to do. The following day I would've looked for another job. After the first strikes and the mass meetings I've begun to understand that we've got rights and they can be defended.[1]

This sense of collective identity was slow to form among the office workers in Italy, but between the winter of 1968 and the spring of 1969 it took dramatic and tangible forms among those employed by the big industrial companies. The participation of white-collar workers in strikes and demonstrations alongside manual workers was itself a new phenomenon. Their autonomous mobilization and development of innovative forms of action and objectives seemed to signal the formation of a new collective identity.

In Italy discussion among Marxists, and in particular among sociologists of industrial relations, had focused on the semi-skilled worker (*operaio comune*). The emergence of the white-collar worker as social protagonist provoked a new debate.[2] Leaflets, articles and conference reports on the question proliferated. Their positions can be divided into two groups: there are those that saw the new white-collar workers (in particular the technicians) as the future makers of a socialist society, in the place of the industrial proletariat; and there are those who identified a progressive proletarianization and radicalization of the white-collar strata. The adequacy of these analyses is best judged by looking at the behaviour of the white-collar workers in the field of industrial relations.

Before and After '68

Before the mass mobilizations of 1968 the *impiegati* enjoyed privileges and a style of life which set them apart from manual workers, and which were sanctioned by the social superiority historically attributed to mental labour.[3] Management paternalism flourished in the offices long after it had been challenged in the factory. In return for the privileges of the monthly salary, sick pay and relative job security, white-collar workers tended to conform to management expectations. Traditionally the *impiegato* turned up for work in times of strikes, thus earning the hatred of other workers. Sometimes this would erupt in violence; a worker at Sit Siemens recalls how in 1967 hundreds of women workers, whistles in their mouths, invaded the offices and literally wheeled out office workers on their chairs.[4] White-collar workers did not think of themselves as members of the working class, nor were they regarded as such by the unions. The CISL encouraged their sense of 'corporate' identity, whilst the CGIL spoke of them as middle-class sectors with whom alliances had to be made. Both bargained and made separate agreements on behalf of their white-collar members.

In the 1960s there was a considerable change in the situation of the *impiegati*. In the engineering sector in the province of Milan they numbered twenty-eight thousand in 1968, and constituted over a quarter of those employed in industry as a whole.[5] The majority were clerical workers in the lowest grades. This change in the employment structure reflected the development of the tertiary sector, and the concentration of management offices in the city and province of Milan. The 'Pirellone', the modernist 1960s office-block of the Pirelli company, and the *centro direzionale* (management centre) near the Central Station, symbolized the changes in progress.

The growth in the number of the white-collar workers is significant in explaining their involvement in the industrial conflict. It is important to bear in mind that the increase in the demand for such employees by private companies and the state was less than the supply. The expansion of the education system and the new aspiration to avoid manual work resulted in the excess supply, which was one of the factors underlying the weakened position of the white-collar worker on the labour market. A survey of the largest firms for the period 1962–70 showed that, whilst skilled blue-collar workers' wages increased by 108 per cent, those of low grade white-collar workers' increased by 86.9 per cent. Although the technical institutes had more than made up for the shortage of technicians by the late 1960s, nonetheless a certain stickiness in the market helps explain the relative buoyancy of their wages, in comparison with those of clerical workers.[6]

In general terms, the expansion of the ranks of white-collar workers, especially in the low grades, and the erosion of their privileged economic position undermined some of the bases of the paternalist system of control. The changes created the conditions for a movement among these workers, but the positions of clerical and technical workers remained very different. Clerical workers and technicians had an unequal 'pull' on the labour market, and a different relation to the manual workers and to management; technicians had more contact with the shopfloor and more independence from management. Yet both groups lacked a tradition of unionism and a sub-culture of the workplace, like that of manual workers. In the late sixties they looked to manual workers and students for a lead.

White-Collar Workers 'Prove Themselves'

If white-collar workers were influenced by mass movements, it was not simply a question of imitation. The borrowing was selective, and certain features of their actions were specific to them as a grouping. They first took strike action because of their exclusion from the benefits accruing to workers from the company agreements won in the factory disputes of spring 1968.[7] At Fiat and Pirelli white-collar workers joined strikes. They reacted angrily to an erosion of differentials that in the past had been automatically restored. The first case of an independent strike was in June 1968 at the Falk steel works in the province of Milan. Clerical workers demanded shorter hours, longer holidays, and incentive payments in line with concessions made to the rest of the workers. There was almost total participation and pickets sometimes included two hundred strikers. The substantial wage concession won by the strikers in July set an example to other white-collar workers in the engineering industry.[8]

The exclusion of white-collar workers from agreements made with manual workers had important implications. Firstly, it signalled a shift in management strategy. The refusal to pass on concessions to white-collar workers meant managements were prepared to buy a truce at their expense and to strain traditional loyalties to breaking point. Management surprise in the face of the office rebellion suggests that they were counting on the passivity of these employees, but the resistance to their demands showed a readiness to suspend a long-standing alliance against the rest of the workforce. Secondly, the isolation of white-collar workers, on which management built its divide-and-rule tactics, sprang from their ambiguous and often estranged relations with blue-collar workers. The situation at the Borletti factory in the winter of 1968, when the majority of the shopfloor refused to support the white-collar strike, was typical; the standard answer to the requests for solidarity was: 'If they've never gone on strike for us, why should we do so for them.'[9] For the white-collar workers, therefore, there was an urgent need to redefine relations with management, with fellow workers, and with the unions.

The breakdown of paternalism was often lived out dramatically, since everyday shows of deference were called in question and managers knew the language of repression and arrogance better than that of conciliation and bargaining. At Borletti an article in the factory paper of the FIM–CISL maintained that differences between white- and blue-collar workers had become insignificant. It denounced the repression of the foremen, but also the haughtiness of management in general. It cited an incident in a lift when a manager waiting for a lift forced a woman secretary, who had said 'full', to get out and walk.[10] At Sit Siemens, a delegation of white-collar workers was brushed aside by a manager:

> Dr Leone, when he rejected our demands in toto had the manner of one saying: 'Go ahead anyway, go ahead. I know my hens; after a day or two nobody will remember this fight of yours'.[11]

Such incidents generated antagonism, especially among younger workers, who were angered by the arbitrary disregard shown by management. The call for the publication of merit awards was significant in this respect.

In the 1960s there had been a considerable extension of the use of merit awards, which were granted secretly, at management's discretion, to 'meritworthy' employees. Their function was to encourage cooperation with superiors and promote competitive and individualist behaviour. By subjecting the merit payment to public scrutiny workers thought that the allocation of the awards could be made accountable to themselves.[12] However, the call was not for their abolition, but for the application of 'objective criteria' via consultation. In the early stages of mobilization, the enemy was seen to be an old-fashioned and arbitrary despotism rather than the very process whereby people were assessed, labelled and allocated a position in a hierarchy.[13]

One of the common features of the movements of 1968–9 was their opposition to authority-figures: police, foremen, headmasters. In the offices, too, resentments and grievances were focused by acts of petty tyranny which would not have been socially acceptable outside the workplace. Clerical workers were no doubt influenced by the refusal of students and others to put up with authoritarianism, but they also proposed their own alternative models of democratic organization. In Milan, the most notable examples were at SNAM Progetti and Sit Siemens.

SNAM Progetti, a unit of ENI, a company which specialized in drilling design and design for the construction of oil refineries and chemical plants, was occupied in October 1968 by its 1,200 workers, most of whom were technicians. The occupation became a *cause célèbre* because of its political objectives and its self-organization. A commission for political relations, set up during the occupation, demanded the establishment of representative organs in the company with decision-making powers over political and economic questions. The general meeting (*assemblea*) was made into the basic unit of workplace democracy, bypassing the union. The SNAM workers demanded the right to study and training in order to reverse the process of de-skilling, which especially affected women who were usually in the lowest grade. They aimed to 'reconstruct workers' dignity and independence'. The SNAM experiment excited the interest of the radical wing of the CISL which was particularly sensitive to the themes of dehumanization and alienation at work. Moreover, contacts with the students of the technical and science faculty of the State University were regular.[14]

The struggle of the *impiegati* at Sit Siemens in Milan has been described as the most significant in the company in 1968.[15] The boom in the telecommunications sector had involved a growth of research and development and of administration; from 1960 to 1968 the number of technicians increased from 1,500 to 2,500, thereby making up 30 per cent of the workforce. The demands they made in November were similar to those at SNAM Progetti; they called for a 'human and anti-authoritarian way of working that enables the valorization of professional capacities'. However, the situation was very different at Sit Siemens in that the relationship between the white- and blue-collar workers was crucial to the balance of forces in the company. Despite eighty to ninety hours of strikes, levels of participation reaching 90 per cent, and a readiness to strike in the interests of other workers, the white-collar workers were defeated in March 1969 because of manual workers' refusal to support them. The latter accepted a separate deal offered by the management. The unions failed to elaborate a set of demands that unified the different sections of workers, but the major obstacle to unity was the manual workers' historic suspicion of people who had traditionally scabbed on them. However, the white-collar workers' struggles at Sit Siemens were important for the way they developed democratic structures independently of the unions.

In the special systems laboratory, workers used their work situation to increase their decision-making role. The technicians of the research team secretly continued with a project leading to a major technological breakthrough, despite management orders to stop the work. Ida Regalia writes:

This experience made the workers independent in the face of management, because their awareness of their own professionalism made traditional deference untenable.[16]

However, these technicians did not cultivate professional elitism. They organized themselves on the basis of open meetings and linked their work to general questions about how science was used in a capitalist society. Contacts were made with the student movement to discuss these issues.

The idea of democracy that was championed by the most radicalized white-collar workers owed much to the student movement, in its stress on active participation and the creation of grassroots organization. The general open meeting was the key structure of discussion and decision-making at both SNAM Progetti and Sit Siemens.[17] The commissions on specific problems (for example, women's conditions) and study groups set up by the white-collar workers, were also inspired by student models. At Sit Siemens the use of a questionnaire to find out about the wants and grievances of fellow workers not only prepared the ground for the formulation of demands, but stimulated awareness of problems. For example, the women workers' study group at Sit Siemens produced a document which discussed grading, the quality of work, wages, and the particular exploitation of women at work. It also pointed out:

> At the end of eight hours in the factory, women work at home (washing, ironing, sewing for the husband and children). They are therefore further exploited in the role of housewife and mother, without that being recognized as real work.[18]

Some white-collar workers cooperated closely with the student movement. The founders of the Sit Siemens study group, set up in March 1968, were members of the FIM, which had connections with Catholic student organizations, whose members participated in their discussions. Cultural and social affinity made for easy exchanges between the office/laboratory and university, while ex-students became Sit Siemens employees.[19] The meeting of two thousand striking white-collar workers in the occupied premises of the Liceo Vittorio Veneto in February 1969, was one of frequent symbolic celebrations of unity.[20]

White-collar workers also looked to the student movement for guidance because of their difficult and critical relationship to the trade unions. Diffidence towards the unions was felt both by those holding on to their 'staff' identities, and those disillusioned by the refusal of the shopfloor workers to help them out. The alternative bodies held more attractions than the unions, for the unpolitical as well as for radicals. Furthermore, the leading militants attacked the unions for being bureaucratic and undemocratic. However, study groups and open meetings renewed and radicalized the unions from below; they did not substitute them.

For a brief period the informal rank-and-file groupings had a lively influence over a wide spectrum of white-collar workers. However, with the decline of the student movement, the example set by the struggles of the semi-skilled workers of the large factories became dominant. Furthermore, the unions began to respond positively to the various practical and theoretical criticisms of their work.

The *impiegati* who refused to join strikes were often the targets of the so-called *spazzate* (sweepings), when groups of workers invaded the offices and drove out the staff. These multiplied in number in mid 1969 and during the Hot Autumn.[21] The attacks were usually 'educative' only in a punitive sense. For the angry young worker it was often 'a moment of total rebellion, an act of liberation that needed visible and tangible effects – doors knocked down, marches, shouting, clashes with the police ...'.[22] For the office workers they were terrifying baptisms of fire.[23] However, during the struggles of 1968–9 this form of action was even adopted by some white-collar workers. The mass picket, demonstrations in railway stations, 'articulated strikes' – all these actions typically undertaken by the blue-collar workers were learnt by their more 'respectable' colleagues.

The intensity of the industrial conflict reached its height in the spring of 1969 when the office-workers of the state sector engineering companies were all in dispute. At Borletti's the office workers proved themselves in the eyes of the other workers, who came out on strike in protest when one of them was arrested. Sectors of white-collar workers looked to the shopfloor for leadership. For many of them manual labour acquired positive connotations, and was identified with the socialist iconography of working-class heroism. Their adoption of egalitarian wage demands, such as lump sum increases, was another sign of their new attitudes.

The development of trust and cooperation between blue- and white-collar workers was a process fraught with difficulties and by no means irreversible. However, in 1969 there were remarkable steps forward in this direction. The white-collar workers' failure to extract major concessions from management by themselves, underlined their need for joint action with other workers. The unions, by the autumn of 1969, drew up demands for a new contract that involved all workers.[24] Union officials and representatives were often more sympathetic towards the white-collar workers than their blue-collar members. The FIM–CISL was especially open to new forms of organization at the grassroots.[25] The formation of delegate structures, the assertion of unions' independence from the political parties, and the unions' consultation of members' opinions – all these developments made the unions more attractive to white-collar workers. Some of them even took a leading role in the unions and won the support of manual workers. At Borletti's workers looked to a white-collar activist, who was 'very good in terms of dialectics', for leadership;[26] at Sit Siemens militant young workers were drawn by the radical ideas promoted by the study group which later became the 'manual and white-collar workers' group' (*Gruppo Operai-Impiegati*).[27]

The militancy of the white-collar workers in industry in 1968 was an important moment of recomposition for the Italian working class. Their struggles, along with that of the semi-skilled workers of the large factories, marked a turning point in industrial relations. The older paternalist system was put in crisis. Clerical workers and technicians expressed some demands of an almost utopian kind when they called for the restoration of skilled and participatory work. Yet these struggles remained relatively marginal in Italy – more so than in France where they were central to the movement for self-management (*autogestion*).[28]

The SNAM Progetti and the special systems laboratory of Sit Siemens in Milan experienced conflicts which raised some of the issues which Serge Mallet identified with the struggles of the new working class. In both instances there were rebellions against the logic of profitability in the name of a higher scientific rationality. The self-organization of work and the democratization of decision-making prefigured a form of society based on control of the work-situation. However, such struggles were exceptional and limited to the companies in question. Mallet's prediction that the technicians, because of their key role in the most advanced sectors of the economy, would make the demands for workers' control a bridge-head in the struggle for socialism was not verified by the events of '68–9. The majority of the demands of the white-collar workers did not substantially diverge from those of the semi-skilled manual workers,[29] who also demanded control over the labour process.

Mallet has been criticized for giving exclusive attention to the work situation of technicians and for his deterministic conception of how revolutionary consciousness developed out of their workplace struggles. Pizzorno has shown that the demand for control is not peculiar to this group of workers, and Low-Beer has shown the relevance of factors such as parental background, career-orientation and images of society in explaining the behaviour of white collar workers. Low-Beer's insistence of the importance of looking beyond the workplace is a salutary corrective in the predominance of *operaist* ideas in Italian studies. His conclusions do not diverge from the 'proletarianization thesis' according to which de-skilling has tended to assimilate most technicians' jobs to those of other workers. However, he also points to workers' lack of interest in their jobs, and their concern over problems of decision-making in society, which they tend to visualize in terms of power rather than status or money. This shift in focus to the 'relationship to the means of decision and control' and away from the 'relationship to the means of production', as Touraine insists, is the key to understanding the struggles which took up the themes first popularized by the student movement.[30]

Notes

1. *L'Unità*, 8 April 1968.
2 Low-Beer, *Protest and Participation*, pp. 1–23.
3. Marchetti, 'Impiegati', pp. 172–8.
4. Silvana Barbieri interview.
5. G. Barile, 'Classe operaia e mobilità sociale: Lombardia e area milanese', *Classe*, 12 June 1976, p. 114; see also *Quaderni di Sindacato Moderno*, 4, 1969, p. 308.
6. Low-Beer, p. 14.
7. Reyneri, 'Maggio strisciante', p. 89.
8. G. Carabelli, *Lotte operaie e sindacato*, vol. 5, p. 137.
9. Rina Barbieri interview.
10. *Dialogo Sindacale*, SAS FIM–CISL, Borletti, December 1968.
11. M. Cavallini, *Il terrorismo in fabbrica: interviste*, Rome 1978, p. 101.
12. *Quaderni di Sindacato Moderno*, 4, p. 259. For a penetrating analysis of how a manager's arbitrary and personal judgement is so effective in undermining subordinates' confidence in themselves, see Richard Sennett's work. He writes: 'The use of badges of ability or of sacrifices is to divert men from challenging the limits of their freedom by convincing them that they must first become legitimate, must achieve dignity on a class society's terms, in order to have the right to challenge the terms themselves.... Power in the organization ... knows about you, what you do not know yourself. The hierarchy's inability to make good on rewards is converted in this way back to a question of who is worth rewarding: the legitimacy of power ... survives only as the powerful can be so very personal'; *The Hidden Injuries of Class*, pp. 153–6.
13. Marchetti, 'Impiegati', pp. 184–5.
14. *Quaderni di Sindacato Moderno*, 4, pp. 16–43.
15. Ida Regalia, *Lotte operaie*, vol. 4, pp. 58–66.
16. Ibid., p. 59.
17. For the function of the 'general meeting' in the first stages of the workers' movement, see I. Regalia, 'Le assemblee', in *Quaderni di Rassegna Sindacale*, September–December 1975, p. 104.
18. Gruppo di operaie della Sit Siemens, *La donna nella fabbrica*, leaflet dated April 1969.
19. I. Regalia, *Lotte operaie*, vol. 4, p. 59.
20. *L'Unità*, 25 February 1969.
21. Marchetti, 'Impiegati', p. 185.
22. An interview with a worker at the Magneti Marelli heavy electrical engineering works in Milan; Cavallini, *Terrorismo in fabbrica*, p. 170.
23. Manual workers' violence towards office workers sometimes had strong sexual connotations. In some sense, all 'pen-pushing' jobs were regarded as not 'real work', not 'manly'. Women clerical workers were the target of overt sexual aggression and abuse. A Fiat worker recalls that during a picket the scabs were humiliated: 'We formed a cordon and the office workers started to come out. I remember that one was wearing a black jacket and that it was whitened by spit. They were made to walk along the human corridor and many were kicked in the backside. Terrible things happened ... workers put their hands under skirts and ripped off knickers ... one woman pissed out of fear.'; Extract from Domenico Norcia, 'Io garanito', in *L'Espresso*, December 1981. 'The commonest thing is to see the office workers running terrified between lines of workers under a rain of insults and spit. The relationship has been almost exclusively determined by worker violence'; *Lotta Continua*, 6 December 1986. Managers began to make their offices into fortresses; *L'Unità* reported that during a dispute at Sit Siemens in July 1969: 'The managers were careful not to leave their armour-plated rooms (the heavy steel doors, it seems, are bullet-proof).', *L'Unità*, 23 July 1969.
24. Marchetti, 'Impiegati', pp. 184–5.
25. Ibid., pp. 190–2; see also FIM–CISL, *Incontro Impiegati*, Clausone, 25–26 April, 1969; 'Documento della FIOM di Milano in preparazione della conferenza nazionale

tecnici e impiegati', *Quaderni di Sindacato Moderno*, 4, pp. 308–14.
26. Rina Barbieri interview.
27. Ida Regalia, *Lotte operaie*, vol. 4, p. 65.
28. Low-Beer, pp. 222–3.
29. Ibid., pp. 38–42.
30. Ibid., pp. 229–40.

14

the hot autumn: from Corso Traiano to Piazza Fontana

Great Expectations

By the autumn of 1969 a social movement composed largely of industrial workers, but also embracing other sections of the population, was already in an advanced stage of development. The movement was not new, in that industrial militancy had a history going back over a hundred years in Italy, but it involved workers who were new to industrial organization and action. The mood in the workplaces expressed the feeling that changes were in the air. It accorded with the process of 'transvaluation' described by Piven and Cloward, in which social disorganization and the traumas of everyday life are perceived as 'both wrong and subject to redress'.[1]

The role of the minority of experienced militants within the factories, and of agitators at the gates, has already been discussed in the case of the Pirelli and other struggles. Their success in promoting mobilization and the awakening of traditionally passive sectors like white-collar workers seemed to prove that something could be done about redressing the wrongs in society. This galvanized activists into feverish propagandizing and organizing. Sections of workers, especially the semi-skilled (*operaio comune*) of the engineering factories, started to move as a group and to organize themselves. Through the struggles of the Hot Autumn similar experiences to those of Antonio Antonuzzo were lived out by hundreds of thousands of people.[2] Individual awareness of and revolt against injustices fused into a collective movement.

Although the surge of rebellion grew out of the discontents and frustrations of everyday lives, these were not new. It required exceptional times to make them explicit and to give them a shape. The renewal of the engineering workers' contract in the autumn constituted such an occasion.

It involved over a million workers, many of whom had already shown their readiness to strike. In addition, the contracts of petrochemical and building workers were due for renewal, and the rubber sector was still in dispute. The anticipation of a great trial of strength between employers and workers focused national attention. Expectations ran high and gained legitimacy from authoritative definitions of the situation. The minister of labour, Donat Cattin, declared himself for change and against the inequalities symbolized by tax evasion:

> By the end of this autumn we shall all be changed people. A system that waves the Italian flag for the workers and the Swiss flag for the industrialists is not a healthy one.[3]

The press likewise predicted momentous events and coined the term 'Hot Autumn' which rapidly entered into popular currency. Its usage is of interest in illuminating the way the strike movement was defined from its onset.

24 Ore, the paper closely associated with Milanese industrialists, was the first to speak of the Hot Autumn (autunno caldo) in its issue of 21 August 1969. The idea probably came from references made in the United States to the time of the race riots as 'the long hot summer'. It was meant to foretell a season of industrial conflict, and the connotations for the readership were certainly meant to be negative. Without undue forcing, this particular metaphor can be seen as part of a genre in which industrial action, demonstrations and riots were described as 'volcanic explosions', 'sicknesses' and 'abnormalities', metaphors which proliferated in the conservative press during subsequent events. However, what is particularly interesting in this context is not these definitions themselves (which are part of the recurrent imagery with which ruling groups define insubordination),[4] but the way in which they were taken over and subverted by the social movement.

Voloshinov writes:

> each living ideological sign has two faces like Janus. Any current curse can become a word of praise, any current truth must sound to many other people as the greatest of lies.[5]

The Hot Autumn exemplifies this point. No sooner had it been pronounced than it was taken up by the movement to describe itself. L'Unità wrote:

> The autumn of the great contract struggles, the autumn that promises to be hot as one of the bosses' papers wrote today ... has already begun in Milan.[6]

During the industrial struggles the outbursts of the *Corriere della Sera* against 'illegal' forms of struggles, and laments on the state of the world were quoted with satisfaction by leaflets and papers circulating in the movement. The catastrophism and fears for the survival of civilization served, ironically, to heighten expectations of change.

Turin Events – Southerners Revolt

The workers' movement of 1968–9 was predominantly northern Italian; it had its centre of gravity in the cities of the industrial triangle. That is not to say that happenings in Porto Marghera or Valdagno were not of great importance in the history of the movement, but they remained isolated. For instance, Venice, the city nearest to Porto Marghera, was a centre of artisanal industry and tourism, with a population which, if anything, resented the very existence of the petrochemical plants. Even in the capital, Rome, the movement was relatively marginal to the life of the city, and had nothing like the impact of the student demonstrations and occupations of the previous year.[7] Further south the movement was weaker still.

In the south there were major struggles as at the steelworks at Bagnoli, an area of Naples, but they were isolated because of the absence of industry or its dispersal into small units, and because of the weakness of the unions and left-wing parties. The structure of social conflict was differently ordered.[8] Pre-industrial forms still had their pertinence. For example, in 1967 at Cutro in Calabria the peasants occupied the land and seized and burnt down the municipal buildings during their fight with the police.[9] In July 1970 the town of Reggio Calabria experienced a major insurrection lasting several days to protest against the transfer of the status of provincial capital.[10] When industrial organization and action did take place, it often faced the possibility of bloody repression rather than conciliation, as happened at Avola and Battipaglia.

The lack of industry in the south meant a lack of jobs, and the necessity of leaving home for the cities of the north – whether in Italy, Germany, or Switzerland. Another option was to enrol in the police or *carabinieri* in those cities (63 per cent of the *guardie della PS, Pubblica Sicurezza*, were southerners).[11] One of the consequences of this labour migration was to transfer the traditions of resistance of the southern proletariat to those cities, and by a cruel irony, to bring the migrant worker and the migrant policemen face to face in conflict.

Turin was a major pole of migration in the late sixties because of the expansion of the Fiat car works. In 1967 alone, with the opening of the Rivalta plant, no less than sixty thousand arrived in Turin. It was

responsible for employing fifty-six thousand in 1968, but the various ·
components firms and the whole local economy depended on Fiat. The
daily national paper *La Stampa*, printed in Turin, was controlled by the
company. In addition Fiat played a major role within the national
economy through the control of 72 per cent of the car market, and in its
capacity as a major exporter.[12] The migrant worker fitted into this scheme
of things as pure labour power; 'he was squeezed like a lemon in the
factory and marginalized in the city.'[13] A fictional autobiographical
account of a Fiat worker's experiences describes the medical tests and the
humiliation of being herded *en masse* into a room with bloodied cotton
strewn on the floor:

> it was not a question of choosing you, but a way of inculcating an idea of
> organization, subordination and discipline.[14]

It was but one of the aspects of the Fordist regime:

> On the production line it was not a question of learning anything, but of
> habituating the muscles. That is, habituating them under pressure to those
> movements, those speeds ... movements faster than the heartbeat ...
> operations that the muscles and the eye had to do by themselves, instantly,
> without the need to think at all.[15]

For many years migrant workers in Turin had had to put up with the
racist discrimination of landlords, the social difficulties and isolation of
the uprooted single man, and savage conditions of exploitation at work.
Yet the experience of social dislocation and poverty had tended to reduce
the capacity and will to resist, which, as studies have shown, depends on
'the workers with firmly established networks ... whilst the newly arrived,
whatever their anger, have great difficulty in forming effective organizations.'[16] It was therefore a necessary precondition to the generalized
revolts in the Fiat plants that the ice was broken in spring 1968 by skilled
workers, and that a workers' movement was already in an advanced stage
of development. The strikes called in protest at the killings at Avola and
Battipaglia, and the union's campaign of action against the 'wage zones',
which institutionalized lower rates of pay in the south, related directly to
the migrant workers.[17] However, in the case of Fiat, it was the students
and political activists who played a more important role than the unions
in providing the network of communications (leaflets, factory gate
presence, meetings in bars) which enabled workers simply to get to know
kindred spirits and to organize. Moreover, the students communicated the
idea of the larger movement in society.

In spring 1969 Fiat was hit by what Reyneri describes as 'a continuous guerrilla offensive'.[18] The demand for regrading whole sections set off a chain reaction so that the interdependence of the productive process operated to the advantage of collective action by workers. Fiat became the *locus classicus* of 'permanent conflict' along with Pirelli. Action stopped completely only for the period of the August holidays. Immediately on return the Mirafiori plant workers, independently of the union, put in a demand for a 1,000 *lire* pay rise. Fiat suspended seven thousand workers to make them all 'pay' for the disruption. The result of the showdown was that the union confederations brought forward the date for action for the renewal of the engineering sector contract. On 25 September fifty thousand engineering workers took part in a national demonstration.

Events at Fiat shook the provincial city of Turin like an earthquake. The student movement had created a cultural and social crisis in middle-class households; the workers' movement shook the very foundations of the social order.[19] In turn, Italian national life was deeply affected. Above all, the rebellion in its most radical forms expressed a refusal of 'industrial culture', of a work discipline that structured life both inside the factory and outside it.[20] Nanni Balestrini writes of this refusal:

> The thing which brought us together was our discovery that work was the only enemy, the only sickness ... the discovery that we all had the same needs and the same necessities.[21]

However, it was not only the Southerners' rejection of socialization into work discipline, but their adaptation of their own traditions and culture of resistance to the Turin situation that determined the forms of their revolt.[22] Thus, in July 1969 a trade-union demonstration over housing was transformed into riots and street battles with the police. Whilst it would be inaccurate to describe the quasi-insurrectionary action as 'southern', nevertheless the rapid resort to violent action and the attacks on the municipal buildings of the 'red areas' (*cintura rossa*) were part of a political repertoire more rooted in the south.

Inside the factories the workers' rebellion expressed a radical antagonism to the factory itself as an institution. In contrast to the Pirelli workers of Milan, the Fiat workers delighted more in disruption than in the autonomous regulation of production. Sabotage was endemic. Such incidents of the conflict have been described as manifestations of 'political primitivism', and as the first glimmerings of trade unionism.[23] A Fiat worker recalls that during the first internal marches there was an incident in which a worker from the south led his workmates, carrying the head of a rabbit stuck on a pole. The 'rabbit' (*coniglio*) was the 'scab'. It symbolized fear and cowardice, and also unmanliness.[24] Such theatrical manifestations of mass defiance certainly had little to do with the 'model' of 'modern unionism'. Moreover, in some respects the identification of the principal enemy in the scab or the foreman indicated a lack of what Gramsci called 'consciousness of the historical identity or exact limits of the adversary'.[25] However, there are gross inadequacies in analyses which dismiss such incidents as expressions of a primitive view of the world.

Approaches which posit an evolutionary development assume a progression from primitive and pre-political forms to modern political forms. Stages of development (often related to the formation of the nation-state or the rise of the market-economy) are said to mark the boundaries between them. Thus, within a Marxist view, utopian socialism and anarchism are stepping stones on the path leading to a scientific politics and party organization.[26] Or, within the perspective of a trade unionist, sabotage and wildcat strikes are often seen as regressive and primitive hangovers from an earlier point in union history. In the postwar period in Italy dominant versions of both Marxism and sociology accepted a model of progress and modernization (hence the endless debates about Italian backwardness).[27] Trade unions, and parties too, competed with one another to appear modern and future-oriented. In other words, much, though not all, of the cultural and ideological perspectives across the political spectrum, were ill-suited to make sense of the strange events in Turin. They were in no way prepared for what took place.

In contrast, there were political and cultural currents, which had grown in influence through the student movement, which welcomed, promoted and theorized primitivism. Or, rather, they maintained that the rebellion in the factories was anti-capitalist. Its very excesses and extremes of behaviour signified a fundamental rejection of the way of life and values of the society of the factory.

In part, this opinion sprang from a revival of revolutionary romanticism.[28] The rebel migrant worker symbolized suffering and resistance. He (it was never a she) was one of Fanon's 'damned of the earth' – outcast, exiled, oppressed and exploited. He embodied images and ideas which reverberated in the post-'68 political culture. But these had an added intensity because they connected up with a rich iconography within Italian culture. In particular, the migrant worker pricked the guilty conscience of the north towards the southerner.[29] He brought to mind films like Visconti's *Rocco and his Brothers*, and images of lonely men with cardboard boxes for suitcases who slept in railway stations. But he was also the fighter, the passionate rebel, and this was the hero who was feted by the young students at the factory gates. It was these positive images which were counterposed to the negative images of suffering and resignation which were associated with Catholic thinking. (Later this positive image appeared in the shape of 'Gasparazzo', a humorous but affectionate cartoon-strip in *Lotta Continua*.[30])

Enthusiasm for the factory rebellion also took more theorized forms. The *operaist* Marxist intellectuals, many of whom had done their apprenticeship in the *Quaderni Rossi*, greeted the Fiat workers' action as the practical correlative of their theories.[31] For them, it was not the migrant worker, but the 'mass worker' who was the embodiment of a new class subjectivity. This is worth noting because in the *operaist* theory the 'weak link in the capitalist chain' was where capitalism was most advanced and, seemingly, strongest; namely, in the modern factory and not in the Third World nor in the person of the poor peasant, the marginals and so on, as a more romantic vision would have it. For *operaisti* the Fiat workers' resort to violent and disruptive methods was not a sign of backwardness, but of their vanguard role. It showed their refusal of capitalist planning and waged labour.

> Above all [Taylorism] has completely and definitively estranged the worker from the content of his work; it has made him understand that the way to freedom lies not in the exaltation of 'productive labour', but in the final abolition of waged work.[32]

The demands raised by *operaisti* and taken up in the worker-student mass meetings during the Hot Autumn expressed a total disregard for normal forms of organization and mediation; the chants 'we want everything' and 'we are all delegates' could make no sense to the trade-union official or the party politician, but they were music to the ears of the *operaisti*.

It is too simplistic to divide the romantics from the *operaisti* even though they came from different cultural currents and milieux.[33] It is interesting to observe, rather, that the factory worker himself became a modern hero, and that the mass-production line had a spellbinding fascination for a new generation of intellectuals, students and others whose origins were not working class. Even if much of the language of *operaist* theory tended to be dry and abstract, it contained moments of poetic intoxication. For example, sabotage was frequently described as an act of joy and liberation. In *Lotta continua*, a paper launched during the Hot Autumn, *operaist* theory and revolutionary romanticism combined in celebrations of rebellion.[34]

The Turin events were of great importance to the development of the workers' movement because they took place in the heart of Italy's largest company.[35] In other words, they mattered politically and economically, and gave a sense of power to the movement in the first days of the engineering contract dispute. But the events need in turn to be related to their historical and cultural significance. Since the time of the factory council movement of 1919–20, workers' struggles at Fiat had been of great symbolic importance for the Italian Communist Party and the CGIL, and for communists of whatever persuasion. A mountain of literature, including, of course, studies in *Quaderni Rossi*, testifies to the interest not only of organizers, but of historians, sociologists and others in the Fiat case.[36] When, therefore, thousands of Fiat workers defied the directives of unions and parties alike and held mass meetings in conjunction with extremist students, their behaviour resonated throughout the political culture of the Left. It dramatically heightened expectations of radical change. In the words of Nanni Balestrini:

> By this point, something had become evident in these meetings; all the workers had the impression that this was a decisive phase in the conflict between us and the bosses.... In fact, frequent use was made of the word 'revolution'.[37]

The Turin events seemed to show that the workers' movement represented something far more radical than the unions and parties, and that, if other cities followed suit, the whole peninsula might be ready for revolutionary change.

Notes

1. Frances Piven and Richard Cloward, *Poor People's Movements*, p. 4, p. 14.
2. See part 1, chapter 3.
3. Sergio Turone, *Storia del sindacato*, p. 486.
4. It would be instructive to map the changes in the use of such metaphors. The metaphor of the 'body politick' and of its 'humours' dates back to the Middle Ages if not further. The continuities, at first sight, are more striking than the differences. For a brilliant essay on crowd-imagery, see Christopher Hill, 'The Many-Headed Monster in late Tudor and Early Stuart Political Thinking', in C.H. Carter, ed., *From the Renaissance to the Counter-Revolution*, London 1968.
5. Quoted by Charles Woolfson, 'The Semiotics of Working-Class Speech' *Working Papers in Cultural Studies*, 9, 1976, p. 170.
6. *L'Unità*, 21 August 1969.
7. Rome was, and is, a city of service industries and government offices. Industry employs relatively few people, and the engineering sector, which was so central in 1968–9, had no companies of the order of Fiat, Alfa Romeo or Sit Siemens.
8. Percy Allum, *Politics and Society in Postwar Naples*, Cambridge 1973, pp. 89–119, pp. 250–61.
9. This incident was an isolated example of a form of struggle which was widespread in nineteenth century Italy before wage struggles prevailed; see Federico Bozzini, *Il Furto Campestre – una forma di lotta di massa*, Milan 1977. It is interesting to note, however, that Renato Curcio, future founder of the Red Brigades, drove down to Cutro immediately and wrote a report of events. For him, Cutro was not the spurt of dying embers but the flame of a proletarian tradition that had to be revived; see Alessandro Silj, *Mai più senza fucile*, pp. 61–3.
10. There was considerable controversy at the time as to whether the revolt was Fascist-led and organized, or a popular insurrection. Whatever the validity of their analyses, there were those who saw the southern revolt as something to be emulated in the north. Far

from being backward struggles, they were greeted as the vanguard; see Luigi Bobbio, *Lotta Continua*, pp. 90–3.

11. *Lotta Continua*, 11 December 1970.
12. G. Guidi, A. Bronzino and L. Germanetta, *Fiat: struttura aziendale e organizzazione dello sfruttamento*, Milan 1974, pp. 17–31.
13. This phrase was a commonplace among a vivid range of images and metaphors used to describe life at Fiat; these include 'monsters', 'infernos', 'labyrinths', 'nightmares'; for example, see M. Cavallini, *Il terrorismo in fabbrica*, p. 29.
14. Nanni Balestrini, *Vogliamo tutto*, Milan 1974, p. 53.
15. Ibid., p. 60.
16. Edward Shorter and Charles Tilly, *Strikes in France*, pp. 272–3.
17. See V. Foa, *Lotte operaie e sindacato*, pp. 171–3.
18. E. Reyneri, 'Comportamento di classe', p. 860.
19. The dramatic effect of these movements on everyday life in Turin was all the greater because of the provincialism and conservatism of the city, in contrast to Milan which was better able to absorb changes.
20. For a fuller analysis of this refusal based on study of the making of the English working class, see E.P. Thompson, 'Time, Work-Discipline and Industrial Capitalism', *Past and Present*, 38, 1967. Thompson's writing stresses that conflicts were to do with values and 'ways of life', and were not reducible to narrow conceptions of the economic struggles.
21. N. Ballestrini, *Vogliamo tutto*, p. 98.
22. Vittorio Foa draws attention to the 'unevennesses' and 'contradictions' in the development of the industrial proletariat: 'There is no linear tendency whereby a proletarian culture progressively adapts to the waged work ethic; the proletariat carries within itself many elements of its autonomous historical culture – peasant and artisan – which appear merely to be extreme defences against bourgeois culture, or nostalgia for a vanished past. Yet, instead, they are weapons of attack with which to overturn capitalism'; Vittorio Foa, 'Il sindacato di fronte alla transizione', *Problemi del Socialismo*, 5, 1977, p. 155.
23. M. Cavallini, *Il terrorismo in fabbrica*, p. 47.
24. A limited, but much referred to, group of animals figured in the language of the movements. Apart from 'rabbits', 'pigs' and 'guard dogs', which played a major role, the 'tiger' was often 'ridden'. The Chinese love of calling enemies by animal names only partly explains this recrudescence of animal imagery. The 'mole', of course, was a great favourite.
25. A. Gramsci, *Prison Notebooks*, p. 273. This anthropomorphism took a more sinister and systematic form in terrorist discourses and action; see part IV, chapter 19, pp. 287–8.
26. This conception is at the heart of Gramsci's writings, which echo his struggles to 'nationalize' an Italian political culture that he saw as backward and provincial; A. Gramsci, *Prison Notebooks*, London 1971, pp. 125–205. For a sophisticated historical account of this kind, see Eric Hobsbawm, *Primitive Rebels*, Manchester 1959. This was translated in 1966 and became an influential book in Italy. Much cruder applications of Engels' model abound. For a critique of this model of history writing in Italy, see Federico Bozzini and Maurizio Carbognin, *Perchè parlare di storia*, mimeographed.
27. Diana Pinto has written of the 'modernization' model as 'the dream that failed to materialize . . . there were "cracks" in the model well before the international economic crisis of the 1970s. Nowhere . . . more analytically visible than in Italy'. But in the 1950s and 1960s its tenets, namely a quasi-mechanistic emphasis on economic growth and a structural-functionalist outlook, were hegemonic. 'An archaeology (à la Foucault) of the term "modernization" would shed light on the essence of our postwar period'; D. Pinto, ed., *Introduction to Contemporary Italian Sociology*, pp. 4–5.
28. This notion needs to be made historical. The connection of revolution and romanticism goes back to the early nineteenth century, but the Risorgimento, especially as represented by Giuseppe Garibaldi, gave rise to a specifically Italian tradition. In 1968, however, it was an international and European phenomenon. The figure

of Che Guevara was emblematic, see John Berger's essay, 'Che Guevara' in J. Berger, *Selected Essays and Articles*, London 1972.

29. The 'myth' of the south has been periodically rediscovered. For example, the earthquake of 1980 brought it back to the centre of Italian consciousness. Gabriella Gribaudi outlines the dominant themes: 'On the one side, there is the tear-jerking image of a south which is peasant, archaic, immobile and solidaristic; on the other, there is its antithesis – a south which is lawless, where people kill each other in the struggle over scarce resources'. These pictures of the south say more about the dominant culture than about the realities they claim to depict. See Gabriella Gribaudi, 'Terremoti', in *Ombre Rosse*, 33, March 1981, pp. 5–10. Images of the immigrant worker echoed this polarization. But there has also been the growth of a literature in which he recounts his experiences, and puts the northern industrial culture into a critical light, for example the writings of Balestrini and Antonuzzo. Furthermore, there have been attempts to speak through the migrant worker, to dig at the racist foundation of Western European culture. See John Berger and Jean Mohr, *A Seventh Man*, London 1975 – a book which is the product of these changes. It must be remembered, however, that the southern worker was still an Italian. His position was therefore very different to the immigrant workers in Germany or France; 'International migrants do not have the nationality of the receiving area. They lack civil rights and are at a serious legal disadvantage.... They have different cultural backgrounds, social values, and customs.... Moreover, internal migrants generally have the same language as the receiving population (despite differences in dialect)'; S. Castles and G. Kosack, *Immigrant Workers and Class Structure in W. Europe*, Oxford 1973, p. 10.
30. Roberto Zamarin, *Gasparazzo – ovvero la nobile arte di fare l'operaio*, Milan 1980.
31. For reflections on this intellectual journey of the 1960s, see Toni Negri, *Pipe-line*, Turin 1983, pp. 85–129.
32. *Lotta Continua*, 6 December 1969.
33. These grew out of the splits in the reviews of the mid sixties; see part I, chapter 3.
34. See, for example, the language of the revolutionary Left press; Patrizia Violi, *I giornali dell'estrema sinistra*.
35. For an account of the Agnelli family's role in Italian history, see Valerio Castronovo, *Giovanni Agnelli*, Turin 1977.
36. Interpretations of the movement's history often took the form of polemics in which the orthodoxy upheld by Communist Party historians was subjected to attack. The *operaist* theorists did not, however, claim the birthright of the past (for example, by showing that the Gramsci of the factory councils was 'real' and 'revolutionary' unlike the Gramsci whom the Party presented to the world). They counterposed the 'productivist' skilled workers' Communism of the early twentieth century, when workers' control entailed greater and more efficient production, to the refusal of waged labour by the modern mass worker. In other words, for the *operaisti* contemporary Fiat workers were rebelling not only against the factory system, but against the productivist politics of the PCI and trade unions; for a 'popularized' version of these ideas, see *Lotta Continua*, 6 December 1969; for a sophisticated theorization, see Sergio Bologna, 'Class composition and the theory of the party at the origin of the workers councils movement', CSE Pamphlet No. 1, *The Labour Process and Class Strategies*, London 1976.
37. Balestrini, *Vogliamo tutto*, p. 106; Balestrini's book has as its title a famous slogan of the movement – 'we want everything'. This fictional autobiography of his journey from the south to the Fiat factories is interesting also as an example of a genre which was an ideal vehicle for revolutionary romanticism. Balestrini made literature and poetry out of the mass worker's experiences. See Pierre Laroche, 'La classe ouvrière dans le roman italien', *Le Monde Diplomatique*, December 1974, p. 31; and M. Caesar and P. Hainsworth, *Writers and Society in Contemporary Italy*, Leamington Spa, 1984, pp. 29–30.

15

the hot autumn in Milan

The Turin events overshadowed developments of the workers' movement elsewhere in Italy from the spring to October 1969. Attention then focused again on Milan because of continued conflict at Pirelli and because of street clashes between demonstrators and police in early November, which drew the state more openly into the industrial disputes. The contract season and the year ended, finally, under the dark shadow of the Piazza Fontana bombing in Milan. These events will be dealt with in turn in the following chapters, along with an analysis of the engineering workers' contract struggle.

Pirelli under Siege

L'Unità announced a 'hot autumn for bosses': 'A massive strike has stopped Pirelli – 11,000 in struggle ... picket-lines include technicians, clerical workers, young workers and women.... A scene which recalls those at the Fiat gates'.[1] A dispute had been simmering since May over questions of union rights – the recognition of elected delegates, a factory council with paid time off, mass meetings in works time. This made the dispute of vital symbolic importance since one of the primary objectives of the unions engaged in all the contract disputes was to win full recognition within the factories. Pirelli was a test case – the company was represented in the highest echelons of the Confindustria. The popular slogan of the moment *'Agnelli, Pirelli – ladri gemelli'* (Agnelli, Pirelli – twin thieves) linked the different struggles against the captains of industry. The fierceness of Pirelli's and other companies' resistance proved much greater on issues of authority than on economic concessions.

The resort by Pirelli workers to their by now well-established tactics of sporadic sectional stoppages met with a company response that increased the stakes, which in turn provoked a radicalization of the conflict. On 23 September Pirelli imported tyres from its Greek subsidiary; the same day lorry-loads of the tyres were set alight and the management declared a lockout, denouncing 'vandalism ... illegitimate forms of agitation ... violence and the threat of violence against persons'.[2] The union confederations in the province of Milan called a one-hour general strike, and the Pirelli workers began *autoriduzione* by 45 per cent. Although the lockout was revoked, a leading militant was sacked for his part in disruptive action. There was a spontaneous strike and a demonstration in which the worker was carried back into the factory. *L'Unità* commented on the 'degree of tension' that could cause such 'unplanned action', while the *Corriere della Sera* horrified its readers with accounts of 'Chinese' subversion, provoking some workers into carrying placards with the words: 'We are not Chinese'.[3]

The Pirelli workers, in a sense, forced the population of Milan to take sides. The city itself became the stage on which the conflict was fought out; massive demonstrations involving up to fifty thousand, and workers' road-blocks were joined by delegations from hundreds of factories and by thousands of students. Milan's everyday life was at a standstill. *L'Unità* wrote:

> The rising fever of union agitation has given the Milanese another day of ferment. Articulated strikes, demonstrations, improvized meetings and road blocks, have transformed the city and its hard-working surroundings into a cauldron of the labour conflicts that have come to a head this 'Hot Autumn'.[4]

For *L'Unità* the sight was impressive for the degree of organization shown by the workers and for their 'coolness and intelligence' in the face of police provocation. The existence of the CUB was not mentioned, nor were most unofficial actions. The sabotage of the tyres was attributed to the activity of *agents provocateurs*. By contrast the *Corriere della Sera* played up the most disturbing elements of the conflict. What seems clear, however, is that the Pirelli workers enjoyed considerable support, to the point that even the Christian Democrat Party federation in Milan condemned the lockout.[5] A protagonist's account of the siege of the Pirelli headquarters gives a vivid picture of how workers rallied to support their fellows:

> The blocking of the Pirelli skyscraper for three days and nights ... meant stopping the brain of an international operation which could not afford to be cut off from the rest of the world for so long.... The participation was enthusiastic, and even included white-collar workers. Thousands took part ...

lorry-drivers gave lifts as did the municipal buses. On this occasion (by way of establishing a tradition) public transport was used without payment ... you simply said 'Pirelli will pay'.[6]

The dangerous escalation of the dispute prompted the intercession of Donat Cattin, the minister of labour, and the signing of an agreement on 14 November which conceded the main demands made by the unions.

Engineering Workers in Milan

The Hot Autumn in the engineering industry in Milan did not have the dramatic and ruptural impact it had in Turin. It was the largest sector of industry but small and medium-sized companies predominated. No single company compared to Fiat in size. In the Milanese engineering industry skilled workers engaged in machine-tool production rather than the semi-skilled assembly workers formed the backbone of the labour force. Moreover, a relatively high percentage were unionized.[7] Even Alfa Romeo, which employed nearly fourteen thousand workers, many of whom were from the south, did not undergo a Hot Autumn similar to Fiat's. In 1966 there were serious riots starting in the Alfa Romeo factory at Arese, but the combination of the firm grip of the unions and the subtler approach of the state-appointed management prevented their repetition.[8]

The struggles of engineering workers in Milan were less radical than those in Turin, and the size and complexity of the city enabled it to absorb the shocks more easily. Nonetheless, they raised demands, and developed forms of organization and action which made them expressions of a social movement. Fundamental questions about the 'social contract' as well as about the industrial contract were opened up. These will be examined under the headings: 'Demands', 'Actions' and 'Organization'.

The Movement's Demands

In preparation for the autumn campaign for the renewal of the engineering contract, the unions launched a massive 'consultation' with workers before drawing up the platform of demands. The level of participation and debate exceeded expectations and, in turn, generated new ones. Meetings in July turned into occasions for freely airing grievances, and took place whilst company disputes were still in full swing. L'Unità reported that there was a 'decisive rejection of the long working day and of heavy workloads', and that the majority of workers favoured lump-sum wage increases, in preference to traditional percentage increases.[9] The lump-sum increase was therefore incorporated into the platform, despite opposition by some officials.

The final list of demands included as its main items: equal wage rises for all; a forty-hour week within three years; progress towards manual–clerical worker parity; the elimination of differentials for those under twenty; union rights inside the factories. The package as a whole represented a considerable challenge since it aimed to make up the loss of earnings in the mid to late sixties, and to end decades of unilateral management in the workplace. Moreover, they were demands with which the workers identified and which were open to control from below, unlike some of the more technical demands.[10]

The demands formulated in the platform and the demands arising in the movement of the Hot Autumn should not, however, be treated as synonymous. Fully to understand the movement's demands it is necessary to look at their informal manifestations in slogans and graffiti, leaflets and papers, and in the whole panoply of demonstrations and strikes. Above all, workers said what they wanted to one another, directly. Unfortunately, studies have tended to concentrate on the formal demands (and those written down), while the language of ordinary workers is neither listened to nor analysed. Certain logics are ascribed to the workings of the movement, which are not explored in relation to the richness of the protagonists' experiences.[11]

The gap between the approach and objectives of the union organizations and the workers on the shopfloor can be seen in the case of Borletti, where a workers' inquiry into the conditions of women workers was carried out in June–July '69. It gives a picture of their preoccupations, as shown by an alternative form of consultation from below, initiated by the factory CUB. The idea of the workers' inquiry was inspired by writings in *Quaderni Rossi*. It was simple enough; workers, it was maintained, knew much more about their workplace than all the parliamentary commissions and experts put together; instead of waiting to be consulted, they should do some research, make known their finding and organize around a set of concrete demands arising from them.[12] These were then framed within a general political perspective; for example, the Borletti CUB report stated:

> To see and understand at first hand what our real working conditions are, to understand how all this is the logical and inevitable consequence of an entire system – this is the first step in becoming conscious of the need to organize and struggle against it.[13]

The inquiry, based on 150 interviews, came up with data on the unskilled nature of women's work (23 per cent learned their job in less than half an hour, 77 per cent in less than a day), and the lowness of wages (83 per cent averaged 70,000 *lire*, whilst the average rent at the time was estimated to be 30–40,000 *lire*). But more importantly, the work situation was related to the personal lives of the workers. 60 per cent of the women workers declared difficulties in making friendships at work ('there's too little time to talk'), whilst for almost half of them between one and two hours a day were spent travelling to and from the factory. The tensions resulting from work were shown to damage physical health; the majority complain of constipation, headaches, breathing and heart problems that had arisen since starting work at Borletti. Furthermore 'a good 90 per cent of women say that they are habitually agitated, sad and irritated', and that this was especially felt through irregular periods and unsatisfactory sex life.[14]

The process of this counter-consultation at Borletti heightened awareness and stimulated demands that the union platform excluded; the opposition to piece-rates sprang from a feeling that they divided workers, and that they encouraged productivity at the expense of health; the demand for the abolition of the lowest grades reflected the discontent of women workers who were systematically paid less than men who did the same work, but none of whom were in the lowest grades.[15] Moreover, the debate and discussion opened up by the workers' inquiry stimulated general awareness of life-problems in relation to work. An article written soon after the Hot Autumn entitled: 'Spontaneous Reflections of a Woman Worker', is full of anger:

> those who do overtime . . . often say there is nothing to life but work. This just shows how thoroughly we have been brutalized by the bosses.

Such is the nature of 'this disgusting society' (*questo schifo di società*).[16]

The movement at Borletti, on the evidence of the leaflets and papers of both the unions and the CUB, made demands speaking as workers rather than as women. Women workers were especially concerned about working conditions. They were among those (migrant workers being another group), who suffered the worst consequences of speed-ups, increased workloads and systematic de-skilling of tasks, which were officially sanctioned by systems of grading and payment.

The vehemency of their demands on these issues emerged in 1969. At the end of April women in the upholstery shop at Alfa Romeo struck for parity, regrading and individual payment of piece-rates.[17] And at Pirelli women were especially combative because they were the main losers from the piece-rate system. It is notable, however, that the demands for the new contract showed no connection with the women's demands for genuine parity in place of the formal parity which the unions had won in 1960.[18]

The gap between the formal demands of the Confederal platform and the informal demands on the shopfloor was most evident in relation to groups of unskilled workers (and in particular migrants and women, and also younger workers). Their grievances tended to be specific and localized, and were therefore difficult to integrate into a general platform. They came into conflict with management over problems of work organization (line speeds, and so on) and authoritarianism. Direct action rather than negotiation through the unions offered immediate and effective redress. Actions were made to speak louder than words, and words were not softly spoken.

Guido Viale described the new modes of self-expression as the 'cultural revolution in Italian factories'; for him, actions such as the burning of Pirelli's Greek tyres were:

> a liberating act consciously and collectively decided upon ... the same is happening in the posters, the writings and carvings which are filling the factories; it began in the lavatories, canteens and dressing-rooms, and now they are also found on the shopfloor and in the offices, done under the very eyes of the foremen.... Workers are learning to put to creative use the instruments of their oppression ... in many factories they are using the foremen's telephones to communicate and organize struggles.[19]

At Borletti and in other factories *dazibao* were attached to the walls, in the manner of the Chinese Cultural Revolution popularized in Italy by the student movement; workers wrote up comments as they wished. Outside every factory the walls became red with spray-paint. Outside a Sit Siemens plant, by the gate, was written: 'Liberty finishes here'.[20] Among the great mass of workers there was a tremendous desire to talk about general issues, about politics in the broadest sense, a desire to have a say, to communicate their feelings to the world and also to listen – a situation that is perhaps only created at the highpoints of popular movements.

The demonstration was the main occasion on which workers addressed the world and shouted their demands in unison. During the Hot Autumn, marches criss-crossed Milan almost every day. They were important moments for the expression of a collective sense of identity. Aldo Marchetti writes:

> Above all, it was perhaps the only moment when the 'working class' effectively appeared *en masse* as one, indivisible and equal. Inside the factory there existed differences of grade, status and pay, in right of access to places and in the language spoken; in the street all that seemed to disappear. The 'working class in struggle' marched through the city as a homogeneous mass and whoever entered its ranks was absorbed.[21]

In this period of mass agitation the differences between union members was of little significance. 'A spirit of solidarity and brotherhood bound everyone together.' It was an experience that was often intensely felt. A description of participating in a workers' demonstration written at a later date by Nanni Balestrini gives a vivid picture of this:

> It is a hot feeling of having sweat all over the body, like a hot bath of pleasure; I am very relaxed and at the same time on fire.... There are tens of thousands of people; it is impossible to count them all. I feel my body involved to its very core, just as when responding to a high-pitched note.[22]

This evocation presents a particular romantic, even sexual vision of the demonstration. Demonstrations also contained an important element of play and theatre. Aldo Marchetti notes that demonstrations bore resemblances to the traditional carnival:

> From the carnival was taken the use of allegorical floats, using lorries decked out in various ways.... Often they carried puppets of bosses and government ministers hanging from the gallows, and these were burnt at the factory gates at the end of the march.... As in a carnival, the demonstration created a sense of the world being turned upside down; for a day or a morning roles were reversed, and the workers became masters of their own time, of the city streets, the business-centre, and of themselves.[23]

And, of course, the demonstration was also an occasion when men and women met and mixed together. The public event created spaces for private encounters.[24]

The demonstration was a form of symbolic communication. The linked arms, the orderly ranks and the often regular step of the demonstrators (and, of course, the very effect of having thousands of people in the streets) projected an image of power with military connotations. This desire to communicate and to count is evident in the chanting of slogans and singing of songs which made demonstrations noisy occasions. It seemed at times as if a thunderstorm was breaking over the city. Often it was not what was being shouted that mattered, but the shouting. Yet slogans also condensed basic demands and produced a sense of direction.

A list of slogans put together by the Sit Siemens factory council for use on demonstrations, gives a fairly representative sample of what trade union activists regarded as popular and appropriate:[25]

Agnelli, Pirelli – ladri gemelli (Agnelli, Pirelli – thieves, the pair of them)

Operai – più sfruttati, padroni ben pagati (Workers more exploited, bosses better off)

Siamo – stanchi – di pagare – tutti – vizi – dei padroni (We are tired of paying for all the bosses' vices)

Mille – miliardi – d'evasioni – questa è la legge dei padroni (Thousands and millions of tax evasions – this is the bosses' law)

La vita – col cottimo – è un calvario – l'affitto – è un furto – sul salario (Life on the piece-rate is a Calvary, rent is theft out of the wage-packet)

The notion of injustice and the sense of moral outrage is strongly present in the slogans, and this accords with some of Barrington Moore's observations on what, historically and cross-culturally, has most often provoked popular protest.[26] It is not so much the fact of inequality and exploitation that anger the lower classes, as what are seen as excesses. The key to understanding this is the 'social contract' which, in Barrington Moore's words, is arrived at by

> continuous probing on the part of rulers and subjects to find out what they can get away with, to test and discover the limits of obedience and disobedience.... The more stable the society, the narrower the range within which this takes place.[27]

It is what is *perceived* as the breaching of the contract which engenders outrage. Such is the case when the law-makers (bosses) break the laws (evade taxes, or, in the case of politicians, take bribes); or, when the money of the workers is spent on luxurious living by idlers, parasites and bloodsuckers; or, when the hard-won wages are 'stolen' in rents. Another slogan popular during the Hot Autumn sums up the feeling of gross injustice: '*ci sfruttano, ci ammazzano, ci sbattono in galera – e questa la chiamano libertà*' (they exploit us, kill us and throw us in prison, and they call it freedom).

The 'contract' that was seen to be flouted was not a formal set of articles. It was, rather, an invisible set of codes governing acceptable behaviour and underpinning the reciprocity of the relationship between rulers and ruled. This helps to explain the strong note of moralism in slogans of condemnation. This also had roots in a morality with an established place in the workers' movement since its inception (note the Proudhonian ring to the slogan: 'rent is theft'), but which was expressed with a new vigour and spontaneity in the Hot Autumn. The dignity of the worker is even lent religious undertones (for example the piece-rate as the 'Calvary' of the worker), by contrast with the moral degradation of the corrupt and inhuman bosses. Wealth is not acceptable, especially if it is flaunted; this was made clear in a letter, addressed by workers of some

Milanese factories to the mayor, in which they told him that the opening night at La Scala:

> will be offensive to the workers if, with the struggle of the engineering workers under way, the traditional ostentation and show of wealth and luxury take place.

The workers threatened a mass picket if it went ahead.[28]

The slogans so far considered should, however, be supplemented by others which were more extreme, and which were not promoted by the trade unions but came from the shopfloor or from revolutionary groups. Examples of these are given by Marchetti:

Tutto il potere – agli operai (All power to the workers)

Più soldi – meno lavoro (More money – less work)

Lo stato dei padroni – si abbatte e non si cambia (The bosses' state is for smashing not changing)

Cosa volete? Tutto. Quando? Subito (What do you want? Everything. When do you want it? Now)

Siamo tutti delegati (We are all delegates)

Marchetti comments that these slogans are striking for their simplicity; they express non-negotiable demands, and evoke a utopia – a world without bosses; they demand immediate gratification.[29]

During the Hot Autumn the shout 'Contract. Contract,' became more and more insistent. It was the simple demand that all the unions' claims should be met. But that call, when shouted in unison by hundreds of thousands of demonstrators, was invested with hopes and expectations of radical social change. And there were slogans which expressed a desire not just for an improvement in the terms of 'social contract' (or its real application), but for a new order of things. The fears and anxieties voiced by the press were more concerned with the range of the testing of the 'limits of obedience and disobedience', than with the engineering contract itself. The challenges to authority, not only in the factories, but in the schools and streets of the cities, seemed to many observers to be going beyond the acceptable realms of carnival.

Strange Strikes

As has been mentioned, strikes were already in progress – or erupting – at Fiat and other companies before the campaign of action was officially launched by the union confederations in September. There was a strike movement in being which arose independently of the unions. The unions then stepped in to programme the industrial action. Firstly, the number of hours of strikes per week were allocated centrally, and each workplace was left free to use them as it saw fit. Secondly, some strikes were coordinated on a geographical basis (by zone, by city and by province, and nationally) in the public and private sectors, or on an industry basis or across industries. This strategy enabled the unions to calibrate the action according to the amount of pressure they wanted to exert, and to deploy the forces of the movement. Thus, as the winter drew on, the action was escalated, and particular pressure was applied, first to the public, and then to the private sectors of the engineering industry.

In Milan there were remarkable possibilities for 'articulating' industrial action by zones, since these often had strong identities historically, which, since 1968, had been strengthened by extensive contacts between factories.[30] It was particularly important given the dispersal of small units. Thus, the small La Crouset components factory, which employed mainly migrant women, became heavily dependent on the Sempione zone for support in its difficult fight against repressive paternalism. In November, the 220,000 workers of the chemical sector in Milan, who were also in dispute over their contract, joined the engineering workers for a day of strikes. However, apart from solidarity action around Pirelli, there was little coordination across industries, although this was called for on the shopfloor. More common was the strike by a whole industry in the province; for example, one hundred thousand engineering workers struck simultaneously on 7 October. The main focus of action, however, was in the various factories where the enthusiasm for strike action often meant that the union quotas of hours were exceeded.

L'Unità reported that during the first four weeks of action in Milan three hundred thousand workers, on average, were in dispute each day.[31] The proliferation of action provoked the Corriere della Sera into introducing a 'calendar of agitation' to guide the readers through the turmoil. At the end of 1969 the resulting total of hours lost in the engineering sector in Milan province was 71,181,182 (96 per cent of which were due to strikes over the new contract).[32]

The statistics on the number of hours lost due to strikes give some idea of the scale of industrial action. However, they only show the tip of the iceberg; the incidence of absenteeism, and forms of non-collaboration which restricted the planned use of labour-power do not appear in the statistics.[33] During the Hot Autumn, the decisive battles were fought 'informally'; the engineering workers took action to control and regulate their working conditions by controlling the speeds of the line, piece-rates, job-assignment, health and safety, mobility, job and wage structure, limits to disciplinary measures, restructuring and regulation of hours as in shift-working and overtime. These questions had traditionally been the almost exclusive prerogative of management in Italian industry, but in the late sixties there was a state of war along what Carter Goodrich referred to as the 'frontier of control'.[34]

The metaphor of 'war' is recurrent in contemporary descriptions of industrial conflict.[35] People spoke not so much about the 'two sides of industry' (a formulation that suggests dependence as well as difference), as about two opposing camps. Nor was it a war, it seems, which was always conducted according to set rules prescribing the use of certain weapons and laying down codes of behaviour.[36] As a popular slogan put it; 'The factory is our Vietnam'; guerilla warfare provided the model for worker 'insurgents', even if managements wanted to stick to the existing rules. A leaflet from the Borletti CUB of October 1969 is of particular interest in this respect. It opens with a quotation from the president of the Confindustria on hiccup strikes:

> these forms of action that cost the industrialists a lot and the workers nothing are illegal. It is useless to come to agreements between generals [the unions and the employers] if subsequently the troops [the working class] do not respect them.[37]

The leaflet goes on to draw some conclusions; namely, that the power of this weapon is borne out by the employers' opposition to it; workers should use whatever means of struggle necessary since 'it is their sacrosanct RIGHT' – 'the only criteria are the interests of the working class'; the 'legality of which they speak is their legality, the same one that allows our exploitation'. There then follows a list of possible actions: the articulation of strikes by shifts and sections, autoreduction ('Pirelli teaches us'), pickets of the RAI Television, and non-payment of television licences.

The strikes were acted out in a multiplicity of performances. They involved not simply the withdrawal of labour power, but the active assertion of workers' power within the factories. A whole repertoire of disruptive tactics was developed according to the labour process, composition of the workforce and its traditions of struggle, the nature of labour relations and other variables.

Great pleasure was derived from what were called 'articulated strikes' (*scioperi articolati*), such as the hiccup strike, which the Confindustria complained against so bitterly. The 'chequer-board strike' was a favourite during the Hot Autumn. The factory was divided up into groups who went on strike for brief periods at different times usually by section or shift.[38] Sometimes formulas were concocted whereby workers with names beginning A to L went on strike, followed later by those at the other end of the alphabet. Whilst the workers amused themselves the production plan fell apart in the hands of frustrated managers. Rina Barbieri refers to workers' feeling of freedom:

> it was enough that you struck for half an hour in the morning and the same in the evening to make the mechanism break down. When you strike, you go around as pleased as punch and you can't be stopped.... When you are busy with a 'chequer-board' action not even the gatekeepers manage to understand the comings-and-goings.... The damage to the bosses was enormous, unlike in the case of pre-organized strikes of previous years.... It was the expression of mass creativity and inventiveness.[39]

This form of struggle was especially popular in mass production factories, like Sit Siemens and Alfa Romeo, which were heavily dependent on the routine cooperation of the workers.[40] Moreover, at Sit Siemens certain sections had played the role of winning gains that were then generalized throughout the plants, so that 'shop' identities were effectively mobilized through articulated action.

No strike action is reducible to purely economic motivation. The strike action undertaken by a movement, such as that of the Hot Autumn, is particularly difficult to interpret in terms of monetary calculation. The arithmetic of the articulated strikes expressed what Giorgio Bocca called the desire to punish a guilty capitalism.[41] The industrial action tended to be expressive rather than instrumental; it was not so much geared to the attainment of precise demands, as functional to the formation of a new collective identity with its stronghold in the workplace. Some of the forms of action achieved this by 'actualizing the objective'; for instance, workers met freely together and moved around the factory when they wanted. The workplace was turned into a place for socializing and making friendships. But before this was possible, it was necessary to break the power of the foreman and disrupt the mechanisms which divided workers.

The role of the foremen varied in the different engineering factories, but it was relatively important in Italy because of management's tenacious grip on its prerogatives. He (for it was very rarely a woman) usually allocated overtime, supervised work, recommended transfers for the troublemakers and promotion for the diligent. The foreman was the immediate enemy on the front-line of the 'frontier of control', and the embodiment of authoritarian and patriarchal rule. Breaking the power of the foreman was often a crucial symbolic moment – a moment which recurs in workers' autobiographies.

Most of the incidences of violence during the Hot Autumn involved foremen. At Fiat the 'red handkerchiefs' (for such were the masks worn by the workers in question) formed a sort of punishment squad which beat up hated foremen or chained them to railings.[42] In Milan episodes of what was called 'proletarian violence' figured less prominently. Mostly it was a case of 'hard picketing'. At Sit Siemens the personnel manager, Ravalico, was chased by workers after he had attacked a woman worker. It required exceptional circumstances to provoke this sort of response, but when such incidents occurred they pushed issues of principle to the fore. A leaflet commented:

> If a worker in a nervous state slaps someone in authority or breaks a window, he risks being sacked. If a manager does the same, nothing happens. All those on the side of the bosses stand up for legality and call chasing scabs (*caccia ai crumiri*) violence.[43]

The violence, of which the foremen were often the victims, represented highpoints of conflict when war was symbolically enacted. Michèle Perrot's observations about strikes in France in the nineteenth century apply to the Italian events:

> Born roughly, suddenly and brutally in the rush of emotion, anger and desire, the strike retains, in part, the whiplash of the primitive wildcat walkout. This spontaneity, which weakens its instrumental consequences, guarantees its expressive richness.[44]

The crisis in the authority of the foreman was also brought about by means other than physical coercion. Physical coercion took place where unions were weakest and managements most jealous of their powers. At Borletti the combination of verbal abuse, humiliations and ribaldry on the part of the workers, on the one hand, and the withdrawal of full management support on the other, drove some foremen to reason 'well, I don't care, I do the best I can'.[45] In a celebrated though isolated case at IBM a foreman denounced his own job as 'supervising exploitation', and his sacking by management provoked a solidarity strike by other workers.[46]

Above all, the crisis in the role of the foremen was the symptom of the crisis of a form of paternalistic management, induced by the collective struggles that culminated in the Hot Autumn. The mechanisms whereby that authority was wielded were challenged and undermined. The remarkable unity created during the Hot Autumn, between skilled and unskilled, workers from different regions, and between men and women workers, made the selective use of rewards and punishments counter-productive. It tended to provoke calls for mass regrading, parity or solidarity against victimization. It was now difficult to give orders from above. Factories ceased to be kingdoms ruled by despots, whether enlightened or not, while the subjects established their rights with a hundred and one informal acts of resistance.

Democracy in the Workplace

During the Hot Autumn the principal organizations of the workers' movement were the trade unions. These played a crucial role in each phase of the mobilizations, and especially in the closing period when they monopolized negotiations over the contract. (This role will be examined in chapter 16). However, before the Hot Autumn, the unions were weakly implanted on the shopfloor, and the vacuum in workers' organization was filled by remarkable experiments in democracy from below. The examples of Pirelli and Fiat were the most visible instances of a wave of democratic self-organization which spread not only in the workplaces, but in the educational institutions, housing estates and in the city generally. Whilst the student movement opened up political experimentation and debate, the workers' movement seemed to offer better possibilities for bringing about changes. It had great power. Strikes, it had been shown, could shake the economy and governments. But workers also developed autonomous organizations which aspired to a more democratic and egalitarian model of society.

Throughout the Hot Autumn the number of groupings of militant activists such as the CUB and the 'worker–student groups' increased. In Turin the worker–student mass meetings dominated the scene. These were regular open meetings in which several thousands participated. In Milan CUBs were set up, following the Pirelli example, at ATM (the municipal transport company), Borletti and Innocenti, where they exerted considerable influence. By contrast with the Turin meetings, the CUBs were tight-knit nuclei of experienced activists. Their role was significant, not so much for proposing or prefiguring a model of self-organization, as for stimulating it. They were at their most influential during the early stages of mobilization, as at Pirelli. Crucially, they helped put workers in touch with the ideas and protagonists of the student movement. However, when the workers' movement launched its strike waves during the Hot Autumn, mass participation and the emergence of a new stratum of leaders from the shopfloor diminished the importance of the pioneers.[47]

The meeting (*assemblea*) in a factory was the first form of workers' democracy to take shape during the mobilizations of 1968–9. It became a regular event in the majority of engineering factories during the Hot

Autumn. It was the product and conquest of the movement. It was a product in as far as a high degree of mutual trust among workers, a sense of common purpose, and a rapid and effective informal network of communication was the precondition for holding meetings. This entailed breaking agreements limiting the mobility of workers in the factory, and defying the foremen. It was a conquest in that workers established the *de facto* 'right' to hold meetings, or, to put it in the terminology of the moment, they 'actuated the objective', before it was negotiated by the unions or conceded by the management. The characteristics of the meetings reflected this process.

Firstly, they took place in the workplace during work-hours, thereby enabling maximum participation. Secondly, they involved all workers, irrespective of union membership. Thirdly, there were moments of open discussion and free exchange of information. And lastly, and most significantly, they had a predominantly decision-making function, and were regarded as the sovereign body in the factory.[48] It was through these meetings that demands were discussed and final agreements voted on, but their main function during the strikes was to decide on the forms of action to be taken; the chequerboard strike, for instance, required considerable coordination based on a detailed knowledge of the labour processes of a section. However, discussion was not necessarily limited to practicalities in a narrow sense. Questions of mental and physical health were related to the labour process, especially through the contributions of the CUB and other groupings. Furthermore, general political issues were discussed; in November 1969, for example, numerous meetings dealt with repression and the police. Instead of being closed off and isolated, the factory was related in discussion to the everyday lives of workers and the problems of society as a whole.

During strikes and meetings, representatives emerged to make up informal leaderships responsible to the *assemblea*. Although there was nothing by way of statutes, the delegate was elected directly by all workers in a section, and could be removed by them. In the summer of 1969 the unions proposed the formation of strike committees to carry on the industrial action, but the proposal was in many cases merely a ratification of an existing practice.[49]

Delegates were elected in the first instance to organize strikes. Workers, who had proved themselves in action by standing up to the foreman, and who commanded the respect of their immediate fellows, made up a 'natural', often charismatic leadership.[50] They owed their positions to force of personality, political acumen, speaking skills and so on, rather than to the fact of being in a particular party or union. They depended on 'spontaneous' support, which could be revoked at any meeting of the section or factory.

A factory delegate during the Hot Autumn strikes was a shuttlecock of frenetic activity. She or he sacrificed a private for a public life, and sought individual satisfaction in collective activities (if, that is, the pressures did not become too great). In their language 'I' was displaced by 'we'.[51] Delegates resisted the separation from other workers which the logics of trade-union organization entailed. Moreover, widespread participation in meetings and strikes made it difficult for leaders to act independently of their constituencies.

The delegates of the Hot Autumn did not spring up from nowhere. The ground had been prepared by the work of independent agitators, and by the encouragement of unions interested in establishing themselves inside the workplaces. However, a new generation of worker representatives had come into being. They tended to be young men, many of whom were semi-skilled or unskilled. Their industrial experience was the product of the 1968–9 mobilizations. These delegates were very different from the older, mainly skilled, and politically affiliated trade unionists who dominated the internal commissions.[52] (Except, that is, for the fact that men still tended to become the leaders even in factories with large numbers of women workers, although there were some signs of change.[53]) This change in social composition corrected the gross disparity which had developed between the representatives and represented within the modern factory.

The election of new representatives meant that the problems of the *operaio comune* were put at the top of the agenda at meetings, and that there was a representative on the spot to deal with grievances over line-speeds or undermanning. The delegates had been elected during the Hot Autumn not to fight a single battle but to lead the everyday skirmishes along the 'frontier of control'. Moreover, the grassroots democratic structures seemed to many to represent the first step on the path to a new conception of democracy within society as a whole. The sight of workers, who previously had been invisible and unheard, debating politics in factories, *piazze* and even universities, inspired visions of a new order in which such a phenomenon would be an everyday occurrence.

The student movement had already popularized notions of direct democracy, but had not been able to create durable structures. The workers' movement had proved more successful. Moreover, it represented the force which in the past had founded soviets and workers' councils. In 1968–9 there was a massive revival of council-communist ideas, which in Italy were historically associated with the Turin movement of 1919–20 and with Gramsci's *Ordine Nuovo* writings.[54] Il Manifesto, the group which was expelled from the PCI in November 1969, was perhaps the most articulate representative of this revival, arguing for a communism in which the factory councils would be the means of struggling for and creating a democracy of producers. This was seen as an alternative to the party-state model which had been Lenin's legacy to the international Communist movement. For Il Manifesto the grassroots democracy of the students' and workers' movements showed that in the complex societies of the West it was feasible and desirable to create more pluralist forms of representation.[55]

The utopia envisaged by Il Manifesto and by other council-communists did touch on the popular utopianism of the times. And the factory democracy of the Hot Autumn embodied aspirations which went beyond those of trade-union organizers. It affirmed values of community, encouraged freedoms of opinion, and gave practical shape to people's desire to 'count' and be respected.[56] However, the ideas of workers' democracy were highly problematic.

Firstly, it was one thing for workers to organize themselves democratically; it was something quite different to propose that workers organize the capitalist labour process democratically. What the skilled worker could do in 1919 could not be repeated by the worker on the mass-production line.[57] Secondly, most models of workers' control assumed that how people organized in the factory could be generalized to the rest of society. Furthermore, they assumed that it was the place where not only goods but society's most significant ideas and values were produced.[58] If the workers' movement tended to confirm this factory-centred view of society (which was also male-centred), it was perhaps a sign of its limitations.[59]

November–December 1969: Blood in the Streets

The workers' movement of 1968–9 had its greatest impact within the factories, but also aimed to change society as a whole. In other words, it was political. In November in Milan its political aspects were increasingly apparent. Two demonstrations ended in violent street fighting. Industrial conflict was framed more and more in terms of 'law and order' in the speeches of politicians and the reports of the media. The sense of a 'state of war' in the factories was translated to society as a whole. There was a shift from a moral panic, in which 'extremists' were identified as the 'troublemakers', to a general panic about social order, in which violence was identified as the symptom of a more widespread malaise.[60]

According to accounts coming from accredited spokesmen, violence was no longer just caused by a minority (*cinesi*, 'extremists', the CUB, etc.); rather, the very intensity of industrial and social conflict was conductive to an escalation of violence. The trade unions and Communist Party were accused of promoting illegality by harbouring its perpetrators. For conservative forces, it was from the social movements themselves that society had to be saved. In the closing weeks of 1969 they made a concerted effort to lay the blame for society's ills on industrial militancy and social unrest, prophesying that worse was to come if action was not taken, and calling for firm steps to re-establish law and order. In the words of a senior official of the ministry of the interior, reported by *Panorama* in July 1969:

> It would be enough at this time if during a demonstration some policeman was killed and if some firearm appeared among the demonstrators. The situation could precipitate in a matter of hours. It would be up to the government and the head of state to declare a state of emergency. That's just what has happened, in point of fact, in some American federal states over the past months.[61]

The first demonstration involving violent clashes between police and demonstrators was held on 6 November in Corso Sempione in Milan, in protest against the RAI television and radio reporting of industrial conflict. Placards were carried saying: 'RAI – the bosses' voice'. A union leaflet called for the checking by union leaders of all transmissions concerning labour relations, and weekly programmes dealing with labour conditions. Several workers from large engineering works were arrested and imprisoned, provoking pickets of solidarity from their factories outside the prefecture of police. *L'Unità* reported that the following day the unions held meetings in all the factories and demanded the disarming of the police. The police were judged to be the guilty party. For the *Corriere della Sera*, by contrast, the fault lay with a 'fanatical minority extraneous to the workers' movement' which was responsible for the 'new explosion of violence'.[62] The second demonstration took place on 18 November; via Larga turned into a battleground between police and demonstrators in the wake of a national general strike for housing reforms. In the turmoil a young policeman from the south, Antonio Annarumma, was killed. *L'Unità* again blamed the police; 'The responsibility for the incident lies entirely with the police authorities.' The crowd was described as 'serious, composed and responsible', the police as 'savage'.[63] It reported similar reactions in the factories; at Sit Siemens seven thousand were said to have voted for the resignation of the minister of the interior, the release of all the arrested and a total ban on police presence at demonstrations.[64]

Annarumma's death provided conservative forces with the opportunity to mobilize the 'silent majority'. The *Corriere della Sera* reported that his funeral was attended by 30–50,000 people and that Milan shops pulled down their shutters, the classic gesture of shopkeeper protest. Its headline on 20 November read: 'A young man has died for our liberty.' On the following day, at a public meeting on law and order in Rome, the Prime Minister, Rumor, was reported as saying, 'Liberty is our most precious asset and we must defend it day in day out'.[65] In the populist discourse of the Right, the southern and humble origins of the dead policeman were counterposed to the comfortable middle-class background of the student agitators (the *figli di papa*) held responsible for the violence. The *Corriere della Sera* spoke of the crowd of 'extremists, Marxist–Leninists, pro-Chinese elements, youth of the student movement, extremist fringes and guerrillas'; for *Il Giorno* it was composed of: 'students, anarchists and ML'; *La Notte* blamed: 'a Chinese and yelling mass'.[66] Such labels had been the stock-in-trade of the conservative press for a couple of years, but they proliferated in the wake of Annarumma's death.

Although *L'Unità* did not report any instances when workers had used violence in the pursuit of the contract struggles, there can be little doubt that many confrontations involved the hurling of ball-bearings, the wielding of batons and banners and the throwing of punches. The paper *Lotta Continua* reported that during the clashes of via Larga:

> groups of workers assaulted jeeps, collecting material ammunition from a nearby building site ... the police were visibly terrorized.[67]

Political groups, such as *Lotta Continua*, actively propagated the use of offensive violence. Attacks on property were common. Some of these were the result of planned, secret actions, such as the burning of the Pirelli tyres, but the use of physical coercion mostly consisted of what Bocca referred to as 'reformist violence'; by this he meant actions like picketing, which were 'mass backed and whose objectives were greater dignity and democracy, not the overthrow of the system'.[68]

However, there were forces interested in using the incidents of violence to present a picture of social chaos and political crisis. The Confindustria stated that:

> workers' power is tending to replace parliament and to establish a direct relationship with executive power. This subverts the political system in all respects.[69]

Giorgio Bocca noted:

> Already there are those who want to make use of the violent incidents and subversion to invite repression. Let us not think of unholy alliances between 'the worse the better' philosophy of the Left and that of the Right; nor of the actions of *provocateurs*; look, rather, at the facility with which certain acts of vandalism have come about in well-stocked factories, suggesting that they were not so displeasing to the owners.[70]

But while for the movement the adoption of violence was mainly expressive and a relatively minor aspect of a wider struggle, during and before the Hot Autumn clandestine operations by groupings of the extreme Right aimed at the strategic use of violence to provoke a backlash against that movement. Some ninety-six openly Fascist attacks on left-wing headquarters took place between early January and 12 December 1969, but another fifty bomb attacks carried left-wing 'signatures', usually claiming to be anarchist-inspired. On 24 April bombs were planted at the Milan Trade Fair and the Central Station – targets which, it seemed, were chosen by enemies of capitalist property. This was the assumption made by the police, who duly arrested known anarchist activists.[71]

Such terrorist acts, which came to be known as the 'strategy of tension', were not much noted during the Hot Autumn, although people like Bocca suspected danger. It took the bomb-blast at the Bank of Agriculture in Piazza Fontana on 12 December to bring them to people's attention. Twelve people were reported dead in what was quickly defined by the police authorities, and then in the national press, as an anarchist-style bombing. The bombing, which occurred four days after the signing of the state sector engineering contract and at a time when strikes against the private sector were escalating, could only be interpreted as political. The *Corriere della Sera*, following police statements, blamed anarchists. The edition of 17 December carried a picture of Pietro Valpreda, one of those arrested, giving a clenched-fist salute. The caption underneath was: 'The propaganda of terror.' The *Corriere* reported:

> The authorities have a precise and concrete idea of the background in which the ferocious plan of destruction was conceived.... The crime found its opening and breeding ground in the anarchist and anarchoid groups where hatred and subversion are preached.[72]

The article then outlined the personal inadequacies of the 'ballet-dancer' which were said to explain his 'irrational hatred for the whole of humanity'. Valpreda was made to represent the 'face of the criminal' in which readers could see the motivations of the terrorist, and the result of two years of social upheaval.

In the immediate aftermath of the bombing the *Corriere della Sera* wrote:

> We are living through the total dissolution of the principles of human society without which democracy cannot survive; we are living through a savage challenge to, in one word, civilization.... Democracy must defend itself.[73]

In an edition at the end of the month following the funeral attended by some three hundred thousand people, it was more optimistic:

1969 opened with a thuggish and fascist-style attack in the name of an irrational and sometimes lunatic denunciation of consumer society.... It was the type of anarchist and nihilist rebellion manipulated by the PCI.... Today, the year comes to an end in a quite different atmosphere – an atmosphere dominated by sadness for the deaths of Piazza Fontana.... The fundamental values of the 'human pact' are getting strong again.[74]

The consensus which the *Corriere della Sera* claimed to see emerging from the ashes of Piazza Fontana was, however largely illusory. The rifts that had developed between social groups and classes in 1968–9 were refracted through their different assessments of the tragedy. The polarizations (in relation to previous clashes) of police demonstrators were repeated. *L'Unità* was careful not to commit itself fully to defending the accused for fear of tarnishing its respectability, but the paper, nonetheless, compared the bombing to the Reichstag fire for which the Nazis had blamed anarchists.[75] In the factories there was widespread scepticism about the official version of events. There was some confusion as to the responsibility for the bombing, but 'it was widely understood to be an attempt to put a break on the workers' movement, which was in a period of growth'.[76]

Far from bringing Italians together to defend 'their' state against its internal enemies, the bombing sowed new seeds of dissent. Giuseppe Pinelli, who fell to his death from a window of the police headquarters became a martyr, and Valpreda became an Italian Dreyfus – the innocent victim of *raison d'état*. A campaign of counter-information linked the bombing to Fascist conspirators with friends within the state apparatuses. Distrust of the state grew rather than diminished. Audiences of the film *Un Cittadino Sopra Ogni Sospetto* (*A Citizen Above Suspicion*), which was widely shown in 1970, could readily recognize the police chief who was given the job of investigating his own crimes. It was an audience familiar with the notion that the plots of public life were stranger and more sinister than fiction.

The campaign, headed by the *Corriere della Sera*, to discredit the social movements was, therefore, largely counter-productive. The movements over the following years were able to draw on the cultural legacy of anti-fascism to outflank such attempts at criminalization. In a longer term perspective, it might be possible to show that the criminalization strategy of the early 1970s laid the foundations for its more comprehensive and successful implementation at the end of the decade.[77] However, analyses like those of the extreme Left at the time, which focused only on the repressive strategies of the state, failed to see how by winning so many of its objectives, the workers' movement established a new relationship with both state and employers. The state was not merely a repressive machine,

but the means whereby contracts in society were drawn up. So although
the workers' movement continued to mobilize over demands, especially in
the early 1970s, conflict was increasingly regulated and institutionalized.

Notes

1. *L'Unità*, 21 August 1969.
2. *Corriere della Sera*, 24 October 1969.
3. *L'Unità*, 3 October 1969; *Corriere della Sera*, 13 October 1969.
4. *L'Unità*, 11 October 1969.
5. *Corriere della Sera*, 25 October 1969.
6. Vito Basilico, 'Pirelli', p. 288.
7. S. Datola, 'L'industria metalmeccanica milanese: 1945–75', in G. Bonvini, *Un minuto più dal padrone*, Milan 1977; G. Beccalli, 'Scioperi organizzazione sindacale a Milano', pp. 101–5.
8. A. Sandretti, *Lotte all'Alfa Romeo*, Appendix XIII–XV, and pp. 31–2.
9. *L'Unità*, 26 July 1969.
10. Marino Regini and Emilio Reyneri, *Lotte operaie e organizzazione del lavoro*, pp. 74–5.
11. For example, the excellent studies carried out by Alessandro Pizzorno's team of researchers sacrifice the richness and diversity of the material they gathered in the interests of fitting evidence into certain categories of variables (for example the cultural dimensions of working-class life at work, and outside, are squeezed into a box labelled 'class composition', analysed in terms of skill, work situation, age, region of origin and education; see A. Pizzorno, Introduction, *Lotte Operaie e sindacato*, vol. 1, pp. 10–11). The project cannot be criticized for doing what it set out to do, but it is worth saying that the work of social historians shows the importance of critical and evaluative use of materials in ways which do not aspire to limiting notions of scientificity. The construction of any set of categories with which to analyse and describe in a 'neutral' manner involves sacrificing some of the richness of the 'natural language' from which they have to be artificially derived. This means that it is always necessary to return to the words used by protagonists to understand what Pizzorno sets out as his object/subject of study – the 'self-consciousness of the collective subject in formation' (*l'autocoscienza del soggetto collettivo in formazione*).
12. Dario Lanzardo, 'L'intervento socialista nella lotta operaia: l'inchiesta operaia di Marx', *Quaderni Rossi*, 5, Milan 1972, reprint.
13. CUB Borletti, 'Inchiesta sulle condizioni di vita delle operaie alla Borletti', in *I CUB: 3 anni di lotte*, Milan 1972, pp. 219–31.
14. Ibid.
15. Rina Barbieri interview. Furthermore, wage parity did not include piece-rates; at Borletti men got 115 *lire*, whilst women got 72 *lire* for the same work; *La Sinistra*, 13 January 1968.
16. *Spontanee riflessioni di una operaia*, Leaflet, undated.
17. *L'Unità*, 1 May 1969.
18. For criticism of unions' attitude to women workers, Nella Marcellino, 'La partecipazione femminile e il movimento sindacale', *Quaderni di Rassegna Sindacale*, May–August 1975, pp. 113–25; Maria Vittoria Ballestrero, *Dalla tutela alla parità*, Bologna 1979, pp. 129–74.
19. Guido Viale, *S'avanza un strano soldato*, Rome 1973, pp. 59–67.
20. *L'Unità*, 15 May 1969.
21. A. Marchetti, 'Un teatro troppo serio', *Classe XIII*, June 1982.
22. Nanni Balestrini, *La violenza illustrata*, Turin 1976, pp. 130–31.
23. A. Marchetti, 'Un teatro troppo serio'; it was this aspect of workers' opposition to society which inspired Dario Fo; he recalled an incident in Milan when workers

organized a funeral cortege with a black carriage, drawn by black horses wearing feathers, and with themselves as mourners. Their factory was threatened with closure, and to draw attention to their case (but leaving passers-by to make apposite inquiries) they set about burying the corpse in good time. A fine sense of theatre! See 'Dario Fo à Vincennes', pp. 24–5.

24. There was perhaps a time when these events were ideal moments for romantic encounters.
25. A typed sheet without dates or instructions (in the private collection of a Sit Siemens factory delegate).
26. Barrington Moore, *Injustice*.
27. *Ibid*, p. 22.
28. *Corriere della Sera*, 29 November 1969.
29. A. Marchetti, 'Un teatro troppo serio'.
30. Workers' organizations in the zones frequently pivoted around the large factories, which set the pace for the smaller ones. Following 1969 there were battles by the latter to win parity with the former. This process tended to unify the movement, but was considerably strengthened by the fact that in 1969 workers and delegates went from factory to factory as never before. The guards could only shrug their shoulders.
31. *L'Unità*, 11 December 1969.
32. B. Beccalli, 'Scioperi e organizzazione sindacale', p. 95.
33. M. Benetti and M. Regini, 'Considerazioni generali sui vincoli posti dalla forza-lavoro occupata alla sua utilizzazione nell'azienda', in P. Alessandrini, *Conflittualità e aspetti normativi del lavoro*, pp. 28–9.
34. Carter Goodrich wrote a book, which has become a classic study in the field of industrial relations, on the basis of observations made inside British engineering factories in the years immediately after the First World War. (C. Goodrich, *The Frontier of Control*, London 1975.) The time-lag between the British and Italian experience in this respect has provoked considerable speculation; see A. Pizzorno, 'Fra azione di classe e sistema corporativi', pp. 949–86.
35. The war metaphor was not new. Engels, for example, greatly admired Clausewitz. Gramsci's writings are full of references to strategies of class warfare in terms borrowed from military manuals; see A. Gramsci, *Prison Notebooks*, pp. 238–9. However, themes of class war re-entered political discussion in a major way in 1968–9. Both the 'spontaneous' and 'scientific' forms of proletarian violence had their advocates and theorists, see part IV, chapter 19, pp. 288–9.
36. Rule-breaking, as Piven and Cloward note, is a key feature of social movements. Poor people can only win concessions by not playing to rules weighted against them. However, every type of conflict is necessarily regulated to some degree. So, for example, during strikes in 1969 workers threw ball-bearings not hand-grenades. No managers were killed; see Eric Hobsbawm, 'The Rules of Violence', in *Revolutionaries*, New York 1973, pp. 209–15.
37. CUB Borletti, leaflet dated 20 October 1969.
38. At Sit Siemens there was considerable experimentation, see I. Regalia, *Lotte operaie*, vol. 4, p. 70.
39. Rina Barbieri interview.
40. *L'Unità*, 14 November 1969.
41. *Il Giorno*, 7 October 1969. The article carried the sub-heading: 'The unions' tough task of convincing the grassroots that a guilty capitalism cannot be immediately and heavily punished if disaster is to be avoided.'
42. However, most of the violence in 1969 was 'spontaneous'. That is to say, that it was not premeditated and carefully organized. Nevertheless, it followed certain patterns; for example, if the honour of one of the parties was called in question ('you're the son of a whore. Perhaps your mother really does walk the streets?'), it had to be vindicated. See Domenico Norcia, 'Io garantito', quoted in *L'Espresso*, December 1981.
43. Gruppo di studio operaio impiegati, leaflet dated 30 October 1969.
44. Michèle Perrot, *Ouvriers en grève* (France, 1871–1890), quoted by Edward Shorter and Charles Tilly, *Strikes in France*, p. 337.

45. Workers enjoyed a good laugh at management's expense by reading their 'human relations' manuals; see part I, chapter 2, pp. 30–31; footnote 32.
46. 'It is the fourth time that IBM … buries a man who refuses to be an instrument of production but wants to use his mind to the full. … It is a question of fighting the arbitrary powers of the few who hold the destiny of millions in their hands'; leaflet entitled; *IBM Democracy has Struck Again*, signed Gruppo dei lavoratori, IBM, 19 September 1969.
47. Marino Regini, 'Come e perchè cambiano la logica dell'organizzazione sindacale e i compartamenti della base' in A. Pizzorno, *Lotte operaie e sindacato*, vol. 6, pp. 168–75.
48. I. Regalia, 'Le assemblee', *Quaderni di Rassegna Sindacale*, 56–7, September–December 1975, pp. 103–6.
49. Ibid., pp. 106–10.
50. Max Weber distinguishes between three types of legitimation of authority in leadership – 'traditional', 'charismatic' and 'legal'; see 'Politics as a Vocation', in Alessandro Pizzorno, ed., *Political Sociology*, London 1971, pp. 27–38.
51. Oral testimonies frequently show this. In my researches I found an extreme reluctance to speak about the personal side of how the movement was lived. This self-effacement points to a collective attitude rather than to modesty.
52. Ida Regalia, 'Rappresentanza operaia e sindacato', in A. Pizzorno, *Lotte operaie e sindacato*, vol. 6, pp. 206–11.
53. See part IV, chapter 21, pp. 325–6.
54. Interestingly, selections of Gramsci's writings on the factory council movement were published in pamphlet form, whereas they had previously been enclosed within large volumes.
55. Lucio Magri, 'Via italiana e strategia consiliore', *Il Manifesto*, 2, 1974, also Grant Amyot, *The Italian Communist Party*, London 1981, pp. 170–93.
56. It is worth noting that the struggle for dignity was closely bound up with work – with being a worker and not a parasite – even when the values of the work ethic were being questioned; see Aris Accornero, *Il lavoro come ideologia*, Bologna 1980, pp. 49–89. But importantly this work was a means of socializing and not just earning money. The factory could be a prison but it could also be a playground; for an account of women who saw work in this double aspect, see M. Boneschi, *Donne in liquidazione: Unidal*, Milan 1978.
57. See Adriano Sofri's critique of the attempt to revive the Ordine Nuovo communism of producers, 'Sur les conseils de délégués', in *Les Temps Modernes*, June 1974. His arguments are taken up in André Gorz, *Farewell to the Working Class*, London 1980, pp. 45–53.
58. This *operaist* vision was most entrenched in the extreme Left, and in the industrial cities like Turin and Milan. It was also shared by currents within the Communist Party and by PSIUP, though from very different viewpoints, as the analysis of the Pirelli struggles has shown.
59. This point is discussed more fully in part IV, chapter 21.
60. For an approach to how a moral panic is transformed into a general panic (or crisis of hegemony), see Stuart Hall et al., *Policing the Crisis*, London 1978, pp. 219–27.
61. Quoted in *La Strage di Stato-controinchiesta*, Rome, 1970, p. 105.
62. *L'Unità*, 7 November 1969; *Corriere della Sera*, 7 November 1969.
63. *L'Unità*, 20 November 1969.
64. *L'Unità*, 21 November 1969.
65. *Corriere della Sera*, 22 November 1969.
66. See P. Violi, *I giornali dell'estrema sinistra*, pp. 173–4.
67. Ibid., pp. 173–4.
68. *Il Giorno*, 7 October 1969.
69. *La Strage di Stato-controinchiesta*, p. 19.
70. *Il Giorno*, 7 October 1969.
71. *La Strage di Stato*, pp. 30–35.
72. *Corriere della Sera*, 17 December 1969.

73. *Corriere della Sera*, 13 December 1969.
74. *Corriere della Sera*, 28 December 1969.
75. *L'Unità*, 20 December 1969.
76. Rina Barbieri interview; Licia Pinelli gives a less sanguine account of the confusion on the Left, much of which was prepared to accept that anarchists might have been responsible; Piero Scaramucci, *Licia Pinelli*, p. 18.
77. The trials and retrials of Pietro Valpreda tell the story of how responsibility for the Piazza Fontana bombing has been allocated according to the political situation in which they have taken place. The theory of the 'convergence of the two extremes' (extreme Right and extreme Left), which explains how Fascists and anarchists can collaborate in terrorist enterprises, has continued to have its advocates. However, there are dangers in attributing grand designs and strategies to 'rulers' who in fact stumble and improvize their way through history. It would be more fruitful to look at how government helped produce 'criminals' (red terrorists, for example) by putting state activities beyond the control of the law; see part IV, chapter 19.

16

the new rules of the game: the unions and industrial relations

During the Hot Autumn a workers' movement developed, especially in the engineering industry which was distinct from the union organizations. Its priorities were not to build formal membership of the unions and to win recognition from management, but to win greater freedom and power in the workplace through organized disruption. It created its own demands, forms of action and organization from below. The unions tended to follow the movement and not vice-versa – 'riding the tiger', as it was called at the time. Nonetheless, the unions did risk the ride and in important respects set objectives and guided the movement. In contrast to the behaviour of the French CGT in the wake of the May events in France, the Italian CGIL and other unions did not try to stem the development of the movement (perhaps in the circumstances of a year and a half of radicalization it would not have been feasible anyway). Instead, they opened themselves to criticism and debate in the light of events. In fact, during the Hot Autumn the unions recouped some of the prestige they had lost in previous months. This enabled them to monopolize negotiations over the contracts and to re-establish control over shopfloor organization. The subject of this chapter is the process whereby the unions used the movement to gain not only a favourable agreement but recognition at both national and local levels.

Renewal of the Unions

The events at Fiat immediately preceding the Hot Autumn marked the nadir of Italian unionism in 1968–9. The movement was not only autonomous of the unions, but hostile to them. Their failure to represent the rank-and-file had many causes which were by no means exclusive to the Turinese situation; unions were identified with particular political parties and their rivalries. Above all, they seemed to have little to do with the everyday problems of the shopfloor, where they were weakly organized and ineffectual. This situation was one of a 'structural crisis' of representation; the unions nationally and locally tended to represent the interests of the better organized, skilled members more than those of the un-skilled and semi-skilled. In the Hot Autumn, the unions aspired to overcome this crisis.

Since 1948, when groups of workers broke away from the CGIL to form rival organizations, the unions had become closely associated with political parties. The CGIL was dominated by the PCI and PSI, and its officials held high party posts, and seats in Parliament; the predominantly Catholic CISL had close links with the Church and Christian Democratic Party; and the UIL had connections with the Republicans and Social Democrats. However, in 1969 the situation began to change dramatically. In the congresses of June–July 1969, ACLI, the influential association of Catholic workers, decided to end its special relationship with the Christian Democrats; the CGIL decided to separate party and union functions, which were thenceforth defined as 'incompatible'; while the CISL was divided, with the industrial delegates most involved in the contract disputes favouring hardline opposition to the government. The tide of votes in favour of a trade unionism freed of party constraints opened the prospect of reunifying the confederations.

This idea was strongest in the engineering sections, which were especially interested in being free of pressures from both the confederations and the parties. (In Turin, the FIOM–CGIL was especially open to these ideas. In Milan, where the FIOM was more tightly controlled by older PCI members, it was the FIM–CISL that was the more radical.) An article in *Dibattito Sindacale*, the journal of the Milanese FIM, in the previous year stressed the need for a positive interpretation of the 'incompatibility' notion. It claimed to identify a new orientation to the union among workers:

> Joining the union is less than ever a reflection of an ideological and party choice, and increasingly activists and members participate in society through the union. . . . The workers are deserting the branches and cells of the parties, because they see that they count for nothing in them.[1]

A questionnaire of the membership in February 1969 found that 72 per cent thought that the union should take on issues usually dealt with by the parties.[2]

The case of the Milanese FIM is an especially interesting example of union renewal; at the time, it was referred to as exemplary. Although it was half the size of the FIOM in the province, it almost doubled its membership in 1967–70, and showed itself open and responsive to the social movements.[3] The dramatic radicalization within the Catholic world found expression and a focus for commitment within the union. There was a shared rejection of the Christian Democratic Party and of a Catholicism which supported the status quo. In a speech to the ACLI conference of Milan province in July 1968 (which, according to *Rinascità*, represented an 'imposing mass organization of some 45–50,000 members, mostly manual workers'), Bruno Manghi referred to the 'strong spiritual force' at work within the ACLI. This was expressed through denunciation of 'intolerable working conditions ... and of the oppression of the personality and humanity of the worker'. *Rinascità* noted:

> no shortage of moral condemnation of those Catholics who are the first to contribute to charity, and yet remain hateful exploiters of men in the factories.[4]

The FIM–CISL, like other sectors of Italian unions, was overtaken by the social movements, but it was quick to adapt to the new climate. There was a desire to get away from the compromises of the past, and to create a new identity for the union. But the legacy of Catholic unionism provided raw materials for this change of direction. For example, the FIM's antipathy to 'ideology', previously bound-up with anti-communism, was developed into a radical pragmatism, which readily borrowed from the student movement and learnt from grassroots opinion. The Catholic humanism of the FIM–CISL opened the way to critiques of the Taylorist organization of work. The pages of *Dibattito Sindacale* in 1968–9 are alive with discussions involving a fundamental rethinking of a tradition.[5] Especially active participants were Milanese Catholic intellectuals, who were engaged in teaching at the Catholic University and in editing the review *Collegamenti*. Yet non-Catholics were also drawn into the ambiance of the FIM, which became a melting pot for ideas coming from the New Left. It became a cultural bridgehead between sections of the Milanese intelligentsia and workers in the factories.[6]

The FIM was capable of rising quickly to the challenge presented by the social movements because of its cultural openness. The early editions of *Dibattito Sindacale* continuously reiterate the theme of 'rebirth' and 'renewal'; for example, Giorgio Tiboni, a member of the secretariat, wrote: 'The union was born in the factory and it is to the factory that it must return';[7] Bruno Manghi referred to 'spontaneous worker protest' as the 'nodal point for any attempt to construct a new union'. 'The union', he wrote:

has to carry spontaneous action into the oganization ... in the sense that it must accept criticism it entails ... it must discover within itself a 'wildcat' attitude to negotiation.[8]

The FIM followed this approach by adopting the demand for egalitarian lump-sum wage increases, despite the resistance of the CISL confederation and of other unions. Similarly, it took up the calls for parity with white-collar workers, and for the reduction of the number of grades. The election of the first delegates was greeted as the sign of a new democracy in the workplace.

The flexibility of the FIM on these issues was partly the result of its traditional rivalry with the FIOM, and this, in turn, was related to differences in their constituencies. The FIOM had a much more clearly defined identity and tradition, with a core membership of skilled workers with strong ties to the Left parties. In 1968–9, the FIOM in Milan, and nationally, opposed egalitarian demands, such as those on wages and grades, because they were thought to undermine differentials based on skill (*professionalità*).[9] The defence of skill was seen as part of the struggle against the imposition of job evaluation, and full capitalist control of the system of pay and promotion. Moreover, the FIOM had a greater stake in the existing structures of workers' representation, especially in the internal commissions, and set a premium on leadership and discipline. Throughout the Hot Autumn, the union hierarchy, though not the ordinary members, supported the renewal of this internal commission, and opposed their replacement by new delegate representation.[10]

The FIM, on the other hand, drew its membership mainly from groups of semi- and unskilled workers and clerical workers, who had had little to do with union organization, let alone political parties. In promoting the struggles of these 'outsiders', the FIM had little to lose and a lot to gain in organizational strength and influence. It was strategically well-placed to take advantage of the structural crisis of representation which overtook the unions in late 1968–early 1969. The membership of the FIM had no interest in defending the hierarchies of pay and grading, and, therefore, shared unambiguously in the egalitarian spirit of the movement. The union's publications openly championed the most radical demands, and even went as far as printing documents of Potere Operaio and the CUB, which actually attacked the unions.[11] In *Dibattito Sindacale*, the FIM intellectuals mounted systematic critiques of the notion of skill, and theorized the role of the *operaio comune* as the spearhead of the attack on the Taylorist organization of work. They wrote of grading, differentials and piece-rates as managerial instruments of social control. The FIM thereby made itself an interpreter of the newest and most radical struggles along the 'frontier of control.'[12]

The Milanese FIM represented a limit-case of union renewal. Union activism involved immense investments of energy and intensive debate, not only in the workplace, but at summer camps. The technical–professional training of militants and officials came second to their theoretical–cultural preparation. Dreams of revolution and a new society were glimpsed in the themes of 'self-management', 'autonomous culture' and 'workers' creativity', which recurred in FIM literature.[13] Not surprisingly, it was labelled 'pan-syndicalist'. However, many of the FIM's proposals were subsequently taken up by the FIOM and by the confederations under the pressure of the rank and file. All the unions stood to gain from the radicalization of the industrial action.

The unions as a whole had an organizational interest in entering the factories from which they had been effectively excluded since 1948. The movement provided the means of entry, and strengthened the hand of left-wing currents within the FIOM and CGIL. At the national congress of the CGIL in 1969, delegates heaped criticism on the leadership for what Rinaldo Scheda called

> the error of holding out against spontaneism at all costs … episodes like the formation of CUB are a severe criticism of our own deficiencies.[14]

Vittorio Foa, the PSIUP member of the CGIL secretariat, insisted on the centrality of workers' control:

> a wage gain, even though it is considerable, is vulnerable to the demands of profitability from the word 'go', unless it is accompanied by greater control over the use of labour.[15]

Yet it took a longer period than the Hot Autumn for the union confederations to come to terms with the transformations of representational structures in the factories.

Nonetheless, throughout this period the unions gave a free rein to the movement and won back their leadership role by democratizing the running of the strikes. Although workers' sense of identification with the unions was marginal to the feeling of being a part of a movement, nonetheless the legitimacy of the unions' leadership was never seriously in doubt. The almost unanimous vote in favour of the unions' final recommendation of acceptance of the contract offers in December 1969 and January 1970, was also a vote of confidence in their leadership. The increase in unionization, which in the province of Milan rose from 30 per cent to 44 per cent of the workforce in 1968–70, was a sign of greater interest in and identification with the unions.[16]

A Plural Society

On 9 January 1970 *L'Unità* reported that Costa, president of the Confindustria, had called for

> the restoration of normality in the workplaces and the infliction of penalties on those found guilty of crimes carried out in the contract dispute of the previous year.[17]

The same day some five hundred cases were due to be heard in Milan. According to the Chamber of Labour (*Camera del Lavoro*), about eight thousand workers had been charged over the previous three years in connection with industrial disputes. What exactly constituted 'normality' was open to interpretation, since the social movements of 1968–9 had destroyed an earlier consensus and interrupted the usual channels of negotiation.

The restoration of the status quo, understood as the management's right to manage without reference to the workforce, was hardly realistic, unless parliamentary democracy was replaced by a military dictatorship. This option was not entirely discounted in some quarters, as evidenced by the launching of the 'strategy of tension', and the attempted *coup d'état* of December 1970.[18] However, it was a bloody and dangerous course of action, which held little appeal for the dominant multinational groups. The report of the Pirelli Commission on changes in the Confindustria, which was initiated in March 1969 and completed in January 1970, welcomed the new spirit of pluralism and modernization within Italian society:

> To pretend that tensions do not exist, or, worse, to know of their existence and to try to suppress them, entails taking a step towards the removal of fundamental freedoms. Order is not the suppression of tensions, even though acute; order is the observation of the rules of civil society.[19]

The principal problem, therefore, was the construction of new rules and norms. The 'explosion of tensions' in the previous months, resulting from 'accumulated social, territorial and sectoral disequilibria', was 'not a reason for industrialists to refuse to recognize the social and political function of responsible and efficient unions'.[20]

The search for formulas for social equilibrium was at the top of the agendas of both the government and the Confindustria. There was an awareness that the status quo could not be restored, but also a desire to put an end to the social movements. The continuous reiteration of the theme of law and order, which reached a crescendo in the wake of the

Piazza Fontana bombings, ran through all the talk of change and reform. Above all, the Hot Autumn and other struggles were defined as an exceptional moment to be bracketed off and superseded. This was the case in the pronouncements of the *Corriere della Sera*, in which the events were treated as a form of temporary national derangement, and in the Pirelli report, in which they figured as manifestations of Italian backwardness and uneven development on the road to modern pluralism. The strategies evolved to deal with the movements, therefore, invoked measures of discipline and coercion, as well as concessions.

A consideration of the engineering contracts and of the labour legislation, which was passed at the end of the Hot Autumn, provides a way of looking at the attempt to construct a new set of rules in industrial relations as part of wider capitalist strategies for bringing the social movements to heel. At the same time, it is necessary to examine the dynamics of the workers' movement itself in relation to the concessions and reforms. Given that they could not be coerced, workers had to be persuaded to abide by new rules.

The Contracts

The engineering contracts were signed on 9 December between the unions and the Intersind, and on 21 December between the unions and the Confindustria. The union platform of demands was largely accepted. The wage increase, which was the same for all, was considerable; it outstripped price rises, enabling workers to buy consumer durables previously made for middle-class or foreign purchasers. (In fact, the share of the National Income going to wage workers increased, while the proportion going in profits declined[21]). Hours were to be reduced to forty a week over a three-year period, and contractual limits were placed on overtime working. The principle of parity between manual and white-collar workers was recognized along with an agreement to implement it by stages, starting with sickness benefits. It gave unions the right to hold ten meetings a year in the workplace, in work time. In addition the unions were to have official noticeboards and the right to issue information.[22]

The new contract was generally seen as a major victory for the workers, and as a blow for the employers. However, its effects on the social movement, which had seen a good contract as a common goal likely to benefit all workers, were complex. The signing of the agreements under-mined and contained mobilization. For many workers it was time to recuperate the wages lost through stoppages. The groups of the extreme Left, for example, argued against acceptance of the agreement, not because they thought it a bad one, but because they knew it would reduce the chances of a political showdown.[23] Yet the contract had been wrested from the employers, taken, not given. The timing of the concessions related to the degree of pressure and disruption brought by the movement. It was clear that the government had all but forced the private sector to give way. There was no question of gratitude, or of concern for the financial situation of the companies. Rather, the lengthy dispute left a legacy of bitterness and recrimination. In January 1970 charges rained down on the heads of workers, whilst the unions published a report outlining cases of management repression in the factories, and organized defence campaigns.

The contract concessions did terminate a particular phase of the movement, but had nothing like the demobilizing effects of the Grenelle agreements in France following the 1968 general strike. Workers fought to implement the contract at a local level: at Fiat they immediately started working a 42-hour week, thereby speeding up implementation. And the movement on the shopfloor continued to press for the abolition of piece-work, for mass regrading, for plant-level wage increases and for the recognition of delegates – none of which had been subject to negotiation in the contract. The contract victory, in other words, proved that collective action was the most effective way of achieving both the material gains and decision-making powers from which workers had ben so long excluded. The gains made through the struggles of the Hot Autumn were the gains of the social movements, for it was the surge of rebellion from below that had forced the Intersind and Confindustria to concede so generously.

However, as has been seen, the unions won back influence during the Hot Autumn, and sealed it with the renewal of the contract. Although there were enormous disparities between the demands, forms of action and organization of the movement and those promoted by the national unions, the contract opened the way for the unions to regulate, and then incorporate, the informal structures of representation created in the previous months. The recognition of the rights of unions (and no one else) to hold meetings was unwillingly conceded by the employers, but it was the necessary precondition to the establishment of defined procedures, lines of communication and set roles in which the union was management's sole interlocutor. The Labour Charter, which was voted through parliament on 11 December 1969 – that is, exactly between the signing of the two contracts – made this aspect of the contract the founding principle of a reorganization of the system of industrial relations in Italy.

The Labour Charter and the General Amnesty

In May 1970 the Labour Charter (*Statuto dei Lavoratori*) became law and, furthermore, parliament gave a general amnesty to those charged with offences connected with labour disputes prior to passage of the new bill. These two measures were the most significant cases of action designed to favour the institutionalization of protest.

The Labour Charter put into law certain rights concerning meetings, recruitment and union activity in general, which had been in the engineering workers' contract. In addition, it contained clauses which made it illegal for employers to discriminate in any way against workers engaged in union activity, and banned company-unionism. Unfair dismissals now resulted in the reinstatement of the worker concerned. Basically, the law sanctioned the recognition of unions in workplaces, and aimed to eliminate repression and the unilateral rights of the employer. The new rights related directly to the conditions of work and union representation rather than to the position of the worker as an ordinary citizen in the factory, which was the case before.[24]

The Labour Charter was a historic piece of legislation. Not since the Constitution had there been such a wholesale redefinition of the rights of labour. The granting of the general amnesty wiped the slate clean, while the new law provided mechanisms for the redress of grievances which were tilted in favour of the employee.[25]

The legislation offered a means of bringing the social movement to an end. Firstly, it aimed to remove one of the causes of the workers' movement – namely, the exclusion of workers' organizations (and workers as individuals) from the benefits of citizenship. Secondly, it aimed to eliminate conflict over fundamental issues (union recognition, above all), and to encourage recourse to the law as the preferred means of resolving conflicts. Respect for the law would, in turn, it was hoped, reduce levels of conflict in society as a whole. The Labour Charter, in other words, was designed to prevent a repetition of the Hot Autumn.

The effects of the Labour Charter and amnesty on the social movements were, however, ambiguous and contradictory. It has been argued, for example, that the general amnesty gave *de facto* legitimation to the use of violence in industrial disputes by absolving the perpetrators of responsibility for their actions. This opened the way for unions and magistrates to interpret the Charter in ways which legitimated or depenalized violent actions.[26] But even if it is accepted that the legislation was used like this, it is misleading to attribute responsibility for violence and terrorism in the factory to judicial leniency.

The question can be put in another way: what would have happened had there been no amnesty? The conflicts of 1968–9, as has been seen, revealed deep-seated and intense feelings of moral outrage on the part of literally millions of Italians. Recourse to violent methods pointed to the fact that people regarded legal methods as inadequate for redressing grievances. It was employers, headmasters and others who had recourse to the law. Therefore, for the state to have sanctioned thousands of trials on charges arising from the social conflicts would have been to risk turning the law courts into the tribunals of popular agitators. The decision to hold an amnesty was a political decision to save the law from becoming too politicized.

The amnesty meant turning over a new page in the law to prevent the blots from previous pages coming through. One of the consequences was that the use of 'reformist violence' (to use Bocca's words) was no longer a sufficient ground for employers to sack workers. The threshold of what was considered acceptable violence was lowered in response to changes in the balance of power inside the workplace, which, in turn, the Labour Charter underwrote.[27] But, without such measures, it would have been extremely difficult to have established new rules to regulate industrial conflicts since they would not have seemed impartial.

In the case of the Labour Charter, however, legislation was never demanded by the social movement. It was drafted by Communist and Socialist Party parliamentarians with the support of the unions, who used the leverage provided by the mass mobilizations to push through the bill. As far as movement activists were concerned, it was through direct action, not in the law courts, that real concessions were wrung from employers and the state. For them, the threat of escalating the actions, not legal niceties, forced through the general amnesty. In Piven and Cloward's perspective, the Charter was an example of legislation designed to strengthen the hand of union organizers over the hotheads of the movement. The problem, in this instance, is that the effects were more contradictory.

As Federico Mancini has noted, this was partly because of the amnesty. But, a distinction needs also to be made between reforms which facilitate and encourage mobilization, and reforms which limit or block it.[28] The Labour Charter did not concede the right to unionize while simultaneously stipulating compulsory mediation, cooling-off periods before strikes and so on. On the contrary, it offered workers protection against sackings which meant that they could take industrial action without fear of management reprisals. (The advantages it gave to workers can be seen by contrasting the position of the *garantiti* and the *non-garantiti* – the 'protected' and the 'unprotected'.[29]) Militancy was invited, especially when it seemed the only way to win concessions. This was the case in the 1970s when Italian governments proved largely incapable of constructing social contracts in which workers gained benefits through state policies in return for their quiescence.

The Pirelli report recommended a package of measures, which included social reforms as well as legal protection. But, between 1969 and 1971, reforms totalled:

> a change in the pension system, a general and not particularly progressive new housing law, and certain promises about the health service.[30]

The state's efforts to reform the health service were as lamentable as its attempts to reform the education system. The number of hospital beds per thousand of the population was the lowest in Western Europe, and the private insurance schemes, pharmaceutical industry and medical profession grew fat off the contributions deducted from wage packets. Giorgi Ruffolo describes the situation:

> The health sector is largely immersed in that vast parasitic area of Italian society that makes up the squalid hinterland of an unevenly industrialized economy; it is the area of rent, middle-men, speculation and clientelistic undergrowth.[31]

In the mid and late 1970s the trade unions were increasingly consulted by governments and were represented in local and national state institutions.[32] But, in the wake of the Hot Autumn, the failure to carry through social reforms from above created some of the conditions for popular mobilizations from below. The workers' movement extended its struggles beyond the factory to support tenants' mobilizations and campaigns of civil disobedience. The strategies of the political elites to reintegrate the movement into normal political channels did not succeed in creating an image of the state as powerful and paternalistic. The Italian state was divided within itself and held in low esteem by its citizens.

Notes

1. *Dibattito Sindacale*, May–June 1968.
2. G. Sclavi, 'Due CISL', *Il Manifesto*, October–November 1969.
3. Bianca Beccalli, 'Scioperi e organizzazione sindacale a Milano', p. 101.
4. Aldo Bonaccini, 'Il soffitto delle ACLI milanesi', in *Rinascità*, 19 July 1969, pp. 9–13.
5. The themes of issues give some idea of the range of discussion: workers' history, '68 and the student movement, and union democracy.
6. A fair sprinkling of sociologists were among them, including Gian Primo Cella, Bruno Manghi and others.
7. *Dibattito Sindacale*, May–June 1968.
8. *Dibattito Sindacale*, March–April 1968.
9. M. Regini and E. Reyneri, *Lotte operaie e organizzazione del lavoro*, pp. 76–7, p. 95.
10. I. Regalia, 'Rappresentanza operaia e sindacato' in A. Pizzorno, *Lotte operaie e sindacato*, vol. 6, pp. 199–206.
11. *Dibattito Sindacale*, September–October 1969.

12. Gian Primo Cella and Bruno Manghi, *Un sindacato italiano negli anni sessanta*, pp. 39–44.
13. The theme of *autogestion* was imported enthusiastically from France where Catholic unionists were keen advocates. Ideas popularized by the May events were filtered through the CFDT; see Serge Mallet, *Le pouvoir ouvrier*, Paris 1971.
14. *Dibattito Sindacale*, September–October 1969.
15. Ibid., p. 16.
16. B. Beccalli, 'Scioperi e organizzazione sindacale a Milano', p. 102.
17. *L'Unità*, 14 January 1970. A union dossier claimed that 14,000 citizens had been charged for offences connected with industrial disputes during the autumn of 1969. 46% were brought by the police, but another 24% were brought by employers. L. Borgomeo and A. Forbice, *14,000 denunce. Chi, dove, come, perchè* (Rome 1970, quoted by Sergio Turone, *Storia del sindacato*, pp. 498–9.
18. Franco Ferraresi writes: 'The Piazza Fontana affair was not unique. One year later, in December 1970, a textbook coup d'état was carried out by Prince J.V. Borghese.... The attempt was mysteriously called off in the course of its implementation.... Later investigations would show that the intelligence services were informed from the very beginning and that they deliberately misled the judiciary'; 'The Radical Right in Postwar Italy', p. 91.
19. 'Relazione della "Commissione Pirelli" sulla revisione di strutture della confindustria', *Mondo Economico*, 8, 28 February, 1970, p. 43.
20. Ibid., p. 51.
21. M. Salvati, *Il sistema economico italiano*, pp. 106–7.
22. V. Foa, *Sindacati e lotte operaie*, pp. 187–93.
23. For Lotta Continua, for example, the problem was how to 'generalize' the factory struggles; the unity of workers and students was conceived of as the first link in construction of a total social revolt. Only the unions got in the way; one Pirelli worker was reported as saying: 'The unions are worse than the bosses. The bosses give you a hard time and sometimes sack you, but the unions will be there in whatever factory you go to'; *Lotta Continua*, 6 December 1969.
24. V. Foa, *Sindacati e lotte operaie*, pp. 193–5.
25. Alberto Melucci lists four factors which inhibited union recourse to the law: i. fear of adverse judgements, ii. distrust of the law and the State, especially among older unionists; iii. preference for local government mediation; iv. fear of exposure to bad publicity. With the implementation of the Labour Charter, judgements were decidedly more favourable in the industrialized north where the magistrates were more progressive and the unions were stronger; see A. Melucci, 'Vers une système de relations professionnelles en Italie', *Sociologie du travail*, 1, 1976, pp. 385–400; see also *Lo Statuto dei Lavoratori: Un bilancio politico*, Bologna 1977.
26. Federico Mancini, *Terroristi e riformisti*, Bologna 1981, pp. 12–13.
27. Gaetano Insolera writes with reference to the social movements in Italy following 1968: 'These illegal practices ... have a specific theoretical foundation.... They have the power decisively to influence the concept of legality itself.... The institutions of political democracy, the system of rights, are not put in question; on the contrary, their maximum use allows claims to be made concerning the substantial legitimacy of prohibited forms of behaviour'; Gaetano Insolera, 'Criminalità politica e illegalita', in Luigi Manconi, ed., *La Violenza e la politica*, Rome 1979, p. 35.
28. The reforms carried out by the Centre–Left government, for example, did virtually nothing to encourage mobilizations of the kind which had brought it to power. For a fascinating analysis of the discussion of reforms and their 'capitalist' or 'anti-capitalist' role, see Paul Ginsborg, 'The Nature of Reforms: Communist Party Strategy and the Agrarian Question in Southern Italy, 1943–48' *History Workshop Journal*, 17, 1984.
29. Unionized industrial workers in large concerns could use their 'muscle' and the skills of their negotiators to advantage. Those in workplaces with less than ten employees were not covered by the law. Given the 'dual' structure of the Italian economy and the conscious strategy of employers to reverse the effects of the Hot Autumn by decentralizing production and 'putting out' work, a large number of workers were

protected neither by laws nor by unions. Women in particular were a key component of this workforce; in the mid seventies an estimated one million or more were homeworkers in the textile and clothing sectors. In the second half of the 1970s this phenomenon (which was referred to as 'black work' – *lavoro nero*) revealed the divisions in terms of pay, conditions, job security, rights and so on which ran through the Italian working class. In these circumstances, the position of the young, of women and of southerners, who were often marginally and precariously placed in the labour market, was very different to that of the workers who had been at the centre of the industrial unrest since 1968. See Massimo Paci, *Mercato di lavoro e classi sociali in Italia*, pp. 220–22.

30. Marino Regini, 'Labour Unions, Industrial Action and Politics', *Western European Politics*, 2 October 1979, p. 58.
31. Giorgio Ruffolo, *Riforme e controriforme*, p. 22.
32. M. Regini, 'Stato e Sindacati nel Sistema Economico', *Giornale di Diritto del Lavoro e di Relazioni Industriali*, 1,1979, pp. 62–6.

17

institutionalization from below: the unions and social movements

The distinctions between strategies and processes of institutionalization 'from above' and 'from below' can be misleading. Firstly, because it suggests a topographical division that is too absolute. For example, the amnesty declared in 1970 was ultimately the result of a political decision taken by the government, but it was also demanded by the social movements, the trade unions and the parties of the Left. Secondly, it suggests a certain coherence of planning or the unfolding of an inevitable logic, while the confusion of events belies such an analysis. Nonetheless, the distinction can be useful if these things are borne in mind. As has been seen, there was no shortage of strategic thinking among the powerful, but it was incoherent and contradictory, ranging from strategies of tension to schemes for an orderly pluralism. By contrast, the unions were more coherent in setting about putting their house in order and in giving institutional shape to the magma of discontent.

Unions in the Workplace

During the Hot Autumn, the unions recuperated overall control of the strike movement, but this involved 'riding the tiger' (that is to say, the movement). It was a movement characterized by non-negotiable demands, expressive forms of action and direct popular participation in decision-making – not the sort of behaviour designed to build union organization. However, in the post-contract period, some of the special conditions making such a movement possible were removed. The signing of the contracts for all the sectors ended the contract season – a key institutional condition for the generalized mobilization. 1968–9 was one of the exceptional moments when popular protest erupted into national politics. But expectations of radical change could not run high indefinitely. It was not only the ruling groups who defined the events as abnormal and exceptional, and therefore a 'passing phase'. The unions, too, were anxious that the mass movement should be channelled into the more stable and durable organization needed for 'normal times'. They sought to make demands negotiable, to direct industrial action towards their attainment, and to standardize the structures of representation. In other words, union officials aimed to discipline the movement so that workers acted through the organization which represented them, and not outside it.

The institutionalization of the movement can be seen particularly clearly in relation to the reorganization of representation. The first moment of the process was marked by the split of the new collective subject formed in the struggles into two components: the participators – the active minority with an interest in power – who tended to become representatives, and the non-participators, who tended to delegate responsibility.[1] One of the most dramatic instances of this occurred at Fiat in Turin, where the campaign of opposition to the formalization of the delegate's role was fought under the slogan 'we are all delegates'. Workers joined the unions and accepted the delegates *en masse*, despite their earlier refusal. Similarly, in Milan, at Alfa Romeo, Pirelli and Sit Siemens, where workers had shown considerable self-organization, especially at shopfloor level, anti-union radicalism had few exponents. Lotta Continua, in particular, argued that the delegates were 'an instrument with which the unions impose their line and repress the vanguards', and that the union structure forced them into 'corporative and sectoral' struggles. It counterposed proletarian struggle and democracy to parliamentarism and phoney democracy.[2] However, such reasoning fell on stony ground.

The split between the delegates and the majority of workers was neither sudden nor absolute, unlike the breakdown in the relations between Lotta Continua-style 'movementists' and the movement in the factories. Throughout 1970–71 levels of participation in meetings remained high, and decisions were taken often against the wishes of the union officials. Many aspects of the delegate structures, which were officially accepted as the basis for union reorganization by the CGIL in December 1970, bore the imprint of the movement from below; for example, delegates were elected by all workers, they represented a 'homogeneous group' (for example the foundry), they were liable to recall and they were empowered to bargain at plant level. Indeed, it was only as a result of the movement's struggles that they first won recognition from management and came to replace the internal commissions.[3] Management resistance was often fierce and workers had continually to fight for their rights. At Borletti recognition was not ceded until 1972, and when the delegates went *en masse* to negotiate they were regularly turned back.[4]

The tendency for the separation between the informal leaders, who emerged during the Hot Autumn, and the rank-and-file workers had numerous causes in the divisions within the working class. Surveys of factory representation in the province of Milan for 1970 and 1973 show that women and immigrant workers remained heavily under-represented, though younger workers and the semi-skilled were better represented.[5] Even when women were in the majority, they usually chose male workers to represent them. It was rare to see a woman's face in positions of authority. Only six of the 185 officials of the engineering unions in Lombardy were women.[6] The lack of representation did not, of course, result directly from the decline of the movement after 1969, but it was exacerbated by it. The participation of women workers in the industrial conflicts had specific characteristics. Ida Regalia has observed in relation to Sit Siemens in Milan:

> There seems to be a negative correlation between militancy and unionization in the moments of fullest mobilization; in this instance the women ... would be the most active (in the marches, pickets and demonstrations) and the most determined to adopt extreme forms of action. The women, typically, use lightning stoppages that are 'expressive', and their demands remain latent, or are ends in themselves (against the speed of the line, foremen and piece-work).[7]

In other words, women workers tended not to be regular members of the unions, but were often the most angry and intransigent during mobilizations. With the return to 'normality', the women workers tended once more to delegate decision-making to the male organizers.

The reasons for this 'unpredictable' behaviour are to be found in a long and complex history – a history which was largely hidden from view until it was brought to light by the feminist movement in the 1970s.[8] The burden of work in the home as well as outside, the high turnover in women's jobs and the dominance of the idea of the male family wage (all of which were taken for granted by the unions) – these were just some of the factors discouraging women's regular participation in the workers' movement. However, the great majority of shopfloor representatives saw women workers as emotional, untrustworthy and difficult. The problem, for them, appeared to be increasingly one of discipline and order rather than the furtherment of democratic participation.

This preoccupation was a general one of how to adapt the union to a less conflictual situation. Many leading activists became full-time union organizers after 1969, while in 1970 up to 50 per cent of delegates resigned.[9] The unions did not invent the turn to organization as the answer to problems in the wake of the Hot Autumn. The revival of

Leninism, to give another example, was but another symptom of a cultural shift away from ideologies of spontaneity and towards those of organization. It was a phase which saw 'organizers' give priority to organizational growth – a tendency which Piven and Cloward have written of as:

> the presumption of most reformers and revolutionaries who have tried to organize the lower classes ... that once the economic and political resources of at least modest numbers of people are combined in disciplined action, public or private, elites will be forced to yield concessions necessary to sustain and enlarge mass affiliation.[10]

Delegates did not understand the private use of collective gains; for example, time saved.[11]

However, whilst among delegates whose formative experiences were as protagonists of a social movement there was an intense desire to represent their fellow workers' interests, sacrificing free time and bonuses in the process, the unions were less willing to be subject to democracy from below. Within them there was considerable resistance to the formation of the new delegate structures. The engineering sections of the unions botched together a compromise at their first unitary conference in March 1970; the factory council composed of delegates was accepted as the new unit of organization in the factory, but on the condition that the union branches and the internal commissions set them up, while continuing to represent workers in their own right. By the time of the conference the following year, some 168 factory councils had been set up in the province of Milan, but without union sponsorship. The conference subsequently accepted the factory councils as the successor to the other bodies. The confederations, however, were more cautious. The CGIL called for the postponement of the decision until after the hoped-for reunification of the unions, before it changed its position in January 1972. Meanwhile the CISL favoured the reinforcement of the existing structures.[12]

Of the unions in Milan only the FIM–CISL consistently championed the new forms of shopfloor democracy.[13] However, even this maverick body showed disquiet about the emergence of forces outside union control. An article, written by a prominant spokesman for the Left in the CISL, urged:

> the task of serious revolutionaries is not to make conjectures about council-communism, reducing the question of the union to its use as an instrument for other purposes, but to apply their energies radically to transform the unions, despite political and bureaucratic opposition.

He warned against the danger of producing an English-style situation characterized by shop-stewards who were 'corporatist'.[14] The Italian unions wanted to make sure that the new democracy was channelled through their organizations.

The union leaderships wanted to prevent rank-and-file democracy threatening the delicate compromises agreed between the confederations. The new organisms had to be subject to what the CGIL called the 'general and binding criteria that give political unity to the structures'.[15] In other words, they had to be compatible with the existing organizations and therefore as much like the internal commissions as possible.

The unions, therefore, sought to institutionalize the movement. This was achieved, especially from 1972 onwards, by several means. Pizzorno writes:

> Above all, candidates were chosen according to union list. Then, especially in cases of clashes between the leadership and the rank-and-file, the electoral constituencies were widened, thereby dissolving homogeneous group representation.[16]

Then, negotiating power was centralized in the hands of the executive committee of the factory council. The delegates became important only in moments of mobilization when an extended network of activists was required. The role of the section and factory meetings was curtailed; from being the sovereign bodies of the movement in which participation involved being physically present, expressing opinions and allotting tasks, they became plebiscitory occasions; they tended to assume the character of demonstrations with long speeches by the representatives, agendas set in line with overall union strategies, and rituals designed to affirm collective identity and minimize shows of dissent.[17]

Although the new forms of representation derived their names and their increased powers from the movement of the Hot Autumn, the aspiration to reconstruct the unions (not to mention society) in their image was defeated. Similarly, the radical demands and forms of struggle developed by the movement were adapted to facilitate negotiation. One of the most significant innovations was the so-called *Inquadramento Unico* which the unions promoted in 1972. This entailed 'squaring the circle' by trying to reorganize the grading system to recognize both skill and demands for parity and reduction of grades. Quintessentially, it required extensive technical knowledge and bargaining skills, and provided a framework for reaching compromises. As such, it privileged the role of the union officials and the construction of a complex apparatus for processing disagreements.[18]

The Unions and Social Protest

The key processes of institutionalization of the workers' movement centred on the 'consolidation' by the unions of the gains of the Hot Autumn. Establishing control over the workers was a necessary precondition of their strategy for winning greater influence within civil society and the state. Pizzorno has formulated this relationship in terms of a 'political exchange' in which the unions guarantee consensus within the system in exchange for benefits conferred by the state.[19] In this framework, the equivalent of the strike is the withdrawal of cooperation. The Hot Autumn involved such a withdrawal (though the unions were not in the first instance responsible for this), and the very success of the non-cooperation put the unions in an unprecedented position in representing a wide spectrum of discontent within society. They were said to have usurped functions proper to the political party. As Vittorio Foa wrote in 1969: 'Today, with the deterioration in the representative institutions, the unions increasingly need a real link between civil and political society'.[20] However, the unions, it seems, were almost fearful of their new power to mobilize protest. The Piazza Fontana bombing threw into relief the political stakes involved in widespread industrial action. In July 1970, they lost their nerve; the confederations revoked a general strike when the government threatened to resign if it was carried out.

The possibilities for the unions to mobilize protest were very considerable in the early seventies, when burgeoning social movements appeared in the schools and further educational establishments, on housing estates, in prisons and in the factories. The factories themselves were no longer isolated within their surrounding neighbourhoods, but connected to them via associational networks (parties, political groups, tenants' organizations and student–worker liaison). The other identities of the worker (parent, tenant, etc.) were being mobilized. Furthermore, there was a willingness to support other groups such as the homeless poor and students. At the grassroots, people were prepared to use their power to disrupt, following the Hot Autumn's successful example.

The unions' response to these developments was contradictory. They saw opportunities to extend their influence in society, and hence to strengthen their bargaining power with the institutions. They also wanted to have a hegemonic role over social movements in order to prevent the emergence of dangerous forms of protest, such as the insurrections in Reggio Calabria in 1970, which, it was believed, had been led by neo-Fascists.[21] At the same time, there was anxiety, especially in national leaderships, about promoting illegal and disruptive actions undertaken by the rank-and-file. This oscillation can be seen in connection with housing struggles, the *autoriduzione* campaigns and the 150-Hours Scheme.

The struggles over housing in Italy grew up in the context of the students' and workers' movements (the first rent strikes in Milan took place in January 1968), but did not come to occupy a central place in social conflicts until 1974 when soaring inflation made it important for the unions to defend living standards outside the factory. However, from 1970, in Milan, protest welled up among the poor in the rundown central quarters and on the estates of the hinterland. One of the papers of the Catholic workers' organization wrote of the plight of these people:

> The contradictions of our society are there before us. On the one hand, there are the families of immigrant workers, who, in the struggle for survival have been thrown into situations of unemployment, slum habitations, overcrowding, high rents and the *laagers* called 'evictee centres'. On the other hand, the authorities build palaces for the rich in areas that were once working class.[22]

Evicted families squatted in municipal housing on the estates at Gallaratese. The following year, homeless families squatted houses in via Tibaldi, and got involved in dramatic confrontations with the police, involving students from the architecture faculty, political groups, and the FIM–CISL. In April 1971, after several evictions from squats, a group of women invaded Palazzo Marini, the municipal headquarters, and hurled furniture out of the windows.[23] By 1976 there were 1,500 squats of public and thirty-seven squats of private housing units.[24]

The protest actions over housing presented special problems for the unions. Firstly, the leading protagonists ('sub-proletarians', student agitators, southerners and women) had little to do with the traditional organizations of the working class. Indeed, the latter had tended to discriminate against sub-proletarians.[25] Secondly, the first tenants' bodies such as the Tenants' Union (*Unione Inquilini* –UI) were formed independently of the unions, and privileged 'movementist' tactics of direct action. Thirdly, the unions themselves were linked to the parties represented in local government and institutions such as the IACP (the municipal housing authority). Some elements of the unions came out in support of the housing struggles; the FIM in Milan was especially active in promoting what it saw as an elementary issue of social justice which justified defiance of oppressive property laws. Similarly, many factory councils were sympathetic. They adopted UI's demands for rents equivalent to 10 per cent of the family wage, for greater public housing provision (in Milan it amounted to 15 per cent of the total), and for the requisition of vacant property.[26] The union Left then campaigned for the setting up of the area councils (*consigli di zona*) to enable representation to reach beyond the factories.[27] But the national leaderships preferred the traditional general strikes and demonstrations in the pursuit of housing reforms, since these gave them greater central control and served to apply pressure on governments. In Milan, the CGIL responded to the housing struggles by creating the SUNIA, a tenants union, and, to keep pace, the CISL followed suit. These organizations acted as lawyers and negotiators for the individual tenant, and as campaign mobilizers. In cases of squats of public housing, they opposed the squatters in the name of the would-be tenant. In this way, the resources of the confederations were used to undermine the protest movement, and to win participation in the local authorities through their ability to guarantee order. This orientation was reinforced in 1975 with the accession of a left-wing junta to power in Milan and in other cities.[28]

The *autoriduzione* campaign of 1974–5 created similar problems for the unions in their attempt to mediate between the institutions of the state and the popular protest movements. Apart from anything else, the unilateral non- or part-payment of transport, gas, electricity and telephone tickets and bills was illegal.

Autoriduzione already had a recent history, as we have seen. But although the term was coined by the Pirelli workers, their reduction-of-output tactic had little to do with these new developments. *Autoriduzione* was now a consumer's rather than a producer's activity. The first real examples are found in the sporadic and spontaneous refusal to pay transport fares by students and workers in 1968–9. Often ticket-collectors allowed demonstrators to travel free of charge, while the latter behaved as if the trams and buses belonged to them. In 1971 young people in Milan enforced price reductions at pop concerts by threatening to sabotage performances.[29] However, it required the activity of factory council delegates and zone committees (*consigli di zona*) to provide the backbone to the resistance to rises in transport fares, and electricity, gas and telephone prices in 1974–5.

Engineering workers and their unions, especially in Turin, where the movement originated, were leading protagonists. Delegates issued tickets at reduced rates on the private buses, and set up organizations to collect the names of those pledged to refuse payment of the increases on the other bills. Although the unions at national level opposed the spreading of the protest, or used it cautiously as a tactic to apply pressure on the government and local authorities, rather than encouraging a new arm of popular action, it was from a factory-based syndicalism that the movement drew its strength.[30] The avowed aim of *autoriduzione* was to defend the gains of the Hot Autumn from the effects of inflation. In the process, groups of workers pushed the unions into acting like political parties and into legitimating illegal forms of struggle, thereby encouraging civil disobedience by other social groups.[31] Whereas the unions' natural adversaries were private and public companies, the logic of the new turn in social conflict made the state into the enemy. However, it was not a logic that was acceptable to the union confederations, and was only canvassed by a small minority of workers close to the extraparliamentary groups. Indeed, the *autoriduzione* campaigns were the last significant mobilizations to uphold direct action politics against the tendency to substitute confrontation by dialogue.

The 150-Hours Scheme, which was incorporated into the engineering contract of 1973, differs from the previously mentioned examples of the unions' relationship to protest movements in that it did not arise directly in response to them. An anecdote has it that the French wife of a trade-union leader was responsible for the idea, which gave workers 150 hours a year paid study leave to help them catch up on their education (in other words, to get the basic middle school diploma – *terza media*). Whatever the immediate origins of the proposal, its germination and particular shape cannot be understood without reference to the 1968-9 debates on workers' access to education and the critiques fo schooling 'from a workers' point of view'. 'Positive utopias' (to use Vittorio Foa's words) such as the 'four hours work – four hours study' idea anticipated the new scheme.[32] The 150-Hours Scheme was part recuperative, part 'cultural holiday'. It was designed to enable workers to get a certificate (an estimated 80 per cent of engineering workers did not have the *terza media*) which affected promotion. But it has been run under union auspices rather than by the state or by private schools. Thus the contents of the courses, the forms of pedagogy, the selection of students and the appointment of teachers has depended on the unions. State examiners, for instance, have tacitly accepted collective assessment.

The implementation of the scheme has led to some remarkable experimentation in group learning and teaching.[33] The student and worker protagonists of 1968-9 were brought together again in the classroom. Groupings of intellectuals in Milan, from the cooperative library of the Centro Ricerche sui Modi di Produzione, the political science faculty of the State University and the Calusca bookshop, channelled great energies into teaching and preparing study notes for the courses.[34] Workers drew on their own experiences and knowledge of the labour process, of health problems, etc. so that sessions involved an exchange between students and teachers. Even if some of the early utopianism disappeared, giving way to instrumental orientations, the scheme showed the unions' capacity for interpreting and channelling forces of protest beyond the confines of the factory. Sections of New Left intellectuals were drawn into the orbit of the unions, which acted as their new 'Prince'.[35]

In 1973-4 the unions reached the height of their influence and prestige among exploited and oppressed social groups, and among radical intellectuals. They, rather than the parties of the Left, had managed to strengthen the hand of social movements and to lead them without suffocating their autonomy. The unions had capitalized on *operaism* (which in the 1960s had been deeply anti-union) to assert the idea of 'workers' centrality' (*centralità operaia*) which they claimed to represent. Workers' organization and methods of struggle had become the model for other forms of social mobilization (tenants' unions, etc.). The making of a 'working-class culture' had become the goal of left-wing intellectuals. The 150-Hours Scheme symbolized the unions' hegemony over agitators both inside and outside the working class. However, that hegemony was fragile and conjunctural. Economic crisis and changes in the confederations' policies created a new situation in which unions lost their leading role within civil society.

Emilio Reyneri dates the change from 1973 when:

> The close connection between factory struggles over wages and work organization, and struggles directed towards the institutions, full-employment policies and the south was broken. The unions tilted the balance decisively in favour of long-term political and economic policies, just as they had always done in periods of crisis and recession.[36]

The consequence of this was that, over the following years, the unions were guided much more by the decisions of the confederal secretariats than by what was discussed on the shopfloor. In other words, there was a return to the practices of the mid 1960s; political parties reasserted themselves at all levels of the organizations; consultation with institutions was privileged over consultation of the rank-and-file; internal democracy withered whilst intolerance towards dissent increased. The gap within the organizations, between the leaderships and the ordinary membership was greatly accentuated, and intellectuals close to the unions grew more and more critical.[37]

To provide an adequate account of the institutionalization of the unions in this period would require analyses of how Italian society changed as a whole. It would mean looking at how the conception of workers' centrality became increasing anachronistic with the marginalization of the 'mass worker', and the rise in unemployment and the 'black labour' market. It would be necessary to chart the electoral swings towards the PCI in the 1975 and 1976 elections, and the replacement of the union by the party as the modern prince.[38] But limitations of space mean that it is only possible to note here how the unions in the mid seventies ceased to represent a broader spectrum of social protest and social movements. In part IV this change is looked at through the movements of social groups, women and youth in particular, which found themselves excluded from the cultural as well as the socio-economic world inhabited by the unions. But what appeared in the 1970s as the redefinition of the unions' role in society, can also be seen as the end of an era in which the workers' movement shaped all forms of social conflict and protest. Institutionalization is too limited a concept with which to make sense of this historical turning-point.

Notes

1. Alessandro Pizzorno, 'Due logiche dell'azione di classe', pp. 28–32.
2. *Lotta Continua*, 7 February 1970.
3. Ida Regalia, 'Rappresentanza operaia e sindacato', pp. 215–16.
4. Rina Barbieri interview.
5. Guido Romagnoli, *Consigli di fabbrica e democrazia sindacale*, Milan 1976, pp. 168–87.
6. Gian Primo Cella, 'La composizione sociale e politica degli apparati sindacali metalmeccanici della Lombardia', *Prospettiva Sindacale*, 1, April 1973, p. 11.
7. Ida Regalia, *Lotte operaie e sindacato*, vol. 4, p. 101.
8. See part IV, chapter 21, pp. 325–9.
9. I. Regalia, 'Rappresentanza operaia e organizzazione sindacale', pp. 220–3.
10. F. Piven and R. Cloward, *Poor People's Movements*, pp. x–xi.
11. Pietro Marcenaro makes an interesting observation on how the politicized workers and activist delegates post 1969 condemned workers who 'saved time' (by working extra fast for short periods, etc.) so that they could play cards. The most minute everyday 'private' resistances were subjected to the collective scrutiny in the person of the delegate; the delegate thought of the factory as 'central to politics and as the point of departure for social change', and abhorred the individual use put to time that needed to be controlled by the collectivity; P. Marcenaro, *Riprendere Tempo*, Turin 1981, pp. 60–1.
12. G. Romagnoli, *Consigli di fabrica*, pp. 68–70.
13. Sandro Antoniazzi, 'Per lo sviluppo dei consigli', *Dibattito Sindacale*, November–December 1970, pp. 5–12.
14. G. Sclavi, *Due CISL*, pp. 23–8.
15. G. Romagnoli, *Consigli di fabbrica*, p. 76.
16. A. Pizzorno, 'Due logiche dell'azione di classe', pp. 28–9.
17. I. Regalia, 'Le assemblee', pp. 107–8.
18. Tatiana Pipan and Dario Salerni, *Il sindacato come soggetto di equilibrio*, Milan 1975, pp. 92–124.
19. A. Pizzorno, 'Scambio politico e identità collettiva nel conflitto di classe', in Colin Crouch and Alessandro Pizzorno, *Conflitti in Europa*, Milan 1977, pp. 407–33.
20. Vittorio Foa, 'La frontiera politica del sindacato', *Problemi del Socialismo*, 39, 1969, p. 223.
21. The concern to maintain public order was also a concern to promote suitable conditions for trade-union activity. Unions since the postwar period feared social chaos. Di Vittorio, secretary general of the CGIL had said: 'To the extent to which the unions make these gains – thereby acquiring sufficient power and prestige to defend the workers' interests in a free and orderly fashion ... bloody uprisings and terrorist attacks ... will become useless and will disappear from the social scene. All society will benefit thereby, as will its degree of civilization'; quoted by A. Pizzorno, 'Sull'azione politica dei sindacati', p. 877.
22. *Il Giornale dei Lavoratori*, paper of the ACLI, 23/24, 17 June 1971; quoted in Mariella Moresco and Giordano Fornasier, *'Lotte "spontanee" per la casa a Milano dal 1945 al 1975 e loro rapporto con le istituzione e le forze sociali'*, Tesi di Laurea,

Universita Cattolica del Sacro Cuore, Milano, Facoltà di Scienze Politiche, 1976, pp. 71–2.

23. Ibid., pp. 44–86.

24. Thomas Angotti, *Housing in Italy*, New York 1977, p. 53.

25. The history of the workers' movement is also the history of how groups of workers have differentiated themselves from the very poorest in society, how the waged have separated themselves from the unwaged. The unions and parties at different moments in Italian history confirmed these divisions, even when speaking up for class unity. The late sixties and early 1970s mark an important moment of questioning of the category 'working class' as defined by the Left orthodoxy. Radical Catholics and the extreme Left discovered the sub-proletariat of south and north, of the prisons and the slums. See Commissione Carceri di Lotta Continua, *Liberare tutti i dannati della terra*, Rome 1972.

26. Mariella Moresco and Giordano Fornasier, '*Lotte "spontanee" per la casa a Milano*', pp. 86–7.

27. Quaderni del Centro Operaio, *Consigli di zona*, Rome 1974.

28. Mariella Moresco and Giordano Fornasier, '*Lotte "spontanee" per la casa a Milano*', pp. 178–90.

29. *Lotta Continua*, 26 June 1971.

30. Eddy Cherki and Michael Wieviorka, 'Autoreduction Movements in Turin', *Semiotext(e)*, 3, 1980, pp. 72–80; Alemanni, Fergio and Ghedda, *Autoriduzione*, Milan 1975.

31. The main forms of *autoriduzione* carried out in the mid seventies required a high degree of coordination, which is one of the reasons why union involvement was so important to their success. However, there were cases of hit-and-run *autoriduzione* in supermarkets, and agitators on the Left 'theorized' or fantasized about 'proletarian expropriations'. A leaflet is reported to have been found after a raid in a supermarket which said: 'The goods we took are ours just as everything which exists is ours because we have produced it through our exploitation.... Not civil disobedience ... not sub-proletarian anger, but the embryo of political struggle against exploitation, parallel to that in the factory'; *Contro Informazione*, November 1974. Dario Fo's play '*Can't pay? Won't pay!*' begins with a scene in which a working-class housewife arrives home after doing the shopping without paying.

32. The impact of the cultural revolution and the factory militancy on the 150-Hours Scheme becomes evident by comparing it with French legislation which was geared more to the needs of industry than to workers' needs, and which was state run.

33. Danilo Giori and Gabriella Rossetti Pepe, '150 ore – per una cultura di classe', *Classe*, 9, 1973, pp. 67–88.

34. These study notes comprised extracts from studies on the labour market, piece-rates, union history and other subjects which were researched by the radicalized sociologists mentioned in chapter 4. An introduction spelt out their political orientation: 'The use of the 150-hours courses is of great importance since it will involve a large number of workers to implement this contract gain, allowing a mass growth in the cultural and political knowledge of the working class.' It warned against subordinating the courses to 'capitalist technological development'; Centro Ricerche sui Modi di Produzione, *Dispense su salari e inflazione*, 2, Milan 1974, p. 2.

35. For an analysis of the trade unions as 'the prince' in the eyes of Italian sociologists, see Diana Pinto, 'La sociologie dans l'Italie de l'aprés-guerre', p. 246. The reviews *Classe*, *Febbrica e Stato* and *Inchiesta* in 1973–74 carry many articles full of enthusiasm for the 150-Hours Scheme. An example: 'For the first time the principle of education as a right in general has been introduced, not tied to company interests, but ... as an attempt to break down the separation between work and study', *Fabbrica e Stato*, July–August, 1973, p. 3.

36. Emilio Reyneri, 'Il sindacato in Italia oggi', in *Il Mulino*, July–August 1977, p. 505.

37. See the analyses of contemporary trade unionism coming from Alessandro Pizzorno, Emilio Reyneri, Marino Regini, Ida Regalia and other sociologists. Within the unions similar opinions were being voiced; Bruno Manghi of the FIM–CISL of Milan wrote:

'Today the unions are treating the political institutions as sacred. A veil of untouchability (*un velo di intoccabilità*) covers local bodies, parliament, the parties, the regions and so on.... It is difficult for the unions, now that they have become legitimated, to do anything but celebrate the institutions without regard to their politics since they have adopted a static and limited role within the political system'; Bruno Manghi, *Declinare Crescendo*, Bologna 1977, p. 31.

38. Vittorio Foa wrote: 'The approach of the Communists to the area of government invites people to think that politics is "in command" (*al posto di commando*), not in terms of class conflict but of mediation and the management of society.... The same council structures ... allow people to imagine a transition from waged worker to producer ... that means a transition from a traditional capitalism to a capitalism with workers' participation'; V. Foa, 'Il sindacato di fronte alla transizione', p. 172.

PART IV

social movements and protest in the 1970s

18

residual and emergent political forms

In the decade following the dramatic resurgence of social conflict in 1968, in Italy and in other Western capitalist countries, there was a spread and multiplication of oppositional movements. Alberto Melucci has listed the main examples:

> (a) worker conflict involving new categories (semi-skilled, young and immigrant); (b) trade union conflicts extended to different occupational groups (especially in the tertiary and public sectors); (c) student movements; (d) urban struggles; (e) feminist movements; (f) youth counter-culture; (g) movements linked with sexuality; (h) regional movements; (i) ethnic conflicts; (j) consumer protest; (k) ecological movements; (k) neo-religious and communitarian movements; (m) anti-institutional protest (over justice, prisons, psychiatric hospitals); (n) struggles linked to the problems of health and medicine.[1]

There are, of course, considerable differences between these forms of action, and they have specific histories, but in various ways they can all be related to the movements of '68–9. It was the students' and workers' movements which provided the models which other movements attempted to replicate, revise or break away from.

The significance of the '68 legacy can be seen in how the thoughts of a generation continually returned to it. The struggles of those years were recounted in epic terms; oral accounts were supplemented by autobiographies, interviews, histories, anniversary editions and reprints which celebrated moments of heroism. The genre which can be called the 'class struggle epic' was recreated. The worker emerged as a mythical figure in the iconography of the period[2], and is the protagonist of a particular type of narrative.

A *leitmotif* of the epic is the protagonist's struggle to transcend individualism, and the celebration of the moment of transcendence. It recurs especially in autobiographical accounts. Antonio Antonuzzo's story about his 'conversion' to unionism is but one example of a phenomenon which was most pervasive in oral form.[3] In the 1970s oral history developed to capture these memories for posterity, and to serve as a basis for reflection on the nature of subjectivities and experience. Above all, worker militants were encouraged to recount their personal histories.[4] An interesting example of this is an interview with a Fiat worker, Franco Platania, recorded in 1974. The story starts with how Platania conducts a personal war with the company (how he outwits foremen and survives the hell of the production-line), and follows his adventures through to the Hot Autumn when, he declares, he changed utterly as a person:

> At that moment my personal biography loses all interest as far as individual motivations are concerned. I joined a Communist organization, Lotta Continua. The important moments of my life tended to become one with the collective moments of struggle that were being shared by the whole working class of Fiat. I felt that every day, as I took on increased political responsibilities, I also took on new dimensions as a human being.[5]

In this instance the epic struggles and the joining of a revolutionary organization are elided, but that is really a secondary element in a typical narrative. More important is the way in which the individual's contingent and haphazard story is subsumed in the story of a class, which is also a future and a destiny.

The re-telling of '68 was an aspect of an important shift in political attitudes. It was necessary, in the wake of the social movements, to legitimate undertakings with reference to an active consensus formed in collective struggles, rather than with reference to institutional definitions of consensus, such as the parliamentary vote. Thus, within the unions, there was a continual evocation of the Hot Autumn, which represented a moment of rebirth. The struggles of '68–9 were, in other words, a fount of legitimacy, and a mythic renaissance for their protagonists. However, the struggles were interpreted in different and conflicting ways, and during the 1970s there was a process of reappraisal. It was said that 'lessons had to be learnt', and that the earlier movements had limited and even prevented the emergence of radically new forms of opposition. By the time of the tenth anniversary of 1968 the number of critical, and even dismissive, analyses had largely displaced the celebratory accounts.[6] Another generation had grown up for whom '68 was a second-hand experience. From a vantage point in the 1980s it is possible to get a clearer picture of how the '68–9 movements left a contradictory legacy, which looked backwards into the past, as well as anticipating future developments.

With the benefit of hindsight, some useful, though necessarily cautious, distinctions can be made between the political and social projects which took shape in the 1970s. These can be broadly divided into 'residual' and 'emergent' forms. These terms are more 'epochal' than the categories of 'movement' and 'institution' so far referred to which are more adequate for the analysis of the shorter term developments. The former are useful in highlighting longer term historical shifts. Raymond Williams offers a useful definition:

> By 'residual' I mean that some experiences, meanings and values, which cannot be verified or cannot be expressed in terms of the dominant culture, are nevertheless lived and practised on the basis of the residue – cultural as well as social – of some previous social formation. There is a real case of this in certain religious values.... A residual culture is usually at some distance from the effective dominant culture, but one has to recognise that, in real cultural activities, it may get incorporated into it.... The pressures are real, but certain genuinely residual meanings and practices in some important cases survive.

> By 'emergent' I mean, first, that new meanings and values, new practices, new significances and experiences, are continually being created. But there is then a much earlier attempt to incorporate them, just because they are part – and not yet a defined part – of effective contemporary practice.... It may be true of some earlier phases of bourgeois society that there were some areas of experience ... which it was prepared to assign as the sphere of private life.... But I am sure that ... because of developments in the social character of labour, in the social character of communications, and in the social character of decision, it extends much further into certain hitherto resigned areas of experience.... thus, the effective decision, as to whether a practice is alternative or oppositional, is now made within a very much narrower scope.... This is usually the difference between individual and small-group solutions to social crisis and those solutions which properly belong to political and ultimately revolutionary practice. But it is often a very narrow line.... A meaning or practice may be tolerated as a deviation, but as the necessary area of effective dominance extends, the same meanings and practices can be seen by the dominant culture, not merely as disregarding or despising it, but as challenging it.[7]

Williams's definitions are primarily made in reference to cultural practices, but they can equally be applied more generally. They parallel Touraine's analyses of 'traditional' and 'new' social movements.[8] Williams differs in putting more stress on how the 'residual' survives and can be reactivated, and he continually underlines the ambiguities and double-sidedness of attempts to counter the dominant order.

Marx's remarks in *The Eighteenth Brumaire* about bourgeois revolutions give a complementary perspective in which political action and cultural practices fuse:

> Men make their own history but they do not make it just as they please; they do not make it under circumstances directly encountered, given and transmitted by the past. The tradition of all the dead generations weighs like a nightmare on the brain of the living. And just when they seem engaged in revolutionizing themselves and things, and in creating something that has never yet existed, precisely in such moments of revolutionary crisis they anxiously conjure up the spirits of the past to their service and borrow from them names, battle-cries, and costumes in order to present the new scene of world history in this time-honoured disguise and this borrowed language.[9]

It is important to note that emergent and new movements can only struggle into existence by drawing on existing traditions. These provide not just easily disposable accoutrements, but the very languages with which to think about social change. At the same time, they impose limits, and make it difficult to communicate experiences for which adequate words do not seem to exist. However, although the new forms can only emerge by selecting, transforming and/or discarding the old, Marx writes that the residual forms can also be revived in ways that parody and that flee from reality, making 'ghosts walk about again'.[10] Indeed, it is Marx's contention that only proletarian revolutions can 'strip off all superstition in regard to the past'; for him they find their 'poetry' in the future. However, a century later, the neatness of this distinction between the 'proletarian' and 'bourgeois' revolution seems dubious in a way it might not have in Marx's lifetime, as the experiences of '68–9 testify.

The social movements of those years can be seen as comprising a rich mixture of residual and emergent forms which contained both 'oppositional' and 'alternative' practices. The student movement is an excellent example. It was a new phenomenon historically, and brought a new order of social conflicts into the open. As Alain Touraine has observed of the French situation:

> the students are representative of all those who suffer more from social integration and cultural manipulation directed by the economic structures than from economic exploitation and material misery.[11]

At the same time, the ideologists of student revolt were deeply influenced by the ideas of Marxism and, to a lesser extent, by radical religious thinking. The movement's symbols were borrowed directly from the workers' movement, as was the rhetoric of its leaders. The 'residual' forms played a significant role in reactivating protest, as has been seen in the case of the Marxist 'heresies' in the 1960s, but the revival of neo-Leninist organizations led to an impasse; the old residues not only were inadequate in the sort of analyses and politics they offered, but they actively resisted the emergence of new forms of social action. Whilst the social movement at its height combined different and often conflicting practices, when it went into decline it fragmented. Subsequently, some of the fragments, such as the neo-Leninist ones, tended to stand in the way of new movements, whilst others contributed to their formation.

It is perhaps possible schematically to distinguish between those forces or tendencies coming out of the late sixties which anticipated and stimulated a 'movementist' politics (emergent forms), and those which proposed organizational solutions (residual forms) to what they regarded as the failings of social movements. As will be seen, this polarization is too simple, there is no clear demarcation between the backward-looking and the forward-looking. History is not a linear development, a railway line connecting past and future. It is notable that what Touraine refers to as traditional forms (industrial militancy, for example) continued to dominate the shape of social conflict in the 1970s, and were themselves extended and realigned in novel ways. Nonetheless, the distinction is not purely an analytic convenience. The increasingly drastic and diverse reassessments of '68–9 in the following decades signalled a real polarization; basic assumptions were put into crisis. It was then no longer clear that the labour movement was the major progressive force nor was it clear what, if anything, was meant by the labels 'the Left' or 'comrade'.

Indeed, the conflicts which emerged in terms of 'movement versus organization/bureaucracy' (itself a frame of reference typical of traditional politics), involved questions of precisely the legitimacy or value of a labelling process, and hence of a political subculture's whole vocabulary and sets of codes. The protagonists of a 'movement' politics did not merely propose a different answer to the question 'how should opposition be organized?', but asked new sets of questions concerning aspects of people's lives which had previously been excluded from politics altogether. They introduced notions of autonomy and control which required social action of a kind incompatible with parties, unions and other organizational models.

The emergence of these new forms of social conflict is the central theme in the sections which follow. These will focus on youth protest and the feminist movement in Italy, since they have been widely seen as the most representative forms of what has been called a 'post-political politics'. Rather than attempt to provide a detailed history or chronology of the formation of these movements, there will be something more akin to a brief outline of their development, which compares them with their forerunners of the late sixties. The recurring question that will be asked is: to what extent were these movements a continuation of tendencies present in the mobilizations of '68–9 and to what extent did they represent a rupture with that past? This question entails looking at the Italian situation (an equivalent examination of the French, German or British case would tell a very different story), but raises the more epochal and general observations of Alain Touraine on the consequences of the transition from a predominantly industrial to a post-industrial society. No answer can be given on this question without a thorough consideration of the changes in the political, social and economic structures of advanced capitalist societies (and this will not be attempted here), but it is possible to undertake the more limited task of seeing how social movements evolved over the seventies. Analysis will centre on how social actors worked with inherited models and adapted them to their needs.

Two chapters, therefore, deal with the youth and women's movements (in that order), but the first chapter will take the case of red terrorism in Italy. This requires some explanation since terrorism (as will be made clear) cannot be considered a social movement. The intention is rather to look at the phenomenon in its early years as a residual form of politics. It, too, was a product of the political upheavals of the late sixties, and no account of the oppositional political developments following 1968–9 would be complete without an analysis of the role of terrorism.

Notes

1. Alberto Melucci, *Sistema politico, partiti e movimenti sociali*, Milan 1979, p. 150.
2. For a discussion of this iconography by historians, see Eric Hobsbawm, 'Man and Woman in Socialist Iconography', *History Workshop Journal*, 6, Autumn 1978, pp. 107–21.
3. See part I, chapter 3, pp. 41–3.
4. There was a rediscovery of a native tradition of oral history before the turn to Anglo-Saxon academic models; see Cesare Bermani, 'Dieci anni di lavoro con le fonti orali', *Primo Maggio*, 5, Spring 1975. Luigi Manconi describes the 'life-history' (*storie di vita*) as the most innovative genre of the post-'68 period; *Nuovo e difficile*, p. 12.
5. Franco Platonia, '23 years at Fiat', in Red Notes, *Working Class Autonomy and the Crisis*, p. 108.
6. Guido Viale's *Il sessantotto* published in 1978 remains caught in a time-warp since it substantially reproduces his ideas of 1968–9 when he was a leader in Lotta Continua. For a spoof celebration, see Cooperativo Centro Documentazione *1968–1978 – Dieci anni di invecchiamento*, Florence 1978 (translatable as 'Ten Years of Ageing'). One cartoon, which shows an ex-leader looking into a crystal ball labelled '68, has a phantom gypsy saying 'Your future is in the past'.
7. Raymond Williams, *Problems in Materialism and Culture*, London 1980, pp. 41–2.
8. Alain Touraine, 'I nuovi conflitti sociali', in A. Melucci, ed., *Movimenti di rivolta*.
9. Karl Marx, *The Eighteenth Brumaire*, in *Selected Works*, London 1970, p. 96.
10. Ibid., p. 97.
11. Alain Touraine, *The May Movement*, p. 355.

19

the Red Brigades: sons and daughters of '68?

Alberto Melucci has referred to red terrorism as 'paradoxically both the most radical result and the most radical antithesis of the new "class movements"'.[1] It is a paradox that commentators have too easily dismembered into one of its constituent parts; they have thereby interpreted '68 as the Pandora's Box of modern Italy, or have written off red terrorism as quite extraneous to the social movements.[2] It is the paradox, however, which is central. Without analysing the ambiguities and the polysemic elements of the subculture created by the social movements of 1968–9, it is impossible to make sense of both the coexistence and the conflict that characterized the relationship between the social movements and the first of the major armed organizations, the Red Brigades, during the course of the 1970s.[3]

In the early 1970s the coexistence between the movements and the armed organizations was often amicable. In the late seventies, however, separation and antagonism characterized the relationship between the majority in the social movements and the project of the armed organizations. An outline of this development is useful in understanding how the Red Brigades represented a residual form of politics which, while being unequivocally oppositional, was fundamentally at odds with the idea of social movements that took root in 1968–9. Or, to put it another way, it was the very radicalness – the total nature of the Red Brigades' opposition to the dominant order – which made them regressive.

The Formative Years: From Sabotage to Assassination

The Red Brigades announced their formation in a leaflet, dated 20 October 1970, in which they described themselves as 'autonomous workers' organizations ... ready to fight the bosses and their lackeys on their own ground as equals'.[4] The founder members had all been active in the movements of the previous two years; Renato Curcio, for example, who was the leading theorist among them, had edited a political review at Trento University.[5] Their decision to take up arms was seen by them as a break with, but also a maturation of, developments in social conflicts. Early documents emphasize the limits of the Hot Autumn struggles; they are described as disorganized, localized and largely subordinate to the capitalist system ('it is not possible to bargain with the bosses for socialism'). The blame for the non-revolutionary outcome of the workers' action is laid at the door of the 'revisionists' (the Communist Party and others), who were said to have contained the movements within the bounds of legality.[6] It is this 'legalism' which is identified again and again by the Red Brigades as the principal weakness of the opposition forces. Respect for the law is seen as a crippling handicap in the presence of a capitalist class which unleashes state violence whenever threatened. The bloody events of Avola, Battipaglia, and the Piazza Fontana bombing seemed to provide irrefutable evidence of this analysis. Yet, in the eyes of the Red Brigades, the working class had shown itself ready to use violence during the mass mobilizations and in everyday clashes with management.

The idea of 'proletarian violence' was by no means exclusive to those choosing to engage in armed struggle. It was widely canvassed within the social movements. Moreover, violent action was a significant, if largely symbolic, aspect of clashes with the police or with foremen. 'War' metaphors abounded in the language of the Left. The Red Brigades could, therefore, legitimately claim to be drawing on a tradition and not just a movement's spontaneous outbursts of rage. Their proclaimed aim of building proletarian counter-power in the factories, which entailed 'dismantling the hierarchies of command', was a basic element in the *operaist* politics shared with other political groupings of the 'extra-parliamentary left', such as Potere Operaio and Lotta Continua.[7] Furthermore, the Red Brigades had ideas about 'proletarian justice' which were common to the Marxist–Leninist tendencies in the movement. This meant that 'the people' had to create its own standards of justice in its struggle against the dominant laws, and that the 'enemy' had to be subjected to its jurisdiction. The cardinal ideas of proletarian justice were not the Red Brigades' inventions; they were present in the social movements. But, as will be seen by looking at the Red Brigades in action, they combined what were disparate elements in the activities of the social movements to produce a systematic terrorist strategy.

The Red Brigades' first target was the Pirelli rubber company in Milan, which had been in the eye of the storm of industrial conflict. In December 1970 the contract for the sector was once more due for renewal. Inside the

Biccoca plant some former members of the CUB had formed a grouping calling itself Collettivo Politico Metropolitano. It was on militants on the inside that the guerrilla actions relied for reports on the shopfloor situation, the listing of potential targets, the distribution of leaflets, feedback and recruitment. It seems that the trade union and Communist Party had regained control of the plant after the crisis in their authority in 1968–9, but there remained bitter and frustrated activists on the Left. A publication by a group of these within the factory council warned against the danger of concluding from the worsening repression that 'fascism is knocking at the door', and that 'we in the name of the working class must accept the level of struggle imposed by the bosses and turn to proletarian violence'.[8]

It was among these kind of militants, who were highly politicized and with experience of daily skirmishes with management, that the Red Brigades won support. Alessandro Pizzorno outlines the consequences of what he refers to as an 'excess of militancy', which became a particular problem with the formation of the right-wing Andreotti government in February 1972, and the exclusion of activists from posts within the factory councils. Pizzorno writes that the latter had

> a bitter taste in the mouth left over from their hopes in 1969–70. Therefore, they either remain on the margins, or they continue to work autonomously exposed to the danger of making their political and trade-union commitments extremist. The sudden brake put on the development of conflict provokes an uncontrolled rush forward.[9]

The first activities of the Red Brigades were geared to this factory-based conflict. It is possible from early communiques to reconstruct the main features of their actions. Seven of these related to actions at Pirelli between November 1970 and April 1971.[10] Communique 1 listed the names of the bosses' agents (*servi del padrone*); thus, Ermano Pellegrini 'has the job of keeping files on political activists, and every day sends a report to the personnel manager, and is in contact with the commissioners of police'; 'Brioschi, Ercole Carlo. Personnel secretary in cable division – champion scab'. These 'spies' are said to 'deserve pillory', and Giovanni Nasi, 'inventor of the Pirelli piece-rate system', 'deserves to be abolished along with his piece-rates'; 'for every comrade they hit at during the struggle, they must pay the price'. Communique 2 called this the principle of 'for one eye – two eyes, for a tooth – the whole face'. The names, addresses and telephone numbers of the 'enemies' are provided with the obvious invitation to workers to make threatening calls and write abusive letters. In Communique 5 the best way of fighting for the contract is said to be 'using the only arm available by making the struggle more incisive and violent'. The actual actions, however, consisted of destroying the cars of managers held responsible for sacking a leading militant, and of setting fire to a warehouse of tyres. Otherwise, there is extensive incitement to sabotage in Communique 7 which detailed the 'intelligent' use of nail and spanner in disrupting production.

The purpose of the Red Brigades' actions was spelt out in the publication *Sinistra Proletaria*. It seems that the principle objective was to educate the workers and to make them see that the state was an organ of class repression which could only be fought with arms:

> It is time to move ahead to a general confrontation in order to establish the principle among the proletarian masses in struggle that 'no one has political power unless they have military power'; to educate the proletarian and revolutionary Left to the need for resistance and partisan actions; to unmask the oppressive and repressive power structures that divide the class.[11]

However, the scale of terrorist actions remained localized, and they were designed to supplement ongoing workers' struggles.

In March 1972, the Red Brigades carried out their first kidnapping (although 'kidnap' is a strong word for twenty minutes in the back of a van). The victim was a manager of Sit Siemens. He was photographed with a placard around his neck with the following inscription: 'Milan 3.3.72, Macchiarini, Idalgo, fascist manager of Sit Siemens, tried by the RB. The proletarians have taken up arms, for the bosses it is the beginning of the end.' Another placard attached to the manager who had now been dumped in the road declared: 'Red Brigades – Hit and run – No one will go unpunished – Strike one and educate one hundred – All power to the armed people.'[12]

In the early 1970s there were important actions around housing (squatting, tenants' strikes), which continued the grassroots politics developed in 1968–9.[13] However, the Red Brigades did not succeed in making any links with them, despite an obvious interest in extending their activities outside the factories. They were especially attracted by the resistance to evictions, which brought disobedience of the law to the forefront:

> the law is the instrument of capital ... it is against this unjust violence that the people will exercise its just mass forms of violence, as it has already started to do in many areas of Milan, Turin, Rome and Naples.[14]

However, the Red Brigades concentrated their energies on the industrial proletariat, and had little time for the urban sub-proletariat, who were the chief protagonists of the housing actions.

Until April 1974 the targets of the Red Brigades remained constant. In June 1973 they kidnapped a manager of Alfa Romeo in Milan, and then in

December a Fiat personnel manager. In addition, they attacked 'yellow union' personnel and property. The kidnappings were for longer periods, and involved the interrogation and trial of the victim. The Red Brigades consciously cultivated an alternative jurisdictional ritual, and put the existing legal system 'on trial' when in April 1974 they kidnapped a judge, Mario Sossi, in Genoa. The terrain of struggle, they now claimed, reached the 'centre of the state-organized counter-revolution'. Sossi was found guilty of crimes against the proletariat but was released unharmed. However, two years later, the kidnapped procurator Coco was executed.

The escalation of operations, which reached their highpoint with the kidnapping and assassination of Aldo Moro in the spring of 1978, turned the Red Brigades into an important political factor.[15] Apart from their military 'professionalism', they showed remarkable ability in manipulating the media to communicate their messages; communiques roneoed and left in public places, or the graffiti with the RB symbol had previously been seen by few people; now, they were read by newscasters and appeared on the front page of newspapers.[16]

Over the years there has been debate about whether changes in the terrorists' objectives reflect a generational turnover, so that some have contrasted the 'Robin Hood' idealism of the founding figures to the cold-blooded ruthlessness of their successors. There has also been speculation about the origins of the phenomenon, including suggestions that a *grande vecchio* or old partisan figure was the mastermind. Clearly, many mysteries remain, and the story is a complex one in which individual biography as well as broader historical developments play a part.[17] The purpose here is the more limited one of identifying the continuities and breaks between the Red Brigades and the social movements from which they came.

The Meaning of Political Violence

In many respects, the political ideas and organization adopted by the Red Brigades were yet another minor variant of the Marxist revival of the late 1960s. For them, the Chinese model was an especial source of inspiration, but that was common enough. The radical difference between the Red Brigades and others lay in the fact that they alone based their notion of leadership and revolutionary action in the systematic use of violence. As Luigi Manconi has observed:

> For the Red Brigades the use of violence is the only form of struggle, the programme, the strategy, the mainspring and the verification of class consciousness.[18]

In the social movements, violence was just one of the many means of protest, and was normally a secondary feature. Usually, the greater the support for a strike, occupation or demonstration, the less the need to use coercion. Violence was also given meaning by the context in which it took place. What the Red Brigades attempted to do was, firstly, to imitate what they took to be popular forms (the threatening letter, punitive actions), and then to substitute them by more professional and military actions (kidnappings, assassinations) carried out 'in the name of the masses'.

Yet the Red Brigades' assumption of a vanguardist role did not alienate the considerable 'area of sympathy' which surrounded them up to the time of the Moro case. Indeed, their daring exploits won them admiration, especially among contemporaries who had taken part in the social movements of the late sixties (even though the Left press regularly condemned terrorist actions as the work of Fascists or *agents provocateurs*). In a sense, figures like Renato Curcio and his comrade-in-arms Mara Cagol had chosen to live out what others had only fantasised; they had sacrificed personal ambitions and safety for the cause. The rescue of Renato from prison, Mara's death in a shoot-out with the police, the treachery of the infiltrator, the ex-monk 'brother Girotto', and the kidnapping of hated managers and judges – all these fired imaginations fed on the 'class struggle epic'. Nor is there reason to suppose that assassinations provoked popular revulsion. For a period, the 'justice' administered by the Red Brigades was attributed a providential role. They were the 'avenging angels', who punished corrupt oppressors. Manconi argues convincingly that the Red Brigades' perception of this

> has led them to stress the connotations of legitimacy and justice in their actions
> – trials/counter-trials; state prisons/people's prisons; army of the bourgeoisie/
> army of the proletariat.... From this flows the whole macabre and grotesque
> ritual of the 'trials', 'interrogations' and 'sentences', of a judicial procedure
> which imitates and inversely mirrors that of the state apparatuses.[19]

The Red Brigades' capacity to attract sympathizers and capture the imagination needs to be related, it should be said, to the state's continued paralysis or deliberate inactivity in the face of social protest. The divide between the *paese reale* and the *paese legale*, between represented and representatives (the first violent expression of which was post-unification banditry[20]), was exploited to the extent that the terrorists could lay claim to a measure of popular support not forthcoming for the government itself. The actions of the authorities in the wake of the Piazza Fontana bombing were a turning-point in this respect. An article by Franco Ferrarotti in 1970 pointed unequivocally to the dangers:

Violence is always basically the response – inarticulate, desperate and often counter-productive – to grave inadequacies on the part of the authorities. It reveals a loss of contact, communication and identification between the top and the bottom of the social system, and to the exploitation by those above of those beneath them. The official holders of constitutional power should be thankful for violence. It is their alarm-bell. . . . It is right to consider alternative solutions such as pacificism or non-violent resistance. . . . But their effectiveness depends on the existence of a common trust and respect for the rules of the game.[21]

However, the politicians and authorities paid little attention to the alarm-bell, and showed an often arrogant disregard for the 'rules of the game', while speaking of their belief in parliamentary democracy. The Piazza Fontana bombing was the first of a long series of cases involving conspiracy and corruption in high places for which no one was found guilty and punished.[22]

Government repression, the 'strategy of tension' involving fascist bombings, the inadequacies or absence of reforms created conditions favourable to terrorist initiatives, Norberto Bobbio has observed how the development of secret government was parallelled by the growth of clandestine organizations:

I call crypto-government the ensemble of actions performed by terrorist political forces that operate in the dark with the various secret services . . . or at least without their opposition. The most disturbing episode of this kind in recent Italian history is undoubtedly the Piazza Fontana massacre. After more than ten years . . . the mystery has not been revealed . . . the darkness has not been lifted . . . I limit myself to recalling the suspicion . . . that state secrecy has been used to protect anti-state secrecy. . . . The degeneration of the Italian democratic system began there . . . if the existence of *arcunum imperii* remains a hypothesis, it is not a hypothesis but a tragic reality to have experienced the return, unthinkable a few years ago, of *arcana seditionis* in the form of terrorism. Terrorism is an exemplary instance of occult power present throughout history. One of the founders of modern terrorism, Bakunin, proclaimed the necessity of an 'invisible dictatorship'. Whoever joins a terrorist group is forced to go underground, wear a mask, and exercise the same art of lying so often described as one the prince's stratagems. He, too, scrupulously follows the maxim that power is more effective the more he knows and sees without being seen.[23]

However, the formation of the Red Brigades cannot be adequately explained as a reaction to state action. The short-lived and desperate history of the Gruppi Armati Partigiani (GAP), which tried to recreate a partisan organization to fight an expected *coup d'état*, was an aberration.[24] The Red Brigades might have grown as a consequence of the state's incompetence, wilful neglect or instrumental exploitation of terrorism, but they were, from the beginning, an offensive not a defensive organization. Their project was conceived in the light of the immense potential for revolutionary transformation that the social movements appeared to reveal. It is necessary, therefore, to examine more closely the chemistry which produced terrorism out of movements from which terrorist organizations were absent.

'68 and the Elements of a Regressive Political Culture

The relationship between the political culture of '68 and the formation of red terrorism has been the subject of extensive debate in Italy.[25] One of the most interesting contributions is that of Nando Dalla Chiesa, who tries to explore the contradictory ideas and practices which led to political outcomes of radically different kinds.[26] Dalla Chiesa suggests six headings under which the problems can be usefully examined. These are: the sovereignty of ideology over theory; the myth of the revolution 'around-the-corner', democracy as a formal problem; the anthropomorphic vision of capital; the disdain for human life; and the mystique of violence.

Firstly, there is the question of ideology – 'the triumph of dogmatism'. Dalla Chiesa writes:

> This element of the political culture is the prior and necessary condition on which the other elements develop ... and what makes them susceptible to terrorist developments.[27]

Although the experience of '68–9 cannot be reduced to its sloganizing, nevertheless, 'ideologism' played a determinant role in structuring the realities of social conflict. The thriving personality cults were the crudest manifestation of a tendency to make society's image conform to the readings of Marx, Lenin and others. This had placed limits on the freedom to construct political alternatives and created a climate within organizations which was inimical to debate and discussion. The ideologues of the Red Brigades were among the most sectarian and fundamentalist in this respect. They recited the writings of Chairman Mao and Lenin *ad nauseam*, and their own tracts made claims and pronouncements (supported with citations from the classics) as if from on high. The slogans around the neck of the kidnapped Idalgo Macchiarini were taken from Guevara and Lenin. For all their claims to novelty and originality (within the Communist tradition), the Red Brigades were exponents of ossified orthodoxies.

Secondly, the myth of incipient revolution common to the generation of

'68 had important effects, not only in motivating action, but in producing acute disillusion many months later. It gave priority to the efficiency, speed and timing of political action, and hence the subordination of means to pressing ends. The notions of the 'militarization of power' and the need to face capital 'on an equal footing' were an extreme version of a widespread fetishization of organization within left-wing organizations. But the Red Brigades interpreted the idea of 'class war' literally. For them, the civil war was not to be awaited; it was to be anticipated in the present by undertaking urban guerrilla action. The Red Brigades saw their task as anticipating the future by making the use of force a choice to be taken now rather than later. History taught the necessity of arming the struggle in its earliest stages. For the Red Brigades, history could be analysed as a series of transitions from spontaneous to organized violence through to civil war. So, while 'the revolution' was not just 'round the corner', the unfolding of the historical process meant that the moment of reckoning could be counted on.

Thirdly, the political culture of '68 contained negative conceptions of democracy, which became the commonsense of many thousands of activists, especially on the extraparliamentary Left. Although the social movements of '68–9 saw remarkable experiments in political participation and unleashed radical democratic forces in Italian society, the existing democratic institutions (parliament, elections) were normally seen as either a formal sham or a palliative. Direct, participatory democracy was counterposed to bourgeois democracy.[28] For the Red Brigades, democracy was just a mask disguising the real exercise of power, and hence the need to strip it away. Such an attitude to decision-making also militated against open internal discussion.

The anthropomorphic vision of capital and the state is the fourth element identified by Dalla Chiesa as part of the political culture of '68 which combined with others to produce red terrorism.[29] The identification of capital with the capitalist (often pictured with a black hat and money bag), and of domination with the dominators, was part and parcel of a traditional socialist propaganda, which was revived during the struggles of 1968–9. As Dalla Chiesa points out, analyses were particularly contradictory when they combined a reductive economism (capitalism as the 'objective' operation of a set of laws), with 'conspiracy theory' in which Agnelli and Pirelli were seen to pull the wires of Italian capitalism. Instead of using Marxist theory to show that the capitalist was not personally responsible for a capitalism of which he himself was victim as well as beneficiary, power was identified with the powerful. Thus the term *servi del padrone* (bosses' lackeys), which was so often used in Red Brigade communiques, by detailing the functions carried out by management personnel and state officials served to confirm their 'objective' guilt. The first targets of the Red Brigades tended to be figures with reputations for fascism or anti-unionism in the workplace, and right-wing judges hated within the extraparliamentary Left. Therefore, their 'guilt' had a subjective dimension in that they had been over-zealous in carrying out their functions. However, the subsequent inclusion of known democrats as targets confirmed the 'objective' nature of the enemy.[30]

The political culture of '68 was contradictory on the question of the value of human life and the relationship between politics and morality. There was a wave of protest against injustice and inhumanity in the world; its targets were not only imperialist war, but the everyday exploitation in the factory which resulted in heavy casualties (significantly, deaths through industrial accidents were referred to as *omicidi bianchi* – white murders), and the toll of backwardness in the south. At the same time, slogans, songs and writings expressed a desire for revenge, and a disdain for the value of the lives of oppressors and exploiters; a favourite quotation from Mao's sayings was: 'The death of a worker weighs heavily like a mountain, while that of a bourgeois weighs as lightly as a feather.' The killings at Avola and Battipaglia in 1968–9 provoked mass revulsion and anger which were infused with these sentiments.[31] What is particularly significant is that responses to exceptional events crystallized into widely-held opinions. The threshold of the acceptability of taking lives in revenge was lowered.[32] This can be seen in the theorization of political violence within the student movement, and subsequently within the extraparliamentary Left, but it was also an aspect of popular thinking. Workers had little time for worrying about injuries suffered by foremen and managers at the hands of the 'red handkerchiefs' at Fiat; these were jokingly referred to as 'industrial injuries'.[33]

The Red Brigades' class view of the value of human life was, therefore, not peculiar to them. Yet they took it a stage further by purging such views of their spontaneous and contingent character, and by making them the basis for an alternative ethic. The idea of the total autonomy of the proletariat from bourgeois morality coincided with a politics in which the ends justified the means.[34] In this schema, lives became commodities to be exchanged; the act of pardon and the act of execution were to be judged only in terms of political criteria. However, the language of the Red Brigades' communiques contains epithets that liken the victims of their actions to animals (pigs). The very term *servi del padrone* is used to disenfranchise and exclude from the human community those that are 'servile'. Marxist-Leninism is then bolstered with references to the Old Testament morality of 'an eye for an eye', while bureaucratic language is used to categorize class enemies.[35]

The exaltation of violence, the last element of the political culture of '68–9 under consideration, was intimately related to the others but was the one which was crucial for the justification of armed action.

Political violence was propagated in the movements not only by the publication of writings by Fanon, Sartre and Latin American authors, but in the leaflets, songs and images that accompanied the social conflicts. The clashes of Valle Giulia between students and police in Rome entered the mythology of the student movement, and the popularity of the song *Violenza* showed a bloodthirsty vein in the protest. Violence was not only accepted as unavoidable, but it was frequently considered baptismal and cathartic. Numerous slogans expressed these ideas. Yet violence in the political culture of the movements was more a matter of words than deeds, and it is too simplistic to assume that the one leads to the other. When violence did take place it was likely to be a by-product and resulted from mass activity, not the pre-planned action of a self-selected minority.

In fact, the Red Brigades were at first criticized for their elitism, rather than for their use of violent means as such. For example, the 'sincere revolutionary vanguards' were criticized by some Pirelli workers,

> because they show through the propaganda of terrorism that they have no faith in the masses, and in attempting to substitute them through exemplary actions, they can only provoke further repression.[36]

However, the line of demarcation was not always so clear. When the chief of police in Milan, Luigi Calabresi, was murdered because he was held to be responsible for the death of the anarchist, Guiseppe Pinelli, in December 1969, a paper closely identified with protest movements declared: 'His death is the result of an act with which the exploited can identify.'[37]

The Red Brigades began by exalting 'mass violence'; the early attacks on property, the threatening of managers and even the first kidnappings sought to imitate things that had been spontaneously carried out by workers. The Red Brigades were attracted to those struggles distinguished for their violence, and studied historical and contemporary examples,[38] but the actions which overtly expressed an idea of popular justice especially interested them. A particular incident that recurs in early Red Brigade documents is the so-called 'pillorying' (*gogna*) of Fascists at Trento in 1970, [39] whereas three years before future members of the organization drove down to Cutro in Calabria where peasants had occupied land, seizing and burning down the municipal buildings.[40] On the one hand, they were searching for a tradition that had been forgotten or censored so as to re-awaken a sleeping historical consciousness. On the other, they wanted to find modern equivalents relevant to the metropolitan capitalist situation.

The notion of creating 'proletarian justice' was not widely propagated within the social movements of 1968–9 when people showed a preference for breaking rather than making laws. Its immediate roots were in Maoism (and its Stalinist antecedents); for example, the Cultural Revolution's trials and self-criticism provided models. It was through the pursuit of 'people's justice', the implementation of which was in the hands of the 'armed party', that the Red Brigades shaped their conception of violent revolution. In doing so, they moved away from the shared political culture of 1968–9. The idea of political violence which attracted the protagonists of the social movements was more likely to be explosive, elemental and passionate – in brief, romantic. The use of violence was, however, considered secondary. For the Red Brigades, by contrast, violence had a quite different status; it was the primary and determining form of struggle.[41] In this sense, the Red Brigades became a fully and exclusively terrorist organization.

In part, the Red Brigades' conception of the primacy of violence was founded on a disdain for human life, and this served largely to lower the threshold at which it was thought acceptable to kill. The most critical elements in the political culture of '68 which combined to make terrorism a legitimate form of action were the weak sense of democracy and the ideological dogmatism. The military and vanguardist vision of the struggle for hegemony meant that politics could ultimately be superseded by force; ideological dogmatism not only facilitated the choice of armed struggle, but was its necessary condition of existence. It cemented the organization together and excluded the possibility of other political choices.

Dalla Chiesa's analysis is largely orientated to uncovering the roots of red terrorism in a diffuse political culture. He is careful to stress that it was not a simple relationship, but a contradictory one:

> conflict is the crucible in which the cultural mix [giving rise to terrorism] is brought together, and yet it is also the most solid barrier against the transformation of those elements into a coherent political project. The decline and containment of conflict, the crushing supremacy of political over civil society, and the collapse of utopianism – all these serve to free those cultural elements . . . the mass movements are therefore, because of their historic characteristics, simultaneously cradle and antidote to terrorism.[42]

However, Dalla Chiesa overplays the elements of continuity. What remained contradictory and complex in the social movements was drastically transformed and simplified by the Red Brigades.

The sharpness of the discontinuity between the armed organization and the social movements is highlighted by the decision to go underground. Clandestinity, as Luigi Manconi has argued, represented the critical step in the formation of terrorist organizations; it was the ruptural point and point of no return.

The choice of clandestinity was, of course, inspired by an ultra-vanguardist conception of political action (in the case of the Red Brigades it was made after a heated debate inside the Collettivo Politico Metro-politano, in which the majority condemned the idea for taking power out of the hands of the masses). However, once decided upon, clandestinity brought with it a whole set of consequences. It entailed a way of life that was, *de facto*, cut off from the everyday experience of most people. The need for secrecy and invisibility meant that activists had to hide their political views, and avoid open political discussions. Thus, they deprived themselves of the means of testing and verifying political hypotheses and projects by discussing them with those (the working class) they purported to represent. While other political organizations had to measure them-selves in terms of the support and participation they were able to win and mobilize, the Red Brigades were only indirectly subject to such pressures. The conditions of underground life functioned as a material basis for the construction and elaboration of a version of reality which did not allow for refutation or questioning. It underpinned a logic which increasingly drove the Red Brigades to impose their own reality, and to make the world conform to their view of it.[43]

The process whereby certain forms of political radicalism which aspire to emancipate people from injustice, regress and come to reproduce some of the worst features of the society they oppose has long preoccupied thinkers.[44] The decline and crisis of movements, the replacement of dialogue by repression on the part of the state, the rise of irrationalism – these are just some of the explanations put forward for the rise of terrorism.[45] Usually, the reasons given by those with sympathies for the Left tend to stress the role of external circumstances, while those more to the Right emphasize the psychological. It is, therefore, interesting to note that in Italy in the late 1970s and early eighties many analyses of the development of red terrorism have looked at the individuals involved without automatically pathologizing them.[46] The terrorists are shown to be not 'monsters' but, for the most part, rational human beings who made a political choice; a choice, moreover, which made sense (that is, was comprehensible) to peers in the social movements.

Nonetheless, the red terrorist option, with its life of clandestinity and military activity, required setting oneself apart from the movements, by internalizing strict codes of behaviour and a claustrophobic morality. For example, life inside the Red Brigades obliged women to adopt male codes. It meant getting rid of 'feminine' attitudes and, not surprisingly, the feminist movement was regarded as petty bourgeois.[47] The Red Brigades spoke of their choice as one imposed by the system and as 'objectively' necessary. Moreover, their actions, which were predicated on the idea that the social order was repressive and authoritarian, functioned to fulfil their prophesies. Their total opposition to the society in which they lived, paradoxically, made them its prisoners.

If red terrorism was partly a product of the social movements of 1968–9, it was also their antithesis and a negation of their main impulses. The movements of the late sixties and, as will be seen, of the seventies, brought with them a rich cabaret of unexpected behaviour and experimentation, and an unleashing of individual energies. They were significant and innovatory precisely to the extent that they did not fit ideological schemas. Faced by their challenge, the Red Brigades turned away and looked for images conforming to their eschatology and desire for purity.[48] The present and everyday realities, so important to the new movements of the seventies, were sacrificed on the altar of the past in the name of a future utopia in which society would be a planned, harmonious whole without pain and disorder. History, fortunately, does not move in such ordered ways, and the crisis of the Red Brigades in the early 1980s marks the end of a peculiarly tragic attempt to 'make the ghosts of the past walk about again'.

Notes

1. Alberto Melucci, 'New movements, terrorism and the political system', *Socialist Review*, 56, 1981, p. 118.
2. For example, Roberto Mazzetti writes of terrorism as a simple extension of the extremist politics of 1968, *Genesi e sviluppo del terrorismo*, Rome 1979. For the opposite thesis, see Roberto Massari, *Marxismo e critica del terrorismo*, Rome 1979. For the more general problem of defining terrorism and types of terrorism, see L. Bonanate, ed., *Dimensioni del terrorismo politico*, Milan 1979.
3. Another important red terrorist group was Prima Linea, which grew out of the more 'spontaneist' rather than orthodoxly Leninist currents in the movements.
4. Soccorso Rosso, *Brigate Rosse, che cosa hanno fatto, che cosa hanno detto e che cosa se ne e detto*, Milan 1976, pp. 70–71.
5. Silj, *Mai più senza fucile*.
6. Soccorso Rosso, *Brigate Rosse*, pp. 63–5.
7. Luigi Bobbio, *Lotta Continua*; G. Vettori, *La sinistra extraparlamentare in Italia*, Rome 1973.
8. Gruppo di Compagni del Consiglio di Fabbrica, *Lotte alla Pirelli*, Milan 1971, p. 18.
9. 'Terrorismo e quadro politico – tavola rotonda', *Mondoperaio*, 4, 1978, pp. 7–9.
10. *Re Nudo*, April 1971.
11. *Sinistra Proletaria*, January 1971.
12. Soccorso Rosso, *Brigate Rosse*, pp. 109–16.
13. See Thomas Angotti, *Housing in Italy*, New York 1977.
14. *Sinistra Proletaria*, June 1970.
15. P. Furlong, 'Political terrorism in Italy: reaction and immobilism', in J. Lodge, *Terrorism: a challenge to the state*, Oxford 1981.
16. For a discussion of the role of the press in relation to terrorism, see R. Lumley and P. Schlesinger, 'The Press, the State and its Enemies', *Sociologial Review*, 4, 1982; R. Wagner-Pacifici, *The Moro Morality Play. Terrorism as Social Drama*, Chicago 1986.
17. See G. Bocca, *Noi terroristi*, Milan 1985; four volumes of research based on interviews with terrorists carried out by the Cattaneo Institute in Bologna is due to be published by *Il Mulino*.

18. V. Dini and L. Manconi, *Il discorso delle armi*, Rome 1981, p. 37.
19. Dini and Manconi, *Il discorso delle armi*, p. 28.
20. E. Hosbsbawm, *Bandits*, London 1972, pp. 23–4; Davis, pp. 59–87.
21. Quoted in Galli, 'La politica italiana', in A. Gambino et al., *Dal '68 a oggi*, Milan 1980, pp. 91–2.
22. See Franco Ferraresi, 'The Radical Right in Postwar Italy'.
23. Norberto Bobbio, 'Democracy and Invisible Government,' in *Telos*, 52, 1982, pp. 54–5.
24. Giorgio Bocca, *Il terrorismo italiano*, Milan 1978.
25. An important debate took place in the period 1978–80 in the wake of the Moro assassination, and included writers, like Leonardo Sciascia (author of the *The Moro Affair*, Manchester 1987), politicians, and trade unionists, as well as academics; see 'La sinistra tra terrorismo e restaurazione – materiali del convegno di Milano del 10–11 maggio', *Quotidiano dei Lavoratori* – dossier supplemento al n. 11, 29 May 1980.
26. Nando Dalla Chiesa, 'Del sessantotto e del terrorismo: cultura e politica tra continuità e rottura', *Il Mulino*, 283, 1981, pp. 53–94.
27. Ibid, p. 73.
28. Norberto Bobbio writes in the Preface to his collection of essays, *The Future of Democracy*, that he wants to reach: 'those who, seeing this democracy of ours, always so fragile, always vulnerable, corruptible and frequently corrupt, would seek to destroy it in order to render it perfect'; p. 22.
29. Dalla Chiesa, 'Del sessantotto e del terrorismo', p. 78.
30. G. Bocca, *Il terrorismo italiano*, pp. 102–3.
31. For example, a student publication listed the names, occupations, place and time of death of twenty-eight people killed by police in protest actions from April 1968 to July 1970; Corrente Proletaria dei Lavoratori Studenti, *Le Lotte dei lavoratori studenti*, Milan 1970, pp. 9–10.
32. On the question of thresholds of violence, see Eric Hobsbawm, 'The rules of violence', in *Revolutionaries*, New York 1973, pp. 209–15.
33. For Fiat workers' attitudes to terrorism, see M. Mantelli and M. Revelli, *Operai senza politica*, Rome 1979; and Cavallini, *Terrorismo in fabbrica*; for the relationship to terrorism of a cross-section of people, from policemen to relatives of victims, see L. Manconi, *Vivere con il terrorismo*, Milan 1980.
34. Dalla Chiesa, 'Del sessantotto e dal terrorismo', pp. 80–83.
35. For an analysis of the language of Marxism–Leninism, see Violi, *I giornali dell'estrema sinistra*, pp. 45–67.
36. *Lotte alla Pirelli*, pp. 38–9.
37. Bobbio, *Lotta Continua*, pp. 105–8.
38. Soccorso Rosso, *Brigate Rosse*, pp. 96–7.
39. *Sinistra Proletaria*, Foglio di lotta, September 1970.
40. A. Silj, pp. 62–3.
41. V. Dini and L. Manconi, *Il discorso delle armi*, p. 38.
42. Dalla Chiesa, 'Del sessantotto e del terrorismo', pp. 91–2.
43. V. Dini and L. Manconi, *Il discorso delle armi*, pp. 41–2. For a fascinating fictional reconstruction of the underground life of a terrorist nucleus, see Luce D'Eramo, *Nucleo Zero*, Milan 1981.
44. For example, the literature produced by ex-Communist Party intellectuals, including Ignazione Silone, reacting to Stalinism in the postwar period; Richard Crossman, ed., *The God that Failed*, London 1950.
45. Bonanate, *Dimensioni del terrorismo politico*.
46. The search to uncover the motivations of terrorists has led to books like Bocca, *Noi terroristi*, Milan 1985.
47. Ida Faré and Franca Spirito, *Mara e le altre – le donne e la lotta armata: storie, interviste, riflessioni*, Milan 1979.
48. On the authoritarian aspects of utopianism and the desire for total solutions, see Sennett, *Uses of Disorder*.

20

the generation of year nine: youth revolt and the movement of '77

Between 1975 and 1979 young people in several major Italian cities entered the political scene as the protagonists of new forms of urban conflict. In Rome, Bologna, Turin, Naples, Milan and other cities, they organized themselves into collectives and 'proletarian youth groups', squatted in buildings and carried out *autoriduzione* (that is, fixed their own prices) of transport fares and cinema tickets, set up free radio stations. At the height of the movement in 1977, tens of thousands of young people were involved in mass protest and street battles with the police.

From February 1977, students mobilized against the *legge Malfatti*, which included a quota system breaking with the principle of the mass university established in 1968, occupying universities and holding demonstrations, such as the 50,000-strong one in Rome on 19 February. Then, on 11 March a demonstrator was shot dead by a policeman in Bologna. Had Francesco Lo Russo been killed in Milan or Rome his death would have provoked less outrage, but the fact that he died in Bologna gave it a special significance. This regional capital prided itself not only on its cuisine and relative peace and prosperity, but on its Resistance traditions and its good government secured by successive Communist administrations.[1] However, the shooting and the subsequent patrolling of the streets by armoured cars evoked an image of the Communist Party as the party of law and order which did not tolerate dissidents.[2] Protest, therefore, became increasingly anti-Communist, culminating in a three-day conference/event in September when Bologna was 'invaded' by the protagonists of the youth movement from all over Italy. Furthermore, the tragedy fuelled the number of those on the Left advocating and implementing political violence, so that before the end of the year the rise of terrorism dominated the horizons of the social movements.

It is misleading, however, to interpret the events only in the light of political violence. The novelty of the new movement sprang from its assertion of a 'youth identity', which had been repressed or displaced in the student and worker politics of the late sixties and early seventies.[3] But that identity was not perceived exclusively in terms of a youth experience or situation; rather it was taken to be emblematic of a situation typical of the modern metropolis. Youth was made to signify exclusion, marginality, and deviance. To be young and working class in a city like Milan meant living in the housing estates of the outskirts (*periferia*) and making a living on the margins of the labour market. In official discourse, this situation was described as a 'social problem' and a 'sickness' that needed to be cured (once, that is, young people began to protest). But, in the language of the movement itself, the identity associated with deviance and marginality was claimed and appropriated by its participants.[4] The 'Metropolitan Indian', who wore warpaint and uttered transgressive chants, did not ask to be 'integrated'; s/he mocked Western 'civilization' and its values.[5] The unemployed asked not for the right to work, but for the right to develop their individual capacities and to enjoy themselves.

The movement of '77 was almost as much a surprise to the New Left, which had grown up in the post-'68 years, as it was to the traditional Left, headed by the Communist Party. Indeed, the 'generation of the year 9' (to use a mock version of the Jacobin calendar with reference to 1968[6]), were also reacting against the older generation. The veterans of '68, and especially the 'leaders' or father-figures, were variously described as people who had made a career out of their radicalism, 'sold out', become mentally sclerotic through excessive orthodoxy and/or nostalgia. The Italian words *sessantottista* and *sessantottardo* (sixty-eighter) evoked an image of the 'has-been'. That sense of difference was expressed in a variety of ways, and age was only a factor in so far as it was perceived in terms of 'dated' language, inappropriate style of presentation and so on. However, the reaction was mainly against the 'institutionalized' forms later assumed by parts of the '68 movements, notably the organizations of the extra-parliamentary Left. In fact, a movement which claimed to represent a complete break with '68 was, ironically, still heavily dependent on ex-sixty-eighters for its intellectuals, leading activists and half-submerged infrastructure of the 'alternative' city.[7] Above all, the fringes of the earlier movement now came to occupy a central place in the new cycle of protest. Yet these previously marginal currents represented polar opposites, in that the blanket term used to describe the new politics – autonomy (*autonomia*) – covered both the so-called 'creative' wing (whose ideas came from artistic avant gardes and the women's movement) and the organized/armed *autonomi* (who were sympathetic to the actions if not the ideas of the Red Brigades).[8] Pulled between these two poles, the development of the movement saw the 'emergent' and the 'residual', the 'new' and the 'old', the 'alternative' and the 'oppositional' intersect, separate and conflict in highly complex ways.

Youth Protest in the Making

Youth politics developed in the 1970s out of a counter-cultural environment similar to that in which feminism took root, but it was primarily male. It was the libertarian and counter-cultural currents coming out of 1968 which incubated many of the ideas, and experimented in the lifestyles that anticipated developments in the mid seventies.

In Milan, the forerunners were associated with two influential reviews, which developed a national readership – *Erba Voglio* and *Re Nudo*, which were both set up in 1970. Their titles give a clue to their identities : *Erba Voglio* refers to the saying : 'The grass I want doesn't even grow in the king's garden', while *Re Nudo* alludes to 'The Emperor's New Clothes'; they affirm children's desires and knowledge in the face of authorities, both familial and state, that attempt to deny them. Both reviews opened themselves to the debates of the early feminist and gay movements.[9] But *Re Nudo* was more important for the formation of a specifically youth politics. It had an extensive circulation (in the summer of 1971 it was reported to sell eight thousand copies in Milan alone), and that figure has to be multiplied to get the number of readers. It also promoted free pop concerts, which drew tens of thousands.[10] *Re Nudo* proclaimed: 'Proletarian youth of Europe, Jimi Hendrix unites us.'[11] Its pages contained a mishmash of American Underground drugs and 'peace-and-love' thinking, Reichian notions of sexual liberation, manifestoes and communiques from the Weathermen and Red Brigades, and Communist visions of cultural revolution. One of the gurus of the Italian Underground (later a convert to Eastern mysticism), Andrea Valcarenghi, summed up the hybrid ambition of this project in the hope that 'the Mao of Western Marxism will grow the long hair of American counter-culture'.[12] Strangely enough, this idea was not so far fetched in the Italian context, and added another chapter (or page) to the country's history of importing cultural goods and models from the United States.[13] But, above all, it meant adapting 'alien' practices to Italian conditions, which, in the early 1970s, meant making them politically left-wing.

At its first national conference the *Re Nudo* collective could claim to have popularized three positive aspects of the underground experience:

1. The organization and generalization of the struggle to reappropriate free time, which reached its climax with the clashes at pop concerts in

1971–2, when the bosses of the music world were forced to reduce the price of tickets for young proletarians.

2. The creation of free, self-managed events and spaces, such as the festivals and counter-cultural centres.

3. The radical critique of the extraparliamentary Left's personal politics, and the recuperation of the themes of anti-authoritarian revolt originating in '68.[14]

When *Re Nudo* was first published, it addressed itself to a readership that was considered to be primarily 'petty bourgeois and student', but, by June 1971, it was talking abouts its public as 'young proletarians'.[15] This term quickly entered into circulation. Although the organization of the extraparliamentary Left consistently attacked *Re Nudo* for its 'remoteness from any form of organization or relationship to the workers', its insistence on the need for a politics of the 'interpersonal, the personal and the everyday', was often more appealing to working-class youth than the sermonizing of the Left.[16] *Re Nudo* had its finger on the pulse of the emerging politics, and addressed the problems of young males living in the big cities. And, in the process, *Re Nudo* had its part in precipitating the crisis of the neo-Leninist groups by giving vent to the dissatisfaction and frustration within them. Although feminists provided the most coherent critiques, the counter-culturalists directed their fire at the moralism which underpinned the militants' sacrifice of the 'private' in the name of the 'public' sphere.[17] The dissolution of this model of political activity was seen as a precondition for the opening up of politics to the lives of those excluded from its coded discourses. The student experiences of '68 were always principally of a university-based movement, and were often a closed book to the next generation. Although the exponents of *Re Nudo* belonged to the '68 generation, they realized this could be a limitation when it came to communicating to a younger generation, and were therefore better at it than those who were unaware of the problem.

Youth had come to mean something quite different by the mid 1970s from what it had meant in the late sixties. Firstly, the distinction between the 'adult' world of regular waged work and youth's transitional situation hardened; the absence of work (or work to match qualifications), and the prolonging of the educational process extended the period of being young of necessity rather than from choice.[18] Then, the divisions between working-class youth and the traditionally middle-class or lower-middle-class student diminished due to the massive expansion of further education, and due to some convergence in their situations. Luigi Manconi and Marino Sinibaldi wrote:

There is a dense network of connections and overlaps between the students' movement and sectors of the proletariat ... the 'strange' figure of the student crops up in the disputes involving door-to-door booksellers, squats of empty property, and in the shape of the unemployed intellectuals going to the labour exchange ... s/he appears equally as the 'strange' worker with the diploma, or the organized unemployed, who study in the 150-Hours Scheme, or go to evening classes.[19]

The youth movement that emerged in the mid seventies was a composite of young manual and white-collar workers, and absentee students. In Milan, an in-depth study of two youth groups showed that one in every five was a manual worker (clearly a minority), but that two-thirds were from manual working-class families.[20] The movement called itself a movement of 'young proletarians', unlike the student movement of 1968, which tended, instead, to make demands *on behalf* of the working class (for example, for greater access to universities). In one Milanese youth group there was even a ban on the participation of non-proletarians because of the fear of being taken over by intellectuals from outside.[21] However, the youth movement was a melting-pot of social and cultural experimentation in which the notion of a 'separate' working-class culture was refuted in practice. In this respect *Re Nudo* played an important part in introducing ideas from the American Underground, which were largely foreign to Italian working-class life, and appropriating forms of 'consumerism' for an oppositional politics. This also meant undercutting many of the ideas, reinforced in the 1968–9 movements, about the need to create an uncontaminated working-class culture.

The changes in the position of youth in the big cities and in their perception of their situation as a group, created a 'crisis of representation'. This was particularly acute in the case of the political organizations of the extraparliamentary Left, which had been formed mainly through the recruitment of young workers and students. The youth movement did not invent a politics *ex novo*; for example, it adapted forms of action such as squatting and *autoriduzione*. Nonetheless, it gave these actions a different purpose and meaning. By examining the forms of action that the movements developed in the period 1975–8, it is possible to explore its particular characteristics.

Taking Over the City: Squatting, Autoriduzione, Free Radio

Squatting was an important form of action for the movement. Squatting had spread in the mid seventies so that in February 1976 an estimated 1,500 units of public housing were occupied. Squats were not now restricted to housing but spread to premises useful as political and cultural centres. In other words, 'needs' were being redefined to mean more than having a roof over one's head. This was particularly the case with the youth groups which started occupying buildings in Milan in early 1975, and had established fifty centres in the city by the end of 1977, involving about 2,000 hard-core squatters, and 3–5,000 occasional participants.[22] A few houses were also occupied; a manifesto issued by a 'youth coordination group' declared:

> We want to live differently from families, and we want to avoid reproducing the same roles within the relationships in the community. . . . We want to live as we choose.[23]

This experiment was relatively isolated, as had been the previous ones attempted by the *Re Nudo* collective. But it expressed a more widespread desire to transform personal relations and win individual freedoms.

In the squats relationships were given priority as ends in themselves. Particular importance was attached to 'being together' (*stare insieme*), and to the exploration of interpersonal dynamics through consciousness-raising. Most activities were pleasure-oriented, with special emphasis on active participation and 'creativity'. In the absence of municipal provision, photographic and music workshops, yoga classes, and so on, assumed 'alternativist' connotations. The very act of taking over a building and running it developed political attitudes.

Although most of the squats were peaceful, some involved ongoing battles with the police, and the threat of eviction hung over all of them. There were also internal dangers, especially heroin addiction which was becoming a major social problem among the young in many cities. Propaganda campaigns through the groups' news-sheets and the provision of help and counselling became a key activity of many of the centres in their desperate attempt to substitute and counteract the repressive measures taken by the authorities against addicts.[24] Social problems were, therefore, continually being defined as political battlegrounds.

Although the social centres of the youth groups were independent of one another, there was a sense of belonging to a movement and sharing common goals. The movement's project was to create a

> different, non-violent and non-competitive politics, which breaks with the cult of leadership and seeks to build egalitarian relationships between men and women comrades.[25]

This alternative sociability was celebrated in pop festivals, such as those held under the aegis of *Re Nudo* at the Parco Lambro in Milan. In 1976, the youth groups in Milan organized a Festival of the Spring, which claimed to revive the pagan and popular tradition of celebrating the 'rebirth of life, renewal and the wish to fulfil needs and desires'. This was a tradition, it further claimed, that 'bourgeois civilization' had destroyed in the name of the work ethic. The Festival's theme was 'Let's take control of our lives' (riprendiamoci la vita); it was part-carnival and part-pop concert, plus a lot of eating, drinking, dancing and dope-smoking.[26]

These festivals and events were expressions of a revolt against the 'ideology of crisis' and the austerity plans propounded by both the government and the Communist Party which included a reduction in the number of feast-day holidays. Opposition to these measures drew together disparate forces around the themes of work-refusal, a shorter working week, and demands for the immediate gratification of a series of 'needs' irrespective of work done. In brief, it was a coalition of counter-culturalists and operaisti based on the principle of 'each according to his needs' as opposed to 'each according to his abilities'. Although there remained fundamental differences between these currents on the means and types of action required to develop the movement, they were united in rejecting the 'ideology' according to which 'labour is the fundamental value in social life and in progress'. Moreover, they questioned the idea that time itself should be organized around the requirements of the productive system rather than in accordance with the needs of human fulfilment. This attitude to waged work did not consist simply of theoretical disquisitions (though there was no shortage of these). Thus, during the enactment of a job-creation scheme for youth in Milan in 1977, eight out of ten job offers were turned down by applicants.[27] What was anxiously debated in the press as 'disaffection from work' could be explained by a number of factors – the growing disparity between the qualifications of the job applicants and the jobs on offer, the preference of some for a life of petty crime or casual working (what was known as the 'art of getting by' – l'arte d'arrangiarsi) and so on. However, individual choices were made in the context of a movement of 'young proletarians', which did not ask for entry to the 'adult' world of work, nor call for the 'right to work'.[28]

The youth movement in Italy developed forms of action (or inaction) which had little to do with the world of work, or were overtly 'anti-work'. Its writings celebrated absenteeism, non-cooperation, sabotage and wildcat strikes as expressions of workers' desires for communism which was defined as the 'abolition of waged work'. It was around consumption and leisure activities that the movement of the 'young proletarians' developed its specific forms of action and established its collective identity.

Autoriduzione of tickets at pop concerts had already been carried out 'spontaneously' in Milan in the early seventies. In September 1977, at a Santana concert in Milan, the practice became formalized; youth groups assured the organizers that the event would not be disrupted in exchange for a fixed price reduction.[29] Earlier, in October 1976, youth groups launched a campaign to force cinemas to reduce ticket prices. A leaflet of the youth groups of *zona* Venezia declared:

> The defence of the living standards of the masses also means establishing the right to a life consisting not just of work and the home, but of culture, amusement and recreation.[30]

The struggle was, it continued, against the monopoly of film distribution and the screening of 'fascist, anti-feminist and *qualunquista*' films. In Milan, about half of the cinemas were concentrated in the centre, and these belonged to the luxury category, while the cheaply-priced cinemas of the outskirts had all but disappeared. In support of their demand for municipal control of cinemas, backing for youth groups and an immediate flat-rate for all tickets, the groups issued tickets themselves. Seven cinemas were hit by *autoriduzione*, but the campaign failed to gain concessions. The president of the Cultural Commission of the *Comune* accused the movement of

> favouring irrational, individual rebellion that only divides citizens ... wanting everything at once, even what it is wrong to want, grabbing at whatever is at hand on board a ship that is sinking.[31]

However, the very obduracy of this response confirmed and publicly underlined the exclusion that was being protested against.

Civil disobedience was at the heart of youth protest. Rule-breaking and the disruption of the routines of city life were practised almost as an art-form – an art-form which fell into the grey area between crime and politics.[32] Classroom behaviour was translated into street politics, and authority in all its guises was held up to ridicule or humorous banter. Yet disruption was more than a last resort of the powerless. It was a means of expression and a source of entertainment, unlike much of the politics offered by the political parties and unions. The slogans of the movement of '77, which were notable for their irony and wit, illuminate this dimension of youth protest.

Umberto Eco commented on the change in semiotic strategies of social movements, contrasting how students, on the one hand, and workers on the other, formulated their slogans against the corrupt government:

> At a recent demonstration the students chanted: 'Gui and Tanassi are innocent,

the students are delinquents.' The irony and provocation are clear. Immediately afterwards a group of workers took up the slogan to demonstrate their solidarity. But they translated in into their own model of intelligibility: 'Gui and Tanassi are delinquents, the students are innocent' ... It was not because they were incapable of understanding the irony, but because they do not recognise it as a means of political expression.[33]

Experimentation with slogans was part of a counter-culture in which the idea of 'transversality' was a vital component. Dadaism, surrealism, the American Underground, all fed into an eclectic poetics of revolt with its special brand of inspirational leaders with names like 'Bifo'.[34]

A favourite tactic was to take the inherited wisdoms of the Left and turn them on their heads. The Communist Party, in particular, was a target. Its thunderings against the 'new irrationalism' and its 'plague-bearers' (*untorelli*) were taken up in a complex battle of signs. The Volsci youth collective in Rome wrote of themselves in their paper:

> We are adorers and worshippers of the P38 magnum, we are abetters and henchmen of terrorism, we are pre-political, unruly barbarians, and we are the so-called raving and desperate adventurists.[35]

Other slogans were ironical about the repression of the movement:

> A hundred policemen per faculty – send the whole army to university (*Cento poliziotti in ogni facoltà – tutto l'esercito all'università*)

> Lama star, Lama star, we want to make sacrifices (*Lama star, Lama star, i sacrifici vogliamo far*) to the tune of 'Jesus Christ Superstar'

> Free radios are a provocation – all power to the television (*Le radio libere sono provocazione – tutto il potere alla televisione*)[36]

The slogans were invented using all sorts of materials, including advertising jingles and popular songs. However, it is worth noting that the importance attached to slogans in the first place, and then the rhyming and vocabulary, exploited the traditions of the workers' movement, and more specifically the post-'68 language of politics. Transversality could only operate in an environment in which the forms to be parodied were already common currency.

To this could be added a more general observation about the role of words in the social movements. In 1968–9 there was an explosion of the printed work as leaflets were roneoed, news-sheets and papers set up, posters plastered to walls; equally, there was an outpouring of the spoken word as meetings multiplied in factories, schools and squares, often lasting for several hours. The combination of the belief of the workers' movement in education, the widespread 'scriptural' attitude to Marxism and the mobilization of students gave a special impetus to political proselytizing with a pedagogic edge. In the mid seventies, this upsurge had been consolidated in the shape of alternative bookshops, small publishers, a multiplicity of journals and sheets and, last but not least, a stratum of activists skilled in producing leaflets, posters and so on.[37] The youth movement, like the women's movement, could, therefore, draw on a wide range of skills and resources in a city like Bologna or Milan.

But the medium with which the movement became identified was radio. Free radios were set up all over Italy in the wake of the Constitutional Court's ruling which declared that the state monopoly of the airwaves was illegal.

That decision was made in July 1975; within a year some eight hundred stations were broadcasting.[38] The majority of these were purely commercial ventures, but in the context of the social upheavals, radio played a significant role as the sounding board and cultural laboratory of the new social movements. It seemed that Brecht's notes on the socialist potential of radio, which were the guiding inspiration of Italian enthusiasts on the Left, could be given practical effect. Radio would, according to this perspective, deal with ordinary people's rich store of experiences, and address the 'real life' problems which the media tended to ignore. Radio would be opened up to contributions by non-professionals. Most importantly of all, the technology was thought to have the potential for making every receiver into a transmitter, thereby replacing the vertical, hierarchical structure and one-way flow of messages with egalitarian organization and horizontal and multiple flows. If in 1968–9 the modern media were seen as an inextricable part of the capitalist and consumerist culture and the enemies of the movements,[39] the utopian enthusiasm for radio helped drastically to change that attitude.

Radio Alice in Bologna and Radio Popolare in Milan, did indeed establish a relationship with the audience which was very different to the one people had come to accept as automatic. John Downing illustrates the difference with the example of the 'phone-in':

> The bourgeois stations generally have a delay-device to put people's voices on the air some seconds after they have actually spoken ... it enables quite effective censorship.... Furthermore, phone-ins are cast very often in the form of interviews with a linkperson. Thus, as a member of the Bologna A/Traverso Collective once put it, they become like a crossword where the person who phones in is faced with something resembling numbered blank squares which have to be filled in with the single correct answer.... By contrast, from a revolutionary radio perspective, the telephone means that a studio is not

essential for public debate. It means immediacy, the most dramatic case being that of Radio Alice during the Bologna insurrection. . . . People can read poetry over the air, sing songs and sometimes speak from workplaces.[40]

This new approach made radio more accessible, enabling members of social groups unlikely to write letters to newspapers to have their say in public, reaching a large audience. Those disadvantaged within a culture which gave priority to the written word, were now seen as rich in oral culture. Special programmes were compiled by and for young people, by and for women, and by and for workers in dispute, while making their problems and ideas known to all listeners. Swearing, denunciation, confession, bearing testimony – an 'unheard of' reality was breaking through taboos and codes. At the same time, new techniques in interviewing on location were experimented with, taking reportage into the streets and factories. The types of music, especially from America, which the RAI never played, suddenly started filling up air-time. Radio stations themselves seemed to float on a tide of enthusiasm bringing in volunteers, people with records or instruments they wanted to play. Some stations, of which Radio Alice was the most infamous, experimented with language, using a 'non-sense' of music and words to 'go through the looking-glass', and not 'mirror' the 'world outside'.[41] In its own words:

> Radio Alice will give a voice to anyone who loves mimosa and believes in paradise; hates violence but strikes the wicked; believes they're Napoleon but knows they could just as well be aftershave; who laughs like the flowers . . . to smokers and drinkers, jugglers and musketeers, the absent and the mad.[42]

Sadly, the fortunes of many of the stations depended too heavily on goodwill and too little on sound finances. However, their demise needs to be related to several factors, including their closure by the police, as in the case of Radio Alice. Not least, was the link between the radios and the mobilization of protest which meant that when the movements declined, so did the audience's size and contribution. Only those with the backing of unions and subscribers, like Radio Popolare in Milan, managed to survive and develop the necessary professional skills and organization which the Brechtian approach had disregarded.[43]

The free radios' failure to articulate and develop autonomous practices should also be seen in relation to the nature of the sub- and counter-cultures in Italy in the mid seventies. Radios could not, of course, create what did not exist in their environment. And that environment in Italy was dominated by a highly politicized subculture, which had arisen in the wake of 1968. This can be highlighted by comparing it to the British situation for the same period. While in Britain youth protest was primarily expressed through music, dress and a reworking of youth subcultural forms (punk, for instance, was contemporaneous with the movement of 'young proletarians'), in Italy a youth subculture had to be invented out of the raw materials of a political subculture (versions of 'autonomy'), with imported elements added.[44] In the latter, cultural spaces and activities were quickly consumed or converted under the pressures of political action. In the Italian context 'alternative' practices were invariably 'oppositional' and politicized. In the late 1970s, the intolerance of the Italian state, on the one hand, and the vitality of the oppositional political subculture, on the other, tended to narrow down the field of conflict. Above all, the theatre of violence imposed its rules on the actors of the social movements.

Two Societies?

Elements of violence were present in the youth movement from an early stage because of its adoption of direct action methods, such as squatting and *autoriduzione*, which often involved confrontation with the police. But violence remained accidental, sporadic and largely defensive, and the primary concern of the movements' participants was to create a cultural and social space for themselves within the city. However, in 1977, the situation changed; a vicious spiral of political violence and repression divided and undermined the movement.

Bianca Beccalli has analysed the process in terms of the blockage of the local political system;[45] the left-wing junta, elected to govern Milan in 1975, was consistently hostile to the demands of the youth movement. They were identified with extraparliamentarianism, and were not, therefore, considered legitimate. Furthermore, local government found it difficult to deal with issues such as heroin addiction, which involved questions of principle, and which needed to be referred upward to national leaderships. Consequently, the movement was defined as 'irrational' and incapable of dialogue. It was first ignored, and then met with repression.

The justification by the Communist mayor of Bologna of the killing of Franco Lo Russo (during a demonstration in March 1977) was the most dramatic instance of the breakdown in communication between the movement and the local institutions. The effect on the movement was to drive it into a confrontational politics; this resulted in the growth in credibility and influence of the so-called Organized Autonomy (*Autonomia Organizzata*), who saw violence against persons and property as the main means of escalating the conflict. This strategy gave them the power to set the agenda for the movements' discussions by simply imposing them. The problems of military strategy, political line, and state repression were made into the key issues.[46] A new version of the neo-Leninist politics, against which the youth and (as will be seen) women's movements had struggled, asserted itself.

The movement's space for manoeuvre was cut away. The refusal of local government to grant financial aid to the social centres, and to make reforms taking demands from below into account, meant that many projects collapsed, or ended up as little more than the 'self-management of misery'. Centres were abandoned and the campaign against heroin addiction given up. Those in the movement were presented with the stark choice between withdrawing into private life – this was the time when the 'culture of narcissism' exploded on the scene – or of supporting the politics of the armed organizations.[47]

The crisis of the movement has been graphically described:

A monumental political immobility today fires the desperate flight into the gothic landscape of urban terrorism, leading in turn to a further retrenchment over law and order and the defence of the state institutions. . . . The symbolic dissolution of the extraparliamentary Left group Lotta Continua on the thorn of feminism; the scattering of the student movement that had briefly survived around the issue of state repression around 1977; the subsequent exodus into the innumerable niches of the 'private' seem to nail inherited politics to an increasingly narrow horizon. Elsewhere, a narcissism, which is incipient to much intellectual activity morbidly fixes itself with its own doomed stare. Critical activity is frequently plunged into a *cul-de-sac* of perpetual mourning, stretched across the abyss between a world that has been lost and a future which refuses to arrive.[48]

It was a crisis which imploded with the forms of youth protest. But it was also more general to the oppositional social movements, which were subjected to the same doom-laden atmosphere, filled with dreams turned to nightmares, chiliasms of hope to despair.[49] Between the politics of terrorism and state repression, there was little space for social movements. For thousands, the journey, which began in 1968-9 and its immediate aftermath, ended a decade later inside, or within the shadow of prison-walls. Indeed, the prison emerged as a powerful metaphor in the political discourse of protest – not as the sign of rebellion as in the late sixties but of the omniscience of power.[50]

The 'defeat' of the 'movement of '77' marked the end of a historical phase of mass mobilizations which began in 1968. The politics of terrorism, based on 'residual' conceptions of the vanguard party, the historical destiny of the working class and the inevitability of violent revolution, triumphed over the emergent forms. Terrorism represented a particular dead-end, but it also illuminated a more general crisis of oppositional politics. It was a crisis of a particular model of political action. Alberto Melucci has written:

> This situation has been interpreted almost exclusively in terms of a withdrawal into private life (*riflusso*).... But I believe that ... it was only a certain politics which prevented important transformations.... To continue to evaluate these phenomena negatively on the basis of a party organization model means not to understand the changes taking place.[51]

In 1968–9 the unions and, subsequently, the Communist Party adapted in order to represent the new oppositional forces in society, such as students and immigrant workers in the big factories. The challenge from the New Left helped revitalize the traditional Left. However, in the late seventies it seemed that a historical shift was making itself felt that presented a much more fundamental challenge to their hegemony of oppositional politics.

Alberto Asor Rosa, first a founding father of Italian *operaismo*, and then a leading Communist Party intellectual, wrote one of the most controversial commentaries on the crisis in progress. In 1977, his 'Two Societies' articles claimed that a new social reality had grown up outside the universe of organized labour:

> Between these two realities – the organized working class and marginalized, unemployed youth – there is a deep divide. This appears in their behaviour, political choices and forms of organization in the Italian and, perhaps, in the European situations.[52]

For Asor Rosa:

> between the system and the forces of student agitation there stand only the unions and the PCI, which represent the first society – the organized and productive one ... they are the only institutions commanding respect in the whole Republic.[53]

While he insisted that the idea of the 'two societies' was metaphorical, Asor Rosa gave a striking picture of a world in which the traditional forces of opposition are in the position of defending the Republic against incipient chaos. The movement of '77, which on 17 February of that year prevented Luciano Lama, the general secretary of the biggest union confederation, the CGIL, from addressing a rally at Rome university, was a sign of the times. It was seen, in fact, as an extraordinary symbolic moment. In 1968–9 trade union leaders were heckled and abused, but even then the movements entered into a kind of dialogue with the workers' organizations. Here, by contrast, there was no language in common between Luciano Lama ('*Lama non l'ama nessuno*' – Lama is loved by no one) and the students occupying Rome University. It was this incident that provoked Asor Rosa's articles.

Asor Rosa's concern in writing about the workers' organizations' failure to represent the *non-garantiti* (the 'second society' which was not protected by state legislation nor by the unions) was that they should extend their area of influence to all forces in society. His aim was to rebuild the bridges between the social groups, as had been done in the wake of '68; this meant playing the role of the critical intellectual who connected up different cultures:

> The pressing problem today consists in asking if and what relationship can exist between the culture which is the expression of the working class, and the culture which essentially wants to 'represent' the crisis of the system... I am convinced that the workers' culture can comprehend the culture of crisis – just as the working class is able to comprehend (*com-prendere*) – to make room for – the rebel, the marginal, the socially outcast, who are a part of its past and who have been its archetypes, even though this might have been forgotten.[54]

For Asor Rosa, the 'dissident' Italian and French intellectuals, who interpreted the 'marginals'' refusal to be integrated as a new form of politics,[55] were simply re-editing a version of 'third-worldism'; they were identifying any group which fell outside the system's mechanisms of reproduction as positive: in the 1960s, it would have been the Vietnamese; in the late 1970s it was the poor and excluded within the metropolitan heartland. For him, instead, the problem was how to integrate them within the cultural sphere of the workers' movement.

This response to the movement of '77 was more intelligent than that of many other intellectuals and politicians on the Left, who sympathized with those taking a hard line against 'irrational' protest, which they treated as coterminous with terrorism.[56] However, the axioms of Asor Rosa's argument were not very different. For him, the problem was to assert the centrality of the industrial working class, and to cast the mantle of Communist Party hegemony over all the forces of opposition within society. The 'infantile', regressive and intellectualistic forms of rebellion had been historically superseded by the disciplined ranks of the labour movement, and this process had to be repeated in modern conditions.[57] Opposition needed to be channelled and educated into assuming attitudes appropriate for future government. Social conflict had, in this sense, to be made political.

However, the redefinition of politics in the 1970s could not so easily be absorbed. The dissident intellectuals Asor Rosa was implicitly referring to, such as Toni Negri, were prone to romanticize the new social actors,[58] but at least they were trying to identify what was changing rather than what remained constant in the organization of society and forms of conflict it produced. What Asor Rosa was attempting to do was to make the new order of conflicts conform to an older model. The tragic demise of the youth movement even lent this project a certain *raison d'être*, given the comparative stability of the political parties and unions. However, its great weakness lay in denying the importance of the autonomy and innovation brought into being by the movements in their struggle to establish new social identities. This was most evident in relation to the women's movement, which came to represent the most radical form of the new politics.

Notes

1. See Max Jaggi, *Red Bologna*, London 1977.
2. See Francesco Alberoni, 'Une opposition de gauche au PCI est-elle possible pour lui?', in Fabrizio Calvi, ed., *Italie '77 – le 'Mouvement', les intellectuels*, Paris 1977.
3. Bianca Becalli, 'Protesta giovanile e opposizione politica', *Quaderni Piacentini*, 64, 1977, pp. 53–8.
4. For a discussion of youth subcultures and marginality, see Stuart Hall and Tony Jefferson, eds., *Resistance through Rituals : Youth Subcultures in Post-war Britain*, London 1977, pp. 223–9: for the debate on marginality in Italy, Massimo Paci, *La struttura sociale italiana*, Bologna 1982.
5. The figure of the American Indian first appeared in the posters of the late 1960s based on old photographs, representing resistance to US imperialism. Now, young protestors themselves dressed as Indians, thereby taking the semiological warfare into the streets to represent their own situation; Umberto Eco, 'Une nouvelle langue: l'italo-indien', in Fabrizio Calvi, ed., *Italie '77*, pp. 123–8.
6. Umberto Eco, 'Anno nove', in *Sette Anni di desiderio*, Milan 1983, pp. 59–63
7. Alternative guide books listed the centres and resources; see, for example, G. Ricci, C. Marras and M. Radice, *Milano Alternativa*.
8. The term '*autonomia*' changed its meaning according to context and speaker/writer. It could be used to mean i) an independent identity/politics of a particular group, eg. homosexuals; ii) anti-reformism. It also referred to a distinct current of Marxism with origins in the previous decade; Christian Marazzi and Sylvere Lotringer write: 'The central theme of Autonomy is the struggle against work, the refusal of work. Ever since the early formulations of Mario Tronti in 1964, the Italian revolutionary movement has been moving towards the refusal of work as a positive productive force of capitalist development. The refusal of work, demand for more money, struggle against unhealthy work ... have all meant forcing capital to develop to the maximum its productive forces.... Only when ... enjoying life becomes a productive fact in itself does freedom from exploitation become materially possible'; *Semiotext(e)*, 3, 1980, pp. 15–16.
9. Corrado Levi, 'Omosessuali fuori', *Erbo Voglio*, May/June 1973, pp. 24–33; see also, Pezzana, *FUORI: Politica del corpo*.
10. Lotta Continua, *Per il movimento degli studenti medi – Convegno di Pavia*, 1971, p. 11.
11. *Re Nudo*, 19, 1973.
12. Andrea Valcarenghi, *Underground a pugno chiuso*, Rome 1974, p. 69.
13. Gundle, 'L'Americanizzazione del quotidiano'.
14. *Re Nudo*, 21, 1973.
15. *Re Nudo*, June/August 1971.

16. Lotta Continua, *Per il movimento degli studenti medi*, pp. 10–12.
17. For example, an article entitled 'Per un modo nuovo di fare politica', said: 'The absence of a language with which to discuss the existential condition of activists has left a lot of problems unresolved, not least because many comrades joined revolutionary organizations starting from their personal contradictions'; *Re Nudo*, June/August 1971.
18. Bianca Beccalli, 'Protesta giovanile', pp. 56–7.
19. Luigi Marconi and Marino Sinibaldi, 'Un strano movimento di strani studenti', *Ombre Rosse*, 20, March 1977, p. 16; see also, Romano Alquati, 'Per un'analisi della composizione di classe degli studenti', *Aut Aut*, 154, July/August 1976.
20. Bianca Beccalli, *The Youth Movement and Public Policy in Milan, 1975–9*, mimeograph, Centre for European Studies, Harvard University, pp. 3–5.
21. *Sarà un risotto che vi seppellirà – materiali dei circoli proletari giovanili di Milano*, Milan 1977, p. 23.
22. Bianca Beccalli, *Youth Movement and Public Policy in Milan 1975–79*, Harvard, 1981, p. 3; Claudia Sorlini, ed., *Centri sociali autogestiti e circoli proletari giovanili de Milano*, Milan 1977, p. 23.
23. *Sarà un risotto*, pp. 39–40.
24. For the politics of hard drugs in Italy in the period, see Giancarlo Arnao, *Rapporto sulle droghe*, Milan 1976.
25. *Sarà un risotto*, p. 40.
26. Ibid, pp. 30–2. The revival of the festival and carnival (and the publication of Mikhail Bakhtin's writings on the subject), were indicative of a cultural shift. Carnival is precisely a suspension of normal rules; see Aldo Marchetti, *'La guerra dei coriandoli: borghesia, carnevale e popolo nella Milano dell'800'*, *Classe*, 1, Summer/Autumn 1986, pp. 71–104.
27. Bianca Beccalli, 'Classe operaia e nuovi movimenti collettivi', in G. Germani, *Mutamento e classi sociali in Italia*, Naples 1981, p. 56.
28. Nino Vento, 'I giovani proletari, l'ideologia, il tempo libero', *Ombre Rosse*, July 1976, p. 25.
29. This form of direct action was, however, self-defeating in that the fire-bombings at concerts simply meant that international bands refused to play in Italy; on music and youth culture in Italy, see Iain Chambers and Lidia Curti, 'A Volatile Alliance: Culture, Popular Culture and the Italian Left', in *Formations of Nation and People*, London 1984, pp. 111–13.
30. R. Sodi, 'Paghiamo il "nostro" biglietto!', *Realismo*, 15, March 1977, pp. 28–31. 'Qualunquista' is a term used to refer to a 'couldn't-care-less' attitude to politics with right-wing overtones.
31. Ibid, pp. 30–31.
32. If *autoriduzione* represented a form of organized semi-legal protest, expropriation was uncompromisingly illegal. For example, a leaflet found after a raid taking goods from a supermarket read: 'The goods we took are ours, just as everything which exists is ours, because we have produced it through out exploitation.... Not civil disobedience ... not sub-proletarian anger, but the embryo of political struggle against exploitation, parallel to that in the factory'; *Contro Informazione*, November 1974.
33. Quoted in Meagan Morris, 'Eurocommunism versus Semiological Delinquincy', in M. Morris, ed., *Language, Sexuality and Subversion*, Darlington 1978, pp. 66–8.
34. Franco Berardi ('Bifo'), *Le ciel est enfin tombé sur la terre*, Paris 1978. (I owe this reference to Malcolm Imrie)
35. *I Volsci*, February 1978.
36. Red Notes, *Italy: 1977–78 – Living with the Earthquake*, London 1978, p. 58: for a comprehensive transcription of graffiti in the universities in 1977, se M.I. Macioti and M. D'Aurato, eds., 'I graffiti dell'università', *La Critica Sociologica*, 41, Spring 1977, pp. 122–51.
37. Goffredo Fofi, 'Piccola editoria', pp. 75–80.
38. Mark Grimshaw and Carl Gardner, '"Free Radio" in Italy'. *Wedge*, 1, Summer 1977, pp. 14–16; Giuseppe Richeri, 'Le système de la télévision italienne: public/privé',

Bulletin de L'Idate, October 1983, pp. 2–4.

39. The key texts for those theorizing the practice of the free radios were Brecht's notes on radio and Enzensberger's essay based on Brecht: Bertold Brecht, *Écrits sur la littérature et l'art*, 1, Paris 1970, pp. 127–35; Enzensberger, 'Constituents of a Theory of the Media'.

40. John Downing, *The Media Machine*, London 1980, pp. 207–8.

41. Berardi ('Bifo'), *Le ciel est enfin tombé*, pp. 130–31.

42. Collectif A/Traverso, *radio alice, radio libre*, Paris, 1977, p. 23.

43. Biagio Longo, 'Fuochi fatui? La resistenza delle radio libere', *Quaderni Il Lavoro dell'Informazione*, 1, 1981, pp. 103–19.

44. Bianca Beccalli explains the peculiar lateness of the emergence of a 'youth movement' in Italy almost entirely in socio-economic terms, thereby denying the cultural any life of its own; see 'Protesta giovanile e opposizione politica'. For a cultural approach to youth, see Hall and Jefferson, *Resistance through Rituals*; and a later Italian study inspired by this work, L. Caioli and others, *Bande. Un modo di dire*, Milan 1986.

45. Beccalli, 'The Youth Movement and Public Policy', pp. 10–13.

46. Luigi Manconi and Marino Sinibaldi, 'Un strano movimento', pp. 18–21.

47. On the phenomenon of narcissism as symptom of cultural crisis, see A. Zanotta, 'La cultura del narcissismo', in *Rassegna Italiana di Sociologia*, 1, January–March 1980, pp. 133–9.

48. Iain Chambers and Lidia Curti, 'Silent Frontiers', in *Screen Education*, 41, Winter/Spring 1982, p. 28.

49. In an interview, Mario Moretti, the literary critic, described his generation as profoundly influenced by an eschatological view of the world; *Panorama*, 12 July 1987; for a mordently humorous account of the mysticism and charlatanry of the seventies, Alberto Arbasino, *Un Paese Senza*, Milan 1980.

50. Michel Foucault's *Discipline and Punish*, London 1977, was read in this light; see *Antigone*, 1, 1985, for an analysis of the role of the prison system and repressive anti-terrorist legislation in Italian life from the late 1970s. For prison literature, contrast the hopeful account of *Liberare tutti i dannati della terra*, Lotta Continua, Rome 1972, with Nanni Balestrini's darkly pessimistic *Gli Invisibili*.

51. A. Melucci, *L'invenzione del presente*, pp. 163–5.

52. The articles were first published in *Rinascita*, and then in book form. A. Asor Rosa, *Le Due Società*, Turin 1977, p. viii.

53. Ibid, p. 66.

54. Ibid, pp. 103–4.

55. For the French intellectuals' petition against repression in Italy (which included Sartre and de Beauvoir among its signatories), see M.A. Macciocchi, *Après Marx, Avril*, Paris 1978, pp. 57–100.

56. Members of the Communist Party were often particularly inclined to see *Autonomia* as part and parcel of terrorism, partly from anxiety of being tarred with the same brush; see Giorgio Bocca, *Il caso 7 april: Toni Negri e la grande inquisizione*, Milan 1980, pp. 146–50.

57. Frederico Bozzini and Maurizio Carbognin write: 'In the culture of the traditional left, the only human element worthy of history is organized social groups. Outside the union and the party, there is no salvation'; *Pechè parlare di storia*, mimeo, 1978.

58. Negri, *Dall'operaio massa all'operaio sociale*.

21

feminism and a new politics

When Marx wrote that 'Men make their own history ... but they do not make it under conditions chosen by themselves', he was no doubt referring to 'Man' as a universal category. However, it is a word that is also revealing of the hegemony of men in the public sphere. Women, it could be said, make history under conditions which are largely 'man-made'. Certainly, the language of politics has historically been fashioned in male terms.[1] The social movements of 1968–9 were no exceptions to this. Women were active participants, but they acted as 'students' and 'workers', and seldom as 'women students' and 'women workers'. Their experience of the strikes and occupations, of the open meetings and demonstrations, were, therefore, contradictory, at least in retrospect. It is from the frictions emerging from the persistence of old roles and the invention of new ones that a women's movement developed in Italy during the 1970s.[2]

The student movement, which was especially significant for the formation of feminism, was lived by many women activists as a great release from stifling social conventions. Parental pressures and institutional tutelage bore down heavily on women students, who were glad to escape from them through solidarity with their peer group. The social movement expressed their anger at injustices, and provided a vehicle for creating new ways of living. It entailed the learning of new skills, meeting people, discovering a whole world through discussion and reading. At the same time, there were limits put on how the freedoms could be used, and channels tended to direct the energies of women students in particular ways. For example, the assignment to women of secretarial functions was so blatant that this role was widely dubbed the *angelo del ciclostile* (the roneo angel). The process of social mobilization in many respects changed women's position in relation to male peers, but the change was for the most part slight, and required a conformity to pre-existing notions of comradeship.[3]

However, it was this change of situation and the assertion of ideas to do with equality and freedom which made long-established injustices intolerable. To duplicate hundreds of leaflets at the behest of some student leader or political activist seemed, suddenly to be a form of complicity in the hypocrisy of those who claimed to be communists.

Feminist anger and criticism were directed first of all against male student activists, who were seen to reproduce dominant values. Although the causes of the women's movement need to be related to a number of structural changes in women's access to education and the labour market, not to mention cultural developments,[4] the initial grievances were directed at the men around them. The 'salesmen of the new inevitability', who did so much to explode the justifications of the dominant group in society (for example, the meritocratic ideal in education), and who provided alternative standards with which to make political judgements, conjured up disaffection from within the movement they led. Their instruments of analysis were turned against them. In Mariella Gramaglia's words: 'Feminism, at least in its first political acts, came into being as revolutionary education for revolutionaries, as living proof of their limitations'.[5] However, the women's movement was not a simple extension of a tendency within the preceding social movements. During the 1970s, feminists wrestled with a legacy of which they were a part, but from which they increasingly sought to escape.

The aim of this chapter is to trace some of the routes taken by feminists which led out of the 1968–9 experience. Perhaps more so in Italy than in many other countries, the women's movement after 1968 was divided along political lines. Women tended to become feminists after they had already been activists on the Left, and the differences within the wider political field were echoed within the movement. In the first section, some of the major tendencies among the pioneering feminists are briefly outlined. The purpose of this is to show how the movement began as a struggle to create a new politics out of an old one; this was a process internal to the experience of the generation who went to university in the mid to late 1960s. The next section deals with the growth of the mass movement around the abortion issue, and with how feminism established its presence in a number of spheres, including the unions and workplaces. However, the women's movement, as the final section argues, remained marginal and antagonistic to the dominant forms of politics on the Left. So, when the latter was in disarray at the end of the decade, feminism seemed to represent a potentially alternative politics.

Pioneering Years

The idea of women's equality was not invented by the generation of '68; it already had a respectable history as part of the more general struggle for democratic and civil liberties led by the Socialist and Communist Parties.[6] The idea of 'emancipation' meant establishing women's full rights as citizens as guaranteed by the Constitution, and their integration into the workforce (and thence into the mass organizations of the labour movement). In the absence of a tradition of 'bourgeois feminism' in Italy, this role was assumed by the Left; as Victoria De Grazia has written:

> Insofar as it actively promoted the rapid and pervasive changes in custom and culture following in the wake of the economic miracle of the 1950s and 1960s, the Left, it could be argued, fulfilled the historical role of bourgeois feminism by modernizing the status of Italian women. In the process, the stage was set for the neofeminist associationalism of the early 1970s; its precedents were not so much early twentieth-century Italian feminist as post-1968 American liberationist.[7]

When the women's movement began, it was therefore vital for its protagonists to differentiate themselves from this tradition. Its shortcomings were discussed at length, with the accent being put on its conservatism; for instance, Togliatti's founding address to the Unione delle Donne Italiane, the PCI's organization for women, was regularly quoted:

> We do not want Communist women to distance themselves from their everyday lives, nor to renounce what I understand to be their duties . . . Nor that they should in any way lose the attributes of their femininity.[8]

In other words, the emancipationist approach of the traditional Left was criticized for making women fit into male-dominated party structures and policies, and for overlooking the inequalities flowing from the sexual division of labour in the home and at work. It was this conservativism and reliance on the institutions which feminists rebelled against, just as the student movement had done in the late sixties.

Carla Ravaioli recalls an incident which brought the new feminism and emancipationists into head-on confrontation. At a conference in June 1970 on 'Women and the Choices facing Italian Society in the 1970s', she writes that:

> a women's voice full of aggression and scandalously out of keeping with the measured decorum of the debate broke in: 'My name is of no importance. I belong to the movement Rivolta Femminile. Over these days I have heard words like "inclusion", "participation", and "integration". . . . It appears to me

that what you want is exactly what already exists.... For you, this culture is fine. The only thing that you're asking is that women be a part of it. The women you want are exact duplicates of the men'.[9]

The attempt to bring women into the orbit of the institutions, without radically changing those institutions, was totally rejected by the early feminists, who worked to create a social movement opposed to them. The defiance and the language of revolt learnt in the social movements of 1968–9 clashed with the procedures and style of parliamentary politics. Yet, the need to act autonomously had arisen because of the failure of the movements to take up women's specific grievances and aspirations.

A statement by the De Mau group (Il Gruppo Demistificazione Autoritarismo), which was founded in Milan in 1966, observed:

> It is quite absurd at a time like this which is characterized by so many radical struggles by young people against authoritarianism, alienation and the division of labour, that no qualitative leap is being made in the direction of an analysis ... that discusses the position of men and women in relation to the division of labour and the rigid fixing of social roles.... You really have to ask why the anti-authoritarian movements don't put this at the very heart of their struggles but instead remain locked into the mystique of the 'political struggle'.... It seems they are too involved in the male logic of the old culture they claim to be attacking.[10]

The De Mau group was short-lived, but it was important in setting up one of the first women's study groups. They studied the family as an institution which reproduced relations of dominance and subordination, adapting the theories of Reich, Marcuse and the Frankfurt School, and asserting the need for women to 'define themselves', instead of seeking integration into the dominant culture. They anticipated developments which led to the foundation of autonomous women's organizations in 1970.

The setting up of formal organizations in the wake of the social movements (Rivolta Femminile and Movimento de Liberazione della Donna (MLD) in 1970, and Lotta Femminista in 1971–2), can partly be explained as a response parallel to that which led to the formation of so many political organizations at the time. Without the favourable conditions of mass mobilization, when small, informal collectives could be formed 'spontaneously' in workplaces and educational institutions, a greater degree of formalization was necessary. However, the response was even more a reaction to the rise of a neo-Leninism which seemed to reinstate authoritarian models. The feminist pioneers saw themselves as developing the anti-authoritarian politics of '68, and rekindling the 'movementist' spirit. Thus, the organizations they set up were very different in structure and methods of working from the others.

As Lesley Caldwell has written, the earliest groups, until 1973–4, concentrated on the importance of the small group which practised consciousness-raising:

> They attempted to confront the internal dynamics of what happens when groups of women meet together, ie, a concentration on work within the group at a series of different levels. . . . So that a politics of the personal, of sexuality, of the body was organized around the possibility/feasibility of beginning to live differently now and according some weight to the relational aspect of masculinity and femininity.[11]

It would be wrong to try and put all the various experiments in feminism into organizational boxes. In cities like Milan, there were complex webs of relationships, which owed their existence to experiences shared inside the social movement – from the acquaintance of 'comrades' to close friendships. These facilitated contacts, arranging meetings and so on.[12] It was seldom a question of membership, as with the extraparliamentary organizations, but rather a participation in intersecting networks and circles. Often a meeting-place, such as the women's centre in via Cerubini in Milan, acted as a focal point where discussion would be combined with the search for new forms of sociality which did not involve men. Nonetheless, in the context of an intensely political subculture, tendencies were identified with organizations. One of the first consistently to discuss the issue of female sexuality was Rivolta Femminile.

The Manifesto of Rivolta Femminile, published in July 1970, is one of the key founding documents of the Italian women's movement. It was uncompromising about the need for autonomy at a time when other organizations, such as MLD, were still open to men. It starts:

> Women must not be defined in relation to men. Consciousness of this underpins both our struggle and our freedom. Man is not the model to be aspired to in women's process of self-discovery. . . . Equality is an ideological attempt to enslave women further.[13]

The Manifesto denounces marriage as an institution of male domination, and declares feminism to be the 'first political stage of a historical critique of the family and society'. Unpaid domestic labour is identified as the work which allows private and state capitalism to survive. Male control of women's sexuality is rejected in the name of a 'free sexuality in all its forms', and the 'right of all children to sexual play', but the target of attack is not only the dominant ideology and institutions, but Marxism itself.

The importance of Rivolta Femminile lay in its pursuit of women's liberation through a return to the sphere of the private, the subjective and the personal, which was seen as fundamental for understanding how power was exercised in society at large. Freedom and difference are counterposed to the idea of equality. The problems of sexuality and the family were brought to the centre of the stage. Carla Lonzi, a leading writer in the review *Rivolta Femminile*, developed a theory relating to sexual behaviour and forms of domination. She denounced the idea that sexual satisfaction could only, or primarily, be derived from penetration of the vagina, and canvassed stimulation of the clitoris as a way of freeing women's pleasures from men's control. Demands for contraception and abortion were framed in terms of increasing women's control over their bodies and their sexuality.[14]

The rigour with which Rivolta Femminile brought the personal to bear on every issue, and the lucidity of their analyses made many other groupings take them seriously, though it was not until 1972–3 that the themes they addressed were discussed more generally within the movement. Even then, as one feminist recalls, 'We had no words for talking about our sexuality, and to speak of our personal problems as crucial during a meeting seemed absurd.[15]

However, it was through rethinking the body as the site of identity and power, with the help of books such as the Boston Women's Health Collective's *Our Bodies, Ourselves* (translated into Italian in 1974), that its relegation to the 'private', and, therefore, 'apolitical', was challenged. Women's experience and the practice of starting from one's own experience and everyday life was counterposed to a politics saturated in ideological formulations. Instead of a politics in which the problem was defined in terms of state power, feminism proposed a new politics based on the transformation of everyday social relations. Thus, it gave a specific content to the rather abstract notions of prefigurative and direct action propagated by the student movement.[16]

The part played by Lotta Femminista in the formative years of the Italian women's movement has been largely identified with their responsibility for the 'wages for housework' demand. While other feminists explored the cultural and social dimensions of women's oppression, the Lotta Femminista collectives focused their attention on the 'material', economic exploitation of women in the home, which, they said, underpinned all the other aspects of their situation. Their analyses are reminiscent of the Pisan Theses, which had been so influential in the students' movement, and which helped make *operaist* Marxism a vital strand of thought in the social movements in the following decade.[17] The Lotta Femminista analysis was simple but novel in its application. It applied Marxist categories to the role of women (as housewives and mothers) in the reproduction of labour-power, and claimed that a vast amount of surplus value was being extracted by capital from the female proletariat. The ordinary woman's position was, in many respect, seen as analogous to that of the prostitute, only she did not even get paid for her services.[18] The demand for wages was, therefore, essential for the 'recomposition' of the proletariat. In the 1971 Programmatic Manifesto of Housewives in the Neighbourhood, Lotta Femminista put forward the vision of a society in which the state would pay men and women for housework. There would be a neighbourhood canteen, a drastic reduction in working hours, the elimination of unpleasant work and night shifts, and the building of free and beautiful houses.[19] A utopia fully in the tradition of 1960s utopian thinking.

In retrospect, the Lotta Femminista approach seems reductively economic. It bears all the hallmarks of a Marxism which is being used to make sense of social processes without relinquishing or adding to the categories supplied by reading *Capital* or the *Grundrisse*. Moreover, as André Gorz has observed, the demand to extend waged relationships into every area of people's lives (thereby reinforcing the *operaist* idea of society as a factory) is not necessarily likely to improve their quality:

> The logical conclusion of this argument is that professional prostitution is an advance over the traditional couple, and that women's liberation requires the transfer of all family-based tasks to the public services. Emancipation will be consummated only when the full-scale statisation of relations has eliminated the family as the last vestige of civil society. This line in demands obviously conflicts with the struggle to redefine relations within couples and to achieve a balanced, freely chosen distribution of household tasks between equal male and female partners.[20]

Nonetheless, the 'wages for housework' campaign provoked a considerable debate internationally as well as in Italy, and brought the issue of domestic labour to the centre of attention.[21]

While acknowledging the validity of criticism made of Lotta Femminista, it needs to be said that they tackled problems which were crucial. As Maria Rosa Dalla Costa's pamphlet *The Power of Women and the Subversion of the Community* shows, their analysis of housework and reproduction brought them to propose and theorize political action around the problems of housing, transport and nurseries, which the main organizations of the Left treated as mere adjuncts to the struggles in the factory. They took up the campaigns of the prostitutes, who had otherwise been regarded only as victims.[22] However, the relative marginalization of Lotta Femminista within the Italian women's movement stemmed from their tendency to bring everything back to the 'fundamentals' of economic exploitation at a time when feminists were trying to deal with the complexities of relations at every level in society. While Lotta Femminista's demands remained on paper, the activities of the radical democratic wing of the movement had much more resonance.

The Movimento de Liberazione della Donna put forward a programme in June 1970 which combined elements of the anti-authoritarian politics of '68 with the perspectives of the Radical Party, to which it was formally affiliated. Unlike the Marxists, they stated that it was no longer relevant in advanced industrial societies to distinguish between struggles in the 'structure' (economic) and struggles in the 'superstructure' (ideological). They were all equally valid, and liberation had to be in all spheres of life. MLD's demands were divided into four sections: firstly, those aiming to win for women the right to control their own bodies (free contraception, legalization and liberalization of abortion with the provision of free medical services); secondly, demands against 'psychological conditioning and models of behaviour' (elimination of gender discrimination in schools, attacks on myths, such as the 'ideal mother'); thirdly, demands for the elimination of economic exploitation (socialization of services, socially controlled public nurseries); and fourthly, legal equalities (civil disobedience against sexual discrimination, against male authoritarianism e.g. surnames, proposals for laws using the referendum). This perspective was important because it promoted a fight against the 'values and behaviour' of a society which was described as 'patriarchal' and 'clerical', as well as capitalist. Furthermore, it put forward a line of action which was neither integrationalist not purely anti-institutional, but envisaged law-making as well as law-breaking.[23]

A radical secular culture and politics has traditionally been weak within Italian society. It has been squeezed between the forces of the Church and Christian Democracy, on the one hand, and the forces of the Communist Party, on the other. Although the PCI had an honourable record in resisting Fascism and actively campaigned against repression in the wake of the 1968–9 movements, it has also shared a certain antipathy for liberal thought, which was in part common to the extraparliamentary Left as well.[24]

In the 1960s, radical opinion was represented primarily through publications like the magazine L'Espresso, rather than through formal political structures; the Radical Party was not refounded until 1967 (after its dissolution four years earlier). Radicals, moreover, played no significant role, as an organization, in the 1968–9 movements. However, they were well-placed to take advantage of the liberatory impulses coursing through Italian society.

The Radical Party itself had a flexible federal structure which was open to collectives as well as individuals who wanted to join it for a limited period and over specific single-issue campaigns. Unlike the democratic centralism of Leninist organizations, this allowed for a sensitivity to demands and pressure coming from social movements 'on their own terms'. The Radicals developed anti-authoritarianism and demands for greater civil liberties – demands which other organizations treated as deviations from the class struggle. They drew on ideas coming from the United States, where the movements of women's liberation and gay liberation were well-established before they had any counterparts in Italy.[25] Although they remained a small force numerically, during the first half of the 1970s the Radicals took a number of crucial initiatives in conjunction with the embryonic new social movements.[26] The most important of these centred on the issue of women's rights.

Growth of a Mass Movement: The Abortion Campaign

The campaign in favour of divorce and abortion, and against sexual violence, which became key political issues in the mid seventies, marked a new stage in the development of feminism in Italy. The activities of the small groups, which were based on the attempt to re-think politics starting from women's 'otherness' (for example, consciousness-raising), were overtaken by 'public' events in the traditional political arena. The sudden and massive growth in the women's movement, which followed the extraparliamentary Left's adoption of the MLD's initiatives, was problematic in many respects for the early pioneers. Rivolta Femminile, for example, rejected the very notions of equality within the male-defined institutions and polity. The idea of the family, which a sizeable part of the pro-divorce lobby said would be strengthened by defending the laws against attacks from the Church, was anathema to these feminists. It looked as if the new politics would be taken over by male-dominated parties and organizations. However, it was out of these conflicts that feminism developed, while the organizations of the New Left, which emerged out of 1968, found themselves riven by contradictions.

The demand for the right to have an abortion as 'a woman's right to choose' was promoted by CISA (Centro Italiano Sterilizzazione e Aborto), following the efforts of the MLD to gain support for a campaign initiated in 1971. Of all the mobilizations, action on abortion was perhaps the most significant for the creation of a mass feminist movement. Demonstrations were enormous; in 1975, demonstrations mobilized a maximum of twenty-five thousand, while in 1976 the number rose to one hundred thousand. The collection of signatures (five hundred thousand were needed to call a referendum) ended by getting the support of some eight hundred thousand people. Furthermore, women organized 'illegal' abortions, and the denounced themselves publicly (*autodenuncia*).[27] Abortion was a single issue, but it was one which embodied in microcosm a whole set of social conflicts.

The practice of civil disobedience and illegality brought activists into confrontation with the authorities, and challenged established procedures and values. They revealed a continuity with the ideas of direct action, control and self-management, and movement, which went back to 1968–9. However, mobilization took off by using the referendum, which was a citizen's right guaranteed by the Constitution. It was, in fact, the Christian Democratic Party which wanted to repeal the divorce law of 1970 that first decided to use the referendum, but it subsequently became a crucial weapon for fighting battles over civil rights.[28] Not since 1968 had there been such a revival in grassroots political activity. But the feminist approach to the abortion issue gave a new dimension to the struggle against the authoritarian power structures in society by showing how they were organized by men and through masculine discourses.

The demand for women's right to free and safe abortion was not exclusive to Italy in the mid seventies, and was common to several countries of the industrialized West.[29] However, it had great implications in Italy because of the power of the Church (through the Christian Democratic Party) in relation to legislation as well as moral attitudes more generally:

> The Church's attitude to the family, in particular its insistence on the primacy of reproduction and the rejection of sexuality, has helped to create and justify a repressive set of formulations ... and even the construction of laws which distinguish the importance of crimes according to whether they are committed by men or women.[30]

The price paid by women was very great; in 1974, the weekly *Panorama* reported that all women had either had an abortion or knew of a friend who had. In circumstances in which contraceptives were not widely available, and ignorance about sex was widespread due to lack of education in schools, abortions functioned as a form of birth control. This phenomenon was not new, but was the product of centuries – a largely unspoken and yet pervasive reality, which testified to an extreme discrepancy between legal and official discourses, and women's experience.[31] In the eyes of the Church, abortion was a terrible sin, and for the state it was a crime punishable by a five-year sentence. But in the mid seventies, the private, individual and clandestine 'solution' was no longer tolerable to many thousands of women, who publically protested their sense of outrage.

It was this dramatic emergence into the public sphere of personal experience not previously regarded as political which made the campaign over abortion quite unlike the mobilizations over labour contracts or educational reform. The role of the pioneering feminists was crucial in this respect; they prepared and anticipated the sudden diffusion of conscious-ness-raising, the search for new vocabularies with which to speak about women's experiences, and the exploration of group dynamics. The very repressiveness of the Italian situation created conditions favourable to the making of connections between the issue of abortion and a whole complex of social relations. In Lesley Caldwell's words:

> The connections between abortion and procreation, between abortion and sexuality, between our ideas of ourselves as mothers and as sexual beings were opened up. Some groups drew parallels between the violence of abortion and the ways in which, at some level, we live heterosexual encounters and pene-tration as violence.... Others ... looked at the way women live their sexuality linked to their biological potential for motherhood and what its implications are; motherhood as something both desired and refused.... They also linked our conscious and unconscious attitudes to this potential to the social conditions that prevent it happening.[32]

In short, feminist politics transformed abortions from being a civil rights issue into a struggle over how power was being exercised in society. This process involved not just the state or the Church as institutions, but the 'micro' relations of power in everyday life.

Through mass mobilizations and a campaign of civil disobedience over abortion, the women's movement established itself as a national force. Political parties looked for ways of responding to the challenge. Above all, the parties of the Left, particularly the PCI, sought to present bills which navigated the dangerous waters between the demands of the movement (and their echoes within their women's sections), and the anxieties of Christian Democratic opinion. When, however, the legislation legalizing abortion was eventually passed in 1978, the law bore all the hallmarks of an unfavourable compromise.

A number of clauses limited women's right to choose by making it compulsory to consult with a doctor or social worker, instituting a seven-day period for reflection, and requiring parental permission for those under eighteen. Most importantly, medical staff were given the right to conscientious objection, and this clause was effectively used by powerful opponents within the hospitals to make it extremely difficult for women to have legal abortions. In other words, the mass movement and the majority vote in the referendum counted for little when their demands were translated into the language and procedures of the institutions. As Gianna Pomata has written, the logic of the party system underpinned the 'systematic collusion between medical corporatism and state power'; the predominantly male doctors had been given the function by the state of supervising the social control of reproduction and the exercise of power over the female patient.[33]

Although the abortion legislation of 1978 did marginally improve women's situation, and opened up some space within the institutions for further struggles, the results were largely delusory. However, the strength of the movement derived from its roots in civil society and its autonomy from the established representative organizations, the parties and unions. The legislative stage had always been regarded as secondary by many in the movement. In this sense, it was very different from the earlier historical movement for women's suffrage, which focused its energies on opening up the institutions to women voters and had a firm belief in parliamentary democracy. The movement in the mid seventies was permeated by a deep antipathy for the state, disillusion with parliamentary institutions seemingly incapable of real reforms, and a suspicion of laws in general, as exemplified by the campaign around rape in 1978–9, which took little interest in actual drafting of legislation.[34]

Instead, much more importance was attached to what could be verified, controlled, changed directly; to what was concrete and easily identifiable. In relation to medical provision, for instance, the movement worked for its own health centres created 'by and for women'. The organizational structures the movement had given itself were not therefore, dependent on what happened in parliament. When mobilization around abortion subsided in the late seventies, organization around the issue, which had given rise to a dense network of collectives, *ad hoc* bodies and friendships, survived; although the movement ceased to be a force *vis à vis* the political system, it continued to be a social force.

The mass movement at a national level had anyway been characterized by particularism, localism and pluralism in its forms of organization and action. Feminists organized around questions of health, sexuality and childcare, and sought to work through their own situations at work or in the community, rather than just through general mobilizations. Bookshops such as the Libreria delle Donne set up in Milan in 1975, or reviews, like *Sotto Sopra*, were run by cooperatives designed to be 'autonomous' from immediate commercial methods and objectives, while health clinics were often self-managed and 'autonomous' from state provision.[35] For the movement, the abortion issue had been crucial because it stood for a whole experience of oppression and injustice; the struggle by women for control of their own bodies was important, moreover, for establishing a sense of identity.[36] It was a starting point for a redefinition of the objects and methods of political action and not an isolated single issue. The struggle for control of biological functions involved criticizing dominant values in society, and how these were articulated in medical, religious and political discourses. Abortion, contraception, and health care focused challenges which ultimately questioned how the 'body politic' itself was constituted.

Women and the Unions

The women's movement of the 1970s was mainly composed of women from middle-class families who had gone through further education. The student movement had been the principal political experience of the pioneers of Italian feminism. While the 'emancipationist' tradition was still strong within the Communist and Socialist Parties and trade unions, the new feminism was largely brought in from outside in the mid seventies. That is to say, it was the women in the extraparliamentary organizations and the women officials in the unions who acted as intermediaries between the movement and women workers. This spread of the movement and its entry (albeit with schizophrenic consequences) into the institutions of the labour movement distinguished the Italian experience from many others.[37] This is particularly well shown by the relationship between the women's movement and the unions in Milan. Here, the role of women identified with the 'union Left' (*sinistra sindacale*) was especially important, notably in a section of the metalworkers' union, the FIM–CISL.[38] They were active in the education, research and training work of the union, which expanded considerably in the early 1970s and in the 150-Hours Scheme. This brought them into contact with large numbers of shopfloor delegates, and with ordinary workers wanting to catch up on their education.[39]

The key figure in bringing ideas of the women's movement into the factories, however, were the women delegates. With the help of the various organizers, they were responsible for setting up women's collectives within sections of the unions, and in establishing women's commissions in factory councils and coordinating bodies that cut across the confederations. In 1976–7, many autonomous women's groupings grew up in this way. Usually these efforts to get together as women met with hostility; when the *Coordinamento delle Donne* met in Milan it was denounced by some officials as a 'sex talking-shop'. This was not surprising since a whole set of assumptions about trade unionism were being called in question, and normal procedures were being broken (women-only meetings, for example, were seen as divisive). The iconography of the workers' movement and the accepted forms of discourses were no longer taken as natural.[40]

One of the first public signs of the new feminism within the unions was the presence of several women speakers on the platform making 'collective interventions' at union conferences. Then, at demonstrations, women workers organized themselves in separate contingents. They carried multi-coloured banners (instead of the obligatory red ones), shouted feminist slogans and publically celebrated sisterhood in a context which had traditionally defined itself in terms of fraternity. And in the workplace too, women held meetings separately from the men in order to talk about their own particular problems and build up confidence in themselves. There was a sense that women had to express their opinions and feelings in their own words, rather than seeking always to follow men. In fact, feminine modes of speaking and listening were counterposed to the masculine. An account of a woman trade union organizer reveals the discovery of a new identity through language:

> It was through listening to a male leader that I too would succeed sooner or later in speaking in the same way; starting calmly, to put people at their ease, accelerating with a slow accumulation of facts and then stirring denunciation of exploitation, and culminating in a rapid crescendo, enumerating struggles and initiatives.... Later, I came to see that my words had no sound ... it was as if I was mute among other women.... Then, I spoke in my own words, laughed, got worked up, contradicted myself.[41]

Within the unions, the application of feminist critiques meant taking apart the abstract definitions of democracy and participation which had come out of the movements of 1968–9. It was becoming clear that most of the demands and gains had not been as egalitarian as everyone proclaimed. Women's wages were on average 12 per cent lower than those of men, while 67 per cent of women as opposed to 23 per cent of male workers were in the lowest grades. They had the worst paid, least skilled jobs and little opportunity to become more qualified.[42] Whereas following the Hot Autumn the representation of un-skilled and semi-skilled male workers increased greatly, women remained heavily under-represented: for example, a mere 6 out of 185 officials of the metalworkers' unions in Lombardy in 1972 were women.[43] However, it was not until the 1970s that they began systematically to criticize the unions for ignoring their needs and aspirations. Women workers too had, in one way or another, accepted a definition of themselves in terms of class and not gender. The language and frames of reference of the unions tended to exclude or stigmatize anything which seemed to encourage division or promote differences between workers. According to their rhetoric, all workers were equal. It took the growth of a mass women's movement in society at large to stimulate and encourage criticisms of union traditions.[44]

Much of the initial impulse behind the criticisms came from within the union Left, which extended an existing repertoire of analyses to examine women's situation in the modern factory. Demands around wage equalization, the reduction of grades and the elimination of piece-work, which had previously been related to the semi-skilled worker in general, were applied specifically to women workers. The issues of health and safety, and childcare provision were especially important in establishing connections between the different aspects of women's lives.[45] Furthermore, the analyses of the *operaist* tradition, which had shown that machinery and technology was not neutral but designed to subordinate the worker, were re-thought to show how they were man-made for men, and therefore excluded women from the labour process. In short, a tradition of rank-and-file militancy forged in the 1960s, and propagated by the extra-parliamentary organizations, was adapted to express the disaffection of a generation of women worker activists, who organized independently of the unions' formal structures.

For the activists of the women's coordinating groups, the union was still the preferred means of bringing about social change; in this respect, their outlook was fully consistent with that of the union Left. However, for feminists, it was not simply a matter of adding 'women's issues' to the union's agenda. The women's movement had developed ways of looking at the world that subverted deep-rooted assumptions about the centrality of waged work to projects of social change. It pointed to the contradictions between women's values and desires, and those sanctioned in the world of work. Paolo Piva, an official of the metalworkers' federation noted:

> Leaving aside domestic tasks, we find our specific nature in our sexuality and maternity, which we do not know how to incorporate into the strategy of the working class. We experience these doubts ... in personal ways in relation to maternity. From time to time, we discover a desire in ourselves to have children, which we have to suppress, or we start to feel that in the end this work is 'not for us'. It is then that we remember there exists a barrier which divides production from maternity. The two processes develop in separate cycles – cycles which come into conflict and are the more highly prized for excluding one another.[46]

Traditionally, women activists had had to conform to the dictates of a 'man's world', and needed to be 'superwomen' to stand on an equal footing with male unionists.[47] What the new feminism proposed, however, was that the work situation should be changed to accommodate the different needs and rhythms of women's lives.

This vision proved difficult to translate into concrete terms. A book entitled *Acqua in Gabbia* (Caged Water), written by two women organizers, is interesting in that it gives a strong sense of women's estrangement from the unions in the late seventies. The water metaphor is evoked to counterpose woman as natural force/movement/life to the cages men construct around their lives. While this recourse to 'essences' played an important part in establishing women's identity (again, it is the body which is the site and symbol for this), it tended to provide a means for condemning the existing state of things rather than for elaborating an alternative. Yet the implications for change were fundamental.

A series of demands, from the call for paid time-off for childcare for both men and women, to proposals for job-sharing and more part-time work, suggested the desire for a drastic reorganization of working hours. Feminist arguments started from the premises that waged work was not the only or most important form of activity, and that it should be subordinated to human needs, and not vice versa. Behind this approach lay a utopia – the dream of a society in which people had much greater control of their time – but it also raised more immediate questions about part-time and flexible working. For the unions, however, this was tantamount to heresy or 'playing the bosses' game', since they were campaigning for more rigidly defined hours within the framework of a fixed working week. Such ideas, it was said, were all very well for intellectuals, but not for workers. The authors of *Acqua in Gabbia* replied:

> Yet, women workers don't only have material needs [i.e. the full wage]. It could be that, on the contrary there is an uneven but positive search to satisfy other needs … many want to do other more stimulating things and to do them straight away, as their participation in the 150-Hours Scheme show.… The real drama is that, while the contradiction between consciousness of the right to live better and the deterioration of working and living conditions gets sharper, the union offers a regressive solution to the problem.[48]

However, the utopian discourse implicit in feminist writings like *Acqua in Gabbia* (which, because it records interviews and discussions with women workers, reflects a more diffuse current of opinion than that of the organizers themselves) sprang up in hard times. From 1976, if not before, the union leaderships were more attentive to the pressures of party politics than to the demands of their rank-and-file, not to mention the new social movements.[49] Their response to the economic crisis following the oil price rise was to concentrate on bread-and-butter issues, and, in the name of realism, to avoid more ambitious and risky projects. While there was a flurry of conferences, inquiries and committees on the 'women's question', demands for paternity leave, fixed quotas of jobs for women, and for changes in production processes designed to accommodate women, went by the board. Nor was the language of realism exclusive to the male leadership. A new generation of women organizers stressed the need to work within the institutions, while those who looked to the women's movement found themselves increasingly isolated. The great hope in the unions, and the labour movement more generally, as a vehicle for women's liberation was eclipsed.[50]

Feminism and the Crisis of the Left

1978 marked a collapse and fragmentation of the social movements and collective action. The anniversary of '68 was more a burial service attended by the so-called veterans than a moment of revival. The disintegration of the New Left, the integration of the unions into the political system, the PCI's historic compromise and forfeiture of its oppositional role, the demise of the movement of '77 and the momentary ascendancy of the Red Brigades, were so many markers in a desolate political landscape. The term '*riflusso*' (the reflux) was often used to indicate that the tide had turned, and that a historic phase was over. The women's movement, too, was deeply affected by this political climate; circuits of information were interrupted and intersecting circles of friendship and acquaintance split apart. In fact the period 1978–80 became known as the 'years of silence' (*Gli anni del silenzio*).[51] The feeling that great changes could be carried through by collective mobilization was weakened by prevailing doubts and uncertainties. Yet, while the feminist project suffered from the crisis, it was not itself at the centre of that crisis; and it was precisely this distance from the dominant forms of oppositional politics, which were the main victims, that made the movement the carrier of hopes for a future regeneration of social movements in the following decade.

During the mid seventies the women's movement had, to some extent, already exercised this function in relation to certain social groups. The formation of a gay movement in Italy owed much to feminist examples (consciousness-raising, critiques of Left politics, social support), and its influence was also felt in parts of the youth movement. Its power was such that it was able to provoke an irreversible crisis in the organizations of the New Left by attacking their authoritarianism and affirming the priority of 'movement' over 'organization'.[52] Its own qualities as a movement consisted of its loose, informal structures (sovereignty of open meetings, small groups); its stress on means rather than ends, and on prefigurative and direct action; and its preference for personal and 'natural' forms of speech and behaviour. In a sense, the women's movement spoke to all those wanting to go back to an anti-authoritarian, 'movementist' politics. Moreover, the women's movement represented a potential alternative politics to that of the workers' movement. The differences between the practices of the women's and workers' movements are succinctly summarized by Alberto Melucci:

> The women's movement affirms a different freedom; it is no longer freedom from need, but the freedom to need: no longer the struggle for equality, but for difference; no longer the freedom to act, but the freedom to be. The rupture and discontinuity with the Marxist and workers' movement tradition appear irreparable.[53]

He argues that the questions raised by the women's movement have effectively displaced those elaborated over the years by the workers' movement:

> It is perhaps not clear what point we have reached, but the questions of identity and difference, the precedence given to the right to be over the right to act, and the demand for living spaces free of society's checks and interference ... are destined to occupy a key position in the field of social conflicts.[54]

While the feminist movement has been a movement of and for women, its effects have transformed the field of political and social action, as shown by the impact of Elena Giannini Belotti's book, *Little Girls*. This study of the socialization of girls in Italy, which was published by Feltrinelli in 1973 and sold 450,000 copies, running into twelve editions, owed a great deal to 1968, giving a new edge to arguments first presented by J.S. Mill:

> Legal equality, equal wages, access to all possible professions, are sacrosanct objectives which have been offered to women – at least on paper – at the moment when men have deemed it right. These rights will, however, remain inaccessible to most women until such a time as the psychological structures which prevent them from wanting and being able to appropriate these rights are modified.... The need to realize and affirm oneself as an individual, the desire for autonomy and independence which women are reproached for lacking, have already been severely shaken in women by the time the fundamental choices of adolescence have to be made.[55]

As Alain Touraine writes, the consequences of feminism were felt by anyone comtemplating radical social change:

> The women's movement is a movement of liberation not only of women but of men by women. One of the most basic aspects is its opposition to all military and financial models of organization.... It represents a will to organize one's life, to form personal relationships, to love and be loved, to have a child....[56]

It is this capacity of the feminist movement to generate new ways of looking at society, and to draw new maps with which to make sense of everyday realities, that has made observers see it as so significant a force for change. It appears (in Raymond Williams' words) as an 'emergent cultural form', creating 'new meanings and values, new practices, new significances and experiences'.[57] Perhaps not since the formative years of the workers' movement has there been such an interrogation of the ground-rules and language of politics. If in its early years feminism borrowed the vocabulary of 'class politics' – as suggested by the titles of some of its publications (*Il compagno padrone*, Comrade Boss; *La donna sfruttata*, Exploited Women) – it subsequently developed its own analyses with which to understand the particular power of men in society, through, for example, the concept of patriarchy. Psychoanalysis was especially important as an alternative to Marxism. Moreover, feminists created a new awareness of the implications of the pervasiveness of a masculine discourse of war within the Left, as seen in the terminology full of 'fronts', 'lines', 'battles' and the glorification of aggression.[58] In addition, the whole notion of unity, which was often as important to the heretics as to the more established Left, was put in question. The diversity, pluralism and differences between and within the movements was made into a virtue; in the words of Anna Rossi-Doria concerning the fragmentation of the movement: 'The aim is not to be "different" from what is "normal", but rather to discover "normality" in difference'.[59]

However, the idea of difference was developed within the women's movement only after it had broken with the traditional discourse of the Left. The initial keywords were not new, except in their inflection, as with 'emancipation' and 'separation', or in their insertion into a new context as with 'liberation' and 'autonomy'. The whole style of the early discourse of the movement was typical of the Left; it was

> full of assertions, permeated with value judgements, and often consisted of demands. The principal preoccupation was that of adapting well-known categories to a new situation, introducing a new 'object' of discourse without dispensing with existing categories, as in the case of the specificity of women's struggle within class struggle. The protagonists who spoke did not reveal themselves in what they said, made very little use of the first person, and frequent use of impersonal forms or the equally impersonal 'we'. The interlocutor was generally an opponent – men, the institutions, the patriarchal order. It was rare for there to be a metadiscourse. Irony and ambiguity were entirely lacking.[60]

Feminist discourse only developed original forms with the shift of the orientation from the 'external' (demonstrations, action in the neighbourhood) to one centred on the 'internal' (consciousness-raising). In addition to the sessions of consciousness-raising, this appeared through forms such as diaries, letters, personal accounts and individual reflections on collective activities. Above all, it was the definition of a new subjectivity that was at stake – the discovery of the first person 'I', and an awareness of the inseparable relationship of language and social dynamics. However, there were usually two phases: an initial phase characterized by 'solidarity among women', in which a common identity was affirmed; and a subsequent one in which differences emerged, often exploding as contradictions within collectives. For some women, this transition was seen in terms of loss and destructiveness, but for many others it meant going beyond the limitations of a situation in which 'the more subjective and experiential the discourse, the more it became indistinguishable from the most abstract and ideological forms of discourse'.[61] Ultimately the refusal to speak because of the feeling that words failed to represent an inner identity showed up the limits of language, an important realization that was 'not necessarily irrational or mystical but something common to everyone's experience'.[62] A movement which began by asserting the priority of voicing opinions and naming problems without a name found itself confronting the gap between the individual and the collective and between words and the non-verbal.

There seem nonetheless to he homologies between the development of the social movements in the 1970s and that of the women's movement, which is hardly surprising given that their history was a shared one. The shifts in discourse discussed above had parallels within the extraparliamentary Left; for example, the newspaper *Lotta Continua* made its letters page into a forum for individual testimonies in 1976–7.[63] The questions of subjectivity and difference were widely debated. However, this development was part of a crisis for the Left, whereas for feminism it also represented an evolution of a current of thought and activity which went back to the origins of the movement.

This difference between the feminist movement and other movements had important consequences for the future. All the social movements went into decline after 1978, and collective mobilization in the 1980s never reached the levels of the previous decade. However, the women's movement did not so much collapse as change its forms; 'Women renounced political organization in order to survive. The history of the 1980s, marked by the abandonment of political confrontation with the institutions and by the search for new politics, has its background in the dispersion of feminism into a thousand little streams at the end of the 1970s.'[64] Some continuity existed in the survival of collectives and consciousness-raising, but this now represented one type of feminism rather than a form of organization common to the movement as a whole.

Indeed the movement ceased to be a public force, with organizations that demanded to be recognized by parties and institutions. Instead it constituted an 'area' with its latent, submerged structures. Informal networks replaced national organizations and even the historic Unione delle Donne Italiane, established under PCI auspices after the war, dissolved itself on the grounds that its national and centralized structures were incompatible with the local realities of the movement.[65] The 1980s saw the redefinition and recycling of skills, contacts and resources developed through the movement in the previous decade on the part of the first and second generation feminists. New professions emerged, especially in the service sector connected with health, and in the media. Feminists began to supply goods and services for a market they had helped to create. Above all, energies were channelled into professional activities and pragmatically making small changes rather than into mobilizing around demands for changes in state provision or legislation.[66] Otherwise activists tended to take their feminist politics into other movements which developed in the 1980s, such as the ecology and peace movements.[67]

Measured in narrow political terms, the women's movement of the 1970s can be judged a failure and the turn away from traditional political concerns in the following decade can be interpreted as a consequence of this. By 1988 still only 7 per cent of the deputies in Italy were women, while the history of the implementation of the abortion law showed the power of sabotage on the part of vested interests in the medical profession. It is also arguable that it was a failure for which the movement was in some measure responsible; like other movements after 1968, its antiparliamentarism was counter-productive when it came to proposing and enforcing legislative changes. However, the movement only concentrated on challenging the political system for the brief period of the mobilization over abortion. Its impact can best be seen not in relation to the political system but with reference to its effects on 'cultural codes and its capacity to produce "other" meanings for society as a whole'.[68]

If it is at all possible to speak of 1968 as opening the door on a cultural revolution in Italy, then feminism perhaps has the best claim to be the most influential agent of that change. However, the changes brought about by feminism have often been called 'molecular' because of the difficulty of identifying them with single events or actions. It is precisely its uncodified and everyday features which have made feminism important, as can be seen in relation to the question of language. While it is extremely unlikely that sexism in language can be effectively legislated against, for a number of reasons to do with the nature of language as a system as well as the Fascist associations of puristic prescriptivism, the new awareness of the linguistic dimensions of sexual inequalities points to the way in which feminism has questioned the most taken-for-granted assumptions. How exactly changes can be brought about in the use of language is difficult to say, yet, as Giulio Lepschy writes, the struggle to abolish unjust distinctions between men and women also has implications for how language is used: 'It is possible to argue that, once the legal possibility exists for women to occupy a certain function, the lack of a term appropriate to indicate that function with reference to women is one of the cultural elements which, however marginally, may hamper them in their progress.'[69] Such developments might seem insignificant when compared with the aspirations of the movement. In fact, in so far as feminism shared the illusion of 1970s that social transformation could be immediate and total, it fell victim to the spiral of disillusionment and despair that affected other movements. However, it is the penetration of feminist ideas into every area of society and their effects on everyday lives which suggests that this movement, more than any other has represented an anticipation of future changes in society and the promise for a renewal of oppositional politics.

Notes

1. The ambiguities of the category 'Man' produced strange situations; for instance, in 1970 Il Fronte Italiano di Liberazione Femminile took out membership in La Lega dei Diritti dell'Uomo (The League for the Rights of Man); U. Eco, 'La donna e nubile', in A. Sartogo, *Le donne al muro*, Rome 1978.
2. Inquiry into the roots of feminism in the prior experience of growing up in the 1950s is, of course, showing that the phenomenon has a longer history; see Simonetta Stella, 'Crescere negli anni '50', *Memoria*, 2, 1981, pp. 9–35.
3. The classic and much quoted definition of the 'comrade' was Che Guevara's which embodied this masculine vision: 'They must be tireless workers who give themselves utterly to the people, and sacrifice their hours of rest, their families and even their lives for the revolution'; cited in L. Aguzzi, *Un liceo: un luogo di lotta*, Milan 1976, p. 295.
4. E. Ergas, 'Femminismo e crisi di sistema. Il percorso politico delle donne attraverso gli anni settanta', *Rassenga Italiana di Sociologia*, 4, 1980, pp. 550–55.
5. M. Gramaglia, 1968 p. 186.
6. See M. Mafai, *l'apprendistato della politica. Le donne italiane nel dopoguerra*, Rome 1979: J. Adler Hellman, *Journeys among Women*, New York 1987; M. Michetti, M. Repetto and L. Viviani, *UDI: Laboratorio di politica delle donne*, Rome 1984.
7. Victoria De Grazia, *Journal of Modern History* 59, 1987, pp. 396–8.
8. Laura Grasso, *Compagno padrone*, Florence 1974, p. 36.
9. Carla Ravaioli, 'La donna', in Antonio Gambino, *Dal '68 a oggi*, Bari 1980, pp. 40–63.
10. Quoted by Lesley Caldwell, *Feminism and Politics in the 1970s in Italy*, mimeograph, unpaged; see also, Rosalba Spagnoletti, *I movimenti femministi in Italia*, Rome 1976, pp. 40–63.
11. Lesley Caldwell, *Feminism and Politics*; see also Lea Melandri, *l'infamia originaria – facciamo finita col Cuore e la Politica*, Milan 1977.
12. Marina Bianchi and Maria Mormio, 'Militanti di se stesse, Il movimento delle donne a Milano', in Alberto Melucci, ed., *Altri codici. Aree di movimento nella metropoli*, Bologna 1984, pp. 128–9.
13. Carla Lonzi, ed., *Sputiamo su Hegel: la donna clitoridea e la donna vaginale*, Milan 1970, pp. 11–18.

14. Ibid, pp. 73–141.
15. Interview with Antonella Nappi, June 1978.
16. Mariella Gramaglia, '1968: il venir dopo', pp. 180–200.
17. Negri, *Dall'operaio massa*, pp. 147–66.
18. Giuliana Pompei, 'Salario per il lavoro domestico', *L'offensiva – Quaderni di Lotta Femminile*, Turin 1972, pp. 35–47.
19. 'Programmatic Manifesto of Housewives in the Neighbourhood', *Socialist Revolution*, July 1971, pp. 84–7.
20. André Gorz, *Farewell to the Working Class*, London 1982, p. 40.
21. See Michèle Barrett, *Women's Oppression Today*, London 1980, pp. 172–86.
22. Mariarosa Dalla Costa, *The Power of Women and the Subversion of the Community*, Bristol 1972.
23. Rosalba Spagnoletti, *I movimenti femministi*, pp. 61–79.
24. See Ferrajoli and Zolo, pp. 68–100.
25. The Italian version of the gay liberation movement was FUORI (Fronte Unitario Omosessuale Rivoluzionario Italiano), which in Italian means 'Out'. It started as a review in December 1971, with women as well as men contributing. At its national congress in 1974 it decided to affiliate to the Radical Party.
26. Massimo Teodori, 'La storia del Partito Radicale', in M.Teodori, P.Ignazi and A.Panebianco, *I nuovi radicali*, Milan 1977, pp. 14–110.
27. Sandra Chelnov, 'Abortion and the Autonomous Women's Movement', *Socialist Revolution*, January/February 1977, pp. 75–92; Ellen Cantarow, 'Abortion and Feminism in Italy', *Radical America*, November/December 1976, pp. 10–30.
28. Donald Sassoon, *Contemporary Italy*, London 1986, 107–8.
29. See Barrett, *Women's Oppression Today*.
30. Lesley Caldwell, 'Church, State and Family: the women's movement in Italy', in Annette Kuhn, ed., *Feminism and Materialism*, London 1978, pp. 70–71.
31. See Luisa Passerini, *Fascism in Popular Memory*, Cambridge 1986, pp. 171–2.
32. Lesley Caldwell, 'Abortion in Italy', *Feminist Review*, 7, Spring 1981, pp. 49–65.
33. Gianna Pomata, 'In scienza e coscienza: donne e potere nella società borghese, *Quaderni Aut Aut*, 1979.
34. Tamara Pitch, 'Institutional Approach to Rape', a paper given to the Women in Italy Conference, Association for the Study of Modern Italy, June 1986.
35. Bianchi and Mormino, pp. 134–6.
36. Ibid, p. 172.
37. Adler Hellman, pp. 208–11.
38. Flora Bocchio and Antonia Torchi, 'L'acqua in gabbia – voci di donne dentro il sindacato, Milan 1978, pp. 27–8.
39. Antonella Nappi and Ida Regalia, eds., *La pratica politica delle donne*, Milan 1978; this book was written as a series of reflections on the experiences of 150-Hour Scheme courses with women workers.
40. Bocchio and Torchi, p. 25.
41. Ibid, p. 126.
42. L. Frey, 'Analisi economica della occupazione femminile in Italia', in L. Frey, ed., *Occupazione e sottoccupazione femminile in Italia*, Milan 1976.
43. Gian Primo Cella, 'La composizione sociale e politica degli apparati sindacali metalmeccanici della Lombardia', *Prospettiva Sindacale*, 1, April 1973, p. 11.
44. Nella Marcellino, 'La partecipazione femminile e il movimento sindacale', *Quaderni di Rassegna Sindacale*, 54–5, May/August 1975, pp. 113–17.
45. Francesco Dambrosio and Mauro Buscalia, 'Ambiente di lavoro e condizione femminile', *Quaderni di Rassegna Sindacale*, 54–5, May/August 1975, pp. 95–109.
46. Bocchio and Torchi, p. 29.
47. 'Women workers today are very interested in discussing the family sexuality, emancipation.... However, when it comes to doing anything, the discussion returns to work questions – grades, rises, discrimination, etc.'; Nappi and Regalia, eds., p. 87.
48. Bocchio and Torchi, p. 65.
49. Bruno Manghi, *Declinare crescendo*, Bologna 1977.

50. Lyn Froggett and Antonia Torchi, 'Feminism and the Italian Trade Unions', *Feminist Review*, 8, Summer 1981.
51. Bianchi and Mormino, p. 130.
52. The emblematic instance was the dissolution of Lotta Continua at its 1976 conference; see Luigi Bobbio, pp. 174–82.
53. Alberto Melucci, *l'invenzione del presente*, p. 180.
54. Ibid, pp. 181–2.
55. Elena Gianna Belotti, *Little Girls*, London 1976, p. 16; first published in Italy as *Dalla parte delle bambine* in 1973.
56. Quoted in Gorz, p. 85.
57. Raymond Williams, *Problems in Materialism and Culture*, London 1980, p. 42.
58. L. Bocccarossa et al., 'Donne, violenza e identità', in Luigi Manconi, ed., *La violenza e la politica*.
59. Anna Rossi-Doria, 'Conservazione e rottura nel movimento delle donne', *Ombre Rosse*, 25, June 1978, pp. 12–16.
60. Valeria Boccia, 'Il filo del discorso', *Memoria*, 19–20, 1987, p. 136.
61. Ibid, p. 141.
62. Ibid, p. 141.
63. Lotta Continua, *Dear Comrades: Readers' Letters to Lotta Continua*, London 1980.
64. Silvia Tozzi, 'Molecolare, creativa, materiale: la vicenda dei gruppi per la salute', *Memoria*, 19–20, 1987, p. 171.
65. Adler Hellman, pp. 217–20.
66. Bianchi and Mormino, p. 169–73.
67. Fulvia Fazio, 'Femminismo e movimento ecologista', in Roberto Biorcio and Giovanni Lodi, eds., *La sfida verde*, Padua 1988, pp. 99–113.
68. Bianchi and Mormino, p. 168.
69. Giulio Lepschy, 'Sexism and the Italian Language', *The Italianist*, 7, 1987, p. 157; see also Patrizia Violi, *L'infinito singolare. Considerazioni sulla differenza sessuale nel linguaggio*, Verona 1988.

22

some conclusions: the difficulties of keywords

The decade of Italian history which runs from 1968 to 1978 has a certain unity that can allow us to call it a period. It begins with the mass mobilizations of the student movement and ends with the movement of '77, when protest quickly fell under the shadow of the armed struggle. The assassination of Aldo Moro in May 1978 and the defeat of the Fiat factory occupations in October 1980 signalled the end of an era in which social movements and social conflict had dominated the language and horizons of a generation as well as the political agendas of governments. The first provoked a systematic campaign of criminalization of extraparliamentary opposition, and the second, the victory of the Fiat management, opened the way for ideological as well as economic revival of Italian capitalism.[1]

Against this background, instant histories were written by protagonists and commentators bent on celebrating or discrediting the politics of opposition which had emerged in the wake of '68. At stake was Italian society's understanding of its recent past – a past which was to haunt it.

Above all it was in the court-room that the histories were not just recounted and debated but put on trial; trials which were in effect conducted as much in the press before the tribunal of public opinion as in court in front of the judges.[2] As Nanni Balestrini wrote of the '7 April' operation against a group of left-wing intellectuals: 'It is now a commonplace to say that the operation was aimed at criminalizing twelve years of struggles by social movements together with their experiences, forms of behaviour, hopes of change, refusal to passively accept the corruptness of public life.'[3]

At the height of the terrorism emergency between 1978 and 1982, such a campaign of criminalization did indeed seem to exist. Symptomatically, the Italian title of Margarethe von Trotta's film about German terrorism,

Years of Lead (English title: *The German Sisters*), which came out in 1982
was almost instantly used to describe the whole decade of the 1970s, not
just the closing years. Terrorism was widely equated with left-wing
extremism. Writings such as those of Toni Negri were cited as evidence of
incitement, while one judge claimed to have uncovered the existence of a
single, all-embracing terrorist organization for whose members almost
every tiny episode of violence was part of a grand design.[4] A teleology of
protest suggested the existence of a logic of progression from the violence
of the picket line to that of armed struggle. 'Utopianism', 'extremism',
'extraparliamentarism', 'anarchism' and 'terrorism' became interchange-
able terms within this discourse of repression.

The criminalization of political opposition, a recurrent feature of Italian
history since the nineteenth century,[5] has overshadowed much of the
debate on the turbulent seventies, leaving its mark on popular perceptions
of a decade whose protest acquired, as a consequence, connotations of
violence and irrationality. However, the most effective campaign to bring
discredit on the strikes and disruption of those years has undoubtedly
come from those who have claimed that they simply represented
outmoded and primitive forms of behaviour.

The situation at Fiat was symptomatic of a change which was both
technological and *ideological*. The implementation of a programme of
robotization went hand in hand with a strategy of imposing mass
redundancies and destroying the power of the unions – a campaign of
action masterminded and enacted by Cesare Romiti.[6] It marked a crucial
phase in the decline of the industrial working class in Italy, not only in
terms of numbers but also of visibility, social status and political power. In
the years 1980–3 alone, employment in Fiat fell from 165,000 to about
100,000. However, the industrial workers that remained were virtually
'dead' as far as the media and sociologists were concerned; as Gad Lerner
wrote in 1988: 'For decades, the background noise of the factory floor
had created a sort of collective guilt complex in industrial societies, and it
was made into a symbol of their unresolved contradictions. Today, such
contradictions are cancelled simply by ignoring them.'[7]

The silence surrounding the working class in the 1980s cannot be
ascribed simply to the success of campaigns launched by big business in
Italy. It is indicative of the profound social and economic transformation
referred to as the transition from an industrial to a post-industrial or information society.[8] The crisis of the oppositional politics of the post-1968
movements in the 1980s can be seen, therefore, as fundamental in nature.
The basic vocabulary of the Left had become problematic; it had become
difficult, for instance, for people to talk about 'the working class', using
the singular and the definite article.

It is this difficulty of language which provides the hook on which to hang some concluding observations. All words, of course, have meanings only in so far as they are socially defined through usage. Meaning is not intrinsic to words but is generated through their relation to one another within texts, and in relation to the cultural context of their users. Words are, therefore, particularly interesting to examine as indices of deeper shifts within a culture. Moments when words drop out of usage, or enter people's vocabularies, and when the meanings of words undergo radical transformation – such moments mark significant changes. As Raymond Williams has written:

> The variations and confusions of meaning are not just faults in a system, or errors of feedback, or deficiencies of education. They are in many cases ... of historical and contemporary substance. Indeed they have often, as variations, to be insisted upon, just because they embody different experiences and readings of experience, and this will continue to be true, in active relationships and conflicts, over and above the clarifying exercises of scholars.[9]

And if conflict and variation is a constant feature of language, it is more pronounced in periods of radical historical change. The late 1970s represented such a period; in the words of Aldo Gargani in a celebrated book on the 'crisis of reason':

> We call the crisis of rationality the realization that the house of our knowledge is in fact uninhabited because of changing social relations – relations between men and women, parents and children, institutions and the governed, and also our knowledge of politics, music, literature and science – is transformed. That crisis is traced in the situation in which we feel an accumulation of energies that go beyond the saturated conventions and rules which at one time coincided with the extremes of our awareness.[10]

A central and recurrent theme of this study of Italian social movements has been the struggle over identity and recognition, over how social groups define themselves, the world around them and their place in that world – struggles in which language has been an intrinsic part. In an earlier epoch, the terminology might well have been religious; in late-twentieth-century Italy, however, it is through the language of politics that most social conflict has found expression. In the post-1968 decade in particular, left-wing politics provided the means with which to make sense of society and attempt to change it. In the words of one of the leading figures in those movements:

> Far from representing a passing fever, politics was the heart and soul of '68. That is, political passion, the conviction that there was a link that held together and demonstrated the meaning of what was happening in the four corners of

the globe; the feeling that one's own life belonged to a destiny shared with so many others in every part of the world. In the West, after the war, political generosity, love of justice, social life itself, were left-wing. Young people in the Sixties didn't discover the Left, they grew up inside it. When the question was asked, it wasn't whether or not to be on the left, but how and for what kind of left.[11]

Although this testimony does not take account of the growth of a Catholic radicalism, it does represent the dominant pattern within the movements.

As has been seen, the relationship between the social movements and the use of political language was never unproblematic. When the same leader cited above writes of '68: 'The eclectic, voluntaristic and populist "Marxism" measured up to the problems it was addressing,'[12] it is a judgement which can only be valid with reference to the mobilizing power of the myths that were appealed to. At the time, words such as 'revolution' or 'the masses' served a unifying purpose, and even when sharp divisions emerged, these were always within a shared framework. If attention is paid instead to their explanatory power, the story is rather different. From the mid to late 1970s, the words proved inadequate to the sorts of new identities to which expression was being given. Moreover, there was a rediscovery of individuality and personal needs which the collectivism of the Left seemed to deny. The relationship between the first person singular, 'I', and the first personal plural, 'we', was being drastically redefined.[13]

The changes in the meanings and usage of political terms can partly be attributed to the fluctuations between periods of collective mobilization and periods of individual withdrawal, between times when relatively greater importance is attached to public duty and times when private concerns are given priority.[14] The swing from the highly politicized language of the 1970s to the so-called hedonistic and narcissistic eighties is a case in point, and was an especially violent turnabout in Italy due to the impact of terrorism. The rise of left-wing terrorism involved a process in which Marxist terms became debased and discredited to the point of being driven out of circulation. To pursue the monetary analogy, the language of the Left had already suffered from a form of linguistic inflation, as indicated by the pejorative label *sinistrese*. However, the propaganda of the Red Brigades seemed a terrible caricature of all that the oppositional movements had stood for, so that calling them 'comrades', as in the expression 'mistaken comrades' (*compagni che sbagliano*) meant that a word which, more than any other, represented the meeting of friendship and solidarity, private and public, fell victim to mistrust.

However, the questioning and doubt surrounding keywords in the language of the Left suggest a longer term historical change in progress rather than a short term oscillation. This can be seen by looking more closely at three of these keywords: 'class', 'the Left', and 'democracy'. It is necessary also to look at the emergence of a new keyword – 'nature'. Finally, there is the important matter of the relationship between the language of oppositional politics and the historical reality it has purported to describe.

The word 'class', in its modern sense, was a product of the period that saw the formation of industrial capitalism and the emergence of new forms of social conflict. As Williams writes:

> The essential history of the introduction of class, as a word which would supersede older names for social divisions, relates to the increasing consciousness that social position is made rather than merely inherited.[15]

It is arguable that an equivalent social transition is currently under way in Western capitalist countries, making notions of class derived from industrial societies inadequate, just as notions of rank were at an earlier date. Alberto Melucci, for instance, has commented on the problems of analysing the new social movements in class terms:

> The term 'class' is not able to express the novelty of the conflicts in late capitalist societies, and should eventually be replaced ... we must stop considering classes as definite empirical groups with a certain culture and way of life.... But then does it still make sense to speak of 'class' struggles? Yes, but the conflicts must be thought of as a network of oppositions centred on the control of development.... Classes have been replaced by a multiplicity of groups which are stratified and intersect in complex ways.[16]

Melucci's reservations are a reflection within the field of sociology of a situation in which the models inherited from nineteenth-century political thought are in crisis.

Within Italy the proliferation of terms to describe social position and social conflict in the late 1970s was difficult to ignore. The terms included: marginals (*emarginati*), emergent groups (*ceti emergenti*), proletarian youth (*giovani proletari*), minorities (*minoranze*), the unprotected (*non garantiti*), the precarious (*precari*), and even plebians (*plebe*). Some commentators even found evidence for the re-emergence of patterns of city life reminiscent of the Middle Ages.[17] It is not that the more consolidated terms, such as working class or proletariat disappeared from political discourse – the marginal or unprotected were often defined in relation to the organized workers – but the significance of being in regular employment was that it enabled fuller participation in society. Social inequalities were increasingly perceived in terms of exclusion from life opportunities rather than of economic exploitation in the workplace.[18] While employment remained, therefore, a key question for the individual and society, its importance derived from norms and values acquired from outside the workplace, marking the end of the 'centrality of work'.[19]

Some political theorists on the Left have greeted the emergence of new forms of marginality and the eclipse of the mass worker with enthusiasm. Tony Negri and André Gorz, for instance, have both seen the changes as opening up new possibilities for radical social movements. In Gorz's *Farewell to the Working Class*, a 'non-class of non-workers', who neither identify with the idea of 'the worker' nor with 'the unemployed' but who fill the area of 'probationary, contracted, casual, temporary and part-time employment', are hailed as the new force of radical social transformation.[20] Unlike the mass worker who is conditioned by the heteronomy of the factory, these new social subjects are said to seek autonomous ways of living in which waged work is subordinate to other forms of activity. They are seen as anticipating a society in which necessary work is kept to a minimum, enabling the development of a flourishing civil society where free association develops unfettered.[21]

However, Massimo Paci, among others, has been more sceptical:

> Up to the time when the conditions of marginality gave rise to innovative and conflictual social and cultural projects, if on the one hand they sometimes constituted a potential source of crises and 'social disorder', on the other, at other times they were a source of vitality and political and cultural change. In the current situation, there are clear signs that an adaptive-functional role is being assigned to marginality, which ... no longer seems to bring people together in visible minorities, and involves the loss of its potential in encouraging cultural innovation, involvement and collective organization on the part of excluded social groups.[22]

He also insists that, historically, forms of marginality have been a recurrent if not constant feature of capitalist development, especially in Italy. At the same time, Paci too sees the need for political perspectives which are based on a recognition of the social and economic changes, proposing, for example, the idea of a social wage payable to all.

The term 'Left' – or rather the Left/Right opposition – lost its sharpness in the late 1970s, though not for the first time in Italian history. From the time of unification there had been many instances of convergence, which the word *trasformismo* has been used to describe; originally it referred to the process whereby the so-called 'historic' Left and Right parties which emerged from the Risorgimento tended to converge in terms of programme until there ceased to be any substantial differences between them. Then the career of Mussolini is a notorious (though not isolated) case of an extreme left-winger becoming an extreme right-winger. In the period studied here the whole question of who was on the Left was hotly debated, not least because of the multiplication of heresies and the emergence of a terrorism calling itself left-wing. There was also the formation of neo-fascist tendencies which claimed common ground with the extreme left,[23] and the phenomenon of the *cani sciolti*, the label of those unloosed dogs who had exited from left organisations, latter day versions of Ignazio Silone's 'ex'.[24] It was in this confusion that Elvio Fachinelli wrote his *Proposal for not using the terms 'Left' and 'Right'*:

> In the political field, in the narrow sense of the term, the polarity Left–Right is losing its clarity and is now used to identify and classify the pre-existing state of things. 'On the Left' is, therefore, what is done or happens within the political space occupied by the forces of the Left. The act of nominating is largely tautological.[25]

Fachinelli's *Proposal* is symptomatic of a suspicion of ritualized categorization that was widespread. This was especially so among the participants of the new social movements for whom the concept of 'difference' had acquired crucial importance – difference meaning the 'demand for the specific, the particular, the diverse, as opposed to the massification and levelling produced by consumer society'.[26] Feminists in Italy had historically seen themselves as part of the Left but found themselves at odds with its traditions in the 1970s. The ecology movement also grew out of the Left but discovered that questions such as conservation were in the hands of political conservatives whereas Marxism, because of its conception of progress, was blind to environmental concerns.[27] Both therefore questioned whether their ideas could be put under the umbrella left-wing without radically redefining what that included. Furthermore, among philosophers on the Left there was a new interest in thinkers like Nietzsche and Schopenhauer, who were associated with the Right, and growing dissatisfaction with the rationalist tradition and Marxism.[28]

All these developments were indicative, however, of a redefinition of terms rather than of a situation in which Fachinelli's *Proposal* could realistically expect implementation. The Left–Right opposition was too well-established to be so easily dispensed with – a spatial metaphor related to human perception in the same way as high and low or near and far, that has not just biological components but the whole weight of cultural tradition from the time of the French Revolution behind it. As such, the terms are lodged within the 'collective imaginary' of western societies and are not restricted to the political sphere.[29] Instead, it is possible to note a process whereby the Left in Italy, and in other countries, has ceased to be synonymous with the working-class movement or with Marxism. The new movements have continued to be egalitarian in that they have aimed to win 'horizontal' equalities – social dignity and real equality of opportunity – without having to renounce differences due to gender or sexual preference. Their politics can, indeed, be seen as largely consistent with the struggle to amplify, specify and realize the principles first enunciated by Liberalism and then taken up by the socialist movement in the nineteenth and twentieth centuries.[30] However, many negative features that came to be associated with the parties of the Left, both parliamentary and extraparliamentary, such as statism, centralism and productivism, were rejected by the new movements. The criticism of the historic and the new Left has changed the meanings of the term not abolished it.

Democracy and control are keywords which were redefined in the wake of 1968 and remained crucial for the movements of the 1980s. This can be seen in the critique of parliamentary democracy in the theory and practice of the movements, and in the proposals for alternative democratic forms. The vicissitudes of the idea of democracy have already been analysed in relation to anti-authoritarian and extraparliamentary politics, to grassroots organizations in workplaces and educational institutions, and to their critical reappraisal by feminism. Yet while the movements revived and experimented with every approach from council-communism to anarchism and Leninism, they cannot be said to have produced any new body of theory. Their significance lies more in painful trial and error. For an evaluation of this and its consequences for rethinking the question of democracy, the most useful work has come from a political philosopher close to the Italian Socialist Party, Norberto Bobbio.

Bobbio's great strength has been his ability to make explicit the political implications implicit in the major movements and transformations of the postwar period. As Perry Anderson has written, his texts form a 'crystalline prism' of that history.[31] For Bobbio the most formative period was that of his participation in the Resistance, but he was also involved, in his role as university professor and father of sons on the extraparliamentary Left, in the conflicts of the post-1968 period. As he later recalled, his initial reaction to the events of '68 was to see them as a threat to democracy:

> For someone who regarded the Resistance as having laid the foundations of a stable democracy and of the Republican constitution, the challenge from the Left with its accompanying delegitimization of the constitution not dissimilar, except in motivation, from that which had always come from the right, was an extremely bitter surprise.[32]

However, Bobbio subsequently came to the conclusion that the movements, unlike Fascism, represented a force for the development and extension of democracy in Italy. Above all they appeared to spread democratic decision-making to those areas of the state and civil society where authoritarianism had previously been the rule – to schools and universities, factories and offices, and even to the army and government administration. They showed up the limits of a model of democracy that was exclusively parliamentary and relied on political parties to mediate between citizens and central government.[33] Democracy, he wrote, could be more subversive than socialism:

> Democracy is subversive in the most radical sense of the word, because, wherever it spreads, it subverts the traditional conception of power, one so traditional it has come to be considered natural, based on the assumption that power – ie. political or economic, paternal or sacerdotal – flows downwards. By conceiving of power as flowing upwards, democracy is in some ways more subversive than socialism, if we use 'socialism' in the limited sense of transfer of ownership of the means of production.[34]

The post '68 movements therefore forced Bobbio and others of his generation to question their own assumptions. Much of his work in the following decade can be seen as an active attempt at dialogue with the protagonists of the movements, from the student movement to the ecology movement.[35] However, he also made sharp criticism of the alternatives to parliamentary democracy that they proposed. For Bobbio, direct democracy, in particular, was misconceived on a number of grounds. Firstly, because of its impracticability; if it was feasible in simple, small-scale societies, it was anachronistic in a complex, technological society. Secondly, because the whole system of revocable mandates and representation based on particular constituencies, like the workplace, was liable to reflect partial interests and not the general interests of the citizen, and was, moreover, exposed to manipulation by leaders, as shown by the experience of the student movement in Italy. Finally, because non-stop involvement in decision-making could easily have an over-politicizing effect which, in the longer term, would provoke withdrawal rather than greater participation. What Bobbio found especially worrying was the utopian idea that somehow politics would fade away in the future socialist society as the government of men gave way to the administration of things. He suggested, instead, that politics was a condition of human existence due not only to limited resources but to differences of opinion over moral questions.

Bobbio's critique of direct democracy in the 1970s was rooted in the debates in the movements at the time over 'leaderism' and hidden forms of authoritarianism, over the crisis of militancy and so on. He also found support for his arguments in the inconsistencies in demands for the extension of rights coming from protagonists who did not recognize the legitimacy of the parliamentary institutions in the first place. What body, he asked, would establish the democratic 'rules of the game' if not parliament, because they could not exist without being guaranteed in law? All in all, the hopelessly ill-considered, rhetorical and sometimes opportunistic conceptions of democracy championed by the post-'68 movements were mercilessly exposed to view.

The difficulties, however, did not arise simply because of confused thinking on the part of those involved in the social movements, and it was their achievement to bring them to light anyway. They derived from the very attempt to combine greater democracy and socialism within a capitalist society. There was the question of exactly how much democracy would be compatible with the maintenance of private property; in Anderson's words, 'the space for radical reform is closed by the very properties of the economic order that calls out for it'.[36] Moreover, especially in Italy, the failure or incapacity of the parliamentary system to respond to demands made upon it has meant that social movements continue to face great difficulties in developing a parliamentary strategy as well as trying to extend democracy outside parliament.

Class, the Left and democracy are keywords in a language of politics which dates back to the French Revolution, if not beyond it. The concept of nature, on the other hand, has tended to be subordinate, especially in the socialist tradition, and has only emerged in the late 1970s and 1980s as a crucial term.[37] If previously reference was made to 'natural rights', now it was claimed that nature and other species should themselves have rights.[38] Given the proximity in time of these developments, it is hard to assess their implications for the future of oppositional politics – whether, for example, the ecology movement represents a movement whose historical significance can be compared with the socialist one at the turn of nineteenth century. What does seem to be the case is that the ecology movement has its immediate roots in the post-'68 movements while representing one of the most far-reaching critiques of those movements.[39]

It is obviously not possible to analyze this movement in any depth in this context, but it is perhaps worth noting the way in which nature has become a key term in contemporary political discourse, and not just in relation to ecology. As Alberto Melucci has written:

> The appeal to Nature has played an important role in the formation of new collective demands. Nature appears as what is resistant to external pressures because it is not liable to instrumental rationality. It presents itself as a 'given', as opposed to the enforced socialization of identity imposed by new forms of domination. But there is, in this appeal, the confused perception that the natural order is a field of action, an object to be produced, and not a 'given'.

The body, desire, biological identity, sexuality are all cultural representations ... 'human nature' can be produced and transformed by social action.[40]

The contradictions and conflicts generated by the increases in human control over or intervention in natural processes is at the heart of the political developments of the 1980s. However, whereas the reality of nature and human dependence on the natural world is at the centre of ecological approaches, there has also emerged what can be called a postmodern perspective in which the very idea of an external reality is questioned. Within an Italian context this polarization, which cuts across any earlier division of politics into Left and Right, can be seen with reference to the writings of two intellectuals, Adriano Sofri and Mario Perniola, who both identify '68 as a watershed in the postwar period, though for very different reasons.

The writing of Adriano Sofri, ex-leader of Lotta Continua, can be taken as an example of someone whose history is intimately bound up with social movements and who now sees the ecology movement as offering the greatest hope for political renewal. Sofri makes no bones about his attachment to his past: 'I cannot go on without briefly doing justice to a feeling too lightly dismissed – nostalgia. The Italian political vocabulary has abused the word; first making it synonymous with Fascism, and then with reactionary ecological sentiments, as if nostalgia for a less ravaged natural world was unfounded.'[41]

Apart from evoking the positive in '68 (the political passion, seriousness, flexibility, eclecticism and poetry of revolt), Sofri focuses on the negative aspects or limits of the 'Marxism' of '68. These include its uncritical attitude towards forms of violence and its exclusion of women, but, above all, its abject failure to confront the relationship between human beings and nature:

> Habituated to shaping cultural history, the history that is made by men ('nature is right-wing', as Ramuz used to say), the Left reacted badly to this intrusion of what is slow, immutable and 'natural'. Faith in discontinuity, in the political genetics of modern man, made the Left (especially the youth with their impatience and voluntarism) intolerant of the very idea of 'human nature', and made it opt for a vocabulary of manipulation and domination over Nature.[42]

Moreover, writes Sofri, 'far from being a critique of industrialism, Marxism is an apology for it'.

In the spirit of '68, Sofri lays claim to the right to learn from the experience of 'sin', from the 'purgatory' that came after the 'inferno' of a politics based on the sacrifice of individuality, human feeling and the present in the name of a remote future; the right, that is, to change. 'What is needed is to find a language that confronts the point of no return reached in our shared history', he writes. '68 cannot be repeated, but it can provide inspiration for exploring possibilities of transformation which were glimpsed at the time but then lost sight of. 1968 was a year when a generation 'discovered a deep feeling of belonging to Europe both culturally and as citizens'. It failed to make use of the parallel experiences of those in Eastern Europe, and to examine itself in the mirror which they represented, as evidenced by the very deformities of the Marxism of the New Left. Yet, the impulse to break down the division of Europe into power blocs was there, and it is to this legacy that Sofri refers:

> The rebellion of '68 had a peculiarly European character. For the first time in a century, Paris became once again the capital of a revolutionary Europe of young people, and its May spoke the language of the German Jew, Cohn-Bendit. The same marches crossed Europe, and brought the students in the West closer than ever before to those of Prague, or Cracow, or Belgrade. A common Europe was the promise of those months.[43]

Sofri's reflections on the meaning of '68 for the 1980s are frankly personal, but he also speaks for a wider constituency, notably those still committed to the politics born of social movements. It is emblematic of a generation's need to address its predecessors and its successors, and, not least, to talk to itself. It is also symptomatic of the return, after a period of withdrawal, to politics and public life in the light of the successes of the ecology movement in Italy and in Europe as a whole.[44]

Sofri represents one broad current of thought which is critical of the '68 legacy but determined to discover and establish continuities. It is admitted that perhaps something was coming to an end rather than beginning: 'Who knows whether it won't turn out to be the beginning of the end of a century which started so late with the revolver shots of Sarajevo and which has rushed anxiously towards its liquidation.[45] Yet Sofri wants to see '68 as a moment of renewal, a starting-point for new projects of changing the world.

By contrast, the writers who can be called 'postmodern' announce the epochal crisis of the notions of political action, subjectivity, and the transformation of the 'real' which underpin the approach represented by Sofri and the ideas of the Greens. Mario Perniola, for example, writes of the dissolution of the traditional distinction between the real and the imaginary. For him, 1968 ushers in the age of the imaginary; the very aspects which others called political culs-de-sac, such as the revival of Marxist orthodoxies, are described as the highways towards the future:

On the one hand, '68 presented itself as radical critique of the society of social and cultural spectacle; on the other, it brings to a paroxysm society's de-realization and culturalization. This latter aspect which has been shamefacedly hidden from sight, appears in the return of all the revolutionary theories of the past (from Marxism and Leninism to anarchism and council-communism) without there having been the slightest chance of a revolution. . . . But, this is exactly what gives one a measure of the degree of de-realization and social culturalization achieved . . . not even being a failed revolution, nor even a dream or illusion, it is a historical event of primary importance, the first historical event that cannot be called 'real' in the old sense of the word.[46]

Perniola's analyses deal with the death of a politics that is seen to originate in the Enlightenment and the French Revolution – a politics based in 'a form of collective representation in which the masses or social groups identify in a way analogous to that which gave rise to the historical consciousness of the people, the nation and the class'. But, 'it is no longer principles, ideas and representations that ensure integration between society and culture', writes Perniola, 'it is simulacra, images, copies without originals; whereas the former continued to presuppose the existence of subjects (if not of persons), the latter move in a space that cancels out all sign of originality, authenticity, subjectivity'.[47]

While Mario Perniola cannot be said to speak as a representative (if anything, such a role would be eschewed by him), his writing nonetheless is part of a current of thought which has won many adherents in Italy and in Europe in the 1980s. In Italy it is especially influential among designers and architects, such as Alessandro Mendini, creator of 'banal design'. Of this tendency Andrea Branzi has written:

The intermediate [as opposed to mass or avant garde] range of cultural forms is boundless, and banal design proposes a use for it, as the only possible adaptation to the post-industrial universe that surrounds us – a chaotic universe born out of a supranational order lacking history or destiny, a discontinuous world created out of what has turned out to be impracticable planning and a medieval culture that is the outcome of progress being turned on its head.[48]

The philosophers of 'weak thought', such as Gianni Vattimo, also have much in common with this approach.[49] The best known theorists of the postmodern, however, are French authors like Jean Baudrillard and François Lyotard,[50] whose work is widely available in Italy in translation. In this context, Perniola, who owes a great deal to Baudrillard, can be said to stand for an important pole in the discussion of the meanings (or meaninglessness) of oppositional politics in the decades after 1968.

Indeed, the positions occupied by Adriano Sofri and Mario Perniola can be seen to encapsulate in miniature a polarization which is found in the areas of opposition, dissent, or refusal, for which the label 'left-wing' appears increasingly inadequate. On the one hand, there is the reaffirmation of history and memory, a narrative that seeks meaning in collective action, a belief in the special role of the intellectual, a discovery of authenticity and irreducibility in nature. On the other, there is the elimination of subjectivity as a category, the replacement of the principle of collective action by that of indifference and neutralization, the dismissal of intellectuals as redundant, the substitution of authenticity by simulation in a world in which everything is seen as cultural. It is as if the positions were mirror opposites of one another, even in their use of language – Sofri's dense with illustration and appealing to the readers' own experience; Perniola's abstract, distant, and self-reflective.

A momentary glance back to the 1960s and 70s shows the distance in time that has been travelled. The certainties, the sense of destiny, the belief in progress, the faith in the power of words: where are they now? The landscape has changed almost out of all recognition. However, this need not be a reason for disillusion and despair on the part of those who see social movements as cause for hope. If the idea of progress as *demythiciz-ation* which was so widespread in those movements is now seen as untenable, 'we have to keep on dreaming while being conscious of the fact that all is a dream'.[51]

Notes

1. Paul Ginsborg, while noting that it is premature to assume some definitive assimilation of the working class into capitalism, writes of the 1980s: 'individualist family strategies have been exalted to a greater degree than ever before in the history of the Republic. Such an outcome is in keeping with the culture and values of the model of modernity which first emerged at the time of the "economic miracle" – a model which appeared to be in dire crisis between 1968 and 1973, but which seems to have entered a golden age in the 1980s'; 'Family, Culture and Politics in Contemporary Italy', in Barański and Lumley, *Culture and Conflict in Postwar Italy*, London 1990.
2. See Alessandro Portelli, 'Oral Testimony, the Law and the Making of History: the "April 7" Murder Trial', *History Workshop Journal*, 20, 1985, pp. 5–35.
3. Nanni Balestrini, 'Anche un processo agli intellettuali', *Alfabeta*, 49, 1988, p. 37.
4. Giorgio Bocca describes the 7 April operation as the product of an agreement between Roman and Padovan magistrates: 'A global theory, an all-inclusive fresco, a Sistine chapel with its last judgement of subversion, the god of justice at the centre, and all around him the saints and the devils, chief among the latter being Professor Negri'; *Il caso 7 aprile. Toni Negri e la grande inquisizione*, p. 135.
5. For a study of the relationship between the 'language of crime' and the 'language of subversion' in late nineteenth century, see the masterly study by John A. Davis, *Conflict and Control: Law and Order in Nineteenth-Century Italy*, London 1988.
6. Cesare Romiti, *Questi anni alla Fiat (intervista di GP Pansa)*, Milan 1988; see also Marco Revelli, 'Defeat at the Fiat', *Capital and Class*, 16, 1982.

7. Gad Lerner, *Operai: viaggio all'interno della Fiat. La vita, le case, le fabbriche di una classe operaia che non esiste più*, Milan 1988, p. 17.
8. See Alberto Melucci, 'Movimenti in un mondo di segni', in *Altri codici*, pp. 417–46.
9. Raymond Williams, *Keywords*, London 1976, p. 26.
10. Aldo Gargani, *Crisi della ragione*, Turin 1979, p. 46: quoted in Iain Chambers and Lidia Curti, 'Silent Frontiers', p. 27.
11. Gianni Sofri, 'La corsa nei sacchi', *Micro-Mega*, 1, 1988, p. 173.
12. *Ibid*, p. 174.
13. Franco Fortini, in response to the violent rejection of individualism in the early 1970s, wrote in verse: 'Better say "I" when meaning "we"/Than saying "we" meaning "I"/I'll be the first person to say goodbye to you/But that first person will be you'; 'Questo e un altro', *L'Espresso*, 20 March 1988, p. 199.
14. Albert Hirschman, *Shifting Involvements*, Princeton 1982.
15. Williams, *Keywords*, p. 52.
16. Alberto Melucci, 'New Movements, Terrorism and the Political System', p. 97.
17. Guiseppe Sacco, 'Città e società verso il nuovo medioevo', in Umberto Eco et al., *Il nuovo medioevo*, Milan 1973.
18. Gian Primo Cella, 'Garantiti e non garantiti', *Prospettiva Sindacale*, 4, December 1978, pp. 56–62.
19. Paolo Ceri, 'Le basi sociali e morali dell'ecologia politica', in P. Ceri, ed., *Ecologia politica*, Milan 1987, p. 106.
20. Gorz, *Farewell to the Working Class*, p. 67.
21. For a critical review, see Boris Frankel, *The Post-Industrial Utopians*, Cambridge 1987; also my 'Socialism: Utopian and Utopian', *Head and Hand*, 13, Summer 1983, pp. 3–8.
22. Massimo Paci, *La struttura sociale italiana. Costanti storiche e trasformazioni recenti*, Bologna 1982, p. 325.
23. Anna Elisabetta Galeotti, 'L'opposizione destra-sinistra: riflessioni analitiche', in Franco Ferraresi, ed., *La destra radicale*, Milan 1984, pp. 269–71.
24. Ignazio Silone, 'The Situation of the 'Ex', in *Emergency Exit*, London 1968, pp. 100–11.
25. 'Una proposta: non usare i termini "Sinistra" e "Destra"', *Lotta Continua*, 27 October 1981; see also Lea Melandri, *L'infamia originale*.
26. Galeotti, 'L'opposizione destra sinistra', p. 270.
27. On the problem of modernity and tradition, see Alain Touraine, 'Le lotte antinucleari', in Paolo Ceri, ed., *Ecologia politica*, pp. 91–7.
28. Massimo Cacciari, 'Sinestreritas', in *Il concetto di sinistra*, Milan 1982.
29. Galeotti, pp. 260–64.
30. Ibid, p. 271.
31. Perry Anderson, 'The Affinities of Norberto Bobbio', *New Left Review*, 170, 1988, p. 33.
32. Norberto Bobbio, *Il profilo del novecento italiano*, Turin 1986, p. 180.
33. See in particular the essay 'Representative and Direct Democracy', in Norberto Bobbio, *The Future of Democracy*; see also Richard Bellamy's introduction.
34. Norberto Bobbio, 'Alternatives to Representative Democracy', in *Which Socialism?*, Oxford 1988, p. 74.
35. For Bobbio's critique of the inadequacies of Marx's (and Marxist) conceptions of politics, see *Which Socialism?*, pp. 31–64.
36. Anderson, 'Affinities', p. 29.
37. The work of Sebastiano Timpanaro is the exception here. As Adriano Sofri has observed, Timpanaro criticized Marx through Leopardi, writing: 'For the Marxist, *historical man* would always put *natural man* increasingly in the shade, and would eventually absorb and supersede the latter entirely. For Leopardi, nature still kept all her formidable destructive power in relation to civilized man'; Adriano Sofri, 'Sempre verde mi fu', *L'Espresso*, 12 July 1987, pp. 136–41.
38. 'It has been widely accepted in the past that it is inadmissable, at least morally, for a human being to be treated as an object, but now nature too can claim the right not to

be treated any longer as an object'; Norberto Bobbio, *Which Socialism?* p. 176.

39. See Roberto Biorcio and Giovanni Lodi, eds., *La sfida verde: il movimento ecologista in Italia*, Padua 1988; also my 'Challenging Tradition: Social Movements, Cultural Change and the Ecology Question', in Barański and Lumley, *Culture and Conflict in Postwar Italy*.

40. Alberto Melucci, *L'invenzione del presente*, p. 140

41. Adriano Sofri, 'Sessantotto. La corsa nei sacchi', p. 171.

42. Ibid., p. 176.

43. Ibid., p. 189.

44. Ibid., p. 175.

45. Ibid., p. 175.

46. Mario Perniola, *La società dei simulacri*, Bologna 1983, p. 8.

47. Ibid., p. 52.

48. Andrea Branzi, *The Hot House*, London 1984, p. 122.

49. Gianni Vattimo and Pier Aldo Rovatti, eds., *Il pensiero debole*, Milan 1986.

50. Important texts by these authors include: Jean Baudrillard, *Simulations*, New York 1983, and Jean-François Lyotard, *The Postmodern Condition*, Manchester 1986.

51. Gianni Vattimo, 'Myth and the Destiny of Secularization', *Social Research*, 2, 1985, p. 360.

bibliography

All major sources cited in the text are listed here; sources referred to in the footnotes are not all included. Because the majority of the leaflets of the student movement are not dated or signed, they are difficult to classify. These are to be found in the Feltrinelli Institute in Milan where they are kept under the general heading 'Movimento Studentesco'. Private collections of leaflets, interviews and fieldnotes are mentioned only in the footnotes.

For the interested reader, the following Italian periodicals were used in research. Daily Papers: *L'Unità, Il Corriere della Sera* (Milanese editions); Weekly and Monthly Papers and Magazines: *L'Espresso, Lotta Continua, Potere Operaio, Rinascità*; Journals: *Aut Aut, Avanguardia Operaia, Classe, Contro Informazione, Dibattito Sindacale, Erba Voglio, Fabbrica e Stato, Inchiesta, Il Manifesto, Il Mulino, Ombre Rosse, Primo Maggio, Problemi del Socialismo, Quaderni Piacentini, Quaderni di Rassegna Sindacale, Quaderni Rossi, Re Nudo, Rosso, La Sinistra, Sinistra Proletaria.*

Accornero, Aris, 'Per una nuova fase di studi sul movimento sindacale', in A. Accornero et al., *Movimento sindacale e società italiana*, Milan 1977.
—— 'Fabbrica diffusa e nuova classe operaia', *Inchiesta*, July/August 1978.
—— *Il lavoro come ideologia*, Bologna 1980.
Adler Hellman, Judith, *Journeys among Women*, New York 1987.
Aguzzi, Luciano, *Scuola, studenti e lotta di classe*, Milan 1976.
—— *Un liceo, un luogo di lotta*, Milan 1976.
Alberoni, Francesco, 'Società, cultura e communicazioni di massa', *Annali della Scuola Superiore delle Communicazioni Sociali, Università del Sacro Cuore, 2*, Milan 1966.
—— *Statu nascenti*, Bologna 1966.
—— *Classi e generazioni*, Bologna 1970.
—— *Italia in trasformazione*, Bologna 1976.
—— *Movimento e istituzione*, Bologna 1977.
—— 'Une opposition de gauche au PCI, est-elle possible pour lui?', in Fabrizio Calvi, ed., *Italie '77*, Paris 1977.
—— 'Movimento e istituzione in Italia tra il 1960 e il 1970', in L. Graziano, ed., *La crisi italiana*, Bologna 1979.

Alemanni, Ferigo and Gheddo, *Autoriduzione*, Milan 1975.
Allum, Percy, *Italy – Republic Without Government?*, London 1973.
——— *Politics and Society in Postwar Naples*, Cambridge 1973.
——— 'Uniformity Undone: Aspects of Catholic Culture in Postwar Italy', in Z. Barański and R. Lumley, eds, *Culture and Conflict in Postwar Italy*, London 1990.
Alquati, Romano, 'Comparizione del capitale e forza lavoro alla Olivetti', *Quaderni Rossi*, 2, 1972.
Amyot, Grant, *Sulla Fiat*, Milan 1975.
——— 'Per un'analis; della composizione di classe degli studenti.' *Aut Aut*, 154, 1976.
——— *The Italian Communist Party*, London 1981.
Anderson, Perry, *Considerations on Western Marxism*, London 1976.
——— 'The Affinities of Noberto Bobbio', *New Left Review*, 170, 1988
Angotti, Thomas, *Housing in Italy*, New York, 1977.
Antoniazzi, Sandro, 'Per lo sviluppo dei consigli', *Dibattito Sindacale*, November–December 1970.
Antonuzzo, Antonio, *Boschi, miniera, catena di montaggio–la formazione di un militante della nuova CISL*, Rome 1976.
Arbasino, Alberto, *Un paese senza*, Milan 1980.
Arnao, Giancarlo, *Rapporto sulle droghe*, Milan 1976.
Arrigo, Giani, ed., *Lo statuto dei lavoratori: un bilancio politico*, Bari 1971.
Asor Rosa, Alberto, *Scrittori e popolo*, Rome 1965.
——— *Le due società*, Turin 1977.
Avanguardia Operaia, *Per il rilancio di una politica di classe*, Rome 1968.
Baglioni, Guido and Treu, T., 'Il controllo sindacale sul potere economico', in *Lo statuto dei lavoratori: un bilancio politico*, Bari 1977.
Baglivo, A. Papa, S. and Pellicciari, G., *Le migrazioni oggi*, Milan 1973.
Balbo, Laura, 'Le trasformazioni del sistema scolastico italiano', in *La scuola del capitale*, Padua 1973.
——— *Stato di famiglia*, Milan 1976.
Balestrini, Nanni, *Vogliamo tutto*, Milan 1974; first ed., 1971.
——— *La violenza illustrata*, Turin 1976.
——— 'Anche un processo agli intellettuali', *alfabeta*, 49, 1983.
——— *Gli invisibili*, Milan 1987; *The Unseen*, trans. Liz Heron, London 1989.
Ballestrero, Maria, *Dalla tutela alla parità: la legislazione italiana sul lavoro*, Bologna 1979.
Barański, Zygmunt, 'Pier Paolo Pasolini. Culture, Croce, Gramsci', in Z. Barański and R. Lumley, eds, *Culture and Conflict in Postwar Italy*, London 1990.
Barbagli, Marzio, *Disoccupazione intellettuale e sistema scolastica in Italia, 1859–1973*, Bologna 1974.
Barbagli, Marzio and Corbetta, P., 'Partito e movimento: aspetti e rinnovamento del PCI', *Inchiesta*, 31, 1978.
Barile, G., 'Classe operaia e mobilità sociale', *Classe*, 12, 1976.
Barrett, Michèle, *Women's Oppression Today*, London 1980.
Basilico, Vito, 'Pirelli: un decennio di lotte viste da un protagonista', *Classe*, 12, 1976.
Baudrillard, Jean, *Simulations*, New York 1983.
Beccalli, Bianca, 'Scioperi e organizzazione sindacale: Milano 1959–70', *Rassegna Italiana di Sociologia*, XXI, 1971.

—— 'The Rebirth of Italian Trade Unionism: 1943–54', in S. Woolf, ed., *Rebirth of Modern Italy*, London 1971.

—— 'Lotte alla Pirelli', *Quaderni Piacentini*, 50, 1973.

—— 'Redaelli', in A. Pizzorno, ed., *Lotte operaie e sindacato*, vol. 5, Bologna 1975.

—— 'Protesta giovanile e opposizione politica', *Quaderni Piacentini*, 64, 1977.

—— 'Classe operaia e nuovi movimenti collettivi', in G. Germani, ed., *Mutamento e classi sociali in Italia*, Naples 1981.

—— *Youth Movement and Public Policy in Milan: 1975–79*, Centre for European Studies, Harvard University, mimeograph 1981.

Beccalli, Bianca and Salvati, M., 'Divisione del lavoro; capitalismo, socialismo, utopia', *Quaderni Piacentini*, 40, 1970.

Bechelloni, Giovanni, *Cultura e ideologia nella nuova sinistra*, Milan 1973.

—— *La macchina culturale in Italia*, Bologna 1974.

—— 'L'università introvabile', *Rassegna Italiana di Sociologia*, 1, 1977.

Belotti, Elena Gianini, *Little Girls*, London 1975.

Benetti, M. and Regini, M., 'Considerazioni generali sui vincoli posti dalla forza lavoro occupata alla sua utilizzazione nell'azienda' in P. Alessandrini, ed., *Conflittualità e aspetti normativi del lavoro*, Bologna 1978.

Berardi, Franco, *Le ciel est enfin tombé sur la terre*, Paris 1978.

Berger, John, *Selected Essays and Articles*, London 1971.

Berger, John and Mohr, Jean, *A Seventh Man*, London 1975.

Bianchi, G., Frigo, F., et al., *Grande impresa e conflitto industriale*, Rome 1970.

—— *I CUB*, Rome 1970.

Bianchi, G., Dugo, A., and Martinelli, U., *Assenteismo, orario di lavoro e scioperi nell'industria italiana*, Milan 1972.

Bianchi, G., and Ellena, A., *Giovani tra classe e generazioni*, Milan 1973.

Bianchi, Marina, and Mormino, M., 'Militanti di se stesse. Il movimento delle donne a Milano', in A. Melucci, ed., *Altri Codici*, Milan 1984.

Bianchi, Sandro 'Lo sciopero a scacchiera', *Prima Communicazione*, April–May 1974.

Blackmer, D. 'Post War Italian Communism' in D. Blackmer and S. Tarrow, *Communism in Italy and France*, Princeton 1975.

Boato, Marco, *Il '68 è morto: Viva il '68*, Verona 1979.

Bobbio, Luigi, *Lotta continua: storia di una organizzazione rivoluzionaria*, Rome 1979.

Bobbio, Norberto, 'Democracy and Invisible Government', *Telos*, 52, Summer 1982.

—— *The future of Democracy*, Cambridge 1987.

—— *Which Socialism?*, Cambridge 1988.

Bocca, Giorgio, *Il terrorismo italiano*, Milan 1978.

—— *Il caso 7 aprile: Toni Negri e la grande inquisizione*, Milan 1980.

—— *Noi terroristi*, Milan 1985.

Boccarossa, Liliana, et al., 'Donne, violenza e identità', in Luigi Manconi, ed., *La Violenza e la Politica*, Rome 1979.

Boccia, V., 'Il filo del discorso', *Memoria*, 19–20, 1987.

Bocchio, Flora, and Torchi, Antonia, *L'acqua in gabbia – voci di donne dentro il sindacato*, Milan 1978.

Boffi, M., Cofini, S., Giasanti, A., and Mingione, E., *Città e conflitto sociale*, Milan 1972.

Bolchini, Piero, *La Pirelli: operai e padroni*, Florence 1967.

Bologna, Sergio, 'Il rapporto società-fabbrica come categoria storica', *Primo Maggio*, 2, October 1973.
—— Class composition and the theory of the party at the origin of the workers councils movement', in CSE Pamphlet no. 1, *The Labour Process and Class Strategies*, London 1976.
—— 'The Tribe of Moles' in Red Notes, *Working Class Autonomy and the Crisis*, London 1979.
Bonaccini, Aldo, 'Il soffitto delle ACLI Milanesi', *Rinascità*, 19 July 1968.
Bonanate, L., ed., *Dimensioni del terrorismo politico*, Milan 1979.
Boneschi, M., *Donne e liquidazione: Unidal*, Milan 1978.
Bonvini, G., ed., *Un minuto più del padrone*, Milan 1977.
Bourdieu, Pierre, 'The production of belief: contribution to an economy of symbolic goods', *Media, Culture and Society*, 2, 1980.
—— *Homo Academicus*, Cambridge 1988.
Bozzini, Federico, *Il furto campestre – una forma di lotta di massa*, Milan 1977.
Bozzini, Federico, and Carbognin, M., *Perchè parlare di storia – contributo dell'area veronese*, mimeograph, 1978.
Branzi, Andrea, *The Hot House. Italian New Wave Design*, London 1984.
Brecht, Bertolt, 'Théorie de la radio (1927–32)', in *Écrits sur la littérature et l'art*, Paris 1970.
Cacciari, Massimo, 'Sinistreritas', in *Il concetto di sinistra*, Milan 1982.
Caesar, Michael, and Hainsworth, Peter, eds, *Writers and Society in Contemporary Italy*, Leamington Spa 1984.
Caioli, L., et al., *Bande. Un modo di dire*, Milan 1986.
Caldwell, Lesley, 'Church, State and Family, the women's movement in Italy', in Annette Kuhn, ed., *Feminism and Materialism*, London 1978.
—— 'Abortion in Italy', *Feminist Review*, 7, Spring 1981.
Cantarow, Ellen, 'Abortion and Feminism in Italy', *Radical America*, November–December 1976.
Capanna, Mario, *Formidabili quegli anni*, Milan 1988.
Capecchi, Vittorio, and Livolsi, M., *La stampa quotidiana in Italia*, Milan 1971.
Castles, Stephen, and Kosack, G., *Immigrant Workers and Class Structure in W. Europe*, Oxford 1973.
Castronovo, Valerio, *Giovanni Agnelli*, Turin 1977.
—— *Italia contemporanea*, Turin 1976.
Cavallini, Massimo, *Il terrorismo in fabbrica: interviste*, Rome 1978.
Cavazza, F.L., and Graubard, S.R., *Il caso italiano*, Milan 1974.
Cederna, Camilla, *Una finestra sulla strage*, Milan 1971.
Cella, Gian Primo, *Divisione del lavoro e iniziativa operaia*, Bari 1972.
—— *Un sindacato italiana negli anni sessanta. La FIM–CISL dall'associazione alla classe*, Bari 1972.
—— 1973 'La composizione sociale e politica degli apparati sindacali metalmeccanici della Lombardia', *Prospettiva Sindacale*, 1, April 1973.
—— 'Gli operai comuni all'Alfa Romeo', *Classe*, 8, 1974.
—— 'Garantiti e non garantiti', *Prospettiva Sindacale*, 4, December 1978.
Centre for Contemporary Cultural Studies, *Unpopular Education: Schooling and Social Democracy in England since 1945*, London 1981.
Centro, Giovanni Francovich, *I comunisti in fabbrica*, Milan 1967.
Centro Operaio (Quaderni di), *Consigli di zona*, Rome 1974.
Ceri, Paolo, ed., *Casa, città, struttura sociale*, Rome 1975.
—— 'L'autonomia operaia tra organizzazione del lavoro e sistema politico',

Quaderni di Sociologia, 1, 1977.
—— 'I quattro volti dell'anti-sociologia', *Quaderni di Sociologia*, 4–5, 1985.
—— 'Le basi sociali e morali dell'ecologia politica', in P. Ceri, ed., *Ecologia politica*, Milan 1987.
Chambers, Ian, and Curti, Lidia, 'Silent Frontiers', *Screen Education*, 41, Winter/Spring 1982.
—— 'A Volatile Alliance: Culture, Popular Culture and the Italian Left', *Formations*, 1984.
Chelnov, Sandra, 'Abortion and the autonomous women's movement', *Socialist Revolution*, January–February 1977.
Cherki, Eddy, and Wieviorka, Michel, 'Autoreduction Movements in Turin', *Semiotext(e)*, 3, 1980.
Cohen, Stanley, *Folk Devils and Moral Panics: the Creation of the Mods and Rockers*, London 1972.
Collectif A/Traverso, *radio alice, radio libre*, Paris 1977 (orig. title: *Alice è il diavolo*).
Colletti, Lucio, 'A Political and Philosophical Interview', *New Left Review*, 86, July–August 1974.
—— 'Le Ideologie', in *Dal '68 a oggi*, Bari 1980.
Comitato Unitario di Base Pirelli, *Linea di massa: documenti della lotta di classe: giugno–dicembre 1968*, Milan 1969.
Commissione Carceri di Lotta Continua, *Ci siamo presi la libertà di lottare: il movimento di massa dei detenuti da gennaio a settembre 1973*, Rome 1973.
Commissione Pirelli, 'Relazione sulla revisione di strutture della Confindustria', *Mondo Economico*, 8, 28 February 1970. pp. 42–53.
CGIL–CISL–UIL, *Fabbrica e salute: atti della conferenza nazionale*, Rome 1972.
Cooperativo Centro Documentazione, *Dieci anni di invecchiamento*, Florence 1978.
Coppola, Aniello, 'Pirelli: una vittoria dell'inventività operaia', *Rinascità*, 20 December 1968.
Corrente Proletaria dei Lavoratori Studenti, *Le Lotte dei lavoratori studenti*, Milan 1970.
Cortese, Luisa, *Il movimento studentesco – storia e documenti: 1968–1973*, Milan 1973.
Corvisieri, Silverio, *Il mio viaggio nella sinistra*, Rome 1979.
Crepet, Paolo, and Pirella, A., 'The Transformation of Psychiatric Care in Italy', *International Journal of Mental Health*, 14, 1985.
Crossman, Richard, *The God that Failed*, London 1950.
Crouch, Colin, and Pizzorno, A., eds, *Resurgence of Class Conflict in Western Europe*, London 1978.
Dalla Chiesa, Nando, 'Del sessantotto e del terrorismo: cultura e politica tra continuità e rottura', *Il Mulino*, 273, January–February 1981.
Dalla Costa, Mariarosa, *The Power of Women and the Subversion of the Community*, Bristol 1972.
Dalmasso, E., *Milan: capitale économique de l'Italie*, Paris 1971.
Dambrosio, Francesco, and Buscalia, Mauro Alberto, 'Ambiente di lavoro e condizione femminile', *Quaderni di Rassegna Sindacale*, 54–5, May–August 1975.
D'Antonio, Mariano, *Sviluppo e crisi del capitalismo italiano, 1951–1972*, Bari 1973.
Daolio, Andreina, *Le lotte per la casa in Italia*, Milan 1976.

—— 'Conflitti urbani e mutamento sociale', *Classe*, 12, June 1976.

Daolio, Andreina, and Tutino, Alessandro, *Pianificazione e conflitto nelle grandi aree metropolitane: il caso Milano*. Seminario internazionale I.U.A.V. Mimeograph, 1975.

d'Arcais, Paolo Flores, *Sinistrese: dizionario dei luoghi comuni della sinistra*, Milan 1978.

Datola, S., 1977 'L'industria metalmeccanica milanese: 1945–75', in G. Bonvini, ed., *Un minuto più del padrone*, Milan 1977.

Davis, John, *Conflict and Control. Law and Order in Nineteenth Century Italy*, London 1988.

De Cecco, M., 'Economic Policy: 1945–51' in S. Woolf, ed., *The Rebirth of Italy*, London 1971.

Della Rocca, Giuseppe, 'Evoluzione delle strutture di categoria', *Quaderni di Rassegna Sindacale*, 49, July 1974.

—— 'L'offensiva politica degli imprenditori nelle fabbriche', *Annali della Fondazione Feltrinelli*, 1974/5.

—— 'Un'analisi sull'organizzazione del sindacato in Italia: il funzionario e l'operatore', *Studi Organizzativi*, no. 2, June 1977.

De Mauro, Tullio, 'La Cultura', in Antonio Gambino, et al., *Dal '68 a oggi: come siamo e come eravamo*, Bari 1980.

D'Eramo, Luce, *Nucleo Zero*, Milan 1981.

Di Ciaccia, Francesco, *La condizione urbana*, Milan 1974.

Dini, V., and Manconi, L., *Il discorso delle armi*, Rome 1981.

Dolci, Luigi, 'Ercole Marelli' in A. Pizzorno, ed., *Lotte operaie e sindacato in Italia*, vol. 3, Bologna 1974.

Donini, Antonio, 'Gli extraparlamentari e il sindacato', *Quaderni di Rassegna Sindacale*, November 1971.

Dorigotti, Giancarlo, 'Il PCI e la scuola', in L. Balbo and G. Chiaretti, *La scuola del capitale*, Padua 1973.

Downing, John, *The Media Machine*, London 1980.

Eco, Umberto, 'L'abito non fa il monaco', in Francesco Alberoni et al., *Psicologia del vestire*, Milan 1971.

—— 'Une nouvelle langue: l'italo-indien', in F. Calvi, ed., *Italie '77*, Paris 1977.

—— 'La donna è nubile', in A. Sartogo, ed., *Le donne al muro*, Rome 1978.

—— *Sette anni di desiderio*, Milan 1983.

—— 'Towards a Semiological Guerrilla Warfare' in *Faith in Fakes*, London 1987, (first edn, 1967).

Eco, Umberto, and Violi, P., 'La controinformazione' in P. Murialdi and N. Tranfaglia, eds, *La stampa italiana del neocapitalismo*, Bari 1976.

Enzensberger, Hans Magnus, 'Constituents of a Theory of the Media', in Denis McQuail, ed., *Sociology of Mass Communication*, London 1972.

Ergas, E., 'Femminismo e crisi di sistema', *Rassegna Italiana di Sociologia*, 4, 1980.

Fachinelli, Elvio, ed., *L'Erba Voglio – pratica non autoritaria nella scuola*, Turin 1971.

—— 'Una proposta: non usare i termini "sinistra" e "destra"'', *Lotta Continua*, 27 October 1981.

Faré Ida, and Spirito, Franca, *Mara e le altre*, Milan 1979.

Farneti, Paolo, 'Partiti e sistema di potere', in V. Castronovo, ed., *Italia Contemporanea*, Turin 1976.

—— 'The Troubled Partnership: Trade Unions and Working-Class Parties in

Italy: 1948–78', *Government and Opposition*, 4, Autumn 1978.

Fazio, Fulvia, 'Femminismo e movimento ecologista', in R. Biorcio and G. Lodi, eds, *La sfida verde*, Padua 1988.

Federazione Italiana della Metallurgia (FIM), *Incontro Impiegati proposte di discussioni*, mimeograph, 1969.

Federazione dei Lavoratori Metalmeccanici, *La repressione nelle aziende*, Milan 1973.

Ferrajoli, Luigi, and Zolo, D., *Democrazia autoritaria e capitalismo maturo*, Milan 1978.

Ferraresi, Franco, 'The Radical Right in Postwar Italy', *West European Politics*, 2, 1988.

Ferretti, Gian Carlo, *Il mercato delle lettere*, Turin 1979.

Fo, Dario, *'Dario Fo à Vincennes'* in *Cahiers du cinéma*, 250, May 1974.

——— *Can't Pay? Won't Pay!*, London 1978.

Foa, Vittorio, 'Introduzione' in G. Levi Arian, ed., *I Lavoratori Studenti*, Turin 1968.

——— 'Note sui gruppi estremisti e le lotte sindacali', *Problemi del Socialismo*, 41, 1969.

——— 'La frontiera politica del sindacato', *Problemi del Socialismo*, 39, 1969.

——— *Note sulla scale mobile*, mimeograph 1975.

——— *Sindacati e lotte operaie, 1943–73*, Turin 1976.

——— 'Il sindacato di fronte alla transizione', *Problemi del Socialismo*, 5, 1977.

——— 'Sul sindacato', *Quaderni Piacentini*, 69, 1978.

Fofi, Goffredo, *Il cinema italiano: servi e padroni*, Milan 1971.

——— 'Piccola editoria: errori manifesti e virtù latenti', in *Quaderni Il Lavoro dell'Informazione*, 1, 1981.

Fornasier, Giordano, and Moresco, Mariella, *Lotte 'spontanée' per la casa a Milano dal 1945–75 e loro rapporto con le istituzioni e le forze sociali*, unpublished thesis, Università Cattolica, Facoltà di scienze politiche, Milan 1976.

Fortini, Franco, 'Questo e un altro', *L'Espresso*, 20 March 1988.

Frabotta, Bianca Maria, *Femminismo e lotta di classe in Italia*, Milan 1977.

——— *La politica del femminismo*, Rome 1978.

Frankel, Boris, *The Post-Industrial Utopians*, Cambridge 1987.

Frey, L., 'Analisi economica della occupazione femminile in Italia', in L. Frey, ed., *Occupazione e sottoccupazione femminile in Italia*, Milan 1976.

Frogett, Lynn, and Torchi, A., 'Feminism and the Italian Trade Unions', *Feminist Review*, 8, Summer 1981.

Galeotti, Anna Elisabetta, 'L'opposizione destra-sinistra: riflessioni analitiche, in F. Ferraresi, ed., *La destra Radicale*, Milan 1984.

Galli, Giorgio, *Storia del PCI*, Milan 1977.

——— 'La politica italiana', in Antonio Gambino et al, *Dal '68 a oggi*, Milan 1980.

——— *Italia sotterranea. Storia, politica e scandali*, Bari 1983.

Garelli, Franco, 'Gruppi giovanili ecclesiali', *Quaderni di Sociologia*, 3–4, 1977.

Gargani, A., ed., *Crisi della ragione*, Turin 1979.

Germani, Gino, ed., 'Aspetti teorici e radici storiche del concetto di marginalità con particolare riguardo all'America Latina', in *Marginalità e classi sociali*, Rome 1976.

Gilroy, Paul, 'Steppin' out of Babylon – race, class and autonomy', in Centre for Contemporary Cultural Studies, *The Empire Strikes Back*, London 1982.

Ginsborg, Paul, 'Gramsci and the Era of Bourgeois Revolution' in J. Davis, ed., *Gramsci and the Passive Revolution*, London 1979.

—— 'The Communist Party Strategy and the Agrarian Question in Southern Italy, 1943–48', *History Workshop Journal*, 1984.

—— *Storia d'Italia del dopoguerra a oggi*, Turin 1989.

—— 'Family, Culture and Politics in Postwar Italy', in Z. Baraǹski and R. Lumley, eds, *Culture and Conflict in Postwar Italy*, London 1990.

Giori, Danilo, and Pepe, Gabriella Rossetti, '150 ore – per una cultura di classe', *Classe*, 9, 1975.

Gobbi, Romolo, *Il '68 alla rovescia*, Milan 1988.

Goodrich, Carter, *The Frontier of Control*, London 1975.

Gorz, André, *Farewell to the Working Class*, London 1982.

Gozzer, Giovanni, *Rapporto sulla secondaria*, Rome 1973.

Gramaglia, Mariella, '1968: il venir dopo e l'andar oltre del movimento femminista', *Problemi del Socialismo*, 4, 1976.

Gramsci, Antonio, *Selections from the Prison Notebooks*, London 1971.

Grasso, Laura, *Compagno padrone*, Florence 1974.

Graziani, Augusto, *L'economia italiana: 1945–70*, Bologna 1972.

—— 'Aspetti strutturali dell'economia italiana nell'ultimo decennio', in A. Graziani, ed., *Crisi e Ristrutturazione nell'Economia Italiana*, Turin 1975.

Gribaudi, Gabriella, 'Terremoti', *Ombre Rosse*, 33, March 1981.

Gribaudi, Maurizio, 1981 'Un gruppo di amici – strategie individuali e mutamento sociale', in E. Beltrami, ed., *Relazioni sociali e strategie individuali in ambiente urbano: Torino nel novecento*, Turin 1981.

—— *Mondo operaio e mito operaio*, Turin 1986.

Grimshaw, Mark, and Gardner, Carl, '"Free Radio" in Italy', *Wedge*, 1, Summer 1977.

Grisoni, D., and Portelli, H., *Le lotte operaie in Italia dal 1960 al 1976*, Milan 1976.

Gruppo di campagni del Consiglio di Fabbrica della Pirelli Bicocca, *Le lotte alla Pirelli: 1968–72*, Milan 1972.

Gruppo di Studio IBM, *IBM*, Milan 1973.

Guidi, Gianfranco, Bronzino, A., and Germanetto, L., *Fiat, Struttura aziendale e organizzazione dello sfruttamento*, Milan 1974.

Gundle, Stephen, 'L'americanizzazione del quotidiano. Televisione e consumo nell'Italia degli anni '50', *Quaderni Storici*, 62, 1986.

Hall, Stuart, 'Deviance, Politics and the Media', in P. Rock and M. McIntosh, eds, *Deviance and Social Control*, London 1974.

Hall, Stuart, and Jefferson, Tony, *Resistance through Rituals: Youth Subcultures in Post-War Britain*, London 1977.

Hall, Stuart, Critcher, Chas., Jefferson, Tony, Clarke, John, and Roberts, Brian, *Policing the Crisis*, London 1978.

Harvey, Sylvia, *May '68 and Film Culture*, London 1978.

Hellman, Steven, 'The PCI's Alliance Strategy and the Case of the Middle Classes', in D. Blackmer and S. Tarrow, eds, *Communism in Italy and France*, Princeton 1975.

Hirschman, Albert, *Shifting Involvements*, Princeton 1982.

Hobsbawm, Eric, *Primitive Rebels*, Manchester 1959.

—— *Bandits*, London 1972.

—— *Revolutionaries*, New York 1973.

—— 'Man and Woman in Socialist Iconography', *History Workshop Journal*, 6,

Autumn 1978.

Horowitz, Daniel, *The Italian Labour Movement*, Cambridge, Mass. 1963.

Illuminati, Augusto, *Lavoro e rivoluzione*, Milan 1974.

Intercategoriale Donne CGIL–CISL–UIL (Torino), *La spina all'occhiello*, Turin 1979.

Jaggi, Max, *Red Bologna*, London 1977.

Jervis, Giovanni, 'Condizione operaia e nervosi', in G. Jervis, *Proletariato industriale e organizzazione del lavoro*, Rome 1975.

Johnson, Richard, *The State and the Politics of Education: Block 1, Part 2 (Units 1–2) in Educational Studies: The State and the Politics of Education*, Milton Keynes 1981.

—— 'Educational Politics: Old and New' in James Donald and Annmarie Volpe, eds, *Is there anyone here from Education?*, London 1982.

Joll, James, *The Anarchists*, London 1964.

Keane, John, *Democracy and Civil Society*, London 1988.

Lanzardo, Dario, 'L'intervento socialista nella lotta operaia: l'inchiesta operaia di Marx', *Quaderni Rossi*, 5, 1972 (reprint).

—— *La rivolta di Piazza Statuto*, Milan 1979.

Laroche, Pierre, 'La classe ouvrière dans le roman italien', *Le Monde Diplomatique*, December 1974.

Lasch, Christopher, *The Culture of Narcissism*, New York 1978.

Lepschy, Anna Laura, and Lepschy, Giulio, *The Italian Language Today*, London 1979.

Lepschy, Giulio, 'Sexism and the Italian Language', *The Italianist*, 7, 1987.

Lerner, Gad., *Operai: viaggio all'interno della Fiat. La vita, le case, le fabbriche di una classe operaia che non c'è più*, Milan 1988.

Lerner, Gad., Manconi, Luigi, and Sinibaldi, Marino, *Agenda Rossa*, Rome 1978.

Levi, Corrado, 'Omosessuali fuori', *L'Erba Voglio*, May–June 1973.

Levi Arian, G., *I lavoratori studenti*, Torino 1968.

—— *Libro bianco sulle associazioni e i giornali studenteschi a Milano*, Milan 1966.

—— *Libro bianco sulla facoltà di architettura di Milano*, Milan 1970.

Lombardo Radice, M., 'Giovani senza rivoluzione', *Ombre Rosse*, 1976.

Longo, Biagio, 'Fuochi, fatui? La resistenza delle radio libere', *Quaderni Il Lavoro dell'Informazione*, 1, 1981.

Lonzi, Carla, *Sputiamo su Hegel, La donna clitoridea e la donna vaginale*, Milan 1970.

Lotta Continua, *Take over the City*, 1971.

—— *Per il movimento degli studenti medi*, convegno di Pavia 1971.

—— *Dear comrades – readers' letters to 'Lotta Continua'*, London 1980.

Lotta Femminista, *L'Offensiva: materiali del movimento femminista: quaderni di Lotta Femminista*, 1, Turin 1972.

Low-Beer, John, *Protest and Participation: The New Working Class in Italy*, Cambridge 1978.

Lucas, Uliano, *Cinque anni a Milano*, Turin 1973.

Ludovici, Emilio Samek, 'Il movimento insegnanti a Milano', *Inchiesta*, 3, Summer 1971.

Lumley, Robert, 'Working Class Autonomy and the Crisis: Italian Marxist Texts of the Theory and Practice of a Class Movement, 1964–79', *Capital and Class*, 12, 1980.

—— 'Socialism: Utopian and Utopian', *Head and Hand*, 13, 1983.

—— 'Challenging Tradition: Social Movements, Cultural Change and the Ecology Question', in Z. Barański and R. Lumley, eds, *Culture and Conflict in Postwar Italy*, London 1990.

Lumley, Robert, and Schlesinger, Philip, 'The Press, the State and its Enemies: The Italian Case', *Sociological Review*, 30, 1982.

Lyotard, Jean-François, *The Postmodern Condition*, Manchester 1986.

Maccacaro, Giulio, *Per una medicina da innovare. Scritti 1966–76*, Milan 1976.

Macciocchi, Maria Antonietta, *Après Marx, Avril*, Paris 1978 (original title: *Dopo Marx, Aprile*).

Mafai, M., *L'apprendistato della politica. Le donne italiane nel dopoguerra*, Rome 1979.

Magri, Lucio, 'Via italiana e strategia consigliare', *Il Manifesto*, 2, 1974.

Mallett, Serge, *La nuova classe operaia*, Turin 1967.

—— *Le pouvoir ouvrière*, Paris 1971.

Mancini, Federico, *Terroristi e riformisti*, Bologna 1981.

Mancini, S., *Socialismo e democrazia diretta: introduzione a Panzieri*, Bari 1977.

Manconi, Luigi, *La violenza e la politica*, Rome 1979.

—— *Nuovo, difficile: una proposta bibliografica sulla produzione culturale delle ultime generazioni*, June 1979.

—— *Vivere con il terrorismo*, Milan 1980.

—— *Il discorso delle armi*, Rome 1981.

Manconi , Luigi, and Sinibaldi, Marino, 'Un strano movimento di strani studenti', *Ombre Rosse*, 20, March 1977.

Manghi, Bruno, 'La spontaneità', *Dibattito Sindacale*, March–April 1968.

Manghi, Bruno, and Montani, G., 'Analisi di una lotta operaia: la Candy', in *Contributi per una sinistra sindacale*, Padua 1972.

—— 'La FIM dal 1969–70 ad oggi', una relazione all'esecutivo nazionale della FIM 30 October 1974, mimeograph.

—— *Declinare crescendo*, Bologna 1977.

Mantelli, Brunello, and Revelli, Marco, *Operai senza politica: Il caso Moro alla Fiat e il 'qualunquismo operaio'*, Rome 1979.

Manzini, G., *Una vita operaia*, Turin 1976.

Marcellino, Nella, 'La partecipazione femminile e il movimento sindacale', *Quaderni di Rassegna Sindacale*, 54–5, May–August 1975.

Marcenaro, Pietro, *Riprendere tempo*, Turin 1982.

Marchetti, Aldo, 'Impiegati, linea sindacale e riorganizzazione del lavoro negli uffici', *Classe*, 13, February 1977.

—— 'Un teatro troppo serio: Appunti di analisi del corteo operaio e dello slogan politico di strada', *Classe*, June 1982.

Mariani, Isidoro, 'Incomes and Employment policies in Italian Economic Planning' in Hayward and Watson, eds, *Planning Politics and Public Policy*, Cambridge 1975.

Martinotti, Guido, 'La partecipazione politica dei giovani', *Quaderni di Sociologia*, XV, 1966.

—— 'Il Movimento Studentesco', *Problemi del Socialismo*, 31, June 1968.

—— *Gli studenti universitari*, Milan 1969.

—— Preface, in Giancarlo Arnao, *Rapporto sulle droghe*, Milan 1976.

Marx, Karl, *The 18th Brumaire of Louis Bonaparte* in Marx-Engels *Selected Works*, London 1970.

Massari, Roberto, *Marxismo e critica del terrorismo*, Rome 1979.

Mazzetti, Roberto, *Genesi e sviluppo del terrorismo in Italia*, Rome 1979.

Melandri, Lea, 'Via Tibaldi e MacMahon', *Erba Voglio*, September 1971.
—— 'Antiautoritarismo e permissività', *Erba Voglio*, 3–4, February 1972.
—— 'Ma esiste il quartiere?', *Erba Voglio*, 6, June–July 1972.
—— 'Operai censurati', *Erba Voglio*, 12, August–September 1973.
Melotti, Umberto, 'La vera natura della società cinese e le contradizioni della nuova sinistra', *Terzo Mondo*, December 1975.
Melucci, Alberto, 'Dieci ipotesi per l'analisi dei nuovi movimenti', *Quaderni Piacenti*, 65–6, 1976.
—— 'Vers une système de relations professionelles en Italie', *Sociologie de Travail*, 1, 1976.
—— *Sistema politico, partiti e movimenti sociali*, Milan 1979.
—— 'New Social Movements, Terrorism and the Political System', *Socialist Review*, 56, 1981.
—— *L'invenzione del presente*, Milan 1982.
Melucci, Alberto, ed., *Movimenti di rivolta*, Milan 1976.
—— *Altri codici*, Bologna 1984.
Merenda, Loretta, 'La donna nelle coppie della nuova sinistra', *Inchiesta*, 27, May–June 1977.
Merli, Stefano, *L'altra storia. Bosio, Montaldi e le origine della nuova sinistra*, Milan 1977.
Miegge, Mario, 'Sviluppo capitalistico e scuola lunga' in L. Balbo, ed., *Scuola del capitale*, Padua 1973.
Milani, don Lorenzo, *Lettere di don Lorenzo Milani priore di Barbiana*, Vicenza 1970.
Moore, Jnr, Barrington, *Injustice*, London 1978.
Morris, Meagan, 'Eurocommunism vs Semiological Delinquency', in M. Morris, ed., *Language, Sexuality and Subversion*, Darlington, Australia, 1978.
Movimento di Lotta Femminile, 'Programmatic manifesto of housewives in the neighbourhood', *Socialist Revolution*, 9, July 1971.
Movimento Studentesco, *Documenti della rivolta universitaria*, Bari 1968.
Nappi, Antonella, and Regalia, Ida, *La pratica politica delle donne*, Milan 1978.
Negri, Massimo, *Scuola di massa in Europa*, Florence 1975.
Negri, Toni, *Dall'operaio massa all'operaio sociale*, Milan 1979.
—— *Pipe-line*, Turin 1983.
Nozzoli, G., and Paoletti, P.M., *La zanzara*, Milan 1966.
Ortoleva, Peppino, *Saggio sui movimenti del 1968 in Europa e in America*, Rome 1988.
Paci, Massimo, *L'evoluzione dell'occupazione in Lombardia e la mobilità delle forze di lavoro*, Milan 1968.
—— *Mercato di lavoro e classi sociali in Italia*, Bologna 1973.
—— 'Vecchi e nuovi conflitti sociali', *Ombre Rosse*, 31, February 1980.
—— 'Marginalità e classi sociali in Italia', in G. Germani, ed., *Mutamento e classi sociali in Italia*, Naples 1981.
—— *La struttura sociale Italiana*, Bologna 1982.
Panzieri, Raniero, *La ripresa del Marxismo–Leninismo in Italia*, Milan 1972.
—— *Lotte operaie nello sviluppo capitalistico*, Turin 1972.
—— *Surplus Value and Planning*, CSE Pamphlet, 1, *The Labour Process and Class Structure*, London 1976.
Parlanti, L., 'Piazza Statuto, 1962', in Red Notes, *Working Class Autonomy and the Crisis*, London 1979.
Parlato, Valentino, 'Rapporto sulla Pirelli', *Il Manifesto*, October–November

1969.

Partridge, Hilary, 'Italy's Fiat in Turin in the 1950s', in Theo Nichols, ed., *Capital and Labour*, London 1980.

Pasculli, Ettore, *Analisi politica delle lotte per la casa a Milano*, Facoltà di Architettura, Politecnico di Milano, mimeographed, 1976–7.

Pasetto, E., and Pupillo, G., 'Il gruppo "Potere Operaio" nelle lotte di Porto Marghera', *Classe*, 3, 1970.

Pasquino, G., 'Capital and Labour in Italy', *Government and Opposition*, 3, Summer 1976.

Pasquino, Gianfranco, and Pecchini, V., 'Italy' in J. Hayward and M. Watson, eds, *Planning Politics and Public Policy*, Cambridge 1975.

Passerini, Luisa, *Fascism and Popular Memory. The Cultural Experience of the Turin Working Class*, Cambridge 1986.

—— *Autorittrato di gruppo*, Florence 1988.

Pateman, Trevor, *Language, Truth and Politics*, Nottingham 1975.

Perniola, Mario, 1983 *La società dei simulacri*, Bologna 1983.

Pertile, Lino, 1984 'Dario Fo', in M. Caesar and P. Hainsworth, eds, *Writers and Society in Contemporary Italy*, Leamington Spa 1984.

Pezzana, Angelo, ed., *FUORI: la politica del corpo*, Rome 1976.

Pillon, Cesare, *I comunisti e il sindacato*, Milan 1972.

Pinto, Diane, 'La sociologie dans l'Italie de l'aprés-guerre 1950–80', *Revue Française de Sociologie*, XXI, 1980.

—— , ed., *Contemporary Italian Sociology*, Cambridge 1981.

Pipan, Tatiana, and Salerni, D., *Il sindacato come soggetto di equilibrio*, Milan 1975.

Pivano, Fernanda, *C'era una volta un beat*, Milan 1988.

Piven, Frances, and Cloward, R., *Poor People's Movements*, New York 1977.

Pizzorno, Alessandro, 'Introduzione allo studio della partecipazione politica', *Quaderni di Sociologia*, XV, 1966.

—— 'On Gramsci's Method', *First Italo-Hungarian Conference of Sociology*, 1967.

—— 'Sull'azione politica dei sindacati', *Problemi del Socialismo*, 49, 1970.

—— 'I sindacati nel sistema politico italiano; aspetti storici', *Rivista Trimestrale del Diritto Pubblico*, October 1971.

—— *Political Sociology*, London 1971.

—— 'Quadro politico delle lotte operaie in Italia', *Quaderni di Rassegna Sindacale*, 51, 1974.

—— 'I ceti medi nei meccanismi del consenso', in F.L. Cavazza and S. Grabaud, eds, *Il caso italiano*, 1974.

—— 'Fra azione di classe e sistemi corporativi', *Annali della Fondazione Feltrinelli*, 1974/5.

—— 'Due logiche dell'azione di classe', in A. Pizzorno, ed., *Lotte operaie e sindacato: il ciclo delle lotte 1968–72*, Bologna 1978.

—— 'Terrorismo e quadro politico: tavola rotonda', *Mondo Operaio*, 4, 1978.

Pizzorno, Alessandro, and Crouch, C., 'Scambio politico e identità collettiva nel conflitto di classe', in A. Pizzorno and C. Crouch, eds, *Conflitti in Europa*, Milan 1977.

Poggi, Gianfranco, 'The Church in Italian Politics, 1945–50', in S. Woolf, ed., *The Rebirth of Modern Italy*, London 1971.

Pomata, Gianna, 'La scienza e coscienza: donne e potere nella società borghese', *Quaderni Aut Aut*, 1979.

Pompei, Giuliana, 'Salario per il lavoro domestico', *L'Offensiva: quaderni di Lotta Femminista*, April 1972.

Portelli, Alessandro, 'Oral Testimony, the Law and the Making of History: The "April 7" Murder Trial', *History Workshop Journal*, 20, 1985.

Procacci, Giovanna, 'Caratteri dello sviluppo economico in Italia dalla fine del secolo alla prima querra mondiale', *Archivio Sardo*, 4–5, 1975.

Rame, Franca, Introduction to D. Fo, *Can't Pay? Won't Pay!*, London 1978.

Rancière, Jacques, 'Le Prolétaire et son double ou le philosophe inconnu....', *Révoltes logiques*, 13, 1981.

Ravaioli, Carla, 'La donna' in Antonio Gambino, et al,, *Dal '68 a oggi*, Bari 1980.

Red Notes, *Italy: 1977–78 – Living with an Earthquake*, London 1978.

—— *Working Class Autonomy and the Crisis – Italian Marxist Texts of the Theory and Practice of a Class Movement: 1964–79*, London 1979.

Regalia, Ida, 'Sit Siemens', in A. Pizzorno, ed., *Lotte operaie e sindacato in Italia*, vol. 4, Bologna 1975.

—— 'Le assemblee', *Quaderni di Rassegna Sindacale*, 56–7, September–December 1975.

—— 'Rappresentanza operaia e organizzazione sindacale', in A. Pizzorno, E. Reyneri, M. Regini, and I. Regalia, eds, *Lotte operaie e sindacato: il ciclo 1968–1972 in Italia*, vol.6, Bologna 1978.

Regini, Marino, and Reyneri, Emilio, *Lotte operaie e organizzazione del lavoro*, Padua 1971.

—— 'Labour Unions, Industrial Action and Politics', *Western European Politics*, 2, October 1979.

—— 'Stato e sindacati nel sistema economico', *Giornali di Diritto del Lavoro*, 1, 1979.

Revelli, Marco, 'Defeat at the Fiat', *Capital and Class*, 16, 1982.

Reyneri, Emilio, 'Magneti Marelli' in A. Pizzorno, ed., *Lotte operaie e sindacato in Italia*, vol. 3, Bologna 1974.

—— 'Innocenti', in A. Pizzorno, ed., *Lotte operaie e sindacato in Italia*, vol. 1, Bologna 1974.

—— 'Comportamento di classe e nuovo ciclo di lotte', *Annali della Fondazione Feltrinelli*, 1974/5.

—— 'La lotta per la produzione e l'organizzazione del lavoro nelle fabbriche cinesi', in Martino Ancona, ed., *Proletariato industriale e organizazzione del lavoro*, Rome 1975.

—— 'Il sindacato in Italia oggi', *Il Mulino*, July–August 1977.

—— ' "Maggio strisciante": l'inizio della mobilitazione operaia', in A. Pizzorno, E. Reyneri, M. Regini and I. Regalia, eds, *Lotta operaie e sindacato, il ciclo 1968–1972 in Italia*, vol. 6, Bologna 1978.

Ricci, Giuseppe, Marras, Claudio, and Radice, Mauro, *Milano Alternativa*, Milan 1975.

Romagnoli, Guido, *Consiglio di fabbrica e democrazia sindacale*, Milan 1976.

Romagnoli, Umberto, and Mariucci, L., *Lo sciopero della costituzione all'auto-disciplina*, Bologna 1975.

Romeo, Maria, 'La disciplina dei licenziamenti: un'analisi comparata', in P. Alessandrini, ed., *Conflittualità e aspetti normativi di lavoro*, Bologna 1978.

Romiti, Cesare, *Questi anni alla Fiat* (interview with G.P. Pansa), Milan 1988.

Ronchey, Vittoria, *Figlioli miei, marxisti immaginari*, Milan 1975.

Rositi, Franco, et al., *La politica dei gruppi*, Milan 1970.

Rossanda, Rossanna, *L'anno degli studenti*, Bari 1968.

Rossi-Doria, Anna, 'Conservazione e rottura nel movimento delle donne', *Ombre Rosse*, 25, June 1978.

Rostagno, Mauro, 'Note sulle lotte studentesche', in *Università: l'ipotesi rivoluzionaria*, Padua 1968.

Rowbotham, Sheila, 'Women's Liberation and the New Politics', in Michelene Wandor, ed., *The Body Politic*, London 1972.

—— *Women, Resistance and Revolution*, London 1972.

Ruffolo, Giorgio, *Riforme e controriforme*, Bari 1975.

Sacco, Giuseppe, 'Città e società verso il nuovo medioevo' in U. Eco, ed., *Il nuovo medioevo*, Milan 1973.

Salvati, Michele, 'Slittamento salariale e sindacato con riferimento all'industria metalmeccanica, 1954–69', *Rassegna Economica*, 6, 1970.

—— 'The Impasse of Italian Capitalism', *New Left Review*, 76, November–December 1972.

—— *Il sistema economico italiano: analisi di una crisi*, Bologna 1975.

Sandretti, Armando, *Lotte all'Alfa Romeo*, unpublished thesis, Università degli Studi di Milano, Facoltà di scienze politiche, 1973.

Sarno, M., and Sinibaldi, M., *Il movimento degli studenti medi in Italia (1975–6)*, Rome 1977.

Sassoon, Donald, *Contemporary Italy*, London 1986.

Scaramucci, Piero, *Licia Pinelli: Una storia quasi soltanto mia*, Milan 1982.

Schianchi, F., *La Università Cattolica*, Milan 1974.

Schioppa, Fiorella, *Scuola e classi sociali in Italia*, Bologna 1974.

Sciascia, Leonardo, *The Moro Affair*, Manchester 1987.

Sclavi, Gastone, 'Le due CISL', *Il Manifesto*, October–November 1969.

Scuola di Barbiana, *Lettere a una professoressa*, Florence 1967.

Sennett, Richard, *The Uses of Disorder*, London 1971.

—— *The Fall of Public Man*, New York 1977.

Sennett, Richard, and Cobb, J., *The Hidden Injuries of Class*, Cambridge 1972.

Siciliano, Enzo, *Vita di Pasolini*, Milan 1978.

Sidotti, Francesco, 'Emancipazione e politiche culturali negli anni '60: Marcuse in Italia', *Rassegna Italiana di Sociologia*, 2, 1974.

Signorelli, Amalia, 'Cultura popolare e cultura di massa: note per un dibattito', *Ricerca Folklorica*, 7, 1983.

Silj, Alessandro, *Mai più senza fucile: alle origini del NAP e delle BR*, Florence 1977.

Silone, Ignazio, *Emergency Exit*, London 1968.

Sivini, Giordano, *Partiti e partecipazione in Italia*, Milan 1969.

Smith, Anthony, *The Shadow in the Cave*, London 1973.

Soccorso, Rosso, *Brigate Rosse*, Milan 1976.

Sodi, R., 'Pagliamo il "nostro" biglietto!', *Realismo*, 15, March 1977.

Sofri, Adriano, 'Sur les conseils de délégués', *Les Temps Modernes*, June 1974.

—— 'Sessantotto. La corsa nei sacchi', *Micro–Mega*, 1, 1988.

Sorlini, Claudia et al., *Centri sociali autogestiti e circoli giovanili*, Milan 1977.

Soskice, David, 'Le relazioni industriali nelle società occidentali', in C. Crouch and A. Pizzorno, eds, *Conflitti in Europa*, Milan 1977.

Spagnoletti, Rosalba, *I movimenti femministi in Italia*, Rome 1976.

Sparke, Penny, *Italian Design. 1870 to the Present*, London 1988.

Squi/libri, *Sarà un risotto che vi sepellirà*, Milan 1977.

Stella, Simonetta, 'Crescere negli anni '50', in *Memoria*, 2, 1981.

—— *La strage di stato: controinchiesta*, Rome 1970.

Sylos Labini, Paolo, *Saggio sulle classi sociali*, Bari 1974.

Tamburrano, Giuseppe, *Storia e cronaca del centro sinistra*, Milan 1971.

Tarrow, Sidney, 'Struggling to Reform: Social Movements and Policy Change During Cycles of Protest', *Western Societies Program Occasional Paper*, no. 15, Centre for International Studies, Cornell University, 1983.

Teodori, Massimo, *Storia delle nuova sinistra in Europa 1956–76*, Bologna 1976.

Teodori, Massimo, Ignazi, P., and Panebianco, A., *I nuovi radicali*, Milan 1977.

Thompson, E.P., 'Time, Work-Discipline and Industrial Capitalism', *Past and Present*, 38, 1967.

—— 'The Moral Economy of the English Crowd in the 18th Century', *Past and Present*, 50, 1971.

Tiberi, Emilio, *La contestazione murale*, Bologna 1972.

Tilly, Charles, 'The Changing Place of Collective Violence', in M. Richter, ed., *Essays in Theory and History*, Cambridge, Mass. 1970.

Tomasi, L., *La contestazione religiosa giovanile in Italia (1968–78)*, Milan 1981.

Tomassini, Roberta, *Ideologia, intellettuali, organizzazione: sul neo marxismo degli anni '60*, Bari 1977.

Touraine, Alain, *Evolution du travail ouvrier aux usines Renault*, Paris 1955.

—— *La conscience ouvrière*, Paris 1965.

—— *Post Industrial Society*, New York 1971.

—— *The May Movement*, New York 1971.

—— *Lettres à une étudiante*, Paris 1974.

—— 'I nuovi conflitti sociali' in A. Melucci, ed., *Movimenti di Rivolta*, Milan 1975.

—— *The Self-Production of Society*, New York 1977.

—— *The Voice and the Eye – An Analysis of Social Movements*, Cambridge 1981.

Tovaglieri, Alberto, 'Sul proletariato come soggetto rivoluzionario', *Quaderni Aut Aut*, 172, July–August 1979.

Tozzi, Silvia, 'Molecolare, creativa, materiale: la vicenda dei gruppi per la salute', *Memoria*, 19–20, 1987.

Trentin, Bruno, 'Organizzazione del lavoro e strategia operaïa' in *Istituto Gramsci, Scienza e organizzazione del lavoro*, Rome 1973.

—— *Da sfruttati a produttori*, Bari 1977.

Treu, Tiziano, *Sindacato e rappresentanze aziendali*, Bologna 1971.

Tronti, Mario, *Operai e capitale*, Turin 1966.

Turone, Sergio, *Storia del sindacato in Italia*, Bari 1976.

Ulivieri, Simonetta, 'La donna nella scuola dall'unità a oggi', *donnawomanfemme*, 4, July–September 1977.

Valcarenghi, Andrea, *Underground a pugno chiuso*, Rome 1974.

—— *Non contate su di noi*, Rome 1977.

Valluari, C., *I gruppi extraparlamentari di sinistra*, Rome 1976.

Vattimo, Gianni, 'Myth and the Destiny of Secularisation', *Social Research*, 2, 1985.

Vattimo, Gianni, and Rovatti, P-A, eds, *Il pensiero debole*, Milan 1986.

Vento, Nino, 'I giovani proletari: l'ideologia, il tempo libero', *Ombre Rosse*, 1976.

Vento, Salvatore, 'Milano' in R. Rugafiori, F. Levi and S. Vento, eds, *Il Triangolo Industriale*, Milan 1974.

Viale, Guido, *S'avanza un strano soldato*, Turin 1973.

—— *Il sessantotto*, Milan 1978.

Violi, Patrizia, *I giornali dell'estrema sinistra*, Milan 1977.

—— *L'infinito singolare. Considerazioni sulla differenza sessuale nel linguaggio*, Verona 1988.

Wagner-Pacifici, Robin, *The Moro Morality Play. Terrorism as Social Drama*, Chicago 1986.

Webster, Colin, 'Communes', in S. Hall and T. Jefferson, eds, *Resistance through Rituals*, London 1976.

Weitz, Peter, 'The CGIL and PCI: from subordination to independent political force', in Blackmer and Tarrow, eds, *Communism in Italy and France*, Princeton 1975.

Williams, Gwyn, *Proletarian Order*, London 1975.

Williams, Raymond, *The Long Revolution*, London 1971.

—— *Keywords*, London 1976.

—— 'Base and Superstructure in Marxist Cultural Theory', in R. Williams, *Problems in Materialism and Culture*, London 1980.

Willis, Paul, *Learning to Labour*, London 1977.

Woolfson, Charles, 'The Semiotics of Working Class Speech', *Working Papers in Cultural Studies*, 9, 1976.

Zamarin, Roberto, *Gasparazzo*, Milan 1980.

Zandegiacomi, Ninetta, 'Critica della società, condizione operaia, potere. Il punto di vista operaia nei giornali dei Consigli di Fabbrica', *Classe*, 9, 1974.

Zanzotta, A., 'La cultura del narcissismo', *Rassegna Italiana di Sociologia*, 1, 1980.

index

Lightning Source UK Ltd.
Milton Keynes UK
11 August 2010

158273UK00001B/60/P